M000033794

No More Deaths

To Trina —
thanks so much for
coming to my talk
at the Sedona Public
Library — Hope we
meet again.

Sue Lefevre
November 2019

No More Deaths

HUMANITARIAN AID IS NEVER A CRIME
SAVING LIVES OF MIGRANTS

Sue Lefebvre

Cover art: Carlos Barbarena
"Santo Pollero" (SRO. Toribito Romo)
Linocut Print 2011
Editors: Leah Downing
Peter Rudolf
www.nomoredeaths.org
www.suelefebvre.com

Endorsements:

In the 1980's, the Sanctuary Movement succeeded in protecting tens of thousands of Central American refugees and forcing change in U.S. policy. In 2003, veterans of that movement organized No More Deaths to take the strategies of civil initiative into the desert borderlands to save the lives of migrants and resist U.S. violations of human rights. This book is essential reading for all who are called to solidarity with migrant families and refugees in this time.

The Rev. John Fife served as Pastor of Southside Presbyterian Church in Tucson for 35 years. He was co-founder of the 1980's Sanctuary Movement and a founding volunteer with No More Deaths."

For ethical analysis to be relevant, it requires occupying the space where oppression flourishes. As an ethicist, I became a scholar on immigration only after walking with No More Death upon these trails of hope and terror. Lefebvre brings to life the trials and tribulations faced by the least of these. A must read for those seeking a better understanding of the human rights crises on our border.

Dr. Miguel de la Torre, Professor of Social Ethics and Latinx Studies at the Iliff School of Theology in Denver, Colorado

We began the desert work in 2004 with a $25,000 grant from PCUSA as an all-volunteer group walking the trails in Southern Arizona dedicated to ending death and suffering in the desert by providing physical aid and by educating hundreds of volunteers and media from all over the world about the border. Today, we cover hundreds of square miles of desert and reach tens of thousands of potential supporters. Brilliant work that continues to grow every year.

In my view, NMD is by far the best grassroots-organized (and, occasionally, disorganized) group of which I have had the pleasure to be a part. We have the most dedicated, selfless workers and imaginative minds on the border.

The best days of my life (so far) have been spent on the trails around Arivaca, Ajo, and Table Top and at Byrd Camp. It was, indeed, the best work I have ever done.

Steve Johnston, writer, publisher, trail-walker, philosopher

copyright © 2019 Sue Lefebvre
All rights reserved. This book or any portion thereof may not be reproduced or used in any manner whatsoever without the express written permission of the publisher except for the use of brief quotations in a book review.

ISBN-13: 9781095045824

*Dedicated to humanitarian aid volunteers
in Southern Arizona*

and

*to Gene Lefebvre for our many years
in loving relationship*

Table of Contents

Gene and Sue Lefebvre in Nogales 2007 (No More Deaths).

This book is written from the perspective of Sue Lefebvre and her husband Gene, No More Deaths volunteers from its beginning in late 2003. As we worked each day, hiking in the desert, volunteering on the border, visiting migrant centers, emailing, planning, attending meetings, fundraising, imagining effective strategies, many other people were doing the same things, but having entirely different day-to-day experiences. Their stories are just as valid as ours; we can only speak for ourselves (and through the voices of the many volunteers who contributed to this book). This book is colored by our personal histories, our No More Deaths experiences, our insights, and our biases—also, our hopes and dreams for progress toward greater justice and equality as expressed by people of conscience, the goals of our faith communities, the promises of the United States Constitution and the Declarations by United Nations.

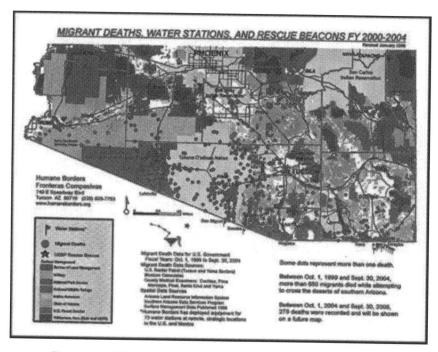

Recovered Human Remains (RHR) in the Arizona Desert

Data for "Apprehensions" comes from Border Patrol. Data for "RHR in Arizona" comes from the Pima County Forensic Science Center. It represents Pima and Santa Cruz Counties primarily but may contain data from Pinal, Gila and Graham counties from time to time. As of May 2012, Pima County is under contract to process RHR for Pinal and Cochise Counties. The RHR data is from the area primarily patrolled by the Tucson, Green Valley and Ajo Samaritans, as well as No More Deaths. The data represents much but not all the Tucson Sector.[1]

---

1 Edgar McCullough, Professor Emeritis, University of Arizona (text modified by author).

2 www.cpb.gov/newsroom/stats/ofo-sw-border-inadmissables-fy (x)

3 Op.cit., McCullough

BP Fed Year	BP Arizona Apprehensions[2]	Number of RHR In Arizona[3]
1994-1995	139,473	
1995-1996	227,529	
1996-1997	305,348	
1997-1998	272,397	
1998-1999	387,406	11
1999-2000	470,449	29
2000-2001	616,346	74
2001-2002	445,675	80
2002-2003	333,648	134
2003-2004	347,263	137
2004-2005	491,771	142
2005-2006	539,079	219
2006-2007	392,074	169
2007-2008	378,239	202
2008-2009	317,696	171
2009-2010	241,673	212
2010-2011	212,202	251
2011-2012	123,285	177
2012-2013	120,000	194
2013-2014	120,939	121
2014-2015	87,915	133
2015-2016	63,397	145
2016-2017	38,657	151
2017-2018	NA[4]	123
2018-2019	NA	NA

4 Border Patrol data not available at date of publication.

Introduction

THIS BOOK ADDRESSES THE CRISIS in the southwestern part of the United States that has desperately needed governmental intervention since NAFTA was enacted in 1994. It documents how, in the meantime, dedicated volunteers have, for more than 15 years, filled the enormous gap left by a negligent government. Additionally, volunteers have provided relevant data to leaders to encourage them to enact immigration reform.

You need to hear this story.

No More Deaths is a humanitarian organization that delivers food, water, and medical aid into the Southern Arizona desert to prevent migrants from dying, and it provides care to repatriated migrants along the border who need a variety of services.

This book chronicles experiences from major efforts of the humanitarian organization (called a movement by many), No More Deaths, from 2004-2019. No More Deaths addresses the political reality that many people don't want migrants from the south to come into the United States. This disapproval is reflected by the fact that since 2004, more than 3,000 Mexicans, Central Americans, and others have died in the Southern Arizona desert. More than 7,000 have died crossing into Arizona, Texas, New Mexico, and California combined. This is an unacceptable outcome of U.S. government policy that forces people into harsh desert terrain for their pilgrimage.

Other solutions are possible and far less expensive. We'll address some of them in this book.

Doris Meissner (former commissioner of the U.S. Immigration and Naturalization Service [INS] from 1993-2000) said in 2000, "We did believe that geography would be an ally to us. It was our sense that the number of people crossing the border through Arizona would go down to a trickle once people realized what it's like." Clearly, that has not happened—people are still willing to escape misery and die for their dreams.

What is it like to die in the desert? Dr. Norma Price is one of the health professionals who provides training and on-call services to both No More Deaths and our sister organization, Tucson Samaritans. She describes it this way:

People in the past have crossed the border back and forth to work in the U.S. while their families remained in Mexico. Following the passage of NAFTA (North American Free Trade Agreement) in 2004, it was anticipated that there would be more people coming north for work, so politicians closed off the traditional border crossing areas. Walls and increased militarization were employed along the border in Texas, California, and Nogales, Arizona; it was thought that the harsh conditions and terrain of the Southern Arizona Sonoran Desert would be a geographical barrier (as expressed above by Doris Meissner). But our government did not understand the determination of people to find work to feed their families. And their labor has always been needed here in the U.S. where many employers—including large corporations—are eager to hire hard-working people from south of the border to whom they pay low wages.

All of this has resulted in a disaster region in the Southern Arizona borderland. Children, women, and men die from dehydration, hyperthermia (heat stroke), and hypothermia (cold exposure or freezing to death). People continue to come out of desperation, the need to feed their families, and in order to reunite with parents and families from whom they have been separated. Until 2011, the number of deaths has continued to escalate. Now fewer people are crossing the border and fewer being apprehended, but the percentage of deaths to crossers has greatly increased.

The more than 7000 known deaths along our southern border are people fleeing poverty, and children, women, and men coming to reunite with family. Since NAFTA was passed in the mid-90s, more than 3 million people have been displaced from their farms in Mexico. NAFTA has benefitted U.S. agribusiness, but has devastated the small Mexican farmer. U.S.-grown and U.S.-government-subsidized corn, sugarcane, and other agricultural products are cheaper for Mexican people to buy in Mexico than the same produce grown there locally.

No one can tell you what it feels like to die in the desert, but it must be a horrible way to go. We do know the causes of death and, in some cases, we know some of the people's behavior prior to their death: bodies have been found where people stripped off all clothing, bodies have been found where the person had been digging in the sand or the earth; one woman who was rescued and taken to an intensive care unit had a mouth full of sand. We can hypothesize but will never know what they thought or felt.

With few exceptions, causes of death are one of three conditions:

* Dehydration–inadequate fluid volume in the body. This includes the intracellular fluid load of the body as well as the circulating fluid (blood and lymph);
* Hyperthermia–body unable to physiologically adapt to heat exposure and organs cease functioning;

* Hypothermia–body unable to adapt to cold exposure. The electrical mechanism of the heart is affected and ceases to pump blood.

Dehydration increases the susceptibility of death from both hyperthermia and hypothermia. Intravascular fluid volume decreases. Cells of the body are starved for oxygen and the cells die, resulting in organ failure. In cases in which the kidneys are severely affected, blood "sludges" through the blood vessels as it tries to perfuse kidney tissue. This results in inadequate perfusion and eventually necrosis and death of the tissue.

Hyperthermia is arguably the most frequent cause of death: overheating of the body that results in organ failure. Dehydration also predisposes death from hyperthermia because those who are dehydrated are at greater risk of succumbing to the heat. The death rate is always higher in the summer months even though the number of those crossing is much less.

Hypothermia is the least frequent cause of death because weather conditions in the Sonoran Desert of Southern Arizona do not usually reach extreme cold for long periods of time. However, we do find people suffering from hypothermia— and not just in extreme winter. Conditions that predispose to hypothermia are dehydration (100 percent of those cross-ing through the desert), fatigue (the journey is extremely challenging—walking in difficult terrain for long hours), wet clothing (either from sweat, rain, or the occasional snow), in addition to sleeping on a cold surface (the ground).

Some of the very ill people who've been found in the des-ert and then taken to the emergency department of nearby hospitals are treated for rhabdomyolysis. This is a serious syn-drome due to a direct or indirect muscle injury, which fre-quently happens in extreme exertion. The breakdown of the muscle tissue then clogs flow through the kidneys, which are already compromised due to dehydration. This can lead to kidney failure. A person may survive the desert crossing but die a premature death if he/she is deported and does not get adequate medical care. They will often need dialysis, maybe even a kidney transplant. Even if the individual doesn't die immediately in the desert, without proper treatment he or she will eventually die an early death from kidney failure.

Possibly one of the saddest ramifications of death in the desert is the unknowing of families. Many, many of the human remains sent to the medical examiner's office are never identified. The families of these people will never know what happened. And we know there are countless more deaths than have been reported or found. Families call looking for loved ones with whom they've lost contact. They call the Coroner's Office, the hospitals, prisons, the Consulate, Border Patrol, and humanitarian groups. Many families will never know what befell their loved ones.[5]

One of Thousands--Tohono O'odham Nation 2008 (Michael Hyatt)

---

5 Submitted by Dr. Norma Price.

When volunteers come across the remains of migrants, they find them in various states of disintegration. The dry desert wind and desert animals have usually already had a field day with any remains in their paths. The remains might be clothed or unclothed, with dry desiccated skin or just bones, intact or scattered around the death site—or possibly recently dead, with oozing sores and maggots in every orifice.

People in Tucson were vividly aware of what was taking place just to the south of them in the desert. Many of those who were concerned had helped migrants before—during the 1980s when death and mayhem were happening in Central America and many endangered people were escaping into the U.S. and beyond.

When No More Deaths was founded, the group of its conveners had a dream that volunteers would come from all over the country, and beyond, to work with us to address this horrendous problem. We knew we had to set up camps in the desert as soon as possible to begin to save lives. We also needed to move quickly to establish our presence and our right to be on public land.

Many of the early No More Deaths activists had previously been involved in the Sanctuary Movement of the 1980s. They found their beliefs and activities to be counter to U.S. government laws and policy, but still well within international law. Thus, it wasn't surprising that when No More Deaths formed, once again, we found ourselves in a state of tension with such government agencies as U.S. Customs and Border Protection (CBP), the U.S. Fish and Wildlife Service (USFWS), the U.S. Forest Service (USFS), and the U.S. Bureau of Land Management (USBLM). When our volunteers experienced distrust, hostility, and/or persecution from these agencies, we shared those pressures with volunteers from Humane Borders and Samaritans, our affiliated humanitarian organizations.

In 2004, and again in 2006, Gene and I took a group of interested people to the little Sonoran town of Altar, a resting place for migrants traveling north. The trip was sponsored by BorderLinks, a nonprofit organization based out of Tucson. We stayed at CCAMYN,[6] a migrant shelter in Altar. One evening after dinner we sat around the room in a circle with the migrants with whom we had eaten. We introduced ourselves and the migrants told of their experiences.

Arturo said: "I'm from the state of Guerrero. I've been sent back from the U.S. and may go across again, or I may go home. I need money to do either. Thanks for your interest in us. Many people don't care. Here, the meals are good, and I am very grateful to be here."

Gustavo agreed and added: "People see us as criminals. *La migra* (Border Patrol) picked me up in Phoenix where I was working in construction. My daughter lives there. I was deported and have no money. I want to see my mother in Chiapas. And, my wife is remarrying."

Salvador told us: "I'm from Los Mochis. I tried to cross into Nogales (the U.S. side of the border) but was caught and deported. I plan to try again."

Arturo added: "When I got off the deportation bus in Nogales (the Mexican side of the border), a *coyote* (a Mexican guide, sometimes called a *pollero*) called to me, 'Hey *amigo*, come with us. I said, 'No, no, I plan to stay here.' He tried to trick me and pressure me, but I still said no. He and his friends beat me up and left me in the streets after dumping me out of their car." Then Arturo spoke about U.S. policy, "I don't know where to start. The U.S. doesn't want too many people to come. They are afraid."

Gustavo: "People in the U.S. are racist. When we travel, we pass through ranchers and vigilantes who don't want us. It's necessary to open doors. But I know there is abuse of the system in the U.S., for example, with food stamps. But people have a right to be scared—to protect what they have." He added another thought, "There are no services for undocumented elderly in the U.S."

Then, Gustavo spoke again: "The Mexican economy is not good. Not many people can improve their lives here. In Chiapas, there is

---

6 *CCAMYN: Centro Comunitario de Atencion al Migrante y Necesitado* (Community Center for the Care and Attention of Migrants) in Altar, Sonora.

no work. The current president (Vicente Fox) tries to create reform but he came into a bad economy. *Mexicanos* blame the U.S. for border problems."

Ignacio said: "There is some work in Chiapas, but there are too many people and no money to pay them."

Arturo continued: "There is a great deal of confusion. Many people pay for the crimes of one. There are good people and bad people. People making policy only see the bad people. Some people look for work only to find doors shut in their faces because of perceptions. The U.S. is always thinking of laws that will close the doors."

Arturo stated: "Things changed with 9/11. Everything got harder. California is more welcoming; Arizona has changed. God gives us life. I'm just glad to be alive. I want to have a job. I am grateful for your concern for the migrants."

In answer to a question, Gustavo said: "In ten years, I want to be someone in this world—here in Mexico, or in the U.S. My daughter lives in Phoenix. I want to find her, and I want to get married. I have faith in God."

Pancho (a local volunteer and the former mayor of Altar): "Migration is a right. These are the protagonists in a real drama. The U.S. can let some in and keep others out, but migration itself is not a crime. We all look to migrate, to create our own needs and desires. Migrants want to meet their most basic needs. They are willing to fight for survival in a new place. These are real people with real dreams. They offer their bodies to make a living. Those who negate migrants forget their own histories. We remember them at Thanksgiving. We celebrate the migrant—people searching for religious freedom. Is it possible for all of us to get our needs met? The prevailing thought is that if *you* get it, I won't. I do have hope. Things are changing in the world. In Venezuela, Presidente Hugo Chavez is aggressive in his talks regarding the U.S. He is pushing Mexico to do something for its own people. There is more to it than just the migrant piece. We need to bring down the border wall—just like it happened in Berlin. The internet violates the borders. Ideas are crossing all the time. We see that President George Bush is the basis for the fear of terrorists."

Maryada Vallet (a young woman from Phoenix living in Tucson who came with us): "Many people think the United States is a war-making country. Both the U.S. and Mexico need to learn how to be good neighbors. We need to educate children about our common history—our common goals."

Pancho: "In Mexico, *we* don't even know who *we* are. Are we mafia? Are we corrupt officials? The deeper question is *"What will Mexico become?"* There is hope we can come together and work together, but it is very difficult to create a healthy relationship with the United States."

Noemi (a nun from BorderLinks) asked those of us from the U.S.: "How do you see the future? Will a change in the president make a difference? Do we in Mexico need a change in our education programs?"

Pancho: "We are hopeful. The categories of left, center, and right need to go. We need to believe more in feelings—we need to be sensitive to the needs of the people of Mexico. We need to get the Mexicans living in the U.S. to vote. The church has a role. Some churches are giving classes in faith and politics for Mexicans. The bishops of Sonora and Arizona have been to CCAMYN to learn what can happen. There have been meetings in El Paso. The bishops want more shelters. And, we need new bills in the U.S. Congress. The violence—I hope it is not growing."

At one point in the conversation, one of the nuns came in and announced: "There's work tomorrow—early in the morning loading melons—for three of you. Gustavo has yard work at a house nearby."

After hearing these voices, those of us from No More Deaths sat quietly, wondering what lies ahead for them, and for us. Their voices touched on most of the issues we have heard before regarding migration to *el Norte*. They also touched our hearts.

PART I
Early Days of No More Deaths 2004-2007

John Fife at Byrd Camp Dedication 2004 (Michael Hyatt)

CHAPTER 1

No More Deaths–Some Background

*When No More Deaths began, we thought we would just
be doing direct humanitarian aid in the desert. But it wasn't
long after starting this work that we heard all the appalling
stories. At that point, we had an obligation to act.*

THE REV. JOHN FIFE
RETIRED PASTOR OF SOUTHSIDE PRESBYTERIAN CHURCH
FORMER MODERATOR OF GENERAL ASSEMBLY OF THE UNITED
PRESBYTERIAN CHURCH

Gene and I speak with many people who ask why the migrants come to the U.S. when it is so difficult for them to get here? "For goodness sakes, why don't they just stay home?" Some remarks are a bit cruder.

The comments of the migrants we met in Altar, Sonora, provided some glimpses into the causes. These people have the same dreams we have—to work, to obtain healthcare...and to be somebody. The inability to fulfill these dreams where they live drives them to seek alternatives.

Many of us are also aware of the impact of the North American Free Trade Agreement (NAFTA) that has devastated small-scale farming in Mexico. Dr. Miguel A. de la Torre, our friend who teaches at Iliff School of Theology in Denver, Colorado, states that since NAFTA was enacted, the United States dumped about $4 billion worth of subsidized corn in Mexico between 1995-2004. This caused a 70 percent drop in Mexican corn prices and a 247 percent increase in the cost of housing, food, and other essentials.[7]

Not surprising, over one million Mexican farmers lost their land within a year of NAFTA's ratification. Our trade policy pushes migrants out of Mexico, while our demand for cheap labor, labor that native-born Americans do not want to do, pulls them toward the U.S. But rather than acknowledge our complicity in causing undocumented immigration, and rather than work toward comprehensive and compassionate immigration reform, our government responded to the predicted increase in immigration by implementing Operation Gatekeeper the same year we ratified NAFTA.

In October 1994, the U.S. Immigration and Naturalization Service (INS) launched Operation Gatekeeper in an effort to move people away from the traditional migration routes in the San Diego area. The number of Border Patrol agents was increased dramatically and construction of a wall between Mexico and the U.S. was underway.

Aviva Chomsky, in her book titled, *"They Take our Jobs!": And 20 Other Myths about Immigration,*[8] places migration in an historical context and sees it as part of a larger global system. It explains that each immigrant comes for individual reasons, but that patterns of immigration have structural and historical causes. While there is not one single cause that explains all immigration, there are, however, several major interrelated factors that have structured immigration in the past and continue to structure it today.

As in the case for most migrant flows, the sending and the receiving countries, such as United States and Puerto Rico,

---

7 Dr. Miguel A, De La Torre, *Latino/Latina Social Ethics* (Texas: Baylor University Press, 2010), 20.

8 Aviva Chomsky, *"They Take our Jobs!": And 20 Other Myths about Immigration* (Boston: Beacon Press, 2007), 123,132.

have a long-standing relationship. The United States took Puerto Rico from Spain in 1898 as part of the spoils of the Spanish-American War and ruled it as a colony until 1952. Globally this kind of long-standing relationship is an important one to look at in understanding migration. People from India and Pakistan go to England; people from Senegal and Algeria go to France; people from Morocco go to Spain; people from Mexico and Puerto Rico come to the United States. Colonization sets the stage for later migration....

That Mexico is by far the largest source of U.S. immigrants is hardly surprising. In addition to sharing a land border with the United States, it was twice invaded by U.S. troops in the 20th century (1914 and 1917), it has been the target of two U.S.-sponsored labor recruitment efforts (during 1917-18 and 1942-64), and since 1986, at U.S. insistence, it has undertaken a radical transformation of its political economy and entered the global market. Moreover, since 1994, it has been linked to the United States by NAFTA, a comprehensive economic treaty that presently generates $250 billion per year in binational trade. Under these circumstances, immigration between the two countries is inevitable, even though Mexico is wealthy by Third World Standards...migration is a result, not a cause of global economic changes.

Mexico certainly carries its share of the responsibility. My husband, Gene, and I have heard about government corruption in Mexico ever since we were children, with some of the bounty mounting to inconceivable levels of American dollars. In more recent years, the Mexican government has continued to neglect community development and refuses to create jobs. They have tried to limit the number of births per family with some success, but lack of education and absence of job opportunities have left people bereft with many mouths to feed. The drug cartels continue to gain power and

5

terrorize people along the border and in Mexico's interior by killing their competitors, including women and children. Thus, people seek a better option.

CONCERN FOR MIGRANT DEATHS—1976–2004

The roots of No More Deaths go as far back as the 1970s when the Manzo Area Council in Tucson took on the plight of El Salvadorans and Guatemalans who had come to the United States seeking asylum. "Manzo," originally a child of the War on Poverty, had had a brief brush with the law once, in 1976, when four of its female staff members were indicted by the Justice Department on charges of transporting and aiding and abetting the presence of illegal aliens in the United States. Essentially what they had been doing was advising undocumented *Mexicans* of their legal rights, driving them to appointments, and otherwise facilitating their lives in Tucson—without alerting the federal government to their presence. As Manzo saw it, did a social agency in the United States have the right to help undocumented people? If they did so without reporting, was Manzo guilty of violating a law?

The issue was never put to a test in court, for as it happened, the election of 1976 brought the Carter administration into office. Margo Cowan, who had been trained by Cesar Chavez, and others in Manzo, successfully put pressure on the Democrats coming into the Justice Department to have the charges against these four staff members dropped. Not only was the case against them dismissed, but the new commissioner of INS, Leonel J. Castillo, shortly thereafter certified Manzo to represent undocumented aliens in the immigration courts. Manzo thus became one of the first grassroots organizations in the country legally certified to get immigrants greater access to the legal process.

Throughout the next few years, Manzo members prepared asylum applications, raised money for bail bonds, and provided social services to refugees, many of whom were in detention in El Centro, California. Within a short period of time, they raised around $30,000 for bond money, and then, folks even put up their homes for the bonds. They bonded out as many as 14 people in one day. They were aided by members of 60 Tucson churches, synagogues, and other religious groups of the Tucson Ecumenical Council, who had set up a task force focusing on Central America. They hired Timothy Nonn, a recent college graduate, as a staffer for $500 per month. Tim moved forward into this type of work, which had little definition.

When many asylum applications were denied by the courts, the religious workers concluded that their work had been futile. INS warned participating church groups that they would be indicted if they continued to aid undocumented Central Americans. So, the churches decided to seek public support.

On March 24th, 1982, Southside Presbyterian Church in Tucson and five East Bay congregations and a handful of churches around the United States publicly declared themselves sanctuaries for Central American refugees. At the time, participants believed the declarations broke the law. A March 23rd, 1982 letter from Southside's pastor, the Reverend John Fife, to the U.S. attorney general stated, "We are writing to inform you that Southside United Presbyterian Church will publicly violate the Immigration and Nationality Act, Section 274(A)." The letter justified the church's actions by noting that the U.S. government was violating both international law and the 1980 Refugee Act by detaining Central Americans and deporting them to places of persecution.[9]

As early as 16 months after the original declarations, attorneys began to advise Sanctuary workers that their actions

---

9 Susan Bibler-Coutin, *Enacting Law through Social Practice: Sanctuary as a Form of Resistance*, 287-290.

could be considered legal under the very laws they accused the government of breaking. Nevertheless, a Tucson Grand Jury indicted 14 movement members on felony charges of conspiracy and alien smuggling. Moreover, in court, Judge Earl Carroll ruled most of the defendants' legal arguments inadmissible. (the conditions in *El Salvador* and *Guatemala*, the death squads, international law, their own personal religious convictions, etc.) Thus, there was nothing to be said in their defense during the trial. When the trial ended with convictions for eight of the 11 defendants who actually stood trial, movement members renewed their determination to continue sanctuary work.[10]

Sister Darlene Nagorski, one of the defendants, had previously said:

> The conditions I have seen and heard, in which our brothers and sisters from Central America are forced to survive, call out to me and all persons of faith and decency.... What could I have done, judge, knowing what I knew? What would you have done if you had experienced what I experienced? If you knew what I knew? How else could I have tried to stop the deportations? What could I have done to follow my call as a School Sister of St. Francis to defend life?[11]

After the judge gave Sister Darlene a suspended sentence with five years' probation and told her to stop her work with migrants, she said, "Judge, you haven't been listening. As soon as this trial is over, I am going to start working with migrants all over again." He was visibly stunned and left the room, but when he returned, he didn't put her in jail.

---

10 Ibid., p. 290.
11 Paraphrased by Gene Lefebvre, president of the Arizona Sanctuary Defense Fund, present at the event.

The wars in El Salvador and Guatemala which had been supported by the United States, were ended by the signing of Peace Accords in 1992. The American Baptist Church v. Thornburg federal court settlement ended deportations to El Salvador and Guatemala and provided temporary legal status for citizens of those countries residing in the U.S. Thus, Sanctuary workers and their many supporters were able to reclaim their lives and turn to other work.

CHAPTER 2

Government Policy Through Deterrence

IN 1992, UNABLE TO DETERMINE who was legal and who was not, Border Patrol was regularly harassing residents of *El Secundo Barrio*, a Mexican-American neighborhood in the downtown area of El Paso. As a result, the students and staff of the neighborhood's Bowie High School brought a civil rights suit against Border Patrol citing routine harassment and abuses. This lawsuit spurred the new Border Patrol Sector Chief Silvestre Reyes to start meeting regularly with community activists and addressing their complaints. In 1993, Reyes mounted Operation Blockade, which intensively deployed Border Patrol agents along the border within the El Paso city limits, successfully halting most urban border crossers and deflecting most illegal cross-border traffic to more sparsely inhabited areas on the edge of the city.

Meanwhile, during the same year (1993) the federal government commissioned a study about new methods of border control from Sandia National Laboratories, a military research facility in New Mexico.[12] The study recommended a strategy of "prevention-through-deterrence by increasing the difficulty of illegal entry through methods like installing multiple physical barriers and using sophisticated electronic surveillance equipment."[13]

---

12 Wayne Cornelius, "Death at the Border: Efficacy and Unintended Consequences of US Immigration Control Policy" (New Jersey: *Population and Development Review*, 2001) Vol 27, No.4, 661-685.

13 Ibid.

In his 2009 book, *Blockading the Border and Human Rights: The El Paso Operation that Remade Immigration Enforcement,* Tim Dunn points out that El Pasoans, tired and frustrated by immigrant streams through their neighborhoods and by Border Patrol harassment of both citizens and legal immigrants, overwhelmingly supported Operation Blockade (later renamed Operation Hold the Line). "Community organizing against widespread civil rights violations by Border Patrol agents proved a major factor in persuading Border Patrol in the El Paso district to adopt a new strategy—one that was described officially as 'prevention through deterrence.'"[14]

Although initially resisted by the National Border Patrol Council in Washington, this strategy later became the prototype of more intensive border control operations in urban areas because of its success in diverting immigration flows to outlying areas. Border Patrol's 1994 strategy statement—which first used the term "prevention through deterrence"—noted that the agency's national strategy was built on El Paso's success. Operation Blockade's model that took the form of massing enforcement resources at traditionally high-volume, mainly-urban, unauthorized crossing areas, inspired the launching of Operation Gatekeeper in San Diego, Operation Rio Grande in the lower Rio Grande Valley (in Texas), and Operation Safeguard in Arizona.

As a result, millions of dollars were poured into diverting unauthorized migrant traffic to more remote, harsher deserts and mountains—called "more hostile terrain" in Border Patrol's strategic plan—by heavily fortifying and policing the customary crossing places in more temperate environs closer to urban centers.[15]

"Although the number of border-crossing deaths had been on the decline between 1990 and 1994, after the launch of the strategy's

---

14 Tom Barry, Review: "Blockading the Border and Human Rights: The El Paso Operation that Remade Immigration Enforcement" (Texas: University of Texas Press, 2009), www.newspapertree.com/features/4171-review-blockading-the-border-and human-rights-abuses.

15 Joseph Nevins, *Operation Gatekeeper: The Rise of the "Illegal Alien" and the Making of the U.S.-Mexico Boundary* (New York: Greenleaf Publishing, 2001).

first phase, Operation Gatekeeper, yearly deaths more than doubled between 1994 and 2005, reaching 472 deaths across the entire border area in just 2005 alone. But the fundamental assumption behind the strategy—that raising the cost would deter migrants—proved wrong. Soaring deaths rates and unabated migrant traffic showed that people were paying the ultimate price rather than be deterred."[16]

The number of deaths was increasing in Arizona, as well, from two or three in 1994, to 134 in 2003. It was this increase in the deaths that had come to the attention of Tucson activists starting in 2000 who then formed Humane Borders, continuing with Tucson Samaritans in 2002, and No More Deaths in 2004.

Birth of the No More Deaths Coalition 2004 (Michael Hyatt)

16 Mary D. Fan, Abstract: "Prevention Through Deterrence and Death Mitigation: Fantasy and Fetishes in Border Law's Symbolic Order," p. 3.

CHAPTER 3

Peopling the Movement

FOLLOWING THE SANCTUARY TRIAL (IN the late 1980s), the humanitarian folks in Tucson started the non-profit organization, BorderLinks, an education and advocacy program that provides cross-border experiences to people from around the world to help them understand the economics and politics of the U.S./Mexico border. Rick Ufford-Chase was one of BorderLinks' first directors and served there for 18 years. During that time, he also spent one year in Guatemala and two years as moderator of the General Assembly of the Presbyterian Church, U.S.A.

Understanding the complexity of the migration and its potential impact on the United States, the Reverend John McMillan Fife, Rick Ufford-Chase, and the Reverend Gene Lefebvre played significant roles in forming Humane Borders, Tucson Samaritans, and No More Deaths.

John Fife, son of a conservative Presbyterian minister, grew up in Pennsylvania and studied for the ministry at Pittsburgh Seminary. For an internship, he spent a year ministering in the Presbyterian Church at Sells on the Tohono O'odham Nation. Later he became pastor of Southside Presbyterian Church in Tucson where he served for 35 years, retiring in 2005. Native Americans, Blacks, Mexican-Americans, and Anglos comprise the congregation of this unusual church. Later John helped design the kiva-style sanctuary now used for worship, meetings, and a variety of celebrations. The church was the first among many churches and synagogues to declare and provide "sanctuary" during the Sanctuary Movement in the 1980s. Southside also started a day labor center and has been a model for church social action ever since.

In 1986, the federal government indicted John, along with 15 other activists, for transporting, harboring, and conspiring to help Central American refugees fleeing to the United States from the death squads in Guatemala and El Salvador. He and the others were convicted of federal felonies and given five-years of probation. In 1992, John took a year's leave from Southside Presbyterian Church and served as Moderator of the Presbyterian Church, U.S.A. While he traveled the country "doing the Lord's work," his wife Maryann designed and built their home in the Tucson Mountains and continued raising their two sons. I've heard John called a leader, a trouble-maker, a forward-thinker, and a "cowboy" (in the sense of someone who heads off in his own direction). He's a good friend to many.

Rick is another story. Rick Ufford-Chase grew up in parsonages wherever his father was serving in various Presbyterian Churches along the east coast. Rick came to Tucson in the late-1980s in his twenties and went to work for the Sanctuary Movement. Rick says that eventually the borderlands became his home, his call, and his vocation. It is a place that holds him and his wife, Kitty, with a magnetic force. It is a place where the poorest, most desperate folks in our hemisphere risk everything on a chance at survival and a future for their children.[17]

Rick would later become director of BorderLinks.

For most of his ministry, Gene Lefebvre has been an advocate for human rights issues: supporting farm workers, promoting Native American rights and civil rights (marching in Phoenix in 1984 and helping effect changes in federal and state laws), fighting for gay rights, participating in peace efforts, and so on. He was a pastor in

---

17 *Presbyterian Social Justice Booklet*, 2006.

California and in various churches in Phoenix. He is a loving husband, father of four, grandfather of eight, and great-grandfather to six.

In the 1980s, Gene became involved with the Sanctuary Movement in the Phoenix area. When church workers were indicted in 1986, the defendants asked Gene to form a defense fund. He felt inadequate to the task, but as there appeared to be no ready alternative, he agreed to take it on. He sought help from church executives in Arizona (heads of Methodist, Catholic, Presbyterian along with other churches and synagogues). They sent him to attorney John Frank, the leading constitutional scholar in Arizona (whose right-hand person at the time was Janet Napolitano—later she became governor of Arizona, secretary of the Department of Homeland Security and president of the University of California).

When Gene walked into Phoenix attorney John Frank's office, John said, "Hello, I've been waiting for you." Then, he called in Ms. Napolitano and asked her to help set up the Arizona Sanctuary Defense Fund.

The defense fund drew together 13 *pro-bono* attorneys, several support staff, a public relations office, and a fundraising team. They contacted some famous movie and TV people to help raise funds through concerts, auctions, and other means. These included: Joan Baez, Ed Asner, Jackson Brown, Stevie Rae Vaughn, Stevie Nicks, the musical group Peter, Paul and Mary, Mike Farrell, and Sweet Honey, and the Rock. Through their support along with support from individuals and groups around the country, the defense fund raised $1.2 million dollars.

THE EXPANDING CIRCLE

In June of 2000, things had been brewing for a while in Tucson when an 18-month-old girl died in the arms of her mother, *Elizama*, shortly after her mother had given her their last drop of water. On

June 2nd, the *Coalition de Derechos Humanos (Derechos)* held a huge vigil to recognize the deaths of migrants, and they invited The Rev. John Fife to be the speaker. They wanted John to help bring mainstream churches and other organizations to bear on this crisis as he had done in the Sanctuary Movement during the 1980s. *Derechos* had been holding press conferences and vigils since 1994 to inform the public, calling them "Stop the Deaths."

In a 1994 national television debate with Senator John McCain about the first 14 migrant deaths in Arizona, McCain denied Isabel Garcia's assertions that NAFTA was potentially the culprit for Mexican migration.[18]

Isabel works as an attorney for Pima County and is a volunteer with *Derechos Humanos*. As a member of *Derechos*, she says, "The issue of the deaths was raised by the impacted community, that is, Mexicans and Mexican Americans. *Derechos* helped give them a voice to stimulate the start of a movement."

About two weeks after the vigil in 2000, faith leaders came together to see what could be done.

"We have allowed *Derechos Humanos* to carry the water on this issue too long," John Fife advised them.

Among other efforts, *Derechos* had been sending *"migra* patrols" out into the desert to follow Border Patrol trucks and assist migrants. The idea of putting out water in the desert came from Father Bob Carney.

Out of that meeting Humane Borders was formed to provide water in the desert to help stop the increasing number of migrant deaths. Starting with 40 stations made of 55-gallon drums, Humane Borders now services more than 85 water stations all across the *frontera* along the U.S.-Mexico border in Southern Arizona. This includes three stations on the Buenos Aires National Wildlife Refuge and two or three on the Tohono O'odham Nation that are managed by tribal

---

18 Luis Urrea, *The Devil's Highway* (Atlanta: Little, Brown, 2004).

members Mike Wilson and David Garcia. These are opposed by the tribal council and frequently removed. The Refuge and the Nation are two large geographic areas within Arizona that share a border with Mexico.

On the occasion of their retirement from Humane Borders, Robin and Sue Hoover wrote about their experience. The original vision crafted at the Pima Friends Meeting House on Pentecost Sunday, June 11th, 2000, included these 8 points: "1) Put water in the desert; 2) Challenge policy; 3) Become an organization of organizations; 4) Appoint a steering committee; 5) Become bi-national ASAP; 6) Organize as faith-based; 7) Utilize media to tell the story of the plight of migrants in places away from the borders." Working with land managers (to make agreements to place water stations) was added later. The first water station was deployed nine months after the founding meeting.

"The death of 14 migrants on May 23rd, 2001, in Cabeza Prieta National Wildlife Refuge[19] catapulted Humane Borders into the world of national and international media. Pima County contracted with us to maintain water stations. Hate mail and death threats toughened our skin. Mission groups and volunteers came from across the country to volunteer, and we saw life-changing results."[20]

Sometime during this period, before 2002, on the road home from a church picnic at the Baboquiviri Peak campgrounds, John Fife and the Rev. Brandon Wert (a youth minister at Southside Presbyterian Church) picked up a migrant by the side of the road. He was weak and completely dehydrated with red-rimmed eyes. He had with him a note he had written to leave with his body, for he was sure he'd not make it. It read—*God, forgive me for being in this forsaken desert and abandoning my family, Jorge.* John and Brandon took the man to Southside Presbyterian Church where he stayed for about a

---

19 Luis Urrea, *The Devil's Highway* (Atlanta: Little, Brown, 2004).
20 Prompromotional literature, "Humane Borders, First 10 Years" (Tucson: Humane Borders, 2010).

week. From there, he went to Brandon and his wife Jody's home for another week or two.

At that point, Gene happened to be in Tucson when John and Brandon told Gene of the young man's plight. Gene drove him back to Phoenix and put him on a Greyhound bus to his family in California. The following Mother's Day, Jorge called to wish Jody a Happy Mother's Day. He also sent thanks to everyone who helped him, especially the people in Southside Presbyterian Church who had saved his life.

After this experience, John Fife said, "We have to do more than put out water tanks."

So, in 2002, the Tucson Samaritans was formed to provide medical personnel and Spanish-speaking individuals to go on daily patrols looking for lost and injured migrants who might be suffering from fatigue, heart failure, broken limbs, heat stroke, or a myriad of other ills. This was followed by the establishment of another group of Samaritans in Green Valley, a retirement community forty miles closer to the border than Tucson. Their volunteers are particularly active in the winter months when all the "snow birds" return to Arizona.

Dr. Norma Price, a retired physician from Atlanta, Georgia, serves actively with Tucson Samaritans. She hikes in the desert searching for migrants who need her attention. In addition, she trains both Samaritan and No More Deaths volunteers in first aid and provides medical consultation to volunteers in the field. She does much more than that—those are just some of her roles. She describes the Samaritan's work from the beginning:

> When we started in the summer of 2002, we hiked off-road about half the time. That first year we did not find as many migrants as we did in the following years. We'd go out to Ajo and Why, park, and hike washes and off-road where cars could not go. I remember that Kitty (Ufford-Chase) and I used to take two sets of car keys so that if one of us returned

to the car before the others, the ones returning did not have to wait out in the heat! Most of the time that first year, I went out Highway 86 and also to Silverbell Mine and Ironwood. We'd leave the car and just hike out in the desert.

We found lots of migrant belongings—a Book of Mormon and a pornographic comic book side-by-side! Sometimes there were trails, but sometimes we'd just hike hours in the washes and desert. Matt Moore, youth director at St. Marks Presbyterian Church, always liked to go down to Arivaca and took other "Sams" there on trips. Once they camped overnight in the desert. The second year, as we found fewer migrants in Ironwood and in the washes off the Tohono O'odham Nation, I also went down to the Arivaca area occasionally.

Matt and maybe some of the other Samaritans went up in a plane with a woman pilot named Sandy. They had walkie-talkies to Sams on the ground and were trying to see if airplane reconnaissance would be of any advantage. We didn't see any. During those first years we found a lot more migrants along the road side. There were no check points along Arivaca Road. But, we also found migrants further into the desert.

As far as water goes: No More Deaths started that, and I don't recall which summer it was—2006 or 2007, I think. After the summer was over and the college and other volunteers had left, Ed and Debbi McCullough (or maybe it was just Ed who was doing all of his GPS work mapping trails) asked if Samaritans would help with the water drops. So, Lois Martin and whoever else was doing the No More Deaths water drops, worked with Ed and the Samaritans to divide up the drops between the two groups.[21]

---

21 Submitted by Dr. Norma Price.

Dia de los Muertos Pilgrimage 2006 with Lupe Castillo (Michael Hyatt)

In October of 2003, Gene was in Tucson for the annual *Dia de los Muertos* pilgrimage organized by Humane Borders to memorialize the deaths of migrants throughout the previous year. They walked from First Christian Church at First Avenue and Speedway to Evergreen Cemetery at Oracle and Ft. Lowell, which is where migrants are buried in the pauper's field. As Gene and Rick walked, Rick began talking about his recent trip to Guatemala where he had watched as various human rights groups and churches work together to address the local challenges. While there, he became convinced that activists in Tucson should start another movement (referring back to the Sanctuary Movement) that would bring groups together in the next step of stopping migrant deaths. He was aware that the number of deaths in the desert was increasing each year. In the fiscal year 2002-2003, it had passed the 200 mark, reaching 203. He thought the name of the group should be No More Deaths (*No Mas Muertes*).

Around the same time, two groups began meeting to search for a solution to the growing misery and increasing numbers of deaths.

One group was convened by Bishop Gerald Kicanas of the Roman Catholic Diocese. The other group was assembled by representatives of the Jewish community. Together, they sponsored several catalytic trips to Altar in Sonora, Mexico, to see firsthand the activity taking place where migrants would gather to begin their journey across the border.

Two months later, fifteen or so key people met at Southside Presbyterian Church where the basic goals and organization of the new movement were established. In addition to Rick, John, and Gene, other participants included: the Rev. David Ragan (from Phoenix Shadow Rock Congregational Church) and his wife, Valerie (a junior high teacher), Liana Rowe (also from Shadow Rock), the Rev. Stuart Taylor from St. Mark's Presbyterian Church, Father Bob Carney (Roman Catholic priest), the Rev. Ken Kennon (Disciples of Christ), Margo Cowan (public defender for Pima County and volunteer for *Derechos Humanos*), Lupe Castillo (instructor at Pima Community College and volunteer at *Derechos Humanos*), Isabel Garcia (volunteer at *Derechos Humanos* and Pima County Public Defender), and Jennifer Hill (a Young Adult Volunteer from the national Presbyterian Church at Southside Presbyterian Church). In January of 2004, the first No More Deaths meeting was held at Southside Church with about 60 people in attendance. They began to organize the work.

No More Deaths developed out of concern for the growing numbers of Mexican and Central American migrants dying in the Sonoran Desert of Southern Arizona (see chart on page xviii). Unlike the refugees of the 1980s who came to escape persecution and death in Central American countries, these migrants were coming to look for work, so they could send money back to their poor families. Others came to join families already in the U.S. Whatever the reason, government policies intentionally forced them into the most treacherous parts of the Sonoran Desert resulting in an untold number of deaths.

CHAPTER 4

Planning for No More Deaths

In January of 2004, the planning for No More Deaths began in earnest with meetings every Monday evening at Southside Presbyterian Church—first in the Kiva (sanctuary), then in the multipurpose room. Everyone was enthusiastic. Representatives came from various coalition groups: Border Action Network (BAN), Samaritans, Green Valley Samaritans, Humane Borders, BorderLinks. All these groups combined with the community at large came to form the No More Deaths coalition. People even came from the towns of Bisbee, Douglas, and Phoenix representing the efforts to help migrants in those communities as well.

During the 2003-2004 year, Jennifer Hill, the Young Adult Volunteer (Presbyterian) at Southside Church, and Melissa Kreek, a young woman who had a few weeks to spare before going to Africa with the Peace Corp, Holly Thompson, and a young student named Lisa provided significant leadership to this group of 65 or 70 people. At the Monday meetings, they'd break into working groups and address the tasks at hand. Toward the end of the meeting, they'd come back together and share what had been decided. Revisions were made to the proposals by the whole group, as necessary.

The group Gene participated in was in charge of planning the opening events leading up to the work in the desert. There was to be a celebration at Hotel Congress in downtown Tucson on Friday night, an event in Douglas on Saturday, and then a march in Nogales on Sunday that would culminate with the placement of crosses on the wall between Nogales, Sonora, and Nogales, Arizona. On Monday, the volunteers would meet the folks who had been on The Migrant Walk in Sasabe.[22] This would be followed by a procession to the newly-established camp on land that was owned by Byrd Baylor, and then, finally, the dedication of an "Ark of the Covenant."[23]

There was a great sense of empowerment at our meetings. When ideas came up, if they seemed good to the folks in the circle, the group would tell them to get five or ten others to join in and "just go do it."

At one meeting, eight or nine fellows wearing black leather flight jackets and glasses arrived at Southside, poked their heads into the Fellowship Hall and asked, "Is this No More Deaths?"

John Fife, in his usual ebullient way, said, "Yes, it is! Welcome!"

"We're so glad we found you!" one of the men exclaimed.

They were members of a Southern Arizona aviation group. They offered their services to fly over the desert, locate people in trouble, and drop food and medical supplies to them. With the prevailing "just go do it" attitude, they had in mind designing a bottle with a map pasted on the outside and water on the inside that could be dropped to the migrants. They intended to communicate with the "ground forces" via walkie-talkies. Fortunately, before this plan was put into action, someone at the meeting remembered that low-flying Border Patrol planes or helicopters cause migrants to scatter so much, that such an effort would likely be useless. We kindly said no thanks. Besides, the Tucson Samaritans had already

22 The Migrant Walk organized by Humane Borders is a week-long hike over Memorial Day called: "We Walk for Life." It calls attention to the human rights crisis at the border and the many migrant deaths. Gene and others in No More Deaths have participated for several years and still prepare a community meal for the final night in south Tucson.
23 In the Old Testament, Israelites carried the "Arc of the Covenant" with them on their journeys as a symbol of their faith.

tried using a plane and decided it was an ineffective method to get the job done.

In the spring of 2004, No More Deaths was sufficiently well-organized to call for a multi-faith border conference to present its principles for immigration reform and offer people the opportunity to get involved in a desert campaign to save lives in the summer of 2004. On April 19th in Phoenix, Arizona Interfaith Network pastors and leaders along with Bishop Kicanas and other multifaith representatives joined No More Deaths on the lawn of the Arizona Capitol Building to urge the government to enact these principles for immigration reform (see Chapter 93). Bishop Kicanas and others expressed concern that No More Deaths was too ragtag and inexperienced to coordinate the event, so they took over most of the program. In the end, however, the job got done.

The first summer (2004), most of the camp volunteers came from within the ranks of the folks in Tucson—the 65 or 70 people who'd been attending the meetings. In addition, Eric Mason and his friends drove over from Santa Fe, New Mexico. Several students came from Colorado College led by their sponsor and driving force, Eric Popkin. Various groups involved put the word out to their email lists—BAN, *Derechos*, Pan Left, and Borderlands Theater. Margo Cowan and Andy Silverman recruited a few others from the University of Arizona.

Matt Moore, youth director at St. Mark's Presbyterian Church, was caught up by the vision and was very active the first year. He felt that putting out water and food was good, but not good enough. "We have to *be* there!" It was decided that an around-the-clock, non-violent, humanitarian physical presence in the desert would be the single most effective approach. The idea of "The Ark of the Covenant" as a name for that presence was Matt's. The following summer he died of a massive heart attack, a tragedy felt keenly by No More Deaths' volunteers and others (his life was celebrated at the opening of camp that year.).

Bill Holliday, a *Bancomun* employee in Nogales, Sonora, helped gather all the equipment and set up camp in Arivaca, Arizona. By 2005, we posted the call for volunteers on our new website. People were also spreading the message by word of mouth. In the summer of 2005, approximately 50 out-of-towners volunteered with No More Deaths.

CHAPTER 5

Philosophy

THE PRINCIPLE OF "CIVIL INITIATIVE" was developed by Jim Corbett, a Quaker, during the Sanctuary Movement in the 1980s to distinguish it from other forms of organizing, such as protest, civil disobedience, or organizing to take power. No More Deaths decided this principle fit the current circumstances as well as those in the 80s and adopted it for this new struggle. As a community, No More Deaths has a sense of law that is more fundamental than formal legal codes.

According to the Sanctuary workers who devised civil initiative, this fundamental sense of law concerns basic human rights which, because they are universally valid, are codified in international and religious law. Tucson Sanctuary workers argued that in the case of U.S. immigration law, the problem was not that the U.S. government had interpreted its immigration statutes in ways that violated the community's consensus but that the persecuted people should not be deported to face further persecution. To correct this misinterpretation, Sanctuary workers decided to act as they felt the government ought to have been doing. They reasoned that this would force the U.S. government to comply with community legal norms in one of two ways. Either the government would fail to prosecute Sanctuary, so they would share their interpretation of the law. (Movement members did not consider the Tucson Sanctuary trial a true test of this theory, since defendants had not been permitted to present their legal arguments.) Participants called their legal strategy civil initiative rather than civil disobedience because they believed that it enforced, rather than violated, federal and international law.

In his most recent book (to this date), Miguel A. de la Torre elaborates:

> Civil initiative is based on international law, specifically the legal response developed during the Nuremberg trials of Nazi officials who tried to exonerate themselves from blame for a multitude of atrocities with the excuse that they were "simply following orders." The court, in *United States vs. Goering* (1946), concluded that international duties transcend individual obligations to obey national states. There is a moral obligation to help victims of human rights violations. Today, probably the greatest human rights violation within the U.S. borders is occurring against Latinos on those borders. Not since the days of Jim and Jane Crow has the U.S. government maintained a policy that systemically brings death to a group of people based on their race or ethnicity. Our immigration policies are killing Hispanics. As our people constantly remind us, this is not a border that separates the U.S. from Latin America, it is a bleeding scar caused by the Third World rubbing up against the empire.[24]

Civil Initiative
By Jim Corbet, Quaker

Civil initiative is formed by this function: Our responsibility for protecting the persecuted must be balanced by our accountability to the legal order. As formed by accountability, civil initiative **is NONVIOLENT, TRUTHFUL, UNIVERSAL, DIALOGICAL, GERMANE, VOLUNTEER-BASED,** and **COMMUNITY-CENTERED**.

---

24 Miguel A. de la Torre, *Latino/a Social Ethics, Moving Beyond Eurocentric Moral Thinking* (Texas: Baylor University Press, 2010).

- **NONVIOLENCE** checks vigilantism. Civil initiative neither evades nor seizes police powers.
- **TRUTHFULNESS** is the foundation for accountability. Civil initiative must be open and subject to public examination.
- Civil initiative is **UNIVERSAL** rather than factional, protecting those whose rights are being violated regardless of the victim's ideological position or political usefulness.
- Civil initiative is **DIALOGICAL**, addressing government officials as persons, not just as adversaries or functionaries. Any genuine reconciliation of civil initiative with bureaucratic practice—the discovery of an accommodation that does not compromise human rights—is a joint achievement: civil initiative can never be based on non-negotiable demands.
- Action that is **GERMANE** to victim's needs for protection distinguishes civil initiative from reactions that are primarily symbolic or expressive. As a corollary, media coverage and public opinion are of secondary importance when our central concern is to do justice rather than to petition others to do it.
- Civil initiative's emergency exercise of governmental functions is **VOLUNTEER-BASED**. The community must never forfeit its duty to protect the victims of human rights violations, but no bureaucracy should be formed that would oppose the return of governmental functions to those constitutionally designated to assume responsibility.
- Civil initiative is **COMMUNITY CENTERED**. To actualize the Nuremberg mandate, our exercise of civil initiative must be socially sustained and congregationally coherent; it must integrate, outlast and outreach individual acts of conscience.[25]

---

25 For more information about Jim Corbett and his ideas, see Ann Crittenden's book: *Sanctuary, a Story of American Conscience and Law in Collision* (New York: Weidenfeld and Nicholson, 1991), and Jim Corbett's book: *Goatwalking, A Guide to Wildland Living* (New York: Viking Press, 1991).

CHAPTER 6

Working in the Sonoran Desert–Claiming our Right to be here–2004

WHEN WE SET UP THE Arivaca camp, and the nearby Organ Pipe Cactus National Monument welcomed tourists throughout the park, back roads were open, and camping was permitted almost everywhere. But as time went by, new restrictions were set in place that prohibited the public from venturing onto any roads except the main highway to Mexico. The Monument staff permitted the public to stay only at the campground next to the headquarters. When we tried to enter Monument lands, we were told these restrictions were set in place "for our protection." Still later, members of the public were allowed to hike a trail in the park with an escort of four armed guards. Although there had been no incidents of violence in the park for ten years, the explanation was that there was "perceived violence."

Our strategy to assert our rights as citizens rendering humanitarian aid on public lands included several components:

* First, we met with Border Patrol's Tucson Sector Chief, Gilbert, to inform him of our intentions. We continued to meet each subsequent chief for the same reason;

* Second, we did not hesitate to meet with government agencies and the press when we thought they were infringing our rights. So, when the U.S. Fish and Wildlife Service cited us for "littering" due to leaving gallon bottles of water on trails, we fought those citations in courts and told the press. We

also challenged their charges by continuing to put out water. Eventually we won in the courts and with the public;

* We used other strategies, as well, to assert our rights to give aid. We created signs for our backpacks and our trucks—to identify ourselves. We enlisted doctors and nurses to help. We organized wilderness first responder courses for our volunteers, and in 2012 we erected a MASH-type first aid tent at our main camp;

* In addition, we took advantage of opportunities to invite people to experience our work first hand. We spoke to groups around the country, elicited media stories, and participated in immigration-related conferences. We invited people to see and hear what we hear on a daily basis.

In addition to helping migrants, we hoped to be sufficiently visible and known that we couldn't be shut down.[26]

THE ARIVACA CAMP–JUNE 2004

Gathering at Byrd Camp (Rick Ufford-Chase left, John Fife center) 2004 (No More Deaths)

26 Submitted by The Rev. John Fife.

Gene and I joined dozens of others in Tucson on Memorial Day weekend in 2004 to initiate the work of No More Deaths in the desert near Arivaca—a small, rural, desert town about 15 miles north of the border. As spelled out by the planning group, the weekend started with an event at the Congress Hotel in Tucson on Friday night, followed by the other events. We then traveled south to Byrd Camp. This was designated sacred ground. Not only was this to be sacred ground in its own right, but the thought was that Border Patrol would think twice about invading this sacred space to look for migrants.

On the way from Tucson to the camp, I kept turning things over in my mind about how the effort would work. Would migrants come into the camp? How would they find it? Would we go out to look for them? Would they stay on cots overnight? Would we cook for them? What if they were injured? What if Border Patrol learned there were migrants at camp? It was difficult for me to imagine how the scene would play out.

The camp consisted of a small trailer, an awning, some shelves containing cans of beans, boxes of pasta, and juice, plus a table with a cook stove, water, and a few plastic crates around about. About 40 people from Tucson and the surrounding area attended. The ministers, John Fife, Sue Westfall, Brandon Wert, Father Bob, and Liana Rowe led the service to dedicate the Ark. The Ark was comprised of a cross, a statue of the Virgin of Guadalupe, and several desert and migrant artifacts. Its purpose was to establish this as a religious site where migrants would be safe to stop and rest.

Byrd Baylor was there as well. I'd heard of Byrd before ever meeting her because her many children's books are among my favorites. That she is a naturalist who loves the earth and the way she connects with Native Peoples comes through clearly in her books with such titles as: *When Clay Sings, The Other Way to Listen, How to Make Perfect Mountains,* and *I'm in Charge of Celebrations,* to name just a few. *The Way to Start a Day* (1979) won a Caldecott Award for both Byrd and her illustrator, Peter Parnell. Parnell has illustrated most of her whimsical stories with charming artistry. She also writes amusing essays that she's published in books for adults. Especially funny is her essay about learning to speak Spanish—class after class, she never gets beyond the present tense. She does readings each year (in English) in Tucson to raise money for the Guatemala Project—a project in which Sarah Roberts, one of our nurses, takes part for three weeks every summer (health professionals working in the highlands of Guatemala).

On the camp dedication day in 2004, tiny Byrd, who weighs maybe 80 pounds, was dressed for the desert in a cotton shirt and pants. With straight white hair and desert-weathered skin, she looked right at home—which she was.

In thinking back to that day, I realize that I wasn't aware how No More Deaths and Byrd connected in the first place. Arivaca residents, a mix of ranchers and hippies, have varied opinions about migrants coming through their back yards, helping themselves to water and occasionally stealing things they need for their journey. Finding someone who'd *actually invite* humanitarians (and probably migrants) onto their land seemed pretty unlikely.

Nonetheless, Steve Johnston gave me her number and I called her. I caught her one day while she was in her truck in front of the Arivaca Mercantile store, and we chatted a bit about how she got involved with No More Deaths. Basically, she told me, "I said yes!" She had gone to the Arivaca dump just outside of town and run across a few folks from Tucson, including her cousin Rudy Byrd. They were removing a Humane Borders water station that had been placed near the dump because Arivaca folks didn't like it being there. They were afraid it would bring out "the wrong elements." Byrd offered to let Humane Borders move the water station to her property about fifteen miles east of Arivaca. So that was done. A couple of weeks later, someone asked about putting a camp near the site of the water tank. She's not sure who that was—maybe

Brandon Wert, from Southside Presbyterian Church—but no matter, she said yes.

Brandon said that he and Randy Meyer[27] went out to see Byrd Baylor about using her property for the No More Deaths desert camp. Brandon had been out previously to see the Humane Borders water station already installed on her property and thought the area could easily accommodate the camp.

He confirmed that Byrd did indeed say, "Yes!"

Byrd Baylor (No More Deaths)

---

27 The Rev. Randy Meyer and his family had recently moved to Sahuarita, a retirement community located between Tucson and Nogales, to be pastor of Good Shepherd United Church of Christ. This church houses a southern group of the Samaritans (called Green Valley Samaritans) and has a large following—over 120 at time of publication.

So, they set up the original camp near that water station but later moved it slightly because they learned the hard way that it was in a waterway. Brandon recalls that by the second summer the notion of "The Ark of the Covenant" became less important, as a number of nonreligious volunteers began to work at the camp and the "Ark" had less meaning to them. Brandon suggested that some of them were just not into Jesus. However, every year people continued contributing artifacts found on their desert treks to the altar. The Rev. Robin Hoover, pastor of First Christian Church and head of Humane Borders, was also involved in those early exploration efforts.

Byrd's house sits on a little hill near Papalote Wash, and it can be seen from the road. She grew up in Tucson, then moved to this charming spot near Arivaca more than 20 years ago. At first, she camped out, but friends from Tucson and Arivaca helped her build her home. She still sleeps outside in a protected area connected to her house. For some time before we arrived, she'd provide migrants with water and food, and occasionally a place to sleep. She told me that Yaqui Indians crossed that area 150 years ago during the Mexican Revolution. Their well-traveled trail can still be seen through the fence right next to the Byrd Camp. The Yaquis were being persecuted and sold into slavery in the Yucatan.

She said, "There've always been people traveling through this area on old, old trails, and there are always going to people traveling through—despite the best efforts of our government to stop it."

GETTING TO TUCSON AND THE OTHER SERVICE LOCATIONS

People arrive in Tucson for No More Deaths adventures from all over the country. Even from around the world. Many of the out-of-country folks are journalists wanting to see firsthand what's taking place to write about our "border problem." Often, they compare it with the border and migrant issue in their own countries—issues that have escalated greatly since the early days of No More Deaths.

Some volunteers drive their own cars or their school's vehicles. Most arrive by plane at Tucson International Airport where they are met by No More Deaths volunteers, or possibly, they climb aboard a shuttle to travel to their destination *du jour*. We've used a few different facilities. During the first few years, volunteers stayed at and were trained at Southside Presbyterian Church—John Fife's former parish. We've also used St. Mark's Presbyterian Church, which sponsors us. Others would come in subsequent years. Each location has its advantages, but the major disadvantage of churches is that they expect to have worship on Sunday mornings. Imagine that! Early Sunday morning, each groggy volunteer would have to gather up his or her sleeping bags and make him or herself invisible. From the church we'd travel to nearby co-opted restaurants, whose Sunday clientele is minimal, to hold our training.

Training is conducted on Saturday nights and Sunday mornings for those going into the desert, and for those going into one of the border towns of Naco, Agua Prieta, or Nogales. The desert folks travel south in No More Deaths vehicles. Those going to the border travel a variety of ways—private cars, commercial vans or buses.

CHAPTER 7

Compassion–The Stretcher–July 4, 2005

JIM WALSH AND HIS PARTNER Sarah Roberts (one of our main health professionals) live in the Tucson Mountains. Jim was trained as a social worker and is a long-time member of the Catholic Worker Movement. He spent many years volunteering with grassroots environmentalists and human rights groups in Korea and Kenya. Among his No More Deaths chores, he serves as our liaison with the Food Bank and started the Dignity Project—which supplies deportees in Nogales with basic necessities. In the early years he volunteered regularly for the Casa Maria soup kitchen in Tucson and has served as a Deacon at Southside Presbyterian Church. He agreed to tell me about "The Stretcher."

One of the best ways to give understanding of what happens to volunteers once they arrive at camp is through a story. We sat on his back porch, looked at his desert garden, and watched birds flutter from tree to tree while he told me what happened:

Jim and Margo Cowan (one of our attorneys and long-time Tucson activist) first found the stretcher in July 2005. The hot, dry weather that summer had caused a record number of deaths in the desert—and volunteers had evacuated many migrants to St. Mary's Hospital in Tucson. Jim himself had evacuated two migrants that very week. A number of the volunteers at Byrd Camp had come from Colorado College; they were kept very busy running patrols along the trails looking for migrants.

Margo and Lupe Castillo (Margo's partner and instructor at Pima Community College) were spending the week at Byrd Camp as camp coordinators. Some of the volunteers were helping in the search for Lucrecia along with her father Cesario (see Steve's story later). Others preferred to search for the living. On July 4th, Jim and Margo were hiking on the Arivaca West Trail, near the road in Buenos Aires National Wildlife Refuge (BANWR). They encountered several migrants and gave them water and new socks. One woman they discovered came all the way from Mexico City and had been with a group who were dispersed by a hovering Border Patrol helicopter. This woman had never reconnected with other members of her group and was totally spent. Her feet were covered with blisters; she complained of chest pains. She was exhausted and wanted to go home.

Jim, Margo, and the woman drove into Arivaca to call Border Patrol. After they called, they sat in the back of the *Roja* (a Dodge pickup) in the front of Arivaca Mercantile watching the traffic go by. They waited at the store for hours, but Border Patrol never came. They took note of the absence of Border Patrol in the field and in town. Lupe, who was fifteen or so miles away at Byrd Camp, suggested by cell phone that they bring the woman there, and she agreed to go. The following day, volunteers could take her to Tucson to see a doctor.

Back at camp, Sun Dog (our acquaintance and caretaker of the old mining town property in Ruby) called to tell the volunteers there was huge activity near the railroad at milepost 16 on Arivaca Road. Seventy people had been taken into custody and one person had died. Early the next morning, Jim and Margo drove to the scene. An entire shift of Border Patrol officers was processing the migrants. Trash lay strewn all around. Jim and Margo learned that a woman had fallen ill, and the other migrants constructed a stretcher, so they could carry her. The woman's friends had carried her almost all the way out to the road. Nevertheless, she died.

The Stretcher 2005 (No More Deaths)

Upon investigation, Jim and Margo found the stretcher about 100 yards south of Ruby Road. The stretcher measured about six feet long, constructed of fallen mesquite limbs and branches (or maybe oak, juniper, or pine). Ripped pieces of garments and a migrant's belt had been used to tie the crossbars to the sides. The stretcher was an extremely awkward and uncomfortable-looking structure.

After finding the stretcher, Jim climbed the trail for about a mile to look for more people. It proved to be a very precipitous trail: deep, rugged, narrow, and steep. Jim realized it took a heroic effort to carry out the mortally-wounded woman—a massive undertaking. One belt holding the stretcher together said "USA USA USA" in white letters on a black background.

Jim said this experience deepened his understanding of the need for people to be out there trying to save lives. Just that day, they had met and helped several groups of migrants. And the temperature was dropping, the sky was darkening, and the winds were kicking up.

Monsoon weather had finally arrived and was horrific—trails were slippery, streams burst their banks, telephone reception was poor if not impossible, migrants suffered unusual foot trauma from wet socks and deteriorating shoes, and the least miscalculation threw migrants and volunteers into beds of cactus and mesquite trees.

The hilly terrain had prevented cell phone reception at milepost 16, so it wasn't until they reached the lake turnoff that a call came through from the camp: four very sick guys had come in seeking help. When Jim and Margo got back from the Arivaca Road scene, they gathered up the four guys and the Mexico City woman and took them into Tucson. As they were driving north, the women from Mexico nursed one seriously ill man by placing cold packs in his armpits and on his lap to help bring down his fever. His sclera (the dense white fibrous membrane that covers the eyeball) was blood red; his speech was slurred. Later on, he had no memory of that day, but it was one our volunteers wouldn't forget. For a long time, until the hiking pattern changed, volunteers made water drops near the stretcher.

Jim said he had been involved in a couple of discussions about removing the stretcher from its place in the desert. But it remained in *situ* and became a monument to migrant inventiveness, tenacity, and care. It was used as a focal point of humanitarian effort—No More Deaths and Samaritan volunteers would take journalists and other visitors to the site and talk about the migrant crisis and their heroic efforts to find new lives.[28] [29]

Just a few days later, on July 9th, Daniel Strauss and Shanti Sells were arrested for driving three men toward Tucson for medical help. This was the beginning of a pitched battle with the government—for the humanitarians to be able to provide aid in the desert and to take sick migrants to hospitals.

---

28 Interview with Jim Walsh (November 2010).

29 A couple of years later this discussion was renewed which led to the removal of the stretcher to a museum site.

CHAPTER 8

Daniel and Shanti–Is No More Deaths
Breaking the Law?–2005-2006

Shanti Sellz 2005 (No More Deaths)

THE MAIN ROAD FROM TUCSON to areas traveled by migrants (Interstate 19) follows the Santa Cruz River through the Santa Cruz Valley. It makes a slight "S" curve as it heads south. A beautiful valley, it offers a wide view of the surrounding countryside. Upon leaving Tucson, one can see the Rincon Mountains on the left and the Santa Catalina Mountains in the rearview mirror. After passing Mission San Xavier del Bac on the right, the long string of the Santa Rita Mountains on the left begin to appear. Its highest peak, Mount Wrightson (elevation 9,452 feet), is a popular location for hiking.

At the base of the mountain range, northwest of Mount Wrightson, is the entrance to Madera Canyon: a holiday haven for bird watchers. More than 200 species of birds have been identified there. The Friends of Madera Canyon website describes the Santa Rita Mountains as a "sky island" above the surrounding sea of desert. Visitors from all over the world arrive in Madera Canyon in search of unusual species, such as the elf owl, the elephant trogon, and sulfur-bellied flycatcher.[30]

Continuing south, on the right are the Sierritas, and ahead, the border mountains, the Tumacacoris, the Patagonias, and the Pajaritos. It is not lost on me that the names of most of the hills, valleys, rivers, and towns in this area of our country carry names from the Spanish, Mexicans, or Native Americans who lived here long before we did. When the United States acquired 55 percent of Mexico's land mass following the end of the Mexican-American War in 1848, more than 80,000 Mexicans are projected to have been living here.

Traveling through this valley in July 2005, Shanti Sellz and Daniel Strauss, young adult volunteers with No More Deaths, were transporting three sick migrants to medical care in Tucson. Along Arivaca Road, in the heat of summer, they were arrested and later charged with two felonies for helping the migrants.

Daniel had graduated from Colorado College and was living in Tucson and working for No More Deaths for his second summer when they were arrested. He had worked at one of the No More Deaths first aid stations in the desert 24/7. Every day volunteers would encounter migrants who were sick and needed help.

---

30 www.friendsofmaderacanyon.org (accessed June 3, 2010).

The previous year (2004), Daniel and eight other Colorado College students had taken a class trip to see what the migrant experience was like. They were among the first college students to work with No More Deaths. They had spoken with migrants in Mexico who were about to cross the border and learned what they were going through, why they had to leave their home communities, the struggles they went through to cross the desert, and why so many people would take that journey and risk their lives. To the college group, the stories were compelling. The migrants were their heroes. They felt like they had to do something to help them.

Shanti had moved to the old Southern Arizona mining town of Bisbee in 2004 to take a job. She was very quickly introduced into the reality of the border and began working with a group in Bisbee putting water in the desert for people who were crossing. From that group she learned of No More Deaths and the camp that Daniel and his school classmates had helped set up (Byrd Camp). She moved to Tucson as a volunteer to participate with them in the camp. She then returned the following summer as a full-time volunteer to help coordinate the camp.

On July 9, 2005, Shanti and Daniel had been out in the desert and drove into Byrd Camp on their way back to Tucson. They learned that nine very sick men had been brought to camp for treatment. The men had been in the desert for more than four days, two of which they spent without food and water. One had been vomiting and said he hadn't been able to keep anything down for days. He also reported finding blood in his stool. Three men had blisters on their feet that prevented them from walking. That month 78 migrants had died; it was the deadliest month on record in Arizona history. The temperature had been over a hundred degrees for forty straight days.

Volunteers at the camp assessed their needs and deemed it necessary for three of the men to be evacuated for further medical care. They had phoned our on-call medical person in Tucson who told them to take the migrants to Southside Presbyterian Church in

Tucson where we have a medical-aid center. They also got agreement from one of our attorneys. When Shanti and Daniel arrived at camp, Steve Johnston was just about to drive the men into town. But Shanti said she was ready to go, so she and Daniel might as well do it. It was agreed. So, they loaded up Shanti's beat-up hatchback and took off for Tucson, with a Samaritans magnetic sign on the side of the car.

The work of No More Deaths had been completely out in the open. We had informed the federal district attorney and Border Patrol of our protocol that included medically evacuating people when our medical consultants advised us to do so. Essentially, we had adopted the protocol of Samaritans until we began to adapt it for our needs at a later time. When we didn't hear back from Border Patrol, we continued doing our work as usual. Daniel indicated that he doesn't know exactly what changed. "One day we passed Border Patrol, waved to them, they waved back; then the next day we were arrested. It was clear something had changed politically, a change in policy, and they wanted to shut down our organization and the work that we do."

The three migrants were taken into custody at the time of Shanti and Daniel's arrest. Two of them were deported immediately with no medical care. The third one was held to testify against the two humanitarian workers. Eventually his story was taped, and he was deported. His story was used to indict the two defendants even though his testimony was completely in favor of Shanti and Daniel, saying that they had saved his life.

Later our attorneys learned the Border Patrol agent was new to the job as was the U.S. Attorney who approved the arrest. Margo Cowan believed that more experienced people would not have carried out the arrest.

Initially, the two volunteers were charged with a felony count of aiding and abetting in furtherance of illegal presence in the United States, basically a smuggling charge. The maximum sentence is five years in prison. They were also given a misdemeanor charge of obstruction of justice. Later in August 2005, they were indicted, and the grand jury dropped the misdemeanor charge, but added another felony of conspiracy which held a ten-year maximum sentence. This brought their potential maximum up to fifteen years in prison and a $500,000 fine!

No More Deaths launched the "Humanitarian Aid is Never a Crime" campaign in response to the indictment. People from all over the world responded to the campaign. We were targeting, at that point, the U.S. Attorney for the state of Arizona, Paul Charlton,[31] who had veto power over this case. We sent fifty-thousand postcards to his office demanding that these charges be dropped, but they were not. This case continued for almost a year and a half.

Humanitarian Aid is Never a Crime 2005 (No More Deaths)

No More Deaths chose the theme "Humanitarian Aid is Never a Crime" to raise money for the defense of Shanti and Daniel and to hook the public into paying attention to the prosecution of these young adults. While No More Deaths volunteers maintained the

31 One of the eleven U.S. Attorneys dismissed by President George W. Bush in 2007.

camp in Arivaca and started a new project in Nogales, the focus of No More Deaths during this period was the defense of Daniel and Shanti. Yard signs reading "Humanitarian Aid is Never a Crime" were distributed throughout Tucson and the state, in part to affect the jury pool who might become sympathetic to the defendants.

For weeks on end, Margo Cowan met at 7 a.m. every morning with Shanti and other No More Deaths volunteers (Daniel had moved to work in Jacksonville, Wyoming) to plan strategy. By the end of some meetings, participants would be in tears from stress over all the work that needed to be done and sometimes the lack of agreement about how to do it. For example, how best to spend the income from the campaign was a common contentious topic. Some people wanted to print more "Humanitarian Aid is never a Crime" signs; others did not—they'd already spent $15,000. Shanti made speaking tours around the country for almost two years to tell people about the case and to raise money for their defense. In addition, members of the group held nine consecutive press conferences.

How the volunteers lived and survived began to be an issue. While Gene and I still lived in Phoenix, Gene learned that some of the young adults working on the Humanitarian Aid campaign were dumpster diving to find food, even though No More Deaths was paying their rent and a providing them with a nominal stipend. (Some volunteers strongly resented the fact that others were being paid.) Many of the treasures they found in dumpsters were quite edible. Often Gene would shop at Costco before traveling from Phoenix to Tucson and then deliver a care package to the volunteers of things like cheese, fruit, almonds, and crackers, with sometimes a gift card to Fry's Supermarket.

In September 2005, a dark cloud still hung over the heads of Shanti and Daniel. Their trial date had been set back numerous times. The magistrate of the court had told attorney William A. Walker (Bill) he wasn't sure Bill should represent Shanti and Daniel because Bill was a participant in No More Deaths. Bill went to two judges for advice, including to Stanley Feldman—former chief justice of the Arizona Supreme Court. After meeting with Shanti and finding her to be a strong, intelligent young woman and a very sympathetic defendant, Judge Feldman called Bill to say he would like to become part of the defense team along with him.

Daniel and Shanti were offered plea bargains if they would plead guilty to committing a crime. They considered this offer over a weekend and then turned it down. When Shanti called to tell her mother, a social worker, she reported there was a momentary pause, then her mother exclaimed, "We're so proud of you!"

On December 13, 2005, (the day before the pretrial hearing) Amnesty International weighed in on the case:

> Amnesty International recognizes the sovereign right of states to control their borders and does not condone contravening the law. However, the organization stresses that no policy of border controls can be at the expense of the international human rights obligations of the state. Amnesty International is concerned that in this case Daniel Strauss and Shanti Sellz face punishment, possibly involving a prison term, solely for providing humanitarian aid to individuals in need of urgent assistance. Given the high death toll among undocumented migrants crossing the Arizona desert, Strauss and Sellz were arguably acting directly to protect and preserve life, a basic human right to which everyone is entitled.
>
> In view of these circumstances, and on the basis of the facts as presented, Amnesty International is supporting calls for the charges to be dropped in this case and considers that, if convicted and imprisoned, Daniel Strauss and Shanti Sellz would be prisoners of conscience.[32]

In court, Border Patrol claimed they had told the humanitarian groups of their change in policy; however, they couldn't produce a

---

32 Amnesty International (December 13, 2005).

document doing so, and the various humanitarian groups claimed they never received notice. U.S. District Court Judge Raner C. Collins, in dismissing the charges, ruled that the U.S. Border Patrol had "at least tacitly" approved the groups' conduct for the three years preceding Sellz' and Strauss' arrests. He said Border Patrol should have responded to the No More Death letters if it found fault with the group's action. The decision to drop the charges sets aside the larger question of whether the group's protocol and transportation of immigrants for medical reasons is legal. That issue must wait for another day, said Collins.

Bill Walker, one of the attorneys, said what the judge said was: "No More Deaths isn't an organization smuggling immigrants."

John Fife, one of the founders of No More Deaths, rejoiced, "This is vindication for our position from the very beginning. And that is *humanitarian aid is never a crime.* In my judgment, this means lives will be saved."

Shanti and Daniel Lead Representative Raul Grijalva on a Desert Trek (No More Deaths)

CHAPTER 9

Volunteers

...Volunteers from such diverse backgrounds
as faith communities and anarchist collectives
come together to expose the hypocrisy of
policies that use death as a political tool.

— CORINNE BANCROFT, NO MORE DEATHS VOLUNTEER

THE WORK OF NO MORE Deaths has been conducted entirely by volunteers—a few of them "stipended" volunteers receiving $1,000/month. Initially this was accomplished through the Presbyterian Church's Volunteer in Mission (VIM) program (later directly by No More Deaths and changed to $1,200). Other than VIMs, workers came from humanitarian groups in the Tucson area—Samaritans, *Derechos Humanos*, Humane Borders, Border Action Network, BorderLinks along with other local folks with concerns about the migrants. The first summer (2004) a group of college students also came from Colorado College in Colorado Springs, Colorado. By the following summer, Walt Staton, a volunteer from Prescott Valley, had put up a No More Deaths website. It attracted more students and young adults from around the country. As people returned home, they told others about their experiences, and the following years more volunteers came.

The in-town volunteers consisted of students from the UA, Pima Community College, and other colleges, and older, mostly-retired people. As students came from out-of-town, some of them stayed on to attend classes here at Pima Community College or at the University of Arizona. Many of the in-town volunteers were drawn from the base of volunteers in the 1980s Sanctuary Movement. This included attorneys Andy Silverman, Bates Butler, Bill Walker, and Margo Cowan; and John Fife, Rick Ufford-Chase, all from Tucson, and Gene Lefebvre from Phoenix.

The young adults moved with altruistic fervor—to carry out their commitment to justice, and most especially, to enact their love of direct action rather than talk to correct perceived wrongs. Many have said, "I've heard groups talk about doing things, but you people do them." Perhaps No More Deaths volunteers should be termed activists, some certainly are "anarchists" as well. Many of the college students have been enrolled in Latin American Studies or worked in migrant shelters or other humanitarian programs around the country. Some of their college programs were in the Departments of Geography with many titles unfamiliar to the older volunteers— Social Geography, Social Ecology, and People and Movements. Somehow, their prior work or studies endeared them to this work.

Except for Sarah Roberts (No More Deaths on-call nurse) and Jim Walsh (who gathers medical supplies and food), we lacked middle-aged volunteers; perhaps because we are too edgy, too risky. Especially for folks with babies and children. No More Deaths is too intense—in the meetings, in the desert, and along the border—for people with a lot to lose to become deeply involved.

CHAPTER 10

The Search for *Lucrecia*

*I may not have saved my own daughter's life, but
I've helped save someone else's daughter's life.*

— CESARIO DOMINGUEZ

PEOPLE WONDER WHY IN THE world that those of us living in Southern Arizona bother with the migrants. They say, it's their own fault that migrants get into trouble and sometimes die. This point of view is not one of compassion nor the result of knowledge and understanding of the complicity of the United States in this crisis through the implementation of NAFTA and cruel border enforcement. Nor are many naysayers aware of the government policy of deterrence which drives people from their homes and causes the deaths and suffering in our backyard. In addition, some people simply refuse to accept the responsibility each one of us has to influence the enactment and implementation of humane policies of our federal and state governments. Not to mention our moral responsibility to love and care for our neighbors.

The following poignant story, told by Steve Johnston, a long-time No More Deaths volunteer who had come to Tucson shortly before this event, reflects the results of our current federal policy. Fortunately, it also demonstrates elements of familial identity, compassion, and care that most humans are capable of showing toward one another. These qualities extend far beyond man-made laws and boundaries that are designed to control the movement of human beings in the face of extraordinary deprivation. Why, if we allow goods and money to cross borders under NAFTA, do we not also allow the needed workers to cross, as well?

This story documents the experiences a woman named Lucrecia had when she was no longer able to feed and fully care for her children in her home in the Mexican state of Zacatecas. She headed north to join other family members and find work. Other people have been coming to the United States from Zacatecas for many, many years and then returning to their families at the end of "the season." But now they face significant barriers to this pattern, which had worked well in past times.[33]

Steve Johnston:

Lucrecia was traveling between Highway 286 and the Baboquivari Mountains about 40 miles north of Sasabe with her 15-year-old son, Jesus, and her seven-year-old daughter, Nora, when she was taken ill. This particular July in 2005, there had been a stretch of 39 days with temperatures over 100 degrees, and many days over 110 degrees. After several days in the desert, Lucrecia had become dehydrated. While traveling at night and urged to move quickly over rough ground, eventually, she was unable to continue. Jesus remained with her, and her daughter continued with the traveling group. Lucrecia and Jesus were soon without water.

Death by dehydration is horrible, as those who have read Urrea's *The Devil's Highway* know. Jesus stayed with his mother

---

33 Aviva Chomsky, *"They Take our Jobs!": And 20 Other Myths about Immigration* (Boston: Beacon Press, 2007).

'til the bitter moment of her death, then, he placed her body in what he thought would be a prominent spot between two washes near an agave century plant since those are uncommon in the low elevation of our desert. He carefully sketched the mountain ranges with Baboquivari on the left and Kitt Peak on the right and marked the location of the agave. He covered Lucrecia's face with a towel and set out to find help.

Wandering for two more days on the 60,000-acre King Anvil Ranch, Jesus finally made his way to Highway 286 where Border Patrol picked him up and promptly bussed him to the Mexican side of Nogales and dumped him—a severely dehydrated and desolate 15-year-old child. He was terrified of Border Patrol and claimed he was 18 years old.

In Nogales, Jesus was able to contact his grandfather, Cesario, who brought ten of his fellow villagers 900 miles from Zacatecas to search for his mother's remains. Cesario and others had crossing visas from working year after year in the U.S. The U.S. government would not allow Jesus, the one person who might be able to locate the body, but, alas, a deportee, to enter the U.S. to assist in the search. After numerous and lengthy delays, Jesus was finally given a 24-hour "compassionate visa." However, the time and trauma from the days of wandering alone had clouded his memory and Lucrecia was not found.

José Lerma, a house painter from Nassau, New Hampshire, twenty years in the U.S. and a citizen, originally came from Sombrerete, Zacatecas, the village of Cesario's family. His wife was a distant cousin of Lucrecia. When José learned of the situation, he flew to Tucson, rented a car, and dealt with the numerous bureaucracies that had given Cesario the runaround: Border Patrol, Pima County Sheriff's Department, Medical Examiner, and the Mexican Consulate. José financed the search for Lucrecia: food, housing, transportation, even the cost of the disposable cameras with which Cesario took pictures of the search areas, developed, and drove to Nogales, Sonora, every night to show Jesus. When asked why he did so much for someone he hardly knew, José didn't seem to understand the question. "We are all family," he said. José, a genuine Mexican-American hero.

The No More Deaths Camp learned of Cesario's search from *Derechos Humanos*, a humanitarian organization in Tucson. José drove Cesario and two other cousins out to Arivaca where they explained the search to us. They spent the night on our cots and before dawn the next morning, we drove the *Roja* (our favorite truck) filled with No More Deaths volunteers 50 miles to the search area.

We spent many days searching with Cesario, crossing scores of miles, in what many of us (including me) considered to be an impossible task: to locate what had to be just scattered remains in a 100-square-mile area. We searched for the lone agave cactus. In the six weeks that he searched, Cesario found three other human bodies before finding his daughter's. This was an area of concentrated migrant deaths and, fortunately, we were able to provide aid to many migrants that we came across during the search. Our mission continued.

Maryada Vallet told me that a Border Patrol commander joined the No More Deaths searchers one afternoon. He seemed to be suspicious of No More Deaths claim to be searching. He quickly fell. Maryada opened up her backpack and started to share a "migrant pack" with him—crackers and Gatorade. She told him, "Wow, I can see the headlines now: Border Patrol Chief of Agents Rescued from Heat Exhaustion by Humanitarians." He snapped back, "That's not funny." This was just a week or so after the arrest of

Shanti and Daniel, so the pressure was on. Then, with this sick agent in tow, they were searching for their trucks again on a dirt road when another agent drove by and saw his boss walking—a bit lost—with the No More Deaths searchers. He said, "Um, sir, did you lose your truck?" The chief seemed mortified! They all piled in the back of the agent's dog-catcher-style truck and he drove them to their vehicles.

One evening in late July, José phoned the camp to tell us that while searching for Lucrecia they had found a badly injured woman far from the highway. A small group of us (Sarah Roberts, Jim Walsh, and I) took the Pathfinder over to Highway 286 and traveled north to the milepost 37 turn-off. A Border Patrol vehicle followed us for five miles and then pulled us over at milepost 27.

Byrd Baylor was listening to her scanner as Border Patrol closed in. She later told us that they made a great joke about "taking us out." Flashing blue and red lights, and then an agent was tapping on our window, shining his flashlight in every corner of the car and laughing, "The rain running you people off? You closing down the camp?"

Border Patrol knew who we were by our distinctive vehicles and bright red *Los Samaritanos*[34] signs—as the 15 minutes of chatter Byrd overheard on her scanner confirmed. After a friendly response, we continued on our way, turned west at milepost 37, and then we traveled ten miles back into open desert to where José, Cesario, and Yolanda were waiting.

Yolanda, in her mid-thirties, came from the state of Mexico. She had been traveling in the desert for four days and had fallen numerous times in the dark. Her knees were the size of grapefruits and, after cutting the shoes off her feet,

---

34 No More Deaths used Samaritans signs until they were asked to create their own in 2007.

we found them covered with open bloody blisters. She had cactus spines in her mouth and all over her body from falling into the desert. She was severely dehydrated, even though José and Cesario had somewhat relieved her pain. She was accompanied by three other migrants, strangers who had encountered her abandoned in the desert. Although they were eager to move on, they stayed to help her. Over that summer, I ran into numerous instances of strangers helping strangers—often to their own detriment—by seeking out the very Border Patrol they were trying to avoid in order to assist a sick or injured fellow traveler. These strangers did not abandon Yolanda. José and Cesario wouldn't, nor would we. We treated her on the ground and phoned medical and legal advisers, who concurred that she required medical evacuation. We treated the blisters of Yolanda's savior companions, for the rain had caused blisters to rise on their feet. We gave them food and water and bid them *buena suerte*.

Cesario said, "I may not have saved my own daughter's life, but I've helped save someone else's daughter's life."

We took Yolanda to Tucson for medical care. She told us that we had saved her life, which was something we heard frequently in July. We giggled like children when we passed the gauntlet of four Border Patrol vehicles parked side by side at Three Points, their headlights shining brightly into our Pathfinder, illuminating us as we turned east onto Ajo Way toward town. We knew that Yolanda could not be thrust out into Nogales, Sonora, without medical aid, so we hid her on the floor. I guess it never occurred to Border Patrol that we were the same group they had followed earlier, and that it had taken us an hour and a half to travel twenty miles down a lonely, rain-soaked highway. You'd think they would've wondered about what we were doing during all that time.

Several mornings each week, Cesario went on the air to ask listeners for information regarding the specific location of his daughter's remains. Among the many pledges of support, four anonymous phone calls came in with invaluable information. Based on the description given by Cesario, these callers separately pieced together an approximate location of Lucrecia's body. The final caller told Cesario that an American flag had been placed near the body in hopes that somebody would find it.

During the third week of their search—and after finding four other bodies—Lucrecia's remains were found. The American flag was there. The body was not intact, but Cesario recognized her three gold rings that were still on her skeletal hand.

**The Rev. Sue Westfall, Shanti Sellz, Margo Cowan
and Cesario (Right Rear) (Michael Hyatt)**

It took two more weeks before her body could be repatriated to Zacatecas. Cesario did not rest. He called the morning show and thanked its listeners. He gathered the many people that helped along the way. Search volunteers and the NGOs involved in the search (including No More Deaths) held a memorial service in Tucson. After the service, Cesario granted quick interviews before catching a plane to Miami. He had been invited to speak about his experience on *Sabado Gigante*, a variety show broadcast throughout the Americas. Cesario's grief for his daughter's fatal attempt to cross the border now had a public face.

Unlike most others, Lucrecia's case would not go away. As soon as the nine days of traditional prayer and mourning were over, Cesario was back in the United States, invited to participate in a congressional delegation to talk about his story with politicians and policymakers. In national interviews and congressional testimonies, Cesario related the history of "...the most difficult task he had ever undertaken: the recovery of his daughter's body."

He forced his way into the public sphere to expose the conditions that make deaths unaccounted for, deniable, invisible, and insignificant. This journey represented a fight against the kind of social erasure that the unrecovered bodies of migrants go through—as in the case of those who "disappear" in the desert. This is a story of a man's work to make a death have meaning. It was no small task. [35]

More of Lucrecia's story was included in Rocio Magana's doctoral dissertation in 2008. Magana adds additional dimension by giving us Lucrecia's full name and where she lived: Lucrecia Dominguez Luna, a 35-year-old woman from the Mexican state of Zacatecas.

---

35 Aviva Chomsky, *"They Take our Jobs!": And 20 Other Myths about Immigration* (Boston: Beacon Press, 2007).

She also tells us that funding for the search came not only from José Lerma, but also from friends, family, and folks who heard about Lucrecia on Spanish-language radio.[36]

Samaritan Volunteer with Baboquiviri Mountain in the Background (sacred to Tohono O'odham Nation) (Michael Hyatt)

36 Rocio Magama, *Bodies on the Line* (Charleston: BiblioBizaar, 2008),138-143.

CHAPTER 11

Broader Concerns Spring 2006–March for Immigration Reform–Sensenbrenner Bill HR 4437

IN THE SPRING OF 2006, Gene and I were still living in Phoenix but thinking seriously about moving to Tucson. Gene and Laura Ilardo, No More Deaths coordinator in Phoenix, had begun to meet with a coalition of immigration rights groups that were gathered together by *Somos America*[37] to plan street actions regarding immigration reform. In the planning leading up to March 25th that year, the groups were asked to contribute $2,000 each to the event. When Gene told the planning group that this would be difficult for No More Deaths (as its coffers were low), the others assured him that it wasn't a problem.

They said things like: "Everyone respects No More Deaths and the work you do in the desert and at the border. You use your money to continue your life-saving efforts. Also, you are doing work that most of us can't do."

We were surprised by their knowledge of the work we do, given the intensity of their response to our dilemma. Gene and Laura continued to meet with planners of the event.

The day of the event, people met at the Fairgrounds at 19th Avenue and Thomas. I was home watching things unfold on television and heard CNN report that Phoenix had 300,000 marchers. The local police reported considerably fewer. When I arrived at the

---

37 An effort across the country convened to oppose the Illegal Immigration Control Act of 2005 H.R. 4437. In some areas of the country this group continues today.

capitol and saw the march along with the subsequent photos, I truly believed the CNN number to be the more accurate.

When I arrived, I met up with two friends in front of the capitol building. We sat in the grass a few feet from the dais and watched as marchers passed by. It was a wildly diverse crowd. Most significant to me were the many Mexican-American families pushing their babies in strollers. The crowd included people of all ages and all races, even though most were Hispanic. It was amazing to see all these people come out of the woodwork—so many excited young families, a group of Buddhist monks, college and high school kids—a number of them waving Mexican flags. The event had been announced on Spanish-language radio stations, which helped generate the large response. This was the first time we were aware that Latino evangelical churches supported such an effort in any numbers.

When the crowd was thick, the speakers (including Liana Rowe, Gene, and his friend, former Senator Alfredo Gutierrez) mounted the dais and spoke to the crowd. With so many people marching together, it was amazing there were no fights or other incidents to mar the day, although a few detractors lined the route.

In Tucson, about 10,000 people marched at Armory Park. I was told the media played no significant role in this march, and that there was a little violence.

Following the local marches, Maryada Vallet, Laura Ilardo, and three other Phoenix No More Deaths people drove all night to Los Angeles where they marched with a reported *one million* people there. They took the "Humanitarian Aid is Never a Crime" banner that was made during the Shanti-Daniel issue and displayed it with pride.

As part of the backlash over the protests and the controversy over the flag symbolism issue (all the Mexican flags flying in marches around the country), a Tucson group calling themselves

"Border Guardians" burned a Mexican flag in front of the Mexican Consulate in Tucson on April 9, 2006.[38]

**Phoenix No More Deaths Volunteers Prepare
Signs for the 2006 March (Laura Ilardo)**

The following day the group proceeded to burn two Mexican flags during another protest in Tucson which was estimated to have had 15,000 participants. After the police seized a student who had thrown a water bottle at the "Border Guardians," they followed the police officers calling for them to let the student go. As the situation escalated violence broke out and six participants were arrested. The next day the leader of the Border Guardians, Roy Warden, was

38 "Mexico says U.S. group burning Mexican flag is unacceptable," accessed April 14, 2006, http://kvos.com/Global/story.asp

arrested for charges including assault and starting a fire in a public park.[39]

In addition to the overall issue of immigration reform (including a path to citizenship), a major theme of the March 25th demonstration was the defeat of HR 4437, a bill sponsored by House Judiciary Committee Chairman, James Sensenbrenner (R WI). A controversial bill, it contained many excellent provisions but also included a number of provisions disliked by immigration reform advocates. Among the ones considered troubling was that the bill would bar states or local subdivisions that prohibit local law enforcement officials from assisting or cooperating with federal immigration law enforcement personnel from receiving SCAAP (federal) assistance. It would also revise the definition of "aggravated felony" to include all smuggling offenses, and illegal entry and reentry crimes where the sentence is a year or more. In addition, it would bar states or local subdivisions that prohibit local law enforcement officials from assisting or cooperating with federal immigration law enforcement personnel from receiving certain federal assistance.[40] These provisions foretold the 2010 legislation in Arizona known as SB 1070.

Another provision authorized the construction of at least two layers of reinforced fencing, additional physical barriers, roads, lighting, cameras, and sensors in five specialized zones.[41] The Sensenbrenner bill was defeated in Congress. What the bill omitted was a pathway to citizenship for migrants who have lived in the United States for many years, what many call "amnesty."

---

39 "United States Immigration Reform Protests," accessed 2/12/2011, www.wikipedia.org, 2.

40 According to the Illegal Immigration Control Act of 2005 H.R. 4437, Sections 201, 225.

41 *The Border Protection Anti-Terrorism and Illegal Immigration Act of 2005*, "Sensenbrenner Bill," Section 1002.

CHAPTER 12

Expanding our Work to the Border–2006–
Mariposa Aid Station

What good is it, my brothers and sisters, if you say you
have faith but do not have works? If a brother or sister is
naked and lacks daily food, and one of you says to them,
"Go in peace; keep warm and eat your fill," and yet you do
not supply their bodily needs, what is the good of that?

— JAMES 2:14-16, BIBLE, REVISED STANDARD VERSION

As EARLY AS 2004, No More Deaths and Samaritans planned an out-reach program to Nogales, Sonora, to provide services to repatriated migrants. In June of 2006, Maryada and others took multiple exploratory trips there "to scope out the place."

Maryada returned to Nogales with Margo Cowan and Maria Ochoa, a member of Southside Presbyterian Church, to meet with their old acquaintance, Sr. Jose Antonio Rivera-Cortes. Maryada told me that she remembers walking into his quiet office and watching him stare out the window at the border wall just a few feet away. Helen Lundgren, Linda Bayless, and Sarah Roberts also went to Nogales at various times to meet with Mexican officials to plan some action.

By summer of 2006, No More Deaths volunteers had become aware that each week thousands of migrants were being dropped off in Nogales and other border towns, hungry, thirsty, and with little or no medical care during their stay with Border Patrol. So, a larger group came together to see what could be done, including Margo Cowan, Maryada Vallet, and Dr. Norma Price. When the program was underway, they were joined by long-term volunteers: Marie Kessler and Charles Vernon (both of whom later became law students at the University of Arizona), Margaret Lordon, and many others in those first months.

Sr. Diego Rivera Cortez and Maryada Vallet 2006 (No More Deaths)

They spearheaded an effort to establish tented shelters at both the DeConcini and Mariposa ports of entry. Margo's previous knowledge of Sr. Diego Rivera Cortes (affectionately known as "*el Profe*") from his days in Tucson as the Mexican Consul helped to facilitate the initiation of the program. Senor Rivera was now the head of the unfunded State Commission for the Assistance to Migrants in Nogales, Sonora.

At the DeConcini port, neighborhood women unofficially cooked beans and made sandwiches in the office of the *Comision*. A *Senor Ramiro* owned the building on the *Comision Estatal* (street) and leased it to the *Comision* so it could be used as shelter for migrants, a place for volunteers to work, storage, cooking, and so on. Sandwiches from the office were distributed to migrants staying under the main town bridge as well as to the aid stations we had established.

In the midst of the campaign to free Shanti and Daniel, No More Deaths along with the Tucson and Green Valley Samaritans set up migrant aid stations to provide water, food, medical care, and information. Sometimes for up to 2000 repatriated migrants a day. At one point, several Mexican states provided beans, rice, coffee, and other foodstuffs to the ports to help feed the deluge of migrants. In addition, volunteers made up of U.S. citizens and migrants—including a *coyote*—prepared the food and worked at the tents. A young man, Gilberto, an on-site coordinator of the Mariposa migrant station for the *Comision*, lived in a small on-site trailer.

The original purpose for providing services in Nogales was to address the vulnerability of migrants as they tried for a second or third time to cross the desert while already exhausted, blistered, and discouraged. They were warned of the risks, counseled not to cross again, and practically speaking, encouraged to rest up for at least two weeks before making another attempt.

Maryada describes some of the initial activities and her reactions:

It was now mid-June and time to make THE MOVE. I'd been living in an apartment on the Mexican side with my friend Jay Ritchie. Bill Holliday from Tucson worked a few days a week in Nogales, Sonora, with *Bancomun*, and accepted our invitation for him to join us in our roach motel.

One day, Jay and I sat for the first time near the Mariposa port of entry with complete curiosity and *naiveté*, asking the informal sector vendors, who would later become very familiar faces, where exactly *repatriados,* repatriated people, might be found. They gave us some *direccion.*

Later we sat on the oversized curb behind the Mexican customs building and flagged down a man selling some deliciously cold fruit *paletas.* They were melting in the heat faster than our tongues could keep up. We wondered how and when the Homeland Security buses would ever come, not realizing that the folks sitting near us had been dumped from the most recent bus. They seemed to be glaring at the borderline in disbelief, unsure where to go or what to do.

We sat talking with our friend Anita about her studies that had brought her to the borderlands. She explained her work with water purification plants in both Nogaleses and the absurdity that a city that used to be unified could now be broken into polar opposites with clean water and sewage treatment found on one side while the desperate giant on the other side was left without these services.

Our car was parked in the dirt lot that would become our project space. It sits at the underpass of the border line with semitrucks waiting above. After about an hour a group of people, 25 or more, came walking toward us. Some wore back packs and some limped. They appeared as though they'd been traversing the desert, so we ventured out to meet them. Most of them were shy, but we chatted a bit in "*Spanglish.*"

I continued to work with people on both sides of the border, in Nogales, Sonora, and in Tucson. I'd lured Micah, a No More Deaths volunteer working in the desert, to come with me to Nogales. Soon I had a project notebook that included maps of Nogales, Sonora, that Walt Staton had printed for me, along with blank pages I planned to fill. With Micah, the project binder, a broom, some dishwashing soap, a cooler, supplies for migrants, and a few personal items, we hit the road.

Little by little, I sensed my geographic perspective shifting; I was now residing in an apartment south of this wretched wall. The 2006 Mexican elections were in full swing.

In the evenings, we sat with Bill to debrief and to beg for his translation of the sights, smells, and systems we were encountering on the daily outings we made in order to make progress with the aid station. On his computer he helped us create our first "bus report" form and an initial attempt at a volunteer orientation packet. This work was frequently interrupted by a squeal from me when another god-awful, large cockroach would appear in closer proximity than my comfort zone would allow. Chemical warfare began, and Bill and our friend Micah were entertained by the "spray" zone I would create around our beds each night.

By the third week of the month, we informed the in town (Tucson) coordinators that we were ready for our first batch of unsuspecting volunteers to be our guinea pigs. It was a challenge to coordinate with Rivera-Cortes to gain access to the office. The volunteers were eager to do their first shift at Mariposa, so we eventually got an office key and were able to store supplies in the office. We received our first "media visit," a southern California independent filmmaker.

On June 25th (2006) I presented a paper entitled "Nogales—Evaluating Summer Efforts and Visions" to a select group of interested folks. We didn't have much effort to evaluate, but we certainly had revisioning to do. I outlined immediate needs that we really could not go on without, ongoing needs, an analysis of what we knew people needed when stepping off the repatriation buses. Then we discussed protocols and the extent of the work. We urged that volunteers REALLY need to be screened before entering this site with such intensive and emotional potential. We also considered our thoughts and concerns about charity (giving things to people) vs. solidarity (working with them), and most importantly we wanted to know, "How can we help the most people with our limited resources?"

Two days later, perhaps as a gift from the monsoon gods, our 19 tons of water arrived ahead of schedule, and nine pickup trucks showed up with volunteers pumped to unload in the heat and humidity of an accelerating afternoon rain.

The binational meeting went well. We talked about wanting to start serving the repatriated migrants by the next Tuesday. And we discussed the need for the participation of local *Mexicanos* to help with the language and culture. We realized we needed to prepare our hearts and minds for a lot of tragedy—pregnant women and even children are returned at 2 a.m. We estimated we will see 15,000 people in just one summer. Unbelievable. We will investigate; we will be compassionate. We hope to bring more national attention to the death and suffering on the border. We want to collaborate with others. We want change. Most attendees sat and listened while Sr. Rivera Cortes and attorney Margo Cowan and a few community representatives discussed the strategy at hand. Most left impressed by the conversation. Slowly the "we hope" turned into "we will" and "we want."

On July 11th (2006) we held a press conference at the Mexican National Migration Institute office at the downtown port. From that point we began 24-hour coverage of the ports of entry. We quickly built a routine, a practice, and a methodology. We were sent forth from the starting line by our organization's and partner's best representatives and politicians. "This is historic," they said, "on your mark, get set, go." With water bottles and socks in hand, we began a fast-paced race of somersaulting—head over heels.

As we go along, no one knows where one day begins and another ends, and we're driven by the dizzying rush of the historic goal: We *will* meet *every* bus—at least during the summer months!

It became almost obsessive-compulsive for all involved, directly and indirectly. We didn't care how it happened as long as it did, and miraculously, the *mana* really did fall from heaven, at least in Southern Arizona, many times at just the right moments.

Gilberto and Felipe arrived around the third week of July. Marie Kessler (YAV volunteer) and I began to feel like "mother hens" with the young men around us. In all, it was a good time with good humor amidst a lot of hard work lifting pots, carrying supplies, and improving our Spanish as we talked with migrants. Before we knew it, we were a circle of friends who cared deeply for one another and for the work.

I wrote in my journal: "Love each migrant genuinely."

I stood in front of the *Comision* office one evening trying to relay these experiences on to a family member in a long-overdue phone call. Watching the wall. People are hard at work doing something and I don't necessarily want to stick around to be known "to have known" what exactly it is they were doing. No doubt I was watching highly-lucrative drugs being passed through the wall. I finished my conversation and stepped back into Rivera-Cortes' office. As I peered out between the curtains into the dark street, I saw a city police truck drive by twice. The second time it stopped in front of the house where the figures bustled around and seemed to join in the clandestine operation.

In my journal I described the organized crime and corruption I had seen in just a few weeks:

1. Watching potentially highly-lucrative drugs being passed through the wall;

2. Discussing police harassment, moneymaking, and involvement in lucrative crimes. It's commonly rumored that Border Patrol agents are bought off too;

3. Watching groups gather and crawl under, through or over the line, even in broad daylight;

4. Hearing about the tunnel systems and where they are purportedly functioning. An old system was found out of the back of the Commission office, and our *colonia* (neighborhood) is well-known for being starting points;

5. Hearing and reading that the rich in Mexico are either part of organized crime (i.e., corporations) or have relationships that are also lucrative (not too different from the U.S.);

6. Learning that our project was threatened by the presence of *coyotes*. I have to turn in the names of those lurking around us to *Profe* so he can decide who to call for enforcement of the area;

7. Discovering that the Mexican *Aduana* (customs) doesn't want us around at night—from *Profe*'s perspective, it's so they could take bribes unobserved.

Maryada soon found that her hesitation turned into confidence and she was able to build relationships in the fast-paced environment. Homeland Security buses dropped migrants ten to twenty times daily, disgorging loads of desert-weary people. These folks needed to be fed, given water, and have their wounds treated. Maryada sometimes expressed that she wondered if she and her coworkers were making any headway…or just building a house on the sand. Border realities are shocking, especially the abuse stories (abuse by *coyotes*, by Border Patrol, by bandits, and by fellow travelers), But, they can also become commonplace for those volunteers who constantly faced those same realities in the field. In town (i.e. Tucson, Green Valley, Sahuarita), many volunteers became committed to the cause, either in the desert or in Nogales. However, Maryada worried about how to articulate effectively their experiences in Nogales to the folks back in town. She reported the work to the No More Deaths in town circle, but said that as she spoke, she felt like each person was trying to internally comprehend what they were embarking on. It was likely different from any humanitarian aid work they'd ever done before.

However, the work in Nogales continued, and by the end of 2006, No More Deaths volunteers had created a mission statement for the work, to wit:

> To acknowledge that the suffering of migrants does not end when they are pulled out of the desert: We will strive to *reduce death and suffering* by giving assistance to returned persons on the Mexico side of the journey and be a *force of hospitality and humanitarian aid*. We will strive to *stop human rights violations* by conducting abuse compilation, and finally, we will commit ourselves to *bearing public witness* to the stories and lives we encounter in order to expose daily economic and border policies.

When Sr. Rivera-Cortes and No More Deaths volunteers began working together, they reached out to local churches, the local employment office, migrant shelters, grocery stores, and local authorities for support. These organizations responded with food, water, and other vital materials.

As Maryada reported, on the first day volunteers met U.S. Border Patrol buses filled with migrants at the Mariposa crossing. A few of the volunteers simply parked beneath the underpass of the international line at Mariposa. They opened the tailgate to their truck filled with a few "desert migrant packs" and waited for a bus to come—not knowing when or where people would arrive or what condition they might be in after their release from U.S. custody. The same situation replayed at the central port during the first night shift. The result: the quantity of basic supplies of food and water needed, the state of physical and emotional distress, the regularity of abuse testimonies, and the large number of women and children encountered far exceeded any prior humanitarian undertaking by these organizations.

Funding, volunteers, and support from both Arizona and Sonora attempted to meet this tremendous need. To give the project an initial surge of energy, an individual donor funded the purchase of the 19 tons of one-liter bottles, which were then trucked into Nogales. The Arizona Food Bank brought in loads of food to the project base at the *Comision* office in Nogales, Sonora.

On July 9th, a press conference in the downtown office of the National Institute of Migration of Mexico *(INM)* officially announced the partnership and the vision. Representatives from No More Deaths-Tucson, *Derechos Humanos*-Tucson, and from the State of Sonora General Direction for Migrants in Hermosillo, Sonora, were all signatories in the partnership. For two months to follow, a presence was maintained at the Mariposa Port (6 a.m. to 10 p.m.) and the DeConcini Port/Centro (10 p.m. to 6 a.m.) to provide bean burritos, sandwiches, water, medical attention, abuse compilation, and orientation to local resources. After the initial summer months, the *Comision* assumed the majority of the daily coordination for the project's efforts with support from U.S.-based groups.[42]

Gilberto, a deportee himself, said, "I see many groups and visitors inspired by the project and want to give and gather support, even if it's juice, soup cups, medicine, or beans. Sometimes the people we give food, water, and socks to say, 'Thank you for your help. You're doing something good.' I have learned a lot from being here the past few months, how to cook better, how to give first aid and blister care, and how the journey really is—how they suffer...and how this project has progressed from nothing! At times it is tiring

---

42 Maryada Vallet, *2006-2007 Year-End Report* (Arizona: No More Deaths, 2008).

but helping them is all I have." Gilberto was separated from his own four children who live in California and found it very painful to talk about them.

At year's end, more than 75,000 individuals (about 75 percent men, 23 percent women, and 3 percent children) had signed *Profe's* yellow pads as they were repatriated by Border Patrol through the port. In some cases, *Profe* was able to use those lists to locate family members estranged from one another and get them back together again. Such a primitive effort—but a beginning!

Mariposa Aid Station, 2006 (No More Deaths)
(from left: Antonio's trailer, *Cruz Roja* trailer, *Comision* tent)

CHAPTER 13

No More Deaths Future Up in the Air–Will We Hang on or Will We Implode?

NO MORE DEATHS DECIDED TO hold a retreat in mid-September 2006 to regroup following the dropping of all charges against Shanti and Daniel. Hurrah! Representatives from the various groups that made up the No More Deaths coalition gathered at Southside Presbyterian Church for the event. Rick Ufford-Chase facilitated the discussions over a two-day period.

Those who had been working on the Humanitarian Aid is Never a Crime campaign, had met with Margo Cowen at 7:00 each morning to plot and carry out strategy. They were exhausted. The exoneration of Shanti and Daniel—though thrilling—left people limp. Many of the same people who had worked on the campaign had also been called upon to put together the summer program: recruiting and training volunteers, purchasing equipment, supplies, and food as well as readying the desert camp. Some other folks expressed that they felt left out of the decision-making process, as they had been indeed. Nothing of major import was taken to the Monday night meetings. Thus, the consensus process that was so valued by many people had been regularly subverted. People were frustrated and angry.

Some participants wanted to move forward strongly by "pushing the envelope" with Border Patrol. No More Deaths volunteers argued that Border Patrol policies were not a true reflection of the law, nor of our rights as humans. It was suggested that we could drive migrants back to the border when they had given up hope instead of calling Border Patrol to come pick them up. We could continue to drive ill or injured migrants to medical care (the same issue in the case of Shanti and Daniel). We could cause disruptive action at ports where Homeland Security stages their buses to gain access to those migrants needing medical care. Still, some wanted to be cautious and avoid any further involvement with the authorities.

By the end of the second day, there was no "meeting of the minds." Rick suggested that everyone stay involved with their various groups while we went on hiatus until after the holidays. Everyone agreed, although it was hard not to wonder if No More Deaths would ever reconvene again.

A FRESH START FOR NO MORE DEATHS

On January 3rd, 2007, Gene and I arrived in Tucson and entered our new home. After we settled in, one of the first events we hosted was a Wilderness Response Training conducted by "Aerie Backcountry Medicine." About twenty No More Deaths volunteers met on our cold, north-facing patio and were led by trainers from Colorado and Montana. By the end of the week, "patients" and "rescuers" stretched across our one-acre piece of desert to demonstrate their first-responder skills when they acted out their final exam among the mesquite, palo verde, greasewood, and other native vegetation. After that, several more trainings took place around Tucson to bring the new volunteers up to date.

No More Deaths took Rick Ufford-Chase's suggestion. After being on hiatus since the previous September, we reconvened February 5th, 2007. But it was a shock to learn that leaders from the various groups comprising No More Deaths[43] had been meeting

---

43 Tucson Samaritans, Humane Borders, Green Valley Samaritans, *Derechos Humanos*, BorderLinks, Border Action Network, the Asylum Program, and others comprised No More Deaths.

privately during the interim to develop a roadmap for the future functioning of the group as a whole. Their plan called for a central committee made up of a member from each of the coalition groups, rather than solely from within No More Deaths itself. After that revelation, for two full months, a group of mostly-young adults pushed back, explaining how much they valued consensus decision-making, how they deplored the others meeting behind the backs of the whole group, how they didn't want a group of mostly-uninvolved people calling the shots, and "who did they think they were anyway? We don't want a board!" they asserted.

The mature were pitted against the young, the new people against the seasoned, the organized-type people against the *laissez-faire*, the Tucson folks against those from the outside, the shy participants against the talkers, and the anarchists against the card-carrying liberals.

Finally, on April 11th (after two months of torturous meetings, proposals and counter-proposals), representatives from each of the various coalition groups met with No More Deaths working groups—with such titles as desert aid (DAWGS), Mexico projects, fundraising, material aid, media, and data. The coalition groups, as well as Cecile Lumer representing the border towns of Naco/Naco, said they had had a change of heart. One by one, each representative indicated that he or she had enough to do to run their own organizations without managing No More Deaths, and they wished No More Deaths all the best.

Of all the representatives, only Margo Cowan (who did not attend the meeting), wanted to continue with in active role with No More Deaths in addition to her other legal work. She represented *Derechos Humanos*. Margo felt so strongly that the coalition should stay together that she had previously threatened to influence people to pull their financial support if the coalition fell apart. Subsequently, she and Mark Townley, the board chair of Humane Borders, continued to participate regularly in No More Deaths meetings.

Thus, No More Deaths became an independent organization (or movement) on its own. Some No More Deaths folks suspected the previous partners believed No More Deaths would go "down the tubes" without them. If they did, they must have been surprised, as No More Deaths continues its vital work with great energy and considerable physical and financial support this day.

Also discussed at that meeting was the need for a centralized group or council to share information, resources, and strategies surrounding migration. It was suggested we break into two groups— those who wanted to start a networking group and those who wanted to start getting No More Deaths organized for the summer.

That's what happened. The coalition representatives formed BorderNet which soon began to meet monthly to discuss topics and issues of interest to everyone. Subsequently, they occasionally met with Border Patrol Chief Robert Gilbert, who was new at the time, to discuss concerns about border issues. These meetings were unproductive, as Gilbert usually told the representatives how things would be and failed to take any of BorderNet's issues to heart. The most grievous issues mentioned to him more than once were: 1) the abuse of migrants while in Border Patrol custody and 2) the lack of medical attention for migrants while in custody for less than 72 hours.

Chief Gilbert indicated that he did not think these issues were a problem. While there exist guidelines for dealing with migrants who have been in custody for more than 72 hours, none exist for less than 72 hours, which is the situation for most migrants at the Arizona border. Walt Staton and Lois Martin, a university professor who retired here from Massachusetts to help on the border, represented No More Deaths at BorderNet meetings.

The "working group" began a budget for the summer. Not having worked from a budget previously, making one proved to be a challenge. After considerable discussion minus important information about previous years, we made a good start that evening. We built upon it over the next few weeks and by the end of May, we had agreed upon a $47,000 budget for the four summer months (June through September).

Fortunately, we had almost $20,000 on hand from the previous year, including the Oscar Romero Foundation prize money awarded to No More Deaths-volunteers Shanti Sellz and Daniel Strauss by the Rothko Chapel for Human Rights Work. Shanti and Daniel shared their part of the prize with No More Deaths. In addition, Rick Ufford-Chase donated $5,000 (part of the money he received from the *Dignitas Humana* Award for Human Rights from St. John's school of Theology and Seminary), and someone at Southside Presbyterian Church discovered $5,000 that had been designated for No More Deaths from an earlier time—which we quickly accessed.

The remainder of our funds would come from fees paid by the volunteers coming to work on the border or in the desert, donations from supporters, and proceeds from general fundraising efforts.

There would be many expenses: feeding and transporting volunteers, making food packets for migrants, providing medical supplies, acquiring, maintaining and fueling vehicles, and funding gallons and gallons of water to carry into the field for migrants.

CHAPTER 14

Decision by Consensus and Other Details

Preparation for the summer of 2007 included establishing new rules for the operation of No More Deaths. The young adults—mostly college graduates who'd become involved during the past three years—insisted we operate on a consensus model, following the model established during the Sanctuary Movement. One of our leaders, Walt Staton, provided training in consensus-based meetings to a small group of volunteers who'd then take turns moderating the weekly Monday night meetings.

The new rules included personal introductions at the beginning of each meeting, as we had some turnover and quite a few visitors each week. When voting, the rule was to use a thumbs-up/thumbs-down method to show support (or nonsupport) of a measure. If a person was new or unsure about an issue, he or she could demonstrate this by putting the thumb sideways. A thumbs-down posture blocked the action, and the issue would be renegotiated until consensus was reached—or it was dropped. If a person liked what was being said, fingers would wiggle to show enthusiastic support.

In addition, it was established that any substantive new proposal must be presented to the group at least one week before being voted on. In the same manner, unanticipated expenses of $500 or more must be proposed one week prior to voting.

Sometimes these rules meant that we took many weeks to come to an important decision. However, the rules gave structure to the meetings, and decision-making proceeded in an orderly manner.

For the first year, we also functioned with a coordinating committee comprised of key people from each of the several working groups.

During the previous September retreat, the group had tried to formulate a mission statement for No More Deaths. A discussion continued about whether we are an organization, a movement, or both. The following statement was adopted in the Spring of 2007.

No More Deaths Mission Statement

No More Deaths mission is to end death and suffering on the U.S./Mexico border through civil initiative; the conviction that people of conscience must work openly and in community to uphold fundamental human rights. Our work embraces the Faith-based Principles for Immigration Reform[44] and focuses on the following themes:

* Direct aid that extends the right to provide humanitarian assistance
* Witnessing and responding
* Consciousness raising
* Global movement building
* Encouraging humane immigration policy

In addition, the principle of civil initiative guides our work, our protocols, our interactions with migrants and the government, and among ourselves.

Universal Declaration of Human Rights

No More Deaths also bases its work on well-founded principles of international law found in various declarations of the United Nations.

As far back as December 10th, 1948, the United Nations adopted and proclaimed the Universal Declaration of Human Rights at the

---

44 See Chapter 93-.

Palais de Chaillot in France. Following this historic act, the Assembly called upon all member countries to publish the text of the declaration and "to cause it to be disseminated, displayed, read, and expounded principally in schools and other educational institutions, without distinction based on the politic status of countries or territories." The Universal Declaration is one of the fundamental documents of the United Nations.[45]

From the Preamble: "Whereas recognition of the inherent dignity and of the equal and inalienable rights of all members of the human family is the foundation of freedom, justice and peace in the world,... And, whereas the peoples of the United Nations have in the Charter reaffirmed their faith in fundamental human rights, in the dignity and worth of the human person and in the equal rights of men and women and have determined to promote social progress and better standards of life in larger freedom,..."

Here are some of the relevant provisions: "4) No one shall be held in slavery or servitude; slavery and the slave trade shall be prohibited in all their forms, 5) No one shall be subjected to torture or to cruel, inhumane or degrading treatment or punishment, 8) Everyone has the right to an effective remedy by the competent national tribunals for acts violating the fundamental rights granted him by the constitution or law, 9) No one shall be subjected to arbitrary arrest detention or exile, 16.3) The family is the natural and fundamental group unit of society and is entitled to protection by society and by the state."

The full document was reapproved at the 60th anniversary of the General Assembly.

RED CROSS PRINCIPLES

In addition, while not formally adopted by No More Deaths, the Red Cross Principles also inform our work:

---

45 "Universal Declaration of Human Rights," Wikipedia, accessed June 3, 2013, https//:en.wikipedia.org/wiki/Universal Declaration of Human Rights.

The objective of humanitarian aid is to save lives, alleviate suffering, and maintain human dignity.

Humanitarian aid agencies do so under generally recognized principles rooted in the Geneva Convention, such as those of the International Committee of the Red Cross/ Crescent: humanity, impartiality, neutrality, and independence. (The ICRC's principles are based on the Geneva Convention.)

* Humanity: that all people have equal dignity by virtue of their shared membership in humanity;
* Impartiality: that aid is given solely based on need;
* Neutrality: that those providing humanitarian aid have a duty to refrain from undertaking any action that furthers the interests of one party to the conflict or compromises those of the other;
* Independence: the agency must be given the information and latitude needed to execute its humanitarian mission.[46]

REDEFINING THE PROTOCOLS

Until 2007, No More Deaths had been using Samaritan (Sams) protocols in the desert. Then Samaritans politely asked us to develop our own protocols—and to make No More Deaths signs for our vehicles (and patches for our arms and backpacks). The Desert Aid Working Group (DAWGs) first took this on, then it went to the whole group for approval. Vigorous discussion ensued. The Sams sign was red; maybe we'd have a red cross, too. No, that's reserved for the American Red Cross. Finally, we settled for a green cross on a white background: about 11"x14" for the car door magnets and

---

46 Terry Fiona, *Condemned to Repeat: The Paradox of Humanitarian Aid* (New York: Cornell University, 2002).

appropriate sizes for other uses. Green is used in parts of Mexico and Central America to designate neighborhood medical clinics; maybe migrants would identify us that way.

We reviewed the Samaritan protocols to use as a model for new protocols for No More Deaths. People in the movement had been calling their efforts "Civil Disobedience." John Fife received a call from an attorney in New York who told him that what the humanitarians were doing was not civil disobedience. That term is used when people are acting against unjust laws. This was not the intent of No More Deaths. We were objecting to the government's lack of initiative in following existing national or international laws. We decided our basic principle should be termed "civil initiative," and feature the following qualities: transparency and accountability. It must be separate and distinguished from law enforcement. Our overall way of operating would be an interpretation of the law, civil initiative, and our mission statement.

Having established the principle of the No More Deaths protocols, the group went on to address the following (check out the No More Deaths website for details):

- Standards for No More Deaths volunteers and programs;
- Protocol for encountering migrants on the trail, roads, washes, etc.;
- Protocol for evacuation of migrants;
- Protocol for persons presenting "endangered persons" criteria;
- Protocol for legally protected persons;
- Protocol for interacting with Border Patrol;
- Protocol for encountering human remains;
- Protocol for patients at camp;
- Protocol for working with the media.

CHAPTER 15

Monday Night Meetings

APPROXIMATELY 25 OR 30 LOCAL volunteers from Tucson and surrounding areas gathered each Monday night at 7:00 at St. Mark's
Presbyterian Church. We met in the Geneva Room (or sometimes in
the Knox Room). We dragged chairs out of the closet, placed them
in a circle, turned on two almost-useless air-conditioning units,
and took our seats. Some of us kept water bottles by our sides and
Kleenex in our hands ready for the sweaty evening ahead.

Just from a few months of Gene's and my full participation with
No More Deaths in Tucson, I could look around the room and know
something about everyone in attendance. Steve Johnston came to
Tucson from Oklahoma 20 years ago. He's a man to reckon with,
more or less 60 years old, with long, grey hair usually fixed in a
ponytail. He wears a great big smile and is very affectionate. For several years, he spent long weekends at Byrd Camp—usually Thursday
through Monday—bridging the gap between the departures and
arrivals of groups of volunteers. He came back to Tucson to report
to the central group during our Monday night meetings.

Walt Staton—a multitalented, young man from Prescott Valley—
graduated at the top of his class and had considered enrolling in law
school this fall. He facilitated meetings, managed our website, fixed
our vehicles, and had something to contribute on every subject. His
eventual departure to graduate school would be a major loss.

Gene, Sue, Antonio, Walt 2006 in Nogales (No More Deaths)

We had known Maryada Vallet since the "Humanitarian Aid is Never a Crime" campaign in 2005. As one of the stipended volunteers in the campaign, Maryada frequently encountered Gene when he went from Phoenix to Tucson for No More Deaths meetings. She was raised in Phoenix as an evangelical Christian and had graduated from Azusa Pacific University in Los Angeles with honors, receiving two Bachelor of Arts degrees in both Global Studies and Political Science with a concentration in International Relations.

Monday night meetings were (and continue to be) pretty lively as we discussed the revision of protocols, the content of training, our newfound status as an autonomous organization rather than a coalition, reports of experiences in the desert and the border, and any other issues. We'd been hearing reports on our work at Naco, Agua Prieta, Benjamin Hill, and Nogales—all in Sonora, Mexico. Plus, we documented abuses by Border Patrol, reached out to other humanitarian groups, followed immigration reform in Congress, and constantly upgraded ongoing efforts. It could be both exhausting and exhilarating.

PREPARING FOR SUMMER

Following the April 11th meeting, serious work for the summer program got underway. Steve Johnston led the charge for Byrd Camp, which intersects one of the main trails used by migrants.

Maryada and a working group made up of representatives from No More Deaths, The Tucson and Green Valley Samaritans, and the Mexican Office of Migrant Assistance, led our continuing work with the Mariposa Aid Station in Nogales, Sonora, Mexico. Unlike most of the desert work that took a break after the long, hot summers, the work at Mariposa continued through the fall and winter of 2006, 2007, and beyond.

Stash of Water Jugs at Mobile Camp (No More Deaths)

As planning for the summer of 2007 in the desert continued, Gene wanted to start a mobile camp that could provide a base for volunteers as migrants changed their paths. He and Dan Millis, a young man recently retired from teaching Spanish at a private school near Sedona, initiated that effort, including the purchase of additional cots, tents, potties, medical supplies, and food—and finding a site for the first base camp.

Dr. Dereka Rushbrook, UA professor, worked on both the migrant center at Benjamin Hill and on the documentation of people who'd been abused by Border Patrol while in short-term custody.

The rest of us took on various tasks that we were suited for—getting insurance for the vehicles, contacting grocery stores for donations of water, updating our website to include an application for summer volunteers, creating an updated training program, revising camp protocols, and more.

Two young women, Carrie Barrie and Andrea Leonard, both recent college graduates who were Young Adult Volunteers from the Presbyterian Church, carried on the work of recruiting and placing volunteers while also managing the variety of supplies that regularly arrived from people around the country supporting our effort. The supplies included water, food packs, socks, shoes, pants, and medical packs. Often large cardboard boxes arrived without warning to our office at St. Mark's Presbyterian Church. It took a huge coordinated effort and cooperation from St. Mark's to make it all work.

SUMMER PROGRAM KICKOFF PRESS RELEASE

These are the people who are changing the world.

Tucson, Arizona—Join No More Deaths this Wednesday, June 6, 2007, at noon at Southside Presbyterian Church for our summer kickoff press conference. We will give a summary of our activities from the past several months, announce the opening of our Arivaca migrant-rescue camp and give an update on our continued aid work in Agua Prieta and Nogales.

Volunteer Shanti Sellz will present the Migrant Courage award—a human rights award that acknowledges the bravery and courage of those people who are forced to leave their communities behind to find a new livelihood to support and unite their families. We have witnessed the daily heroic acts of these individuals and will share some of their heartfelt stories.

The press conference will also feature statements from Tucson Samaritans, Green Valley Samaritans, *Derechos Humanos*, Humane Borders and others.

For its fourth consecutive summer, No More Deaths is committing to around-the-clock presence in the Sonoran Desert of Southern Arizona. Year after year, this region has proven to be the deadliest to migrants with summer daytime temperatures easily exceeding 100 degrees. Almost 100 people have already died since October 1st, 2006. Doctors, nurses, EMTs, Wilderness First Responders, and other medical professionals have already enlisted as summer volunteers to assist with No More Deaths life-saving work.

…No More Deaths demands safe, legal, and dignified avenues for people to cross the international boundary and opposes the fundamentally flawed ongoing approach of border militarization.

Debbie McCullough created an art piece featuring a spoon with the words: "How far would you walk to feed your child? The award is dedicated to the migrants; We're not the heroes, the migrants are."[47]

Following the press conference, volunteers headed home to pack for going out to the desert or heading south to the border.

---

47 No More Deaths, *Press Release*, (June 1, 2007).

CHAPTER 16

An Historical Perspective

AT THIS TIME (2007), No More Deaths conducted training on Saturday evenings and Sunday mornings for those going into the desert and those going into the border towns. These folks received on-site training, as well. Over the years, experimentation took place regarding content, venue, and length of time spent on training.

Here's a taste of a one-hour training on Southwest history given by Lupe Castillo, an instructor at Pima Community College. Here, I am paraphrasing what Lupe had to say in the first few trainings I attended. Many people from other parts of the country or world who come to Tucson to volunteer had a lot to absorb about the Southwest before venturing into the field to begin their work. This information provides background and context to the volunteers for understanding the current crisis in the desert:

> We in Southern Arizona live in profoundly indigenous lands. Prior to the coming of the "white man," migration had been from the north to the south, not east to west as we later know it. People traveled across the Bering Strait and headed south leaving native colonies all along the way. Arizona alone has 26 indigenous communities started in that way. I am Tohono O'odham. I am Mexican. Maybe my parents and grandparents were born here, but I still identify myself as Mexican. I can assert Mexican and American identities equally.

The Mexican flag expresses the mythology of the beginnings of Mexico. The leader of a group of people traveling from the north had a dream in which their god, *Huitzilopochtli*, commanded them to find a crested bird perched on a cactus devouring a snake. After two- hundred years of wandering, they found the promised sign on a small island in Lake Texcoco. There they founded their new capital, *Tenohctitl* (later called Mexico City). The center crest of the tri-colored flag represents this story. The three bands of color represent the following: green–hope, joy, and love; red–hardiness, bravery, strength and valor; white–peace and honesty. (Note: there are other interpretations of the meaning of the colors.)

The first Europeans (Spaniards) arrived in 1540. They landed near the area now known as Mexico City. They were inveterate adventurers and traveled as far as San Francisco to Texas, and even into Louisiana, establishing *presidios* (forts) and towns from which wars could be fought and the people and land could be protected. Tubac, a little town south of Tucson (now a flourishing tourist attraction), was a Presidio, and Tumacacori, next to Tubac, became a mission outpost.

Institutions came into being; the Spanish language spread, and Spanish Colonial system governed the land. Spain maintained its power for 300 years in Central and South America, as well as in North America. It proved to be a spiritual conquest, as well, as Christianity (mainly Catholicism) was promulgated throughout the area. However, the indigenous people transformed Christianity into an indigenous religion with idols placed behind altars to receive adorations and petitions, and parades held to honor both Christian and indigenous gods. Throughout the Americas profoundly diverse communities emerged.

The basis of the developing economy in the southwest was Mexican workers—mining, driving cattle, exploring rivers, working in reclamation projects, and farming. Workers in southern California and Arizona were subsidized by capitalist demand for workers from Mexico, with funding from France, Germany, and Russia, as well as the United States, to finance multiple projects. It became an early form of globalization. When World War I broke out in 1917, the need for workers increased dramatically and the economy of the U.S. and Mexico became intricately connected.

In 1882 the U.S. passed the first major immigration act—The Chinese Exclusionary Act. We wanted immigrants from England, Scandinavia, Germany, and France, but no religious Jews, Italians, Chinese, or other eastern Asians to enter our "pure" land. Mexicans, however, could still come and go as they pleased. Two or three agents (the beginnings of Border Patrol) were assigned to the southern border to keep out the Chinese who resided in Mexico.

With a "Texas Ranger" mindset—let's restrict the blacks, the Mexicans and the Indians in Mexico—the U.S. passed the 1924 Immigration Act. Again, it favored Europeans.

By 1942 the U.S. was at war again. Under the federal agreement with Mexico, four-million Mexicans came to work in the United States as *braceros,* or wetbacks (named from migrants swimming rivers to get across the border). Much exploitation took place, with *braceros* offered inadequate housing, food, and transportation. The education of their children was overlooked, as well. This program ended in 1964 as a result of new immigration laws that failed to recognize historical realities of border migration and the continuing need for workers.

In 1970 we provided more law enforcement as we implemented the war on drugs.

The year 1994 saw the beginning of anti-immigration fervor in California—"Let's get rid of the Mexicans—"that continues today. Our economy was in shreds as the cold war ended. President Clinton spoke even more strongly than California's then governor, Pete Wilson. "We will go after the migrants."

During the 1994-95 session of Congress, the North Atlantic Free Trade Act was passed. This act, plus conditions in Mexico have forced people to migrate north. Since then, the United States has struggled to address our schizophrenic attitudes toward Mexicans and Mexican labor.

Lupe went on to address what she believes needs to happen next:

Immigration is not about policing. We also need to address this issue holistically.

Those who are crossing are changing our world. They are risking their lives for mothers, fathers, brothers, sisters— for others, not for themselves. We hope with their example we will change the world. They are not looking for a better life for themselves; they have been here before and will come again in order to make a life for their families. Every major research shows that immigrants contribute more than they cost to the U.S. economy.

Homeland Security is designed to protect us from terrorism. To this date, not one terrorist has come through our southern border. Why are we spending so much money to protect it? The heightened militarization we continue to believe will save us only causes upheaval and chaotic conditions in both Mexico and the United States. We all feel the heavy burden of 9/11.[48]

---

48 Guadalupe Castillo, No More Deaths trainings (2008-2011).

There is so much more to say, not the least of which is that our governmental policies are driven by fear and uncertainty. Think about what causes these emotions! And what they are costing us, not only financially, but also in our hearts.

CHAPTER 17

Back in the Desert–Ben and Laura–
Mobile Camp–June 2007

No More Deaths had already established a camp at Byrd Baylor's place, which was well-known around town. Sometime in 2005 or 2006, a man named Ben encountered a No More Deaths volunteer in town and mentioned that he and his wife, Laura, owned 10 acres of land where another camp could be located. So, when Gene and Dan were looking for a site for mobile camp in the spring of 2007, Ben and Laura's names came up.

Ben and Laura were among many people who've found respite from city life in the area surrounding the small Southern Arizona town of Arivaca. The rural setting provides rolling hills, ever-changing skies, exquisite sunsets, seasonal variety, and vast spaces. These and other features enticed Ben and Laura to build a life here. They located a 10-acre piece of land just off Arivaca Road at milepost 9.2 with a small house and several artifacts from the past—signs that large numbers of cowboys had been fed outside. There was also a dry streambed that floods during the summer monsoons. They decided to purchase it. Ben worked as a handyman both around town and on their own property. Over time, they added a large trailer to the house with private bedrooms, and they fenced the yard for their dogs. Laura, an attorney and a Buddhist, home-schooled their three children (the oldest is about eight), and thus their new life began to take shape.

**Laura and Ben (seated) Receive an Award at
an Event in Tempe (Laura Ilardo)**

They soon learned about the migrants passing through while traveling north from the border. Before long they became aware that migrants walked or ran along the Cerro Colorado wash only a hundred yards from their house. Across from the wash, the *coyotes* had set up a temporary camp. Ben and Laura were sympathetic to the people who stopped by, and they occasionally provided them with water and food.

Gene and Dan talked with them, and they all decided on a nice spot near the Cerro Colorado (Red Hill) wash at the point where it crossed Ben and Laura's land. The Cerro Colorado hill loomed nearby. Running water and electricity were available to run a pump to water the area.

A small shed surrounded by large, protective cottonwood trees, and a flat area where Rick Ufford-Chase's RV along with some various tents could be placed, added to the location's advantages. The plan was that this would provide a base camp from which mobile groups could depart to explore areas previously unserved—north of Arivaca Road, west and around the town of Arivaca—mostly in the Batamonte area. The mobile groups would stay out in the field for a night or two, then return to the camp at Ben and Laura's place for rest and replenishment.

One day during the first week of June, while setting up the mobile camp, Gene and Dan stopped for lunch and were relaxing at the little table inside the RV, when Dan looked up and saw fire out the window. He hollered FIRE! and raced out of the RV with Gene at his heels. At three spots along the extension cord, fire was licking at the ubiquitous buffel grass that covered the entire area defining the camp. Dan ran to the pump, unplugged the electrical cord, and began fighting the fire with a slender hose, parts of which were melting from the fire. The dense buffel grass caused the fire to flare up like a gasoline fire.[49]

Meanwhile, Gene grabbed gallon jugs filled with water for migrants and began dumping them in another spot. As the fire crept closer to "camp central," it burned a large canopy, an ice chest, and part of Dan's backpack. Gene could see fire licking the undercarriage of their truck. He jumped into the truck and moved it to a safer spot. He and Dan kept fighting the fire as it burned in every direction.

At one point they thought they'd lost it. Gene called 911 and was told that someone would arrive shortly from either the Arivaca or Green Valley Fire Departments. The fire quickly moved east toward the neighbor's house, toward the shed, and toward Ben and Laura's home. Gene and Dan continued to fight the fire even though they might lose the battle.

---

49 Buffel grass is an invasive shrubby grass up to 1.5 feet tall and 3 feet wide. It looks like a bunchgrass plant when small. Older plants branch profusely and densely at nodes, giving mature plants a messy appearance. These nodal branches produce new leaves and flower spikes very quickly after light rains, making buffel grass an extremely prolific seed producer. See Wikipedia for more information.

Finally, they got the fire under control, which was a very good thing, since the volunteer Fire Department didn't arrive. Gene drove into Tucson, bought a new canopy and took it back to camp to set it up.

Cleaning up the Mess After the Fire (Dan Millis)

Mobile Camp opened a couple of weeks after Byrd Camp in the summer of 2007. Gene and John Fife slept overnight at the camp and spent time making sure everything was ready for the volunteers. Volunteers for this camp were carefully selected because their upcoming tasks required experience—they would be mapping new areas as well as leaving water out on trails for migrants. They required previous training and experience with No More Deaths, plus knowledge of using GPS. They also needed to be able to take care of themselves with no fuss or bother.

When John and Gene got up the first morning of camp (no volunteers yet), they moseyed on over to Ben and Laura's house (John needs coffee ASAP). There, Ben was serving "breakfast" to 25 migrants—pizza and cokes. [50] Gene and John offered fresh migrant packs, but Ben said the migrants preferred pizza. Laura told John and Gene that Ben loved to cook for the migrants, and that he did this two or three times a month.

One day, Gene and Dan went out early from Tucson to check on Mobile Camp, and it was empty of volunteers. Gene stopped by the RV to look inside.

Dan called, "Look here!"

There in the nearby shed were 17 sleeping migrants lying on top of one another for warmth and to stay clear of the inclement weather. Dan woke them up, and Gene went into Arivaca for food. They also called over to Byrd Camp for help with medical needs. Two volunteers arrived about 45 minutes later—a man trained in first aid and a woman who spoke fluent Spanish. They set up a triage unit, and while Gene and Dan fixed eggs and pancakes, the newly-arrived volunteers triaged and treated a variety of wounds, mostly blistered feet.

No More Deaths ran that camp for five weeks that summer and served several new geographical areas frequented by migrants. Toward the end of the five weeks, Laura mentioned that the migrants were coming by more frequently and becoming more demanding. One *coyote* told her that he would pay her to have water and food ready when his groups came through. Of course, she refused, but she found him to be mean and intimidating. The *coyote* came three times within one month. The third time he demanded to use her

---

50 Laura and Ben's property is situated near Arivaca Road with a No More Deaths-friendly pizza place located nearby—close to the town of Arivaca.

phone. Laura was alone with the children and became very worried. Soon after that, Border Patrol raided the migrant camp across the wash and rounded up 20 migrants along with their *coyote*. Things calmed down a bit after that.

Laura also spoke to Margo Cowan about her concerns, and Margo brought the issue of migrants at Mobile Camp to a Monday night meeting. No resolution was reached, but after a couple of weeks, everyone moved to Byrd Camp. This significantly increased the census of volunteers at Byrd Camp (15 volunteers are ideal), but they managed to make it work through the rest of the summer.

CHAPTER 18

Food and Water from Humanitarians Denied

Volunteer Marking Water Bottles (No More Deaths)

And if you see no present fruit yet persevere. Be not overcome with evil, as all are who avenge themselves. But overcome evil with good. Conquer your enemies with kindness and patience.

ROMANS 12:21 EXPLANATORY NOTES ON THE
WHOLE BIBLE BY JOHN WESLEY

THROUGHOUT THE SPRING AND SUMMER of 2007, the newly formed BorderNet group met monthly with Chief Gilbert of Border Patrol. Representatives of the various humanitarian organizations expressed concern to Chief Gilbert about hearing migrants receive inadequate amounts of food and water while in detention. In addition, Gilbert was told that Border Patrol agents were no longer permitting humanitarians to approach migrants being detained at Border Patrol vehicles or at Wackenhut[51] buses to provide water, food, and first aid. The humanitarians asked that these services be permitted to resume, as migrants are obviously in poor shape. In response, in November of 2007, Chief Robert W. Gilbert sent the following message to Border Patrol agents in charge and unit supervisors:

While Border Patrol recognizes the humanitarian purpose of immigrant care organizations, the primary responsibility of the service for those in custody is their security, safety, and wellbeing. For this reason, civilians are precluded from

---

51 Wackenhut is a security services firm founded in 1954 in Coral Gables, Florida, by George Wackenhut and three partners (all former FBI agents). By 1964 Wackenhut had contracts to guard the Kennedy Space Center and the U.S. Atomic Energy Commission's nuclear test site in Nevada. In 2002 the company was acquired by a Danish Corporation Group 4 Falck which then merged to form British Company G4S in 2004. Over the years the company has expanded its services to include permanent guarding service, disaster response, emergency services, control-room monitoring, armed security, special-event security, security patrols, reception/concierge service, emergency medical technician service and ambassador service. http://en.wikipedia.org/wiki/Wackenhut.

providing care and/or food to Border Patrol detainees, to include those waiting for transportation or on Wackenhut buses or Border Patrol vehicles. This will prevent a detainee from possibly becoming ill from food from an outside source.

Agents are to ensure that detainees are not contacted by civilians while in Border Patrol custody, to include the acceptance of any consumable items for individuals in custody.

By doing so, the Agency retains a controlled environment and better assures that aliens in custody receive any necessary care and food.

Drinking water will continue to be available for agents to distribute to detainees in the field as needed.

This did not sit well with the humanitarian groups, and they began to question the value of these meetings with the Border Patrol chief. Our offerings of food included sealed packets of tuna, fruit, or other non-perishables, not egg salad sandwiches that admittedly might spoil and make someone sick. It seemed that BorderNet was just feeding information to Border Patrol about what we were doing and about our concerns, which could then be turned against us. This was not the first example of this happening, nor the last.

In May 2007, under the headline, "Wackenhut Worries: A company with a sketchy record has quietly taken over transportation duties from Border Patrol," Adam Borowitz, in the *Tucson Weekly*, describes the new arrangement Border Patrol (instead of Homeland Security) has made with Wackenhut to transport migrants:

> The change took place quietly last October in Tucson and involves the nation's entire border with Mexico as part of a five-year, $250 million deal between the United Customs and Border Protection Agency and Wackenhut, the domestic subsidiary of the U.K.-based security giant Group 4 Securicor.

What's odd, he goes on, is that a portion of our nation's border security was taken away from Border Patrol and handed over to a private company without much notice from media or officials—despite national attention on the area and even a recent visit from the President.

Stranger still is that Wackenhut was given a contract to work with the U.S. Border Patrol the same year they were fired for providing inadequate security at the Washington D.C. headquarters of the parent organization of, ironically enough, the U.S. Border Patrol.

The article goes on to describe a variety of accusations of abuses and incompetence by Wackenhut, but Wackenhut officials assured Border Patrol they will be professional in handling their work. John Fife is quoted in the article as saying, "The number one thing is account-ability—what standards are they expected to meet, and how can we actually get some accountability from them? With their human rights history, globally, how did they ever qualify for this contract?"

No More Deaths continued to approach Wackenhut buses to provide water, food, and first aid to migrants—and we continued to document abuses when migrants were returned to the ports of entry.

WANDERING IN THE DESERT—SUMMER 2007

One hot day in late June, Dan Millis and Gene Lefebvre drove into an area of the desert mountains northwest of Arivaca called *Guihas*. They came across three migrants, one in his 40s and the other two in their 20s or 30s. The older man was suffering from exhaustion and the younger two refused to leave him behind.

Gene called Border Patrol and told the operator a man needed help. He gave the operator the longitude and latitude coordinates from his GPS. After an hour or so, no one had come, so Gene called back. They told him someone was on the way and gave Gene's num-ber to the agent in the field. The agent—when he finally realized he was lost in the desert—called Gene for help. He asked for more information about the location—the names of the roads, for example.

Gene told him there aren't many names, and when there are, they change along the route. The main road is Batamonte, west and north from mile post 17 ½ from Arivaca Road. After another couple of hours, the agent called again and said that he couldn't find the location.

Gene asked if he'd gone through a ranch with two gates. The agent said that he had, so Gene knew he was still going west. Gene told the agent to come on up the road and then turn south. Gene could leave Dan at the location to go to find the agent.

The agent replied, "No don't do that. I'll come on, and in a little while I'll honk." In a few minutes he honked, and Gene honked back. They did this maneuver three times before finally connecting.

Two Border Patrol agents emerged from the truck. They were very personable and kind to the migrants. They permitted Gene and Dan to send water and food for the migrants in the truck with them. As they started to leave, one of the agents casually asked, "How are you going to get out of here?"

Gene said, "We're going to Arivaca—we'll take this road south."

The agents said that they wanted to go toward highway 286 where they'd find a Wackenhut bus waiting.

Gene told them to go straight west and pointed the way. "Any road you see going west will take you there."

"What is that map?" The agent pointed to Gene's topographical "topo" map. The agent asked about the squiggly lines and blue lines.

Gene explained the map to him. All the agents carried was an 8"x10" paper map of major roads, but he'd never seen a "topo" map. The agents didn't have a GPS, or even a compass, with them.

It was shocking to see how poorly trained these new agents were. Congress authorized 4000 new agents to be trained. Prior to that, no more than 500 had been trained in one year. We hoped it would get better over time.

CHAPTER 19

Nogales-Mariposa Work Continues

ANTONIO ZAPIEN WAS PART OF the glue that held our Nogales program together. Frequently he drove from Tucson to Nogales—usually paying for his own gas—to carry supplies, water, and perishables to the Mariposa operation.

He was born in the rural town of Numaran, Mexico, the second son of a *compesino* couple, his mother a seventeen-year-old. His father was a farm worker who would travel to the United States, save up some money and then return home. Antonio recalls going with his father when he was six years old to the bus stop at the edge of town to leave for America. His father never returned. Antonio traveled with his mother wherever she found work. A friend suggested she place him at *INI (Internado Nacional Infantil)*, a home for about 1,200 young homeless boys. He said for the first time in his life he had three meals a day, a bed, clothes and a uniform.

One day Susan and Hugh Hardyman, a Scotsman and an American, went to the school looking for six boys to live with them on a farm outside Guadalajara. Antonio was one of the six who were chosen. Two teachers, the Hardymans, and the six boys boarded a bus for their new home. There Antonio learned to care for animals and fruit trees and more, and he learned to take care of tools and the house. He was told to "try your best always. We are here to help you."

The Hardymans owned many books, and Antonio learned to read both English and Spanish.

Antonio studied hard and transferred to junior high school where he studied to become an agricultural engineer. He met his future wife when some Americans came to his village to start a kindergarten. Then he studied at the University of Guadalajara; he became a veterinarian doing research on cattle production. He started his professional life in the tropical region of Mexico. Over the next 30 years, he traveled back and forth between Mexico and Tucson where he earned a master's degree and a PhD at the UA.[52]

Antonio and his wife lived in Tucson from 2006 to 2012. Antonio volunteered with both Samaritans and No More Deaths and was a resource for other humanitarian groups. His wife was associate dean at the University's College of Public Health. Antonio's son and daughter were married and have children. All are bilingual. He says, "Our family is binational, and we like that."

Email: December 8, 2007, 7:55 a.m.
To: Mexico Projects/No More Deaths
From: Antonio Zapien

Hola, yesterday afternoon I went to Mariposa. The voluntarios were there, had coffee to give away, were cooking rice, etc. Very cold afternoon. Gilberto and Griselda told me that between the cooking space they have at the small trailer and the small stove they have outside, it's enough space to cook. According to both of them, there is no problem for cooking.

I left Mariposa by 6:30 p.m. and went to the DeConcini port[53] to talk with Mexican official people there. By the time

---

52 Ann Snowden Crosman, *The New Immigrants* (Washington: Book Publishers Network, 2012) 1-8.
53 The main port between Nogales, Arizona, and Nogales, Sonora.

I left Mariposa, very few deported migrants had arrived—22! What happened after? No idea. At DeConcini, they told me that during the day, several small vans came with small groups of people. Looks like at least yesterday more people were deported at DeConcini than through Mariposa.

The Mexican voluntaries are very much taking care of Blanca Guadalupe Gonzales, the new voluntaria. She is 22 years old, five or six months pregnant, waiting for her husband to be deported (he's in jail somewhere in California) and has almost nothing. In the meantime, she is helping at the port. I asked her to give me a list of personal items she needed: sweat pants (size seven), a jacket, hand cream, deodorant, a hair brush, tooth brush, tooth paste, a small blouse, etc. I will try to do something with that. If some of you can help also that would be great.

In 2012, Antonio and his wife moved to Guadalajara where he could continue working with the *Hacienda*, the orphanage that had taken him in as a child. He left Southern Arizona in frustration that more had not been done to help the migrants in Nogales.

The above email from Antonio foreshadowed some of the changes taking place in the flow of migrants—changes which we had no knowledge of beforehand. One day deportees were being dropped at Mariposa, the next day at DeConcini. Sometimes they were dropped in the morning, sometimes at night—even women and children at night, which was not supposed to be happening (according to international agreements). There had been much discussion about moving all the deportations to the DeConcini port. However, that port dumped people right into downtown Nogales, a highly-congested area that is frequently unsafe. Also, changes were about to take place in the running of the *Comision* (Profe's responsibility)—Mexican elections had transferred power from *Partido Revolucionario Institucional (PRI)* to the *Partido Accion Nacional (PAN)* and those changes would be felt at the port after the first of the year. Maryada and the others in our "Mexico Working Group" planned a celebration of *Profe's* work at Mariposa in January, as he would soon be replaced.

Most volunteers at the Mariposa port refused to be daunted by the reality of working in a third-world country such as Mexico. Small houses and shacks on the hillside, the railroad in the middle of town, young children at the port selling Chiclets, runny-nosed babies, old men and women wandering the streets, venders everywhere, people sweeping their front stoops, unfamiliar smells, and crummy buildings all give an unexpected and unsettling ambiance. The environment also included business people hawking their wares, groups of young men hanging out "trying to decide what to do next," and people sleeping in the cemetery. Nevertheless, volunteers saw that they could be of help, and many became attached to their work and the people.

Other organizations were trying to help also: The Catholic Church, *Grupo Beta*,[54] and various nonprofit groups providing temporary housing. At times we were able to join forces with them. Somehow, we were all able to overlook that the systemic problems in both Mexico and the U.S. were insurmountable. New migrants will be needing help tomorrow. The volunteers do not question that their work feeding people at the port, listening to their stories, and mending their broken feet has to be done. Although in the back of their minds they hope and pray things will change.

MARYADA'S NOGALES JOURNAL

When people fear their government, there is tyranny;
when the government fears the people, there is liberty.

THOMAS JEFFERSON

---

54 *Grupo Beta's* central task is the search and rescue of migrants in Mexico. A type of Mexican Border Patrol, they provide water, first aid, and directions to migrants going north, or heading back home. They also patrol the southern border of Mexico for migrants coming into Mexico. They were founded about 1991.

Throughout her work in Nogales, Maryada kept a running journal of her activities and thoughts. The following passage is from her journal:

Arizona's freshman U.S. Representative Gabrielle Giffords[55] seems to need a dose of our border reality. No More Deaths Steve Johnson continually harasses Gifford's immigration aide, meaning multiple emails are sent back and forth asking her to come down with us for a visit. In the end, only excuses are given. This visit never takes place.

Last evening as I relayed stories from the day to Walt Staton, I became emotional and desperate myself, thinking about the lives destroyed, the suffering, and my own feelings of helplessness as we are not able really to be a human being to one another. We just give support in small ways and say goodbye.

Shura Wallin (from Green Valley Samaritans) plans a grand birthday celebration for Gilberto. She asks *Profe* ahead of time if she can kidnap him during her regular Green Valley Sams visit and take him to lunch at the famous and fancy "La Roca" restaurant. At the last moment *Profe* decides it is too important for Gilberto to be at the port that day, for whatever reason. Everyone is tremendously disappointed. The next week Shura has instead arranged for the party to come to Gilberto! She hires a group of *Mariachis* to come and play at the tent! I also bring a pathetic cake from *Casa Maria*.[56]

---

55 Giffords was gunned down in Tucson in 2011 during a meet and greet at a local grocery store. She survived and after much physical therapy still weighs in on issues of gun safety.

56 *Casa Maria* is the Catholic soup kitchen in Tucson where Maryada lived and volunteered for several years. It receives cast-offs from residents and local restaurants, including pathetic cakes.

Kathryn Ferguson and Shura Wallin (Tucson Samaritans)

Cruz Roja (Mexican Red Cross) plans to send a large medical trailer. It's hard to imagine that we have the space in our little spot next to the Mexican Customs (*La Aduana*), but it's exciting to think about having a separate and more sanitized clinic space to work in.

I have ethical questions and struggles: The transition has ended; we are partners but in a different way, no longer the day-in-day-out coordinators. A new community is forming at the port apart from the U.S. volunteers and including them. Too bad the politicians and some of the blinded public seem to be disinterested completely in the beauty that migrants can bring to community. They teach us what is worth dying for—and living for.

In the late spring of 2007, Maryada flew back to Washington D.C. to speak at a banquet as an "Emerging Leader" for *Sojourners* organization. She was recognized for her ability to make things happen in a local community—in this case, with No More Deaths at the border of Mexico, especially at the Mariposa Aid Station in Nogales.

From my Journal

That I may consider it a blessing—
my sense of urgency,
my tears, my feelings of compassion,
my innocence,
my carrying the weight of the world on my shoulders.
We must change it!
One abuse is too many, one hungry family and
one person so desperate
he or she is driven to insanity on the street is <u>too much</u>.
One life ruined because of walls,
and greed, and corruption means—
we as a society, have gone <u>too far.</u>
But not too far to turn back. To start over.
To imagine something new.
To create dignity, caring and community.
To speak truth to power.
To LIVE FREELY.
To free our minds of fear.
Maryada Vallet

CHAPTER 20

Selecting Stipended Volunteers

IN 2004, NO MORE DEATHS reached out to the national Presbyterian Church for help funding volunteers who would be paid a small stipend to cover their living expenses while working for the cause. The Volunteer in Mission Program of the Presbyterian Church (VIM) came to the rescue, and in 2004-2005, Jonathan Scanlon and Marie Kessler were chosen as our on-site, stipended volunteers. No More Deaths paid $5,000 for each volunteer and those who were selected matched these funds. These funds were doled out to the volunteers on a monthly basis, with some amount deducted for the program's overhead. The individual volunteers are called "VIMs."

The Rev. Brandon Wert coordinated the Volunteer in Mission Program which included a fall retreat for the group of six or seven volunteers who were spread out among several humanitarian groups with regular meetings throughout the year to provide support, training, and a final debriefing. They shared common housing in south Tucson, lived and cooked together, and shared a vehicle or two as well as bicycles provided by the program.

In 2006-2007, Andrea Leonard and Carrie Barrie became our second pair of VIMs. Andrea (from Dallas Texas, and Atlanta, Georgia) worked part-time for St. Mark's church and part-time for No More Deaths, while Carrie (from St. Louis) was full-time with No More Deaths. Both were fresh out of college. Andrea processed all the applications coming from potential volunteers around the country.

Carrie managed the logistics for the program—from arranging for volunteers to be picked up from the airport, to providing transportation into the field, to making sure the vehicles were drivable.

Toward the end of their tenure and after lengthy discussions, we decided to advertise for and interview our own stipended volunteers rather than using the VIMs from the Presbyterian Church. We looked to hire the first one in September of 2007. Several volunteers from around the country applied, but a newly-formed personnel committee hired a young woman who had been working in the desert throughout the summer. Danielle Alvarado came from San Jose, California, with Spanish language and computer skills along with demonstrated interest, skills, and advocacy experience from working with Hispanic issues in the northwest part of the country. She had just graduated from Whitman College in Washington state in May. She took off running when Carrie and Andrea finished in early September and handled the recruitment and vetting process for volunteers for the next summer. Little did we all know there would be an Alternative Spring Break Program to deal with as well. Later we would address the need for a separate logistics coordinator.

CHAPTER 21

2007 Year-End Report

In 2007, No More Deaths completed its fourth year of trying to save the lives of individuals crossing the Arizona desert. During much of that time, No More Deaths has been documenting the treatment of people in detention. Every day we see people who haven't been given water or food since being picked up by Border Patrol and people who were physically or verbally abused while in custody.

Volunteers working at the Mariposa Aid station included 60 regular Green Valley and Tucson Samaritans, 20 visiting volunteers, and 40 out-of-town volunteers. In addition, a number of Mexican volunteers who worked at the aid station, there were many media visits, and other organizations (such as BorderLinks and churches) who brought groups to Mariposa to see the work and talk with the humanitarian workers and migrants.

Between June and September 2007, No More Deaths maintained two desert camps near Arivaca, Arizona, where volunteers established bases from which they scoured the desert in search of lost, disoriented, hungry, or ailing travelers. Approximately 400 individuals were encountered and given assistance. 39 people requested help to return to Mexico because they were sick and discouraged. Border

Patrol was called to assist them. Four were in serious enough condition to be evacuated by helicopter to Tucson hospitals.

Humane Borders Water Station 2007 (Michael Hyatt)

Humane Borders, a sister organization, maintained water stations throughout Southern Arizona to assist thirsty and dehydrated travelers. In addition, No More Deaths deposited more than 3,000 gallons of water supplied by people in Phoenix and Tucson along the trails in the main corridors of travel. These have since been taken by migrants. We continue to pick up used bottles and other trash left behind as this trash defiles the desert and is quite a source of distress by local ranchers and the various government agencies.

- Local experts from the University of Arizona, Pima Community College, No More Deaths, Samaritans, and Humane Borders provided training (desert survival, organization protocols, emergency health care, humanitarian sensitivity, and other aspects of importance) to the summer volunteers who were trained in Tucson, in addition to fifty-one volunteers trained in Phoenix. They volunteered in the desert camps, at the Mariposa Aid Station, at the Agua Prieta Migrant Center, and in Tucson. Twenty local volunteers received Wilderness First Responder Training in preparation for the summer.

* Volunteers distributed and used hundreds of pounds of medical supplies donated by Medical Bridges, Southwest Medical Aid, World Care, Carondelet Health Systems, and the University Medical Center, in addition to medical supplies donated by individuals.

* No More Deaths in Phoenix made and distributed almost 600 migrant packs, collected 500 pairs of socks, shoes, clothing, bulk foods, and medical supplies destined for Agua Prieta and Arivaca. Many other migrant packs were prepared by churches and individuals and distributed as well.

* Work continued at the Agua Prieta Migrant Center, the newly opened shelter at Naco, and the Mariposa Aid Station. Emergency work continued in the desert during winter storms. Weekly trips were made into the desert to distribute gallons of water along the trails south of Tucson.

* In 2006, Morgan Luce and Richard Alun Davis started a No More Deaths program in Flagstaff out of Northern Arizona University. Folks from Tucson and Phoenix provided training of local folks to work in the desert. Soon, Christa Saddler began to help with trip coordination and what became many educational and working trips to the border and to the central corridor operated by Phoenix No More Deaths. Dr. Robert Neustadt, professor in Global Languages and Cultures at Northern Arizona University in Flagstaff, became involved and

subsequently involved many students in these trips to the border and raised thousands of dollars for No More Deaths with the sale of CD's he developed and produced.

As the year 2007 came to an end, it occurred to many No More Deaths volunteers that we'd had only minor skirmishes with our federal adversaries this year. No major problems about which we had worried so often.

CHAPTER 22

How We Grow–2007

No More Deaths Volunteers 2007 (No More Deaths)

EMAILS, LETTERS, AND REFLECTIONS FROM volunteers began to fil-
ter back to the local No More Deaths volunteers. We knew many
locals who had spent their younger years working with young adults
in summer camps, excursions, work camps, and other settings (often

church sponsored). In those programs, they frequently built in opportunities for questions and reflection about their activities that would demonstrate to participants how these experiences were helping them grow and mature. Psychologists tell us that these ages are ideal for gaining fresh points of view, for expanding world concept, for making new and closer relationships, and for becoming affiliated with others with similar goals and aspirations. Here in Southern Arizona, many experiences need to be processed both intellectually and emotionally. Some of this takes place before volunteers go home, and some after they arrive.

In border towns, violence increases week by week. In the desert, a number of groups with guns vie for the space. The ranchers protect their land, Border Patrol seeks elusive migrants, *coyotes* seek to protect their valuable cargo, drug runners hide their packages of drugs, cartels fight over turf, and vigilantes, with their guns, too, join the mix. Only humanitarian organizations and migrants enter the Southern Arizona desert unarmed.[57]

Several leaders began to realize that the warlike experiences were having a profound impact on No More Deaths participants. As an example, here are the final three paragraphs of volunteer Reena Burton's statement about her experiences with No More Deaths:

> It was then that I realized this work is not just about the work. It is not about the numbers, the best hikers, and the lack of rest. In this work of humanity, it is not about mimicking the suffering we see around us. We cannot do work of hope and replenishment by internalizing the sorrow we see and the crashing repentance on our hearts. I have heard volunteers say they dislike reflections at night after our patrols,

---

57 In May 2007, just south of Naco an estimated 50 gunmen assaulted the town of *Cananea* (a mining town). They killed 22 people, including five cops. Twenty of the town's 52 police officers resigned, devastated by the violence. Metro Networks Communications, Inc. (2007), www.cox.net.

they wish to process what we are seeing alone. Although this is important, I want to stress the profound necessity of our sharing, our connecting, and our caring about what we are doing—not just doing it. Perhaps I do not have immense experience hiking through the desert, reading maps and plotting the GPS, or wilderness medical training; but I do have one thing to offer this work, my heart.

I found comfort in the principles of No More Deaths written in our reader passed out at training. It is rooted in the deep emotional investment that those who started this program had for the people crossing the border. It reads, "We come together as communities of faith and people of conscience to express our indignation and sadness over the continued death of hundreds of migrants attempting to cross the Mexico-United States border each year. We believe that such death and suffering diminish us all. We share a faith and a moral imperative that transcends borders, celebrates the contributions immigrant peoples bring, and compels us to build relationships that are grounded in justice and love. As religious leaders from numerous and diverse faith traditions, we set forth the following principles by which immigration policy is to be comprehensively reformed. We believe that using these principles—listed from the most imminent threat to life to the deepest systemic policy problems—will significantly reduce, if not eliminate, deaths in the desert borderlands.

Last Sunday I attended the service at Southside Presbyterian Church, and was overcome with joy at being in worship again. In his sermon, Larry Graham-Johnson stated that in the work of humanitarian aid, love is always the bottom line. As a summer volunteer for No More Deaths and someone who will take home my experiences here to share with my community in California; I would like to rally for more love. For sharing and connecting, hand holding and tears, hugs and eye contact. I would like to stress that we take things personally, get overwhelmed, reach out to each other, and allow ourselves to be truly, deeply, and irreversibly affected by what we see here in the desert. It is not in numbers, reports and statistics that minds are changed, hearts are opened, and inequality is balanced; it is in the connection from one hand to another. It is only the sight of another's tears that will soften the hardest of eyes.

Annie Swanson, too, after a year of work in a house of hospitality in El Paso for those who had recently crossed the border in Texas, expressed the transformative nature of her border experience and its impact on her life-planning decisions:

My life changed during that time. Everything seemed simpler, starker. The priorities of the rest of the world were backwards. All that really mattered was water. And a heart full of love, a heart that was resilient and could be broken open time and time again. A heart capable of tremendous compassion in the sense of "suffering with" others. I came to see how upside down the world in general was and the reality of the border in particular. I contemplated dropping out of school, renouncing a long-term relationship, giving up everything to do with this work. I ultimately decided not to break these commitments, to take a year, with the promise that I would return as soon as possible.

Longtime volunteers began to discuss what we could do to maximize this opportunity to help people solidify their new understandings. More volunteers than just Reena and Annie found their desert and border experiences to be mind-shaking and life shaping. No doubt this had been considered before, but once again we explored more effective techniques for training, on-site education, and follow-up to change our collective hearts.

We are grateful to Reena and Annie as well as many others who point out to No More Deaths the potential for personal transformation while participating in humanitarian work. It may be that this is all about the migrants, but it's also all about us.

Little could we predict the interesting and challenging issues that lay ahead.

PART II
Doing the Work of No More Deaths
2008

Beginning of a Migrant Trail - Sonora 2004 (Michael Hyatt)

CHAPTER 23

Humanitarians Meet the Government

HARVEST

Desert wind sighing through saguaros
whispers
(Romero, Ileana, José, Hilario)
Sullen sun over Sasabe Road
threatens
(bandidos, la migra, sed, hambre)
Discarded remnants on rocky trails
recall
(Guanajuato, Oaxaca, Sonora, Chiapas)
Harvest moon hangs on mountains,
beckoning
(Virginia, California, Florida, Colorado)
Coyote begs of the night:
What will my harvest be?

LAURA DRAVENSTOTT, COLORADO NO MORE DEATHS

NO MORE DEATHS VOLUNTEERS AND other humanitarians started the new year with the naive expectation that our services in the desert and at the port were, if not welcome, at least tolerated by the federal agencies. However, by the end of January, Samaritan Kathryn Ferguson had been accosted by agents from the Bureau of Land Management (BLM). By the middle of February, Dan Millis had been ticketed for littering on the Buenos Aires Wildlife Refuge (BANWR) by their officers. By the middle of the year, Dan had been to court, found guilty, and sentenced. By December, Walt Staton had also been ticketed on BANWR for "knowingly littering." All around, it was an interesting and challenging year. By the end of 2008, we had 40-45 people attending our Monday night circle to help make decisions regarding the challenges ahead.

We also had the naive expectation that National Immigration Reform would take place within the next two or three years, and our work would be mostly finished.[58]

KATHRYN FERGUSON[59] FACES THE BLM–JANUARY 2008

After running a desert patrol, Gene and his patrol mates stopped at Arivaca Mercantile, the main store in the southern desert town of Arivaca. It sells everything one might need in rural Arizona— bread, milk, fish hooks, bubble gum, gasoline...you name it. The woman behind the counter asked if he was one of those people who helps migrants. When he said yes, she told him, "There's one of your people over there in the corner. She's pretty upset."

Gene looked where the clerk had pointed and saw one of the regular Samaritan volunteers, Kathryn Ferguson, talking on her cell phone and looking distraught. Gene recognized her. She goes out in the field regularly, usually with a doctor, searching for migrants needing help and providing them with water, food, and first aid. Kathryn is knowledgeable of border issues, tall, very creative, beautiful, and not afraid to speak her mind. When she finished on the phone, Gene asked her what had happened, and she told this barely-believable story.

---

58 During the 2016 presidential debates, Hillary Clinton said she thought 2007 had held the greatest promise for immigration reform.

59 Kathryn Ferguson died spring 2017.

She, along with a doctor friend, Robin Redondo, and her son, Liam, had been checking migrant trails and placing water in strategic places. As usual, their car was identified with a 12" x 12" magnetic Samaritan sign on the door. Just southwest of Arivaca, they pulled off the road next to a stand of mesquite trees because they were being followed.

A truck pulled up behind them and just sat there.

After a while, Kathryn and Robin got out of the car to get water from the back and saw the men staring at them. Kathryn went to the driver's side and asked if she could help them. Three large men jumped out. One got right up into her face and mocked her with a high voice, "Can we help you?"

He continued mocking her when she asked to see his ID. He pulled it out quickly and snapped it shut before she could get a good look. It was obvious they were federal agents, but they were wearing plain clothes and wouldn't say if they were Fish and Wildlife, Forest Service, Buenos Aires National Wildlife Refuge, or Border Patrol. It turned out they were from the Federal Bureau of Land Management.

Agent Ruiz, the driver, indicated he wanted to see their drivers' licenses. Kathryn went back to her car to get them. When she walked around the back of the men's vehicle to take down their license plate number, Agent Ruiz became very angry, stormed up, and hit her hard across her collarbone and then against her jawbone. She fell back a few feet.

She accused him of hitting her and said, "You can't *do* that." Ruiz roughly put her hands behind her back and cuffed her, "You're under arrest for interfering with law enforcement." Then he searched her very inappropriately. The ticket said that she was "causing a nuisance."

Kathryn describes the "frisking," or so the agent called it:

He places one of his hands on each of my feet and touches my shoes. As soon as I feel that touch the ground shifts.

Balance is a curious thing. You never think about it until it's not there.... He pushes my legs apart. Then he forces them apart again, wider. I almost fall forward on top of him. At first his movements are furtive, like a rodent. He plants his hands on my feet. He stretches his neck, pats my shoes, and pats my socks. He pats my calves. His hands stop. His warm palms cup my calves. He lifts his torso and stretches his neck on the side, like he has all the time in the world, like he is getting ready to settle into a task. But he doesn't look in my eyes. Then he moves his hands slowly, up behind my knees the way an insect crawls under your clothes and you try to hit it before it strikes. Even through denim, I feel warmth from his palms. He slows his hands as they spread up the inside of my thighs. They don't pat, they rub. Then his hands move to my hamstrings, alternating, as one goes high the other goes down, like milking a cow. Then he moves his hands from the hamstring back to the inner thigh. Even slower. Rubbing. In circles. As his hands get higher, I say, "Don't."[60]

While this was going on, Robin was waiting inside their car. She called our attorney, Margo Cowan. When she announced, "I'm calling our attorney," the agent jerked his hands away from Kathryn. Certain of her imminent arrest, Kathryn sent Robin and Liam back to Tucson. Margo, meanwhile, got on the phone with federal officials and after some time, along with some challenging dialogue, plus a few phone calls to and from several higher-ups, the men cut Kathryn loose with no explanation. The assumption was that Margo's phone calls must have worked some magic with the U.S. Attorney.

The BLM truck took off unceremoniously leaving Kathryn on the side of the road—with no ride. Fortunately, another official truck had stopped across the road. The driver, a federal officer as

---

60 Kathryn Ferguson, *The Haunting of the Mexican Border A Woman's Journey* (Albuquerque: The New Mexico Press, 2015), 180-181.

well, saw what had happened and took pity on Kathryn. He drove her into Arivaca.

When Gene heard her story, he was appalled. He tried to comfort her, but by that time she was furious and didn't feel like being comforted. She had already arranged for Robin to come back from Tucson—an hour-and-a-half drive away—to pick her up.

This was the first time since Daniel and Shanti were arrested in 2005 that a federal agent had stopped one of our humanitarian vehicles and pursued an arrest. Why on earth were the Bureau of Land Management agents involved? The Samaritans weren't even on BLM land but rather on a public highway with legal right-of-way. We wondered what it would mean for the future of humanitarians if all federal officers could pursue us, especially on a public road, away from their own territories with no legitimate reason?

CHAPTER 24

Border Towns–Naco, Benjamin Hill, and Douglas

IN ADDITION TO THE WORK in the desert and at the port of entry at Mariposa, at some point No More Deaths expanded its work to include supporting migrant programs in Naco, Benjamin Hill, and Agua Prieta, all towns in Sonora, Mexico.

NACO

Naco (native word for "cactus") is the name for towns southeast of Tucson, on both sides of the international border with Mexico. Before the arrival of Europeans, the area was dominated by the Nahua and Opata peoples. Naco came into being in 1897 as a border crossing to connect the copper mines on both sides. Naco, Arizona, has remained small—fewer than 300 people, but Naco, Sonora, has grown to almost 6,000 inhabitants, over half of whom currently deal with the influx of migrants, both from the north and from the south.

Cecile Lumer played a vital role in assisting migrants in the Naco area. She lived in nearby Bisbee. She had a PhD in biology and sometimes taught at Cochise Community College. She loved and appreciated Mata Ortiz pots and drove into Mexico to the town of Mata Ortiz to purchase their exceptional pots. Here she tells about the beginnings of the migrant resource programs in Naco, Sonora:

The story of the Migrant Center and Shelter in Naco, Mexico, really starts in about 2004 when a group of people in Bisbee, Arizona, formed Citizens for Border Solutions. Local folks began by holding educational forums, having cross-border events, binational fiestas and putting out water and picking up trash on known migrant trails in the desert near Bisbee.

As the anti-immigrant situation escalated, we found that the water was destroyed, whether by vigilantes or Border Patrol, or both. *Frontera de Cristo*, the Presbyterian office in Douglas, donated a truck. Humane Borders gave us tanks and flags. Several of us went out twice weekly in the summer to clean and fill 50-gallon tanks. In the winter we usually went out once a week. During these water runs we would see migrants waiting to cross and so we began carrying food as well as water.

For several years, a small group of people (Citizens for Border Solutions), living in and around Bisbee, were upset by the militarization of the border with Mexico, as well as by the rising number of people dying in the desert. We began by holding town forums and letter-writing campaigns to our state and federal representatives. We put water on known migrant trails in the United States, but this water was vandalized. As a result, we began to put out water in Mexico, eventually partnering with *CRREDA*[61] a drug and rehabilitation organization in Naco, Mexico.

---

61 *CRREDA (Centro de Rehabilitacion y Recuperacion para Enfermas de Drogaddicion y Alcoholismo.)* The program at Agua Prieta is one of 29 located between Baja California and Chihuahua states. It offers prayer, education, humanitarian aid and legislative action to help drug addicts recover and heal. 92 beds serve recovering alcoholics, geriatrics, mental cases, and incorrigible children. The center is open to all. (www.JessicaWunderlich.com)

We also wanted to demonstrate our friendship with our neighbors and so we held binational fiestas in conjunction with the local government in Naco, Mexico. These fiestas were on the border, one mile from the port of entry at Naco. Here there was no wall, only a vehicle barrier. We put a volleyball net on the barrier, tables with food on both sides of the border, and had music and dance on both sides. In this way we shared food, music, dance and friendship. We were able to have the fiestas for four years until the new wall was built. Late in 2007 we realized the need to do something more due to the number of migrants funneled through Arizona and the increasing number of deaths which resulted from this activity.

The only services in Naco for migrants have been the hotels from which the *coyotes* operated. In 2006 a center for helping migrants opened in Agua Prieta (across the border from Douglas, Arizona). The *Centro de Recursos para Migrants* started by *Frontera de Cristo* provided food, medical care and other types of help to migrants when they were repatriated by the U.S. Border Patrol. Members of Citizens for Border Solutions decided that a similar center was needed in Naco. We began the search for a building to house a center.

Friends who had opened a small restaurant (Taco Fish) moved to Hermosillo. Their building was vacant and in the perfect location for a migrant center—close to the border where the migrants were left by Border Patrol. This building is actually on the sidewalk and they had rented the sidewalk from the city of Naco and then put up the building. When we asked the folks in Hermosillo about the building, we were told, "Yes, the building is ours and you can have it, but the sidewalk belongs to the city." Our work with the local government putting on the binational fiestas, had built relationships in the community which made it possible for us to negotiate the needed permission to take over the building without paying any rent.

A small grant from the Center for Human Rights and Constitutional Law in Los Angeles helped to jump start us. With an OK from the center in Agua Prieta, we adopted the same name, *Centro de Recursos para Migrantes*, and opened our doors in January 2006. At that time, and continuing today, we are staffed mostly by Americans who are all volunteers. Basically, we offered the same services then as we do now: food, medical care, and a phone to call family in the United States. We offered people a safe place to just "be," a place where they could relax and make life decisions.

We also began working with the Mexican Consulate in Douglas, Arizona. Many of the migrants are separated from family members during the detention process. The Mexican consulate conducts searches for people and we connected people to this process. As an example, a woman may come to the Center saying she was separated from her husband in custody and doesn't know where he is. We call the Mexican consulate and initiate the search. Or, a family is looking for their son who crossed in Naco. Additionally, if people decide they do not want to cross again and would like to return home, the consulate helps with the bus fare. Perhaps what sets us apart from other similar centers is the fact that from the first day we opened, we were the only place in Naco which offered free help to migrants.

Within a short time of opening we realized the importance of keeping statistics to document the reality of what was happening on the U.S./Mexico border. Over time we refined our intake procedure, sending information to the Mexican consulate and to No More Deaths. Among other things, we began documenting the number of people who come through, where they come from in Mexico, the number of hours they were held in custody, what, if any, food they were given in custody, as well as abuses of all kinds.

This information is shared with the Mexican consulate and with No More Deaths. I found that when I told people that we worked with other groups to change the laws in the interior as well as along the border, they were often eager to help. In addition to obvious physical abuses, we considered family separation an abuse, lack of medical care an abuse, lack of food to be an abuse, a prison cell that was too cold or too dirty to be an abuse, a prison cell so crowded that people couldn't sit was also an abuse. This information has been included in the 2008 report by No More Deaths, *Crossing the Line.*

BENJAMIN HILL

In 1939 a small ranch became a town—Benjamin Hill—when the railroads *Ferrocarril Sonora Baja* from the west and *Ferrocarril Sud Pacifico* from the south joined at the ranch. It is an excellent resting place for migrants coming north and has a small migrant center. No More Deaths provides periodic supply drops at the center. We have $285 in our monthly budget for Benjamin Hill, but the money doesn't always get translated into beans, rice and flour to be taken the 75 miles south of Nogales each month. In 2008, the Phoenix No More Deaths group constructed wooden benches for the shelter and transported them to Tucson. From our backyard, Margo Cowan made the delivery to Benjamin Hill. In the year 2005, there were 5,285 inhabitants there, a few in farming, and some in an auto parts *maquiladora*. In addition, small cattle ranches send calves to the United States.

Children Crossing at Naco (Cecile Lumer)

OUR NEIGHBORS IN DOUGLAS/AGUA PRIETA

Like Naco, Douglas lies along the southern border of Arizona with Mexico. Its population is fewer than 20,000, while across the border, the town of Agua Prieta boasted a population of almost 110,000 in 2007.

Douglas' early history is filled with western lore dating back to the 1500s when Spanish explorers established a route north from Mexico during 1535-1536. This region was part of the *Nueva Espana* during the 1700s with the *San Bernardino presidio* established near the initial settlement of Douglas to defend the territory. In 1878, Company C of the U.S. Cavalry was sent to the area as part of the Apache Indian Campaign and to challenge the activity of Geronimo and his band of Apaches. Geronimo surrendered in 1886.

The military maintained a presence in the area with the U.S. Calvary, the Buffalo Soldiers, and Camp Harry J. Jones. This camp was established in 1911 to deal with border troubles during the Mexican Revolution and remained an important part of the area for more than 20 years. In the early 1900s, Phelps Dodge selected the Douglas area to establish a smelter to process nearby Bisbee's rapidly growing copper production, as well as copper from *Nacozari, Mexico*. Developers installed electricity, telephone services, and other basic needs, quickly making Douglas a thriving little town.[62] Smelting operations continued until the plant closed in 1987.

Of interest for today, Douglas was named one of the top 100 small towns in America in 2014. Today's city council has business-friendly policies that make the town poised to capitalize on the growth potential of the state. The development corridor is positioned for investment by a number of regional companies, and the town has leveraged its location to support international trade and do more global business. Already several *maquiladoras* have settled across the border in Agua Prieta and are able to ship a variety of products, including window blinds and auto seatbelts, through Douglas into the United States. Workers are drawn there from all parts of Mexico.[63]

---

62 City of Douglas (accessed August 7, 2016, http://visitdouglas.com).
63 "100 Top Small Towns in America," accessed August 7, 2016, http://www.free-press-release.com/news-100-small-towns-in-america-douglas-arizona.

FRONTERA DE CRISTO

Welcome to Douglas, Arizona (Mark Adams, Frontera de Cristo)

Frontera de Cristo is a Presbyterian border ministry located in the sister cities of Agua Prieta, Sonora, and Douglas, Arizona. As it has responded to border needs, *Frontera de Cristo* has developed six individual ministries:

1. The New Hope Community Center is a local collaboration designed to improve the quality of life in an outlying community of Agua Prieta;
2. The Mission Education Ministry focuses on building relationships across borders;
3. The Family Ministry shares the gospel with unchurched persons in the *Nuevo Progresso* community and beyond, holding parenting classes, Bible study, marriage enrichment and other workshops;
4. The Church Development Ministry works with the *Presbytery de Chihuahuain* in the development of two churches and in the support of continued growth with one another;

5. For more than 15 years, the Health Ministry has provided health education and services in the New Progress Community in Agua Prieta. Services include prevention of cervical uterine cancer and breast cancer, as well as dental hygiene to the population;

6. The Migrant Resource Center, a binational project, is a partnership of many different organizations and people with the common goal of helping migrants. Migrants have many basic humanitarian needs—fresh socks, something to eat, medical attention. The Center participates in abuse documentation, both on their own and in coordination with No More Deaths. On June 30, 2016, the center celebrated its 10th anniversary.

In 1998, Mark Adams graduated from Columbia Theological Seminary and arrived in Douglas, Arizona to begin his ministry with *Frontera de Cristo*. He is married to Miriam Maldonado Escobar, also a Presbyterian church worker, and together they have three children. Miriam is from the Mexican state of Chiapas. She worked as the community garden facilitator to help rehabilitation centers and families of the church, the community, and the schools grow their own food. Named Mexican Coordinator of *Frontera de Cristo* in 2014, Joca Gallegos (Rosario Jocabed Gallegos Viesca) first came to the border in 1990 when her father undertook the same position. Trisha Maldonado was born and raised in Phoenix, while her grandparents migrated to the United States from San Luis Potosi, Mexico. Trish serves as office manager for *Frontera de Cristo*.

In 2009, a No More Deaths supporter from the Midwest offered some land north of Douglas to the organization. Paul Barby, Lois Martin, and I made the two-hour drive from Tucson to Douglas to see the site—with a side trip to the county offices in Bisbee to identify the exact location. Located north of Douglas, just a mile or so past current development, we found a fully-developed outline for a future subdivision by roads that had been carved out by a rough tractor pass. We were able to identify our site and took a few photos of flat land covered with mesquite trees and the Peloncillo Mountains visible in the distance. Our sponsor, Tucson Unitarian Universalist Church, accepted the gift of land in the name of No More Deaths. Worth little at that point, perhaps it will yield income in the future.

**Meeting Family and Friends at the Douglas/
Agua Prieta Border (Frontera de Cristo)**

For several years, volunteers took the Arizona Shuttle from Tucson to Douglas to work for a few days, or sometimes weeks, in their migrant program of choice. A sister from the Racine, Wisconsin Dominican Order stayed in our home both before and after her few days volunteering in Douglas. She was so impressed with the work there, she suggested No More Deaths apply to her order for funding. We took her up on it and for three years, the order gave No More Deaths $10,000 in grants. These funds were used along the border in Naco, Nogales, Douglas, and on the Tohono O'odham Nation. The major portion was directed to the Abuse Documentation Project which has produced several important reports regarding the behavior of Border Patrol toward migrants. Visit the No More Deaths website to access these reports (www.nomoredeaths.org).

CAFÉ JUSTO Y PAZ IN CHIAPAS, MEXICO

"*Café Justo*"[64] (Just Coffee) is a remarkable success story that may serve as a model for remediation of border problems. Randy Campbell says that the story of Café Justo is about economic justice, religious relationships, mutual respect and trust, persistence, and the commitment to a vision despite many obstacles, cultural and financial. Mark Adams has said it is the best response to the issues surrounding migration that he's ever seen.

Mark encountered David Cifuentes, a Mexican who had been displaced from the south by the bottoming out of the coffee business in the early 90s. Mark and David discussed the issues of migrant families living in Agua Prieta and in David's home state of Chiapas, which is a mecca for growing coffee. Together they brainstormed ways of helping these displaced workers now living in Agua Prieta who preferred to stay in Mexico. Mark and David considered the amount received by the growers compared to the amount Americans are willing to pay for a cup of coffee. They brought Tommy Bassett, a self-styled hippy and friend of No More Deaths, into the discussion. Tommy had previous business experience, so he helped figure out how the middleman could be eliminated by having the coffee shipped directly to Agua Prieta for roasting and distribution, thus providing a living wage to both the growers and those working in

---

64 Full name is *Café Justo y Paz*.

Agua Prieta in the Café Justo plant. Mark applied to the Presbyterian Church for a microgrant; David went to Chiapas to round up growers. Mark got a paltry, but meaningful, $20,000 grant and David got 25 families to sign up, followed the next year by ten more.

First one roaster was purchased, then another. The sales of Café Justo coffee grow each year. It is distributed regularly throughout Southern Arizona, but also around the country. With a grant from the Presbyterian Hunger Program, Café Justo applied for and received certification as an organic product.

Several families now live in Agua Prieta working in the Café Justo program. These, plus the families in Mexico growing the coffee beans, means many families can now stay in their home country and make a living wage.[65]

It's a program that works for everyone!

Douglas Fence in 2018 (Mark Adams, Frontera de Cristo)

---

65 Margaret Regan, "Roasting Revolution," *Tucson Weekly*, February 8, 2007, accessed May 2, 2018.

CHAPTER 25

Some Laws Affecting Immigration

IMMIGRATION ACT OF 1990

THE FEDERAL GOVERNMENT HAS PRIMARY responsibility for laws affecting immigration. "Enacted on November 29, 1990, the Immigration Act of 1990 was an amendment in United States immigration law that increased the number of legal immigrants that entered into the United States every year. In addition, the amendment introduced a 'lottery' system which assigned visas to immigrants randomly. The main reason for this was to change previous United States immigration law that prohibited the granting of visas to immigrants from certain countries. Other immigration law changes that were included in the act was a stipulation that prevented immigrants from entering the United States because of their homosexuality. Another restriction that was lifted as a result of the enacted United States immigration law was restrictions against immigrants that are HIV positive."[66]

This act represented the first major overhaul of the U.S. immigration system in twenty-five years. Subsequent laws build on this one.

FEDERAL LAW 287(G)

Passed in 1997, the 287(g) program authorized the federal government to enter into agreements with state and local law enforcement

---

66 Law at immigration.laws.com/immigration-act-of-1990, p 1.

agencies in order to designate local law enforcement officers to identify, process, and detain immigration offenders they encounter during their regular daily law enforcement activities. Training is provided to local officers by U.S. Immigration and Customs Enforcement (ICE).[67]

While an agreement was signed between ICE and Maricopa County (think greater Phoenix) and the Arizona Department of Public Safety in 2007, it wasn't until 2008 when Pima and Pinal Counties signed on as well. In Tucson, the signing of this agreement caused considerable concern among the Hispanic population and immigration activists. Fear increased that the local police would stop dark-skinned people along the road, in their cars, or in their homes and ask to see their papers, which could possibly break up families. While ICE has many partnerships with state and local agencies, only the 287(g) program allowed state and local officers to directly perform specific immigration functions in place of ICE officers.

Humanitarian groups including No More Deaths began to wonder how they could help local Hispanic families deal with this new challenge. It would be some time before our volunteers began riding with police, organizing community groups, organizing against Arizona SB 1070 (2010 anti-immigrant legislation), and forming a group called Keep Tucson Together. These efforts were yet to come.

OPERATION STREAMLINE[68]

Sixty-two men and women were sitting in the courtroom when we entered. The first thing I noticed was the metallic sound of chains rattling as they shifted in their seats. They were handcuffed, the

---

67 Migration Policy Institute, *Delegation and Divergence: A Study of 287(g) State and Local Immigration Enforcement* (Washington, DC: Migration Policy Institute, 2011).

68 This section was originally written as a research paper for a rhetoric course sponsored by Coursera. Parts of it were published in the February 2015 issue of *Sojourners Magazine*.

handcuffs tightly bound to a chain around their waists, their feet shackled with chains as well. The fifteen women sat on a bench at the front of the court, separated from the men. All the people were dressed in the same clothes in which they had crossed the desert and in which they had spent one to five days in detention. It was clear they had not been given a chance to bathe, wash their faces or even their hands. Many were limping when they walked. All of them looked exhausted and many seemed confused, sad, and ashamed. A number slumped in their chairs without looking around. A few looked back at us and tried to smile. *Christa Sadler, Flagstaff No More Deaths*

In 2004, the North Atlantic Free Trade Agreement (NAFTA) was passed in the United States, Mexico, and Canada. Under this agreement, the United States could continue subsidizing corn, while Mexico was not. As a result, billions of tons of excess corn from the U.S. were shipped to Mexico, undermining sales of their now more expensive crop. Within one year, over one million Mexican farmers lost their farms and began searching for a new way to make a living. Many of them fled north to the U.S., and since then, other factors have increased the flow of migrants to the U.S. including: a major hurricane in 2005 and the growing presence and menace of the drug cartels which continues to this very day.

In 2005, a program was devised (using existing laws, policies, and procedures) to take all illegal crossers into federal court and put them through a process known as Operation Streamline. Below is according to a fact sheet put out by the ACLU and the National Immigration Forum in July of 2009:

Operation Streamline is a Bush Administration program implemented in 2005 ordering federal criminal charges for every person who crosses the border illegally...Operation Streamline forces undocumented migrants through the federal criminal justice system and into U.S. prisons. Those who are caught making a first entry are prosecuted for misdemeanors punishable by up to six months in prison, and those who reenter after deportation may be prosecuted for felonies punishable by up to 20 years in prison. Under this fast-track program, a federal criminal case with prison and deportation consequences is resolved in two days or less.[69]

Started in southern Texas in 2005, this program was eventually implemented into 8 of 11 jurisdictions along the border. It moved into Arizona in 2008—where 50 to 70 migrants are taken to federal court each day for prosecution (considerably fewer than the "all" mandated by the program). No More Deaths and other humanitarian organizations based in Tucson would visit the court each weekday afternoon to observe the proceedings and offer tacit support to the migrants who are shackled at their hands, legs, and waist while waiting for their justice. These undocumented migrants spend 30 minutes or less with a court-appointed attorney—obviously insufficient time to explore the facts of the case—to determine if the individual is already a U.S. citizen or eligible for asylum, or to see if the individual is eligible for a variety of federal visas. When asked by the judge if they are guilty of crossing into the U.S. illegally, almost all say *"culpable"* (guilty). Then they are sentenced according to their status (first-time or repeat offender or other special circumstance).

The abrogation of civil rights of the undocumented immigrants combined with such misuse by the federal criminal justice system resulted in Operation Streamline being called unconstitutional.[70] According to the Chief Justice Earl Warren Institute on Race,

---

69 Ted Robbins (NPR Southwest correspondent), *Border Patrol Program Raises Due Process Concerns* (Washington, DC: NRP, September 13, 2010), www.npr.org/templates/transcript.php?storyId=129780621.

70 Joanna Lydgate, *Assembly-Line Justice: A Review of Operation Streamline* (Berkeley: The Chief Justice Earl Warren Institute on Race, Ethnicity at University of California, Berkeley Law School, January 2010),1, available at www.law.berkeley.edu/files/Operation_Streamline_Policy Brief.pdf.

Ethnicity and Diversity at the University of California Berkeley Law School, "The program's voluminous prosecutions have forced many courts to cut procedural corners. Magistrate judges conduct *en masse* hearings, during which as many as 70 defendants plead guilty at a time."[71] One of the most troubling aspects of Operation Streamline has been that prosecutors are denied "prosecutorial discretion," a feature which had previously allowed them to prosecute the most egregious of the crimes—drug smuggling and human trafficking, for example. Instead, they must now prosecute everyone caught and charged.

Violations observed by many were so excessive that the ACLU took the program to federal court. As a result, in December 2009, the 9th U.S. Circuit Court of Appeals held that Operation Streamline's *en masse* plea hearings in Tucson, Arizona, violated federal law. They said that by focusing court and law enforcement resources on the prosecution of first-time entrants, Operation Streamline diverts attention from fighting drug smuggling, human trafficking, and other crimes that create border violence. The Warren Institute concluded that Operation Streamline is not an effective means of improving border security or reducing undocumented immigration.[72] That was 2009; yet the program currently continues with few modifications.

In fact, Grassroots Leadership (an organization committed to reducing incarceration of undocumented migrants) reports that while considerable belief exists in the efficacy of Operation Streamline in Congress and elsewhere, decades of research indicate that economic forces—particularly shifts in employment and real wages—are the actual drivers of immigration trends, and the recent weakened condition of the U.S. economy is no exception.[73]

---

71 Ibid.

72 Ibid.

73 Grassroots Leadership, *Operation Streamline: Costs and Consequences* (Austin: Grassroots Leadership, September 2012), 2.

Although Latinos made up only 16 percent of the U.S. population in 2008, in 2018 they make up 23 percent of all the prisoners in U.S. prisons.[74] The majority of these people came here from Mexico or Central America to look for work or reunite with family. They have no prior convictions.[75] According to Grassroots Leadership, "Southwest border districts apply an inferior standard of due process to those charged with immigration offenses. The expedited procedure combines arraignment, plea, and sentencing hearings into one court appearance, churning out groups of ten or more immigrants at a time (ed: usually six in Tucson)." Several magistrate judges have referred to Streamline as "assembly-line justice." At the present time attorneys defending the undocumented immigrants earn $110-125 per hour to meet with clients and appear in court. They are not always able to meet with clients individually resulting in violation of attorney-client confidentiality. In addition, checking on citizenship (or asylum claims) can take considerable time. Clients who may have legitimate claims to citizenship or asylum are easily overlooked due to these time constraints.[76]

A case-by-case analysis by the Transactional Records Access Clearinghouse, a research center at Syracuse University, during fiscal year 2013, immigration prosecutions reached an all-time high nationwide, with new cases being filed against more than 97,000 defendants. Over the last decade, the number of new cases has grown more than 300 percent.[77] "This is quite a new phenomenon. It has nothing to do with the individual or infraction," Tucson attorney Margo Cowan said, "it's about sending a message as a matter of policy: Don't come north."

---

74 "Blacks and Hispanics are overrepresented in U.S. Prisons," last modified January 12, 2018,
accessed September 30, 2018, www.Pew Research Center, 1.

75 Op. cit., Lydgate.

76 Op. cit., Lydgate.

77 *TRAC Immigration*, Syracuse University, available at http://trac.syr.edu/immigration/reports/336/.

The supporters for the continuation of Operation Streamline includes for-profit prison corporations: Corrections Corporation of America (CCA) and GEO Group (GEO). These are the two major companies that dominate the prison market. CCA made $1.74 billion (43 percent from the feds) and GEO made $1.61 billion in 2011. Both entities' income has increased significantly since 2005.[78] CCA had been a major supporter for the election of the anti-immigrant Arizona Republican governor, Jan Brewer (2010). Additionally, cities and counties using the federal court process, derive significant income as a result of this program, including those fees paid to local public defenders. It seems no one wants off the gravy train.

End Streamline Protest 2013 (No More Deaths)

Looking ahead: What could be done to stop this expensive, constitutionally questionable program? In Tucson, during 2012-13, several humanitarian organizations formed a new group they called the "End Streamline Coalition," with the goal of getting the program halted. That fall, the End Streamline group took action to

---

78 Op. cit., Lydgate.

stop the busses from carrying the 70 or so undocumented immigrants from the prison to federal court. At least for that day, the prosecutions were halted as volunteers lay chained under the buses; several members of the group were arrested. The coalition called for Attorney General Eric Holder (now resigned) to visit the Tucson federal courthouse to see the tragic proceedings for himself. "This is a terrible, unethical way of processing people," said Leslie Carlson, an activist with the End Streamline Coalition. "We shouldn't be criminalizing people whose only crime is crossing the border."

The courts, the ACLU, and many other organizations have recommended improvements in the Operation Streamline process. Such changes would be costly; for example, providing each defendant one hour of private time with an attorney before going to court; and are unlikely to be implemented. The mood of some in Congress was such that proposed immigration legislation called for the program to be tripled!

The first recommendation by the Warren Institute calls for "the administration to replace Operation Streamline with a comprehensive and effective approach to border enforcement." Secondly, they say "this administration should also restore U.S. attorneys' discretion to initiate prosecutions as they see fit along the Border.

On October 19, 2014, in the *Arizona Republic* (and elsewhere), several well-informed writers noted that Operation Streamline is costly and does not work. They said, therefore, Operation Streamline should be stopped.

CNN reported (November 8, 2014) that President Obama hoped to stop the limitation on "prosecutorial discretion" before the end of the year. This would go a long way toward increasing prosecutions of the smugglers, bandits, and traffickers, and allow administrative action to deal with first-time crossers. While focused primarily on undocumented persons present in the U.S. for an extended period of time, at a minimum the action would require the administration to revisit Operation Streamline to ensure no one who is in the action's protected categories is swept up in the wrong net.

LEGAL ARIZONA WORKERS ACT 101 (ARIZONA EMPLOYER SANCTIONS LAW)–1987

Included in the ramping up of Arizona laws against migrants was the Legal Workers Act 101 (Arizona Employer Sanctions Law), under the local belief that the federal government was failing to do its job of enacting and enforcing immigration law.

From Muzaffar Chrishti and Claire Bergeron of the Migration Policy Institute, January 16, 2008:[79]

> A new Arizona state law (passed in late 2007) targeting businesses that "intentionally" or "knowingly" employ unauthorized immigrants went into effect January 1, 2008.
>
> Under the Legal Arizona Workers Act, employers with unauthorized workers could have their business licenses suspended for up to ten days and be put on probation. A second offense could lead to a revocation of the license. The county attorney's offices across Arizona's fifteen counties will enforce the law.
>
> The new law also requires that all employers in Arizona check the employment eligibility of those hired after January through E-Verify. Formerly called the Basic Pilot Program, E-Verify is an online federal database through which employers can check whether an individual is authorized to work in the United States....
>
> ...newspaper reports suggest the law is already having an impact. Some employers have begun to lay off workers, some are abandoning plans to expand their businesses in Arizona, and some are shifting their operations to neighboring states, even to Mexico.
>
> Arizona Governor Janet Napolitano reluctantly signed the law last July amid strong speculation that a more punitive

---

79 Migration Policy Institute, 2008, accessed at www.migrationinformation.org/ UsFOCUS/PRINT.CFM?id-669.

version would be enacted through a popular referendum. In expressing her reservations, Napolitano called the law a "business death penalty."

In November 2006, voters in Arizona overwhelmingly supported three propositions to counter illegal immigration and a proposition to make English the state's official language.

The Arizona Employer Sanctions law was appealed, and in June of 2008, the Supreme Court upheld the law making it clear that states can play a role in what is generally a federal system of immigration regulation. The key issue was the denial of a license to businesses who failed to comply. Critics fear the Arizona law will be replicated by other states. However, in Arizona it took several years before any business or employer was charged under the law.

These are just a few of the many state and federal laws and regulations that affect immigration, but these also greatly affect humanitarian efforts in Arizona. A full listing of recent Arizona bills can be found in Appendix A.

Hamilton College Trip–January 2008

IN JANUARY OF 2008, A group of students from Hamilton College in New York, led by Corinne Bancroft, went out for a few days to patrol the desert. Since the Mobile Camp at Ben and Laura's wasn't used during the fall months of 2007—the desert operation had taken place only in the hot summer months—the group used it when they arrived. They brought their own gear and food. Corinne, whose home is in Tucson and whom Gene had met when she volunteered in the summer of 2007, did warn the students that it could be very cold in the desert in winter, but did they pay attention? On the first morning when Gene arrived at Ben and Laura's from Tucson to check on them, the students all stood around shaking, with their blankets or sleeping bags wrapped around their shoulders, nudging each other for a place by the fire. Gene came back to Tucson and got down the stash of sleeping bags we kept in our attic and took them back to camp. *Ahh, warmth!*

The Hamilton students made regular patrols on hilly trails looking for migrants. One day, while they were back at camp, all huddled in Rick's RV for warmth, they heard migrants running by in the Cerro Colorado wash. They were so near, and it was oh so cold! At our house in Tucson, we had an unusual inch-and-a-half of snow.

Josseline–February 16, 2008

Josseline Jamileth Hernandez Quinteros **2008 (Source Unknown)**

*"I can't imagine her fear and anguish, having
been alone for two weeks before she died."*

STEVE JOHNSTON

JOSSELINE JAMILETH HERNANDEZ QUINTEROS, A fourteen-year-old *joven* (young person) from El Salvador, was traveling north with her uncle and ten-year-old brother to reunite with her parents in Los Angeles, when she became dehydrated and exhausted and fell behind. She urged her family members to go on without her. When her uncle and brother arrived in Tucson, they notified the Salvadoran Consulate that Josseline was missing. No More Deaths received a call from Kat Rodriguez of *Derechos Humanos* in Tucson after she heard from the El Salvadoran Consulate that the family was worried. An alert went out and volunteers from several humanitarian groups searched for her for several days, to no avail. It turned out they had been looking too far south.

A couple of weeks later, No More Deaths volunteers Dan Millis, Clint Kalan, and Maria Wilz happened upon Josseline's remains while taking a shortcut between two well-traveled trails on their way to a very busy water drop. Dan said when he saw her green shoes beneath the mesquite tree, he thought someone might be near. He called out in Spanish, but just as he began to speak, he spotted her lifeless body.

Imagine how she had felt after two weeks of abandonment. The inclement weather had included freezing temperatures every night at 4,000 feet where she'd been left behind. It seemed as though she carefully removed her shoes and placed her feet in a pool of water. Then she had died.

She had been lost for three weeks and dead for one week when they came across her body. Later, Josseline's brother said she had been vomiting before she dropped behind. Dan called the Pima County Sheriff's Department whose recovery team took several hours to arrive. Dan reported back to us that the deputies "...bagged her, dragged her, and strapped her..." to their truck. A full lunar eclipse followed them all back to Tucson.

Steve Johnson reflects that Josseline was found in a deep rocky canyon between two trails—one a very busy trail and the other next to a road that would have taken her to Joe and Janet Arachy's house (neighbors of Byrd Camp). Ed McCullough and Steve had passed by on the busy one while mapping trails a few days before. If she had stayed on a trail, she probably would have been assisted by other migrants. But Josseline is not to blame. When hikers become dehydrated, at some point, they become disoriented. Frequently they wander off the trail into less hospitable terrain and out of sight of other migrants or volunteers.

A few weeks later, Josseline's aunt and uncle, two cousins, and her grandmother (all with a citizenship or green card), hiked with members of the Salvadoran Consulate, Dan, and other humanitarian group volunteers to the spot where Josseline had been found and created a shrine in her memory. They almost had to carry her *nana*. Josseline's undocumented parents and brother couldn't come because they lacked proper identification. They wouldn't have made it past the checkpoints. Father Bob Carney conducted mass for the group.

The previous year, at the end of summer 2007, after the intense summer No More Deaths program was over, Dan was fortunate to find a free place to live near San Xavier, in a little house owned by No More Deaths supporters, Jim and Loma Griffith. By February, when he found Josseline, he'd been hiking trails for more than eight months putting out water and food. Dan was deeply affected by this experience. He spoke little at subsequent No More Deaths meetings, but he continued walking the trails throughout the spring along with a couple of other volunteers.

Dan has returned to the site of her death many times since February. Several memorial services have been held there, and a beautiful cross with her name has been erected. Dan reported that at the end of September, the cross had survived the bad weather and other trials of summer.

In October, a well-attended memorial service was held in her honor at *El Tiradito Shrine**[80] in Tucson. Many of us shed tears for Josseline and for her family and for their lost hopes and dreams.

---

80 El Tiradito Shrine, located between La Pilita Museum and El Minuto restaurant, is the third site (within a close area) of a historic shrine in Tucson. Many

BUENOS AIRES NATIONAL WILDLIFE REFUGE (BANWR)– FEBRUARY 18, 2008

A couple of days after finding Josseline's remains, Dan Millis was doing his usual thing—picking up trash and leaving bottles of water for people in need. He was with three others: Max Garcia, from the Florence Project, Chris Fleishman from Phoenix No More Deaths, and Sebastian Rodriguez, Tucson No More Deaths volunteer, when they ran into Border Patrol while hiking on the Buenos Aires National Wildlife Preserve (BANWR).

When the agents discovered several sealed gallons of water that the volunteers had left behind for migrants, they issued a citation for littering. Dan convinced them that as the leader of the group, he was the most culpable, and the agents confined their ticketing to him. If he failed to pay the $175 fine, he faced six months of jail time or a $5,000 penalty.

Agents Kirkpatrick and Kozma seized 22 gallons of water from the trails along with eight gallons from Dan's vehicle. They took lots of photos—of the people, the water, the truck, bags of trash, and the contents of Dan's notebook.

Dan says this ticketing is particularly ironic and absurd given the U.S. government's responsibility for creating the problem, continuing human rights abuses, and impeding attempts at direct relief. (See Part III)

The volunteers were surprised to learn that not only is it against Fish and Wildlife regulations to put out water, but that it is also illegal to pick up trash. Both activities require a Special Use Permit that is available but is also subject for approval at the BANWR

---

people visit the little shrine, known as a place to make their dreams come true. At the present time a small but faithful group meets on Thursday nights to recognize lost migrants. Stories abound regarding the origins of the shrine. The process of putting it on the National Registry of Historic Places saved that area of Tucson from destruction by the construction of the Butterfield Express in the 1960s. The shrine dates from 1870. www.tiridito.com

Headquarters. Dan's group had collected five large bags of trash while hiking. The agents weren't interested in that.

Dan commented, "I was kind of bummed they didn't take the trash while they were at it."

Sebastian told the agents, as they were leaving, "Humanitarian aid is never a crime."

Agent Kirkpatrick replied, "It is a crime, and you're about to find out that it is."

CHAPTER 27

Seeking a New Non-Profit Home–Spring 2008

ST. MARK'S PRESBYTERIAN CHURCH, WHERE No More Deaths was housed and whose non-profit status we used, received the strong recommendation from its legal advisor that No More Deaths cease working under the auspices of St. Mark's Church—using their non-profit status. We had never reported to St. Mark's financially or otherwise, so there were no records on St. Mark's books about our financial activity. We hadn't kept very detailed records ourselves but had used their non-profit status to handle our donations. This raised a huge red flag for their auditors.

In the beginning of No More Deaths, the co-pastors, The Rev. Stuart Taylor and The Rev. Sue Westfall, were deeply involved in No More Deaths and had welcomed its move from Southside Presbyterian Church to St. Mark's. They were doing more than their share by allowing us to use office space and meeting rooms and by taking midweek meals to our folks in the desert throughout each summer. We continued to pay overhead for our space. In 2007, there was no rift with St. Mark's itself. Relations with St. Mark's preachers, staff, and all committees remained excellent. Sue left to take another call and Stuart was very busy trying to keep the graying congregation together. So, when the auditors didn't like what they saw, or didn't see, there wasn't much for us to do but recognize our faults, strive to make changes, and look for another sponsor.

We spent several months exploring options, particularly various organizations that sponsor non-profits and let them use their 501(c)3 status to operate, and several local churches. Nothing seemed to be a fit. By January, I was totally frustrated with our processes and decided to take a break from Monday night meetings.

When I returned a couple of months later, I learned it had been suggested that we become part of a charter school on whose board of directors Margo Cowan and Lupe Castillo sit. Arizona is one of the leading states for charter school sponsorship, with many different types of programs offered through various schools. In a former life in Phoenix, I had been asked to be on the board of a charter school that had just fired its director and was faced with many problems. I served for a while, then later became co-director with a friend. . We tried to pull the school out of its problems, but finally it had to close. Over the two years I was involved, I attended many trainings, studied the charter school law, met with other charter school directors, and became quite thoroughly indoctrinated in how charter schools should and could work.

After doing research about the basis for this particular school recommended by Margo, I came to the conclusion that its only purpose was to run the charter school, unlike some entities that are incorporated to conduct a variety of non-profit activities, such as a charter school, a food program, a child care center, an after-school program, etc. Not this one.

Based on my previous experience of administering a charter school, I expressed my belief that it would be unlawful for the charter school to adopt No More Deaths, and I told people why. But the train was in motion, and I felt my concerns were not being heard. Margo gave all the reasons why we should do it, and after all, she's the lawyer and on the school's board, so what could be the issue?

Seriously concerned, I called the Arizona Charter School Association and spoke with its director, Mark Francis. I knew Mark from a previous time when the charter school I worked for was having trouble. He's the director of a school in Phoenix that focuses on arts education and is always at the top of the states' AIMS achievement scores. At this time, he was head of the Arizona Charter School Association. I thought if anyone knew the ropes, he would.

We talked for quite a while in "hypotheticals"—a certain charter school in Tucson planned to take a certain nonprofit (edgy) organization under its wing and let the nonprofit use the charter school's 501(c)3 status with the feds. As we got further into the conversation, it became very heated. Mark demanded to know which school was involved and which nonprofit. I said I wouldn't tell him. He said I had to. I countered, no I did not. He yelled at me and I yelled back. Finally, I promised I would let him know who was involved if it looked like any action was really going to be taken. Mark wasn't satisfied, but we left it at that.

A couple of days later, Rick Ufford-Chase called the house to talk with Gene. While we waited for Gene to come to the phone, I told Rick that I had called Mark about the issue. Rick became angry. *How could I go behind the back of No More Deaths? Why wasn't I being loyal?* I told him I wasn't going behind anyone's back. I was trying to get clarification on what I believed would be a very wrong step for No More Deaths. I told him that I had background with charter schools and just didn't believe it would be right for us to align ourselves with one. I didn't want to cause problems for the school, and I didn't want us to get into something we'd eventually have to get out of. He wasn't satisfied with my position either.

Next, there was a meeting of a small group of people—I don't remember the topic—I do remember that attorneys Margo Cowan and Andy Silverman were there, and Ed McCullough. I told them about my research and that I strongly believed that linking No More Deaths with the charter school would be wrong. I didn't fully understand the No More Deaths consensus process at that time, but in essence, I blocked the decision, and it was never discussed again in an open meeting. It was humbling to realize I had that much effect on the process. However, I was prepared to leave No More Deaths if they went ahead with the charter school; right or wrong, I felt that strongly about the issue.

In the spring, Walt Staton, who is a member of the Unitarian Universalist Church of Tucson, suggested we talk with their folks. I didn't know much about the "UU's," but it turns out they are very social-justice oriented, and their principles align with those of No More Deaths.[81] This Tucson Unitarian Universalist church already had a border-action committee, and the pastor, The Rev. Diane Dowgiert, expressed interest in working with us. Walt, Paul Barby, Margo Cohen, Lois Martin, and I worked out the details with their Empowerment Team. No More Deaths volunteers made presentations to the congregation and by June 30th the congregation voted to adopt us as a mission of the church; we were very grateful to have a new home. Paul and Margo went on to work out the reporting, liability, and insurance details, and things began to fall into place.

---

81 See "Unitarian Universalist Statement of Principles" in Appendix B.

CHAPTER 28

Spring and Summer Work–2008

THE FIRST ALTERNATIVE SPRING BREAK PROGRAM–MARCH 2008

WHEN CORINNE BANCROFT WAS IN Tucson in January with her Hamilton College group, she and Gene discussed what might be involved in having an alternative spring break program for college and university students. Many colleges across the country were developing alternative programs rather than have their students spend their holidays "cutting up" on nearby beaches. Corinne and Gene took their idea to the Desert Aid Working Group (DAWGs) which said, collectively, we're too busy to take that on. Gene and Corinne would not be deterred—college kids, outdoors, on a mission, in the springtime, that's his idea of a good and meaningful time. So, a DAWG subgroup was formed to plan for spring break—two months away—and bring the details back to DAWG. The plan was formulated and approved.

Corinne went back to school and put her ideas into a plan which she quickly shared over telephone and email with the subgroup (subject to changes, of course). An application was put up on the website, and notices were sent out to our email list of former volunteers. Over 100 people, mostly students, responded. Those who were accepted came to Tucson from Colby College, Hamilton College, Washington State, Oregon State, USC, UCLA, Warren Wilson College, North

Carolina State, and Notre Dame. In subsequent years, other colleges and universities joined in.

Programs were offered for three weeks in March after the schools responded with their particular spring break dates. The program used Byrd Camp and two satellite camps to accommodate the numbers of applicants. This first year, one satellite was located at Chavez Crossing, and the other on Arivaca Road across from Universal Ranch Road (the road to Byrd's place). A man named Karl Hoffman permitted the group to use part of his horse pasture to put up tents, create a kitchen area, and store gallon jugs of water. Electricity and water served the area, so Gene and I bought a refrigerator off craigslist and towed it out to camp. Giovanni Conti designed and constructed a shower.

A number of changes put in place for spring break carried over into the summer program: adjustments to the daily schedule, the hours of hiking, the number of people in each hiking group, and improvements in the protocols. For example, college students will not drive No More Deaths vehicles (because our insurance won't cover people under 25 years of age). College students will not be left in the desert for extended periods of time to treat or accompany migrants. Lois Martin insisted there should be more in-depth education to challenge these students, which was conducted before they left Tucson for camp. Things like map-reading, using the Global Positioning System (GPS), and some first aid training had to be dealt with on site.

By 2016, alternative spring break programs had been conducted with nearly 1,000 young adults.

FEEDING THE VOLUNTEERS

When people like Dan went out with a small group, they provided their own food. However, when a large group of out-of-town volunteers comes in for spring break or the summer program, it's an entirely different story. That's when our food team kicks into gear.

**No More Deaths Volunteers (Steve Johnston,
Front Left) (No More Deaths)**

Jean Rooney and Stephanie Keenan:

"Simple," you may say on reading the title, "what could be hard about that?" Pardon the pun, it is NOT a piece of cake to feed 10-30 hungry volunteers who are walking trails in a remote desert area for a week with no electricity and no refrigeration! They have a four-burner gas stove and four large camping coolers (and dishes, etc., all which they wash—no paper stuff!).

The challenge is finding fresh produce and staples that can withstand desert heat, insects, and animals, while creating as little garbage as possible. Add to this challenge—young appetites that are vegetarian or vegan or gluten-free or any combination thereof. Meals must be somewhat appetizing as well as nutritious to support long days of walking desert trails. We follow a strict budget, but we can't resist sending a treat now and again—Victor's specialty is fresh salsa and bean dip. The biggest treat for the volunteers is Wednesday, when Gwynn Roskie and her team from St. Mark's Church prepare and deliver an incredibly delicious dinner. The volunteers say that they spend Tuesday anticipating the meal, Wednesday evening eating it, and Thursday remembering it.

SO, here's what we do, in teams of two or three people (imagine this happening in 110 degrees Fahrenheit):

1. Midweek - the Volunteer Coordinator (or a reasonable facsimile thereof) sends us a list of the following week's volunteers and their food preferences. So, we find out how many volunteers will be at the camp, and add in some visitors, maybe media people, who might show up with little notice;

2. Thursday or Friday - maybe someone shops at the Community Food Bank for food and beverages for migrants (and picks up free breads, pastries and produce for volunteers);

3. On or near the weekend the Costco Team shops for such things as coffee, beans, cheese, tortillas, cereal, cookies, peanut butter, jelly, bread, condiments, pasta, pasta sauce, etc.;

4. Saturday afternoon - check local markets giving away produce that might last a few days;

5. Sunday morning - the Produce Team shops at the local farmers' market (Sunflower) for fruit and vegetables and eggs. Get a good selection and lots of it—think about five pieces of fruit for each volunteer and vegetables for lunch and supper;

6. Get all of this to the local church being used for training by noon to be loaded into vehicles along with the

volunteers going to the camp. Buy bags of ice to put with the most perishable produce—hopefully in a big cooler that someone remembered to bring back from the camp. Then hope it gets to the camp within two to three hours—especially if it's only in boxes.

As you can imagine, lettuce and peppers and peaches and bananas, in this heat, are pretty much eaten or spoiled by midweek. A call to or from the camp will tell us if we need to send out more food with the Wednesday dinner providers, since we may have underestimated the number of people or the amount they would eat.

So that's all (!!) there is to it.... In addition to keeping in touch with someone at the camp through the week, evaluating what is being used and not used, checking up on staples and their containers periodically (bins of rice, lentils, beans, etc.) to reduce waste and overbuying, as well as occasionally re-organizing food storage (different volunteers each week).

For next year, food shoppers would like to discuss the cuts for sandwiches, salad stuff, cookies, and fruit. Helpers include Margret Fusari, a retired bookkeeper, Lazaro Medrano, a local volunteer, Kat Sinclair, a statistician at the UA, and others. I think I've also seen Annie Swanson and Kevin Riley lurking in the kitchen.

CHAPTER 29

Ben and Laura Pull Up Stakes–April 2008

MOBILE CAMP AT BEN AND Laura's place operated off and on through-out the winter of 2007 whenever people were available to go out from Tucson. Dan Millis rode with Corinne Bancroft on trails on bicycles looking for migrants. They discovered that flat tires impeded their progress. But they were successful riding the bikes while mapping trails in some of the less hilly areas.

Ben and Laura, however, had had their fill of the migrants and decided to pull up stakes. Laura's brother in Colorado was ill and Laura wanted to help him, so that was drawing them away from Arivaca. They put their ten-acre spread on the market. Some No More Deaths folks thought about buying it and then offering it for use to No More Deaths. But these were just passing thoughts as people real-ized anyone else living on the property would face the same hassle with the *coyotes* and migrants as Ben and Laura had experienced.

Chip, the husband of my cousin Nancy, showed some interest also. One day he and Nancy and Gene and I went out to take a closer look at the property. Laura was home so after she greeted us, she sent us out to scout around. Nancy and I were checking out the No More Deaths camp area. I stood about 20 feet away from her when she opened the door to Rick's trailer, then shut it again quickly. She pointed and mouthed, "There are people in there."

I walked over and opened the door. Inside huddled seven or eight migrants together, both men and women.

I assured them they needn't be afraid of us. They had come into the trailer after being scattered by a Border Patrol helicopter earlier in the day. They were really terrified they were going to be picked up and sent back to Nogales. One pregnant woman cried softly. I tried speaking with them in Spanish, but the man closest to the door spoke perfect English so we switched to that, translating a bit for the others. I suspected he was the *coyote*. They were waiting for nighttime to move on.

Later we told Laura about the discovery, thinking it to be an unusual experience. She said, "Oh no! They do that all the time—hide in the trailer. It scares me to death. That's one of the reasons why I want to move."

Their property stayed available for a few months, but then someone local purchased it. We struck the mobile camp and moved the trailer over to Byrd's place. It had been a great idea while it lasted.

Annie Speaks

*Which of them would not be walking this earth at this
moment if it were not for our presence in the desert?*

— ANNIE SWANSON, VOLUNTEER

DESERT AID–SUMMER 2008

ANNIE SWANSON IS A VERY thoughtful young woman who came to
Tucson from school in Washington, D.C. She made significant contributions to No More Deaths both in the field and later serving as
our volunteer coordinator. She authored the following:

> I had promised to return. That ended up being May of this
> year (2008) and this is how I came to be sitting on an isolated
> dirt road with *Martín* that day.
>
> I try to remember the lessons I have learned over the
> past few years as both a graduate student and a humanitar-
> ian aid worker, a scholar and an activist, the times I have
> had a moment of realization or a deepening of understand-
> ing that really altered my way of seeing things. I try to make
> the connections between the human encounters I have had
> at the border and the broader questions I have grappled
> with in an academic context. Sometimes the correlations

are clear, sometimes they are not. At times I feel that I am nothing more than the keeper of this enormous repository of stories....

So many names, so many faces....

Annie's Friends

* *Felipe* with the six-year-old daughter with neurological problems *que Dios les mando* (that God sent) and *Vincente* who made us laugh;

* *Ruben* who never smiled and who would have given up days before if it weren't for his sick mother waiting for him;

* *Juan* who sobbed as I sat with him and who had a fever of 105 degrees; *Juan Carlos* and *Javier* who were just boys;

* *Elva* who was the sole woman in a group of ten men;

* *Gemmy,* who we promised medical attention to as he lay prone on the desert floor, his face contorted with pain, and who was deported a few hours later;

* *Felipe* who was medically evacuated and *Pedro* who he didn't want to be separated from (when I close my eyes, I can still see little *Pedro* sitting all alone after they had taken *Felipe* away, surrounded by people in uniforms, so far from *Oaxaca*);

* *Elizabet* who carried her two-year-old daughter over two mountain ranges while wearing flip-flops.

* *Elfren* and his sister *Elvia,* who was so scared and so grateful to find herself with other women;

* *Ignacio* with the postcards from *Puebla* and *Cruz* who believed his open and bloody feet were a punishment from God for causing his family to suffer;

* *Martin* from *Oaxaca*; the other *Martin* with the twins in *Guanajuato*;

* *Felipe* who was walking all the way to Tucson and had trouble keeping his eyes open for exhaustion;

* *Edgar* who picked lemons in California;

- *Cristine* and *Jorge* who were *sonando de agua pura* (dreaming of pure water) and who vomited after drinking our water;
- *Jesus* and *Cruz* who played soccer with us; *Ignacio* with the sprained—perhaps broken—ankle.

I can't possibly remember each of them forever, with their unique stories and their own individual hopes and terrors. I don't even know where any of them are right now. Which of them would not be walking the earth at this moment if it were not for our presence in the desert? Is it even worth thinking about? *Hacemos lo que hacemos, ya basta.*

In the U.S. Immigration Policy course I took at Georgetown University, we dedicated an entire seminar to the phenomenon of "devolution." Devolution is the practice, increasingly widespread, of authorizing local law enforcement to play a role in enforcing immigration law. In its most extreme manifestation, a county can petition for a "partnership" under a law known as Section 287(g), meaning that local law enforcement officials are delegated the authority to perform immigration law enforcement functions. "287(g) counties" are notorious for being extremely anti-immigrant, often home to a blatantly racist sentiment. This has concrete effects on the lives of many, many human beings.

I have met numerous people this summer who have lived in the U.S. for years but have been unable to regularize their immigration status simply because there *is* no legal channel through which they can do so. Our immigration system is broken, and this is never clearer to me than when I meet someone who has lived north of this border for most of his or her life, yet who is forced to put his or her life in jeopardy to return to a family, to a job – to return home.

When I met *David* for the first time in the desert, I asked him where he was from and his response was "well, here." "Here" was Santa Paula, California, where he had lived since he was nine. A few weeks before, he had been driving back from a church function when he was pulled over and arrested for driving without a license. His immigration status was checked, and he quickly found himself deported to Nogales, Sonora, hundreds of miles from his wife and daughter, from his job on a local ranch, and from his home of more than 20 years. David rested with us for a few days before continuing to walk north. I can only hope he is with his family now, but I have no way of knowing.

Immigration enforcement happens at the local level because the system is broken elsewhere. Devolution is a problematic response to an even more problematic situation at the federal level; there is no path to citizenship for the vast majority of the nearly 12 million undocumented individuals who live in this country. While it is unthinkable that anyone should find themselves risking their life to cross a border, it is especially ironic in situations like David's, where he has lived in the U.S. for most of his lifetime, from an economic viewpoint, a productive member of the workforce and a taxpayer, and from a noneconomic viewpoint, a unique and beautiful human being who certainly contributes to the richness of this country in many ways.

A few weeks ago, my friend Darby and I walked a few miles with *Concepción* and *Tomás*. Concepción is from a small town near Puebla in México. She was a police officer there, and she has three teenage daughters. Her husband left her when the girls were little, and she is also the primary caregiver for her alcoholic brother's three little girls, all under age ten. She was also two months pregnant. She had never met Tomás before, but she fell down as they were walking, scratching her face and bruising her knee, and he refused to leave her. The *coyote* wouldn't wait, and thus they were left behind together, with no idea of where they where or how to get where they were going, miles from the nearest town.

We developed a relationship of trust in the time we spent together, and as Darby talked with Tomás and I sat with Concepcion, I tried to touch sensitively on the question of her safety during the crossing. There are so many stories about rape and sexual violence, but I have never had anyone talk directly about it with me and have never felt that it was appropriate to ask them to. I asked Concepcion tentatively if she felt that as a woman, the risk or dangers were greater for her. She looked directly at me and said "Anita, let me tell you, the risks here in the desert are nothing, *nothing*, compared to sitting down to eat with your children and knowing that you haven't been able to put enough food on the table."

I have heard this expressed in various ways by many people regarding the suffering of the journey, but I know that I will never forget her words or her face as she said this to me. She asked me to be the *madrina* of her baby, who is due early next year, and she promised to call when she gets to New York. The morning after, we returned to the trail where we had last seen the two of them, and they were gone. The area was thick with Border Patrol that day, and I have no idea whether they made it or not but can only hope and pray.[82]

---

82 Provided by Annie Olson Swanson in 2008.

CHAPTER 31

Joe Arpaio/Isabel Garcia–July 2008

SHERIFF JOE ARPAIO CAME TO town! In the middle of summer! Surely you don't have to ask, "Who is Joe Arpaio?"

Joe Arpaio, sheriff of Maricopa County, purports to be the toughest sheriff in the country. He has about 80 percent support of the people in his district and has been elected and reelected four times. He's past his 80th birthday.

The humanitarian groups in Tucson decided to protest his visit at a Barnes and Noble bookstore. When we parked outside the bookstore, he was still on the porch talking with supporters. Minuteman Roy Warden was there taking notes for his blog. Others milled around trying to catch a snatch of Arpaio's words.

A few minutes later he sat inside facing a large bank of chairs squeezed between the racks of books inside the store. The table in front of him held a microphone and a few stacks of his latest book, *Joe's Law: America's Toughest Sheriff Takes on Illegal Immigration, Drugs and Everything Else That Threatens America* (2008: Joe Arpaio and Len Sherman). He was getting ready to conduct a radio program. The technician sat off to his side.

At 6:00 p.m. the program began. He started by introducing himself, Sheriff Joe Arpaio, the most famous sheriff in the land. He'd just returned from a world tour with his book and declared that everywhere he went people knew who he was. Even on small islands, if he said he was from Phoenix, Arizona, people said, "Oh, you must be Joe Arpaio!"

His reputation as the world's toughest sheriff comes from the tent city he built in Maricopa County for prisoners, the pink underwear he makes them wear, and the old-fashioned black and white striped shirts and pants. According to legend, he feeds the inmates moldy baloney sandwiches. He's taken on illegal immigration as a cause.

Meanwhile, the humanitarians gathered outside, eventually forming ourselves into a large circle with maybe 60-80 protestors. We walked in a circle chanting, "Hey, hey, ho, ho, Joe Arpaio's got to go." Young and old joined in. Other people were continuing to enter the bookstore hoping to find a seat. One staunch Arpaio supporter said to me, "You people need to get an education."

According to the *Arizona Daily Star*,[83] "Arpaio talked mainly about his reasons for using his department to enforce immigration laws, and about his conflicts with other politicians and activists over his aggressive anti-illegal-immigration comments and activities." Isabel Garcia of Coalition of Derechos Humanos took to the microphone outside and spoke in her eloquent way about the abuses of Arpaio's office and the need for immigration reform. This was followed by young people carrying an effigy of Sheriff Joe, about four feet tall, with a photo of Sheriff Joe pasted on the head with fake handcuffs hanging from the waist. A few young people showed up with 4-foot long sticks and started banging on the effigy, eventually knocking off its head and ripping into its body.

Some people made quite a fuss about Isabel Garcia taking part in the demonstration, as she is a public defender for Pima County in addition to being a volunteer for Derechos Humanos. Later I attended a Pima County Board of Supervisors meeting where a number of people spoke both for and against her. Ultimately, her job was safe since she was protesting on her own time, but this

---

83 Friday, July 12, 2008.

assurance followed several days of criticism and concern in the public arena.

While we were preparing our house in Phoenix to sell in order to move to Tucson, Gene picked up a young man from a day-labor center to help us. He said he worked three jobs, so he can send home money to his family in Guadalajara, Mexico. A really good worker, he labored for several days. We talked some about Joe Arpaio's stand toward the day labor centers and how he was trying to prevent workers from getting day jobs. These folks are thrilled to get work for $8 to $10 an hour plus maybe a sandwich for lunch. With a history of working hard to meet their own needs, they will paint, fix things, do yard work, or whatever else needs to be done. And they will do all these jobs well. This young man was very aware of Sheriff Joe's opinions.

When we lived in Phoenix, for several years Luz Lugo and her sister, Minerva, cleaned house for us one or two days a month. After we moved to Tucson we learned from a friend in Phoenix that Minerva had been picked up by one of Sheriff Arpaio's minions in Scottsdale for speeding. He asked her for "papers" and when he found she had none, he arrested her. When we learned about her situation, she was in prison in Florence, a prison-filled town halfway between Phoenix and Tucson.

We got on the phone with Margo Cowan who agreed to do what she could before Minerva's arraignment the following Tuesday. Margo interceded in the arraignment, did her work, and by the following Friday, with $5,000 in hand for the bond, sister Luz was able to "spring" Minerva. Thus, began a protracted series of court appearances in Tucson. As of 2016 her case was yet to be finalized. At the first appearance, the judge said to Margo something like, "I'm sure you need time to prepare your case, let's set the next hearing after Christmas—six months away." He seemed sympathetic to the tenuous state of the law which could change at any time and the strong desire of people to stay in the states. Minerva had lived here for almost 20 years.

Subsequently, Joe Arpaio was put on trial in Phoenix for a variety of federal crimes and found guilty of criminal contempt by Judge Susan Bolton on July 31, 2017. She stated that Arpaio evidenced flagrant disregard for another judge's order that had halted his immigration roundups. Bolton's findings were set aside by a pardon of Joe Arpaio by President Donald Trump on August 25, 2017.

CHAPTER 32

Three Angels–July 1, 2008

Mysterious Form Near a Migrant Camp, 2005, (Michael Hyatt)

GENE AND ANNIE AND JENNIFER came across a mother and her two children (babies, really) in the mountains near Apache Well.

The three No More Deaths volunteers parked the FJ Cruiser in a wash and started hiking the trail up to Apache Well. Each of them carried at least four gallons of water about 150 feet up a small hill. When they reached the crest, they could see the mountain ahead of them split in two, as a backdrop for the small body of water filled by a local wellspring. From that well area, trails lead up Apache Saddle and Apache Peak.

As they hiked along, Annie called out in Spanish, "*Buenos dias; podemos ayudarles; tenemos agua y comida.*" Suddenly a woman popped up out of the weeds. Soon, she called out her young children who were hiding in the bushes behind her. The woman, *Aurora*, introduced herself and her children, ages three and five, *Cynthia* and *Vanessa*. They all sat down and visited and ate some food and drank some water, with Annie translating. Aurora told them how she and her children had been forced to drop out from their group because they simply couldn't keep up. She became very frightened for her children.

At one point in her story she said, "I've been praying for an angel, and God sent three, calling out *buenos dias!*"

The *coyote* made a point to take them to an area where fresh water had been placed by No More Deaths activists. He assured her someone would come along soon to replace the water and would be glad to help her little family.

Annie, Gene, and Jennifer finished distributing their jugs of water, and then called the Mexican Consulate to come for Aurora and her kids, which they did. It has been our experience that the Mexican Consulate is quite willing to come when children are involved—even teenagers. They come quickly and drive right through the Amado checkpoint on their way back to Tucson. We're not always sure what happens next. I suppose it depends (*!Depende!*).

Gene reflected later on the text from Hebrew 13:1-3:

> Let brotherly love continue. Be not forgetful to
> entertain strangers: for thereby some have entertained
> angels unawares. Remember them that are in
> bonds, as bound with them; and them which suffer
> adversity, as being yourselves also in the body.
>
> — *Holy Bible: King James version.*

This may be one of God's creatures sent to help *us*. We the volunteers are helping them and in the process are transformed ourselves. This happens frequently when people work with migrants.

Profe, in Mariposa, reported that he saw many more women and children crossing than in past times. When the border was more porous, the men would travel to the U.S. to work and then return home to their families during the off-season. However, more stringent border policies have made such journeys very dangerous. Thus, the women seeking to reunite with their men in the U.S. take the risks of travel upon themselves and their children.

Profe with a Migrant Child (No More Death)

In her book *The Death of Josseline,* Margaret Regan tells the three angels' story as told to her by Annie Swanson (Margaret was also in the desert at the time and participated in the part of the story she tells). She also tells Dan Millis' story of finding Josseline, hence the title of her book. Check it out: (Boston: Beacon Press, 2010), http://www.beacon.org/The-Death-of-Josseline-P873.aspx.

DAN MILLIS' TRIAL BEGINS JULY 25, 2008

In 2007, Dan Millis came to No More Deaths from the Verde Valley School in Sedona, Arizona. Recently, he bought Gene's Toyota Forerunner and spent a great deal of time on the trails, alone or with others. He'd been mapping trails, dropping water, and looking for migrants in need. He's a very talented and responsible leader.

Dan was ticketed for "littering" on the BANWR on February 18, 2008, and by July 25th his trial was underway. A contingent of No More Deaths supporters gathered outside the federal courthouse at Congress and Granada to provide energy for Dan. Then many of us squeezed ourselves into the federal courtroom to hear the proceedings. The next day Dan emailed his friends:[84]

> The trial yesterday morning went pretty well, I think. Lots of nice people said I did a good job of testifying on the stand. That was good to hear because speaking before a judge and a packed courtroom is tough. I felt like I was taking some sort of oral SAT test while speeding down a blurry tunnel with a cardboard toilet paper tube lodged in my throat.
>
> By the time it was done, I was so spent that I pretty much spaced everything I was going to say at the press conference afterwards. That was OK, because only a couple of cameras were there anyway. Still it was great to talk to reporters with a

---

84 Dan Millis, "Borderstoked Blog," used by permission, July 26, 2008.

crowd of friends and family behind me, some holding color-ful, hand-painted signs saying "PROUD TO LITTER," "WE NEED MORE DANS," or "TRASH THE WALL," etc. Some of the supporters were wearing black-and-white collars given to them by *Jesus.*

What about the outcome of the trial? Well, the moment came that we all waited for, and at the end of the proceed-ings, the judge spoke, the verdict was...not given. No, he decided to take it "under advisement," which means that within a month or so he will let everyone know what he has decided, and I will need to be back for acquittal or sentenc-ing or whatever. To me it seems like a win-win for the move-ment. A "guilty" ruling might result in public outrage, an appeal, and a great excuse for a No More Deaths fundraiser; while "not guilty" would keep my record baby-bottom clean and set a precedent that puts us ever so slightly closer to sane border policy. Stay tuned. Dan

**Volunteers: Annie Swanson on left, Dan
Millis on right (No More Deaths)**

CHAPTER 33

Denver JustFaith Group Visits the Border–Late Summer 2008

SOMETIME DURING THE SUMMER OF 2007, Heidi Parish, a friend of ours from Shadow Rock Congregational Church in Phoenix who had moved to Denver, called to see if John Fife or Gene could come to Denver to speak with people in their church about No More Deaths. Gene suggested that Heidi and a few others come to Tucson first to visit the borderland themselves, and then decide what would be the best type of presentation to make for their congregation.

Four people came in the fall—Heidi, Laura, Terry, from St. Andrews church, and a young pastor, from Iliff Seminary. Iliff has Methodist roots but educates anyone going into the ministry and those taking work for graduate degrees. Iliff and St. Andrews had worked together in the past and thought that migration issues might provide a good vehicle to work together again.

The four women experienced a very moving trip. They spent a day and a half at Byrd camp going on patrols along the trails. Then they visited the migrant aid center at the Mariposa port of entry in Nogales. Along the way, they talked with many people about border and immigration issues.

In December of 2008, John Fife and his wife, Maryann, flew to Denver with Gene and spoke to several groups. Then again in April of 2009, Gene, John, and I flew to Denver and talked some more—mainly to the church's JustFaith[85] group, to their social justice ministry group, and to the young people. John participated in a panel discussion along with Dr. Miguel de la Torre from Iliff Seminary, a Representative Tom Tancredo's staff person (Tancredo, an avid anti-immigration member of Congress, did not run for reelection), along with some others. Gene and I drove south to Colorado Springs to speak with a group of students there.

While in Denver, we stayed in the home of Rob and Laura Dravenstott and their three children. Rob is a computer guru and Laura graduated from Harvard in Literature. Laura stays home with their children and participates in many justice activities in St. Andrews Methodist Church. Carol Harr and others provided delicious meals for us all.

We returned home with commitments from the Iliff Seminary people to travel to the border at the end of August, and from the St. Andrews Methodist Church people to come mid-September. This was just the beginning of a long-term, and personally meaningful, relationship.

IS NOW A TIME FOR A STRATEGY OF RESISTANCE?

On the plane coming home from Denver, John Fife began drafting a paper about the current border situation for the humanitarian aid groups. We realized on a daily basis that government agencies were pushing back against the humanitarian aid provided by No More

---

85 JustFaith is a 30-week, justice-formation process with a focus on poverty. Meeting weekly, groups employ books, videos, lecture, discussion, prayer, retreats and hands-on experiences. The intent is to provide a tapestry of learning opportunities that emphasize and enliven the remarkable justice tradition of the church. Started within the Catholic Church, JustFaith has spread to many other churches, including St. Andrews Methodist Church in Denver. Note: JustFaith now has its third round of participants at St. Andrew's. Folks who previously came to the border provide part of the leadership and have tied their border experiences into the JustFaith curriculum. (https://justfaith.org).

Deaths. John's resulting paper titled, "Is it Now Time for a Strategy of Resistance?"[86] starts out like this:

For the past eight years, humanitarian aid and human rights groups in the borderlands have attempted to cooperate with Border Patrol and U.S. government officials in order to be effective in saving the lives of migrants in the Sonoran Desert. But over the past eight years, the government has closed down the space and opportunity to save lives and provide humanitarian aid.

- When Humane Borders began, Border Patrol agreed not to target water stations with electronic or human surveillance. That agreement was terminated in 2004;
- When Samaritans began, our protocol to transport migrants in medical evacuations under the direction of a physician was agreed to by Border Patrol. That agreement was terminated in 2005;
- The No More Deaths camp was placed under daily and sometimes nightly surveillance in 2004;
- For six years, food, water, and some other humanitarian aid were permitted to be given to migrants in custody in the desert (often waiting in the sun next to a bus to be transported). That has been terminated;
- Two volunteers were arrested and charged with felonies in 2005 (Shanti Sellz and Daniel Strauss). One Samaritan volunteer was cited for a misdemeanor after being threatened with incarceration (Kathryn Ferguson).

John went on to point out the following: " The evidence is abundant that the U.S. government is determined to continue to violate basic human rights in the borderlands and throughout the country."

---

86 John Fife, "Is Now a Time for a Strategy of Resistance?" (provided by John Fife, 2008).

- No More Deaths, The Florence Immigrant and Refugee Rights Project, and the Border Action Network have documented the human rights abuses of Border Patrol in the detention and deportation of migrants. There are no standards or oversight to which the government is held accountable;
- The Arizona Denial Prosecution Strategy will directly lead to many more deaths in the desert and puts humanitarian aid workers in an ethical quandary;
- ICE raids across the country have devastated and separated families. Local law enforcement officials are now acting to enforce federal immigration laws. Racial profiling is pervasive;
- Hate speech, bigotry, and overt racism have increased dramatically in this election year;
- The devastating effects of Free Trade Agreements will escalate in 2008, as all agricultural tariffs are ended. Mexico estimates that at least one million more small farmers will be displaced by subsidized imports from the U.S. and Canada.

"Therefore, we have no choice as people of faith and conscience. We must move from a strategy of cooperation for the sake of humanitarian aid—to a strategy of active nonviolent resistance. This strategy of resistance must also continue to provide humanitarian aid to the victims of government policy that uses the death and suffering of the poor as an enforcement policy."

Among a number of other recommendations, John cites the following as part of a resistance strategy:

- **A strategy of resistance to the human rights abuses in the desert, detention, and deportation system:**
  - A letter advising Border Patrol and Wackenhut employers that they are acting in violation of human rights and international law;

* Constant documented demands by physicians and nurses to assist migrants in custody in the desert;
* The timely release of abuse documentation and demands for standards and oversight.

* **A strategy of resistance to the Arizona Denial Prosecution Strategy:**
    * Recruit and train thousands of volunteers from faith communities, universities, and peace and justice organizations to walk a spiritual pilgrimage in the Sonoran Desert;
    * Use our experience and training to provide leadership to groups of pilgrims.
    * Foster existing relationships with hospital and court staff to follow the enforcement strategy;
    * Continue to provide food, water, and medical care to migrants in the desert.
    * This component would provide active, non-violent resistance in the desert.
        * It would be spiritually based;
        * It would confound the enforcement strategy with the clutter of pilgrimages in the desert;
        * It would increase the provision of humanitarian aid;
        * It would be legal;
        * It would contribute to the education and organizing of volunteers and their communities across the nation.

* **A strategy of resistance in dialogue with Border Patrol and government officials:**
    * For eight years humanitarian aid organizations have tried to engage in a cooperative dialogue with the U.S. government. Now we must initiate this dialogue from the position of asserting our right and responsibility to protect basic human rights and aid the victims of human

rights violations by the government. Civil Initiative requires that we continue to seek opportunities for dialogue, but the relationship and tenor of the conversation will change under this strategy.

This paper became the basis for discussion in No More Deaths meetings. While not formally adopted, we held the strategy in the back of our minds as we moved forward, and it informed our program planning and our ongoing relationships with government institutions.

CHAPTER 34

Kidneys, Ambulance, and Border Patrol–August 2008

I have met many migrants, but I have never met one who wanted to be a migrant. They never expressed happiness at walking away from their country, leaving culture, family, children, and familiarity behind. The migrants I have met were forced to migrate. They were displaced, economically. If they did not move, they would die.

JEAN BOUCHER, NMD VOLUNTEER COORDINATOR, FORMERLY WITH ANNUNCIATION HOUSE, EL PASO, TEXAS

Migrant Being Placed in Ambulance (No More Deaths)

At a Monday night meeting in the middle of August, Maryada explained why she looked so drained. She and Joshua Sutton (formerly known as Oskar Pawpaw) had been up all night looking for a migrant who had been taken to a hospital in a Green Valley ambulance. He was frightened—she and Josh had promised to stay by his side at the hospital where he was to be treated for renal failure. They tried everything they could think of but were unable to locate him after the ambulance drove off.

Later Maryada and I met for lunch at La Salsa on Speedway, and she told me more of the story.

Danilo, a Mexican man who was approximately 18 to 20 years old, had walked into Byrd camp on a Friday; he was very ill. He told the volunteers that he had been walking five or six days, and that he had drunk from a cow tank (nasty, nasty water). He also reported that he had not urinated for four days. As it happened there were four EMTs in the camp plus a few Wilderness First Responders; they began to assess Danilo's condition. Then, they monitored him closely for the next 24 hours.

Throughout the following day they offered him something to drink every half hour until he consumed a little less than 500 milliliters. His yellow/brown urine output went from 10 ml to 50 ml. After consulting with Dr. Norma Price by phone in Tucson, the group decided to get Danilo to the hospital due to the threat of kidney failure. Danilo freaked out at that suggestion and simply wanted to go back home. Every time he tried to eat he became nauseated. Norma instructed the volunteers to keep trying to persuade him to go the hospital.

Saturday, after dinner, Dan Millis came into camp with another migrant he had found way out on the trail who was slumped over near a water tank. The man was in really bad shape; he was very weak and throwing up. They placed him on a cot near Danilo and assessed his vital signs while Lindsey DePew, a college student and local volunteer, was explaining how serious kidney failure was. Danilo took all this in. Then, Maryada called Dr. Norma back, to report the new arrival.

Norma talked more about kidney failure: "You can't tell when it will happen, maybe tomorrow, maybe next week; maybe later in life you will suffer the effects."

Maryada asked her what to do if they couldn't get consent from the patients.

Norma told her to keep trying to put the "fear of God" into them.

The second "guest" was a bigger guy. His blood pressure was very low, and he was not able to take in fluids. Norma instructed the volunteers to take him to the hospital. For us, this means calling 911 and letting whoever responds to handle the situation, but the man still said NO.

Suddenly, Danilo piped up and said, "I'll go." That was around nine or ten at night. The dilemma then was whether to call 911 for Danilo right now and call later for the other man, or to wait and call later for both.

Everyone moved into the "Tarp-Majal" where the two men were resting. Two of the volunteers sat with the men and checked them every few minutes. Finally, they called 911 for Danilo.

The Arivaca Fire Department arrived around 11:00 p.m. in the form of two men in their personal vehicle—so they wouldn't have to backtrack from their nearby homes to the fire station and then drive to the camp. They conducted their own assessment. According to Maryada, they were kind and professional. Josh wanted to go with them to the ambulance but was told he wouldn't be permitted unless he was family. The medics assured him that they would let him know to which hospital they would take Danilo—probably St. Mary's in Tucson or Holy Cross in Nogales. The fire department volunteers said they could meet up at the Arivaca Fire Department where an ALS (advanced life support unit) would meet them. Maryada and Josh followed in a No More Deaths vehicle.

At some point, Danilo was transferred into the Arivaca ambulance and later into the Southwest ambulance from Green Valley. Maryada said that inside the Green Valley ambulance sat a man wearing a green uniform. *Holy Shit! Border Patrol! He's already in custody.* They learned the agent was not from BorStar, Border Patrol's emergency medical group; he was just there to take Danilo."

When they arrived at the fire station and left their cars, the agent went up to Maryada and Josh and chewed them out immediately saying, "You had an illegal in your camp and you didn't call us!"

Josh told him, "We're not cops. We're medics."

"If he needed help, why was he still in your camp?" the agent shouted.

Maryada responded, "Until an hour ago, we didn't have his permission to take him for help. The moment we got consent, we called 911."

"Consent?! From whom?!"

From whom? W*hy, the patient, of course.*

Well-established protocols for EMTs and WFRs[87] require "consent to treat" if the person is coherent, as Danilo certainly was. In addition, EMTs and WFRs must hand off ill or injured persons to someone who is equally or more highly-trained than they are—like another EMT or a nurse or doctor.

As Maryada moved away from the ambulance she could see the Green Valley medic cut through Danilo's clothes from his feet all the way up to his shoulder. Those, of course, were the only clothes Danilo owned. The medic proceeded to examine Danilo.

Then the paramedic said to Maryada, "You had a renal failure and you didn't call us?"

Maryada told him, "We *did* call you when we had his consent."

The agent asked, "How old is he?"

Maryada said, "He told us he is 18, but his identification says 20. He seems to have lied out of fear."

The agent remarked sarcastically to the paramedic, "He's not the only one lying here tonight."

---

87 Wilderness First Responders.

Maryada was beside herself with frustration. *Is this how profession-*
als trying to provide the best standard of care treat each other?

Maryada and Josh were invited to leave for the second time.
The ambulance driver refused to tell them to which hospital Danilo
would be transported. Then the driver told them that HIPPA[88] says
we don't have to tell you! *Really?*

Josh and Maryada waited a while, then decided to go to the
Cow Palace Restaurant in the little town of Amado and wait. If the
ambulance turned left on the highway from Amado, they'd know
that Danilo was being transported to Tucson. If the ambulance
turned right, they would know he was going to Nogales. No need
to be ambulance chasers. When the ambulance arrived in Amado,
it turned left. Maryada and Josh followed from a distance. So far
behind, in fact, they didn't see the ambulance turn off into Green
Valley instead of proceeding to Tucson.

Maryada and Josh continued north into Tucson and pulled into
St. Mary's Hospital. No Danilo. Then they called around to other
hospitals looking for him to no avail. Finally, at five in the morning, they concluded that Danilo had been taken into Border Patrol
custody, processed, and deported. In essence, he had "disappeared."
Without clothes? Without definitive care?

A day or two later, Dr. Norma Price spoke with the Green Valley
Southwest Ambulance dispatcher and was told the patient "refused
medical care" so he wasn't taken to a hospital.

A few days later, one of the volunteers heard by phone from
Danilo's brother. Danilo was in Nogales—still sick, scared to
death, and trying to get back home to Vera Cruz. The second
migrant had remained at camp. He slowly improved and then
went on his way.

Unfortunately, news of these unsettling activities didn't reach
Gene before he left for camp with a group from Iliff Seminary on

---

88 Health Insurance Portability and Accountability Act.

Sunday. He wasn't aware Border Patrol may have upped their reactions to our efforts. In her new position as a reserve EMT in the Tubac fire department, Maryada overheard some Border Patrol agents telling the fire department personnel that they planned to "drop a 2000" on those people (No More Deaths). *Whatever is a 2000?*

Iliff Seminary Students Visit During the Democratic National Convention in Denver

Then the King will say to those on his right, "Come, you who are
blessed by my Father, inherit the kingdom prepared for you from
the foundation of the world. For I was hungry, and you gave
me food, I was thirsty, and you gave me drink, I was a stranger
and you welcomed me, I was naked, and you clothed me, I was
sick, and you visited me, I was in prison and you came to me."
Then the righteous will answer him, saying, "Lord, when did we
see you hungry and feed you, or thirsty and give you drink? And
when did we see you a stranger and welcome you, or naked and
clothe you? And when did we see you sick or in prison and visit
you?" And the King will answer them, "Truly, I say to you, as you
did it to one of the least of these my brothers, you did it to me."

— *BIBLE, REVISED STANDARD VERSION, MATTHEW 25:31-40*

GENE AND DR. MIGUEL DE la Torre[89] scheduled the Iliff Seminary
(in Denver) trip to the border for August 23-31, 2008. When they
arrived in Tucson, some folks expressed disappointment at missing

---

89 The Rev. Dr. Miguel de la Torre is professor of Social Ethics and Latino/a
Studies at the Iliff School of Theology in Denver, Colorado. He has served as the
elected 2012 president of the Society of Christian Ethics and currently serves as the
executive office for the Society of Race, Ethnicity and Religion.

the Democratic National Convention (DNC) back in their own hometown. Nevertheless, emails had flown back and forth between Gene and Dr. de la Torre as they planned for a successful experience for ten students and Miguel. Their plane arrived late, around 5:00 p.m. on Saturday evening. Gene and Miguel picked up a van for their transportation for the week and collected the students.

Maryann Fife had prepared a dinner of braised beef and an alternative dish for the vegetarians, with tossed salad and brownies for dessert. We ate outside on the patio. From the living room and from the patio, the Tucson Mountains frame the left side of your view, while down below you can see the hills and valleys, and then the lights of Tucson. In the distance the majestic Catalina Mountain rises 9000 feet above our mere 2500 feet. What a view!

On Sunday morning, the Iliff group attended services at the Southside Presbyterian Church, previously served by John Fife. In the Presbyterian Church system, former pastors aren't permitted to linger after they retire, so the current assistant pastor, our good friend Brandon Wert, recounted the history of this most unusual church. Founded as a mission church to the Tohono O'odham (then known as Papago), the church was initially named Papago Presbyterian Church. The church also served the Mexican and Chinese people who lived in the area. Since its founding, Southside's congregation has included a diverse mix of Native Americans, Chinese, Latinos, Caucasians, African Americans, and others. The present-day neighborhood is mostly comprised of Latino and Native American families living in modest single-family homes.

On Sunday afternoon, Gene and John Fife took the Iliff group to the No More Deaths training at St. Mark's Presbyterian Church from 2:00 p.m. to 5:00 p.m. There they heard presentations on the history of our border with Mexico, immigration law that applies to our work, the No More Deaths protocols, the principle of Civil Initiative, privilege, first aid, and other topics. Unfortunately, little did they know that in the room next door, volunteers were debriefing the Danilo situation to Dr. Price and Nurse Sarah Roberts. Such knowledge of Border Patrol behavior might have made them wary of what could occur this week.

Following the training, the group drove out to Byrd Camp. On the way, at milepost 13 on Arivaca Road east, they saw six men beside the road. They stopped and asked if the people needed water and food. Three men accepted some, but when asked about their health they replied that they were tired but okay. They asked if our group would take them to Phoenix. When Gene declined, the migrants said that then they wanted to go back to Mexico. *Would we call Border Patrol?* Gene called Border Patrol (their number is programmed into our phones), and the operator said he'd send someone. Soon after that, about 7:00 p.m., Gene saw two Border Patrol trucks coming southwest down Arivaca Road. He flagged them down, and one vehicle pulled over. The officer, a captain, came out of the truck. He had not heard of Gene's call but was willing to take the migrants into custody. Another officer arrived; they loaded the migrants into one of their trucks and left with thanks to our group who continued on to camp. Gene and John were slated to be camp coordinators.

At camp on Monday morning, Ed McCullough, our GPS (Global Positioning Systems) guru and former geography professor and vice-provost at UA, helped Gene train the new volunteers on the use of maps, GPS units, desert survival, and more first aid. Ed, along with others, including Dan Millis and Kevin Riley, has mapped over 2000 miles of trails in the mountains and valleys of the area served by No More Deaths and Samaritans. Ed has entered all this data, including waypoints, into the GPS units, and he regularly printed out fresh 9"x12" maps of each critical area for the volunteers. After the training, and throughout Tuesday, the group split up and went out on patrols.

I expected the group to return to Tucson on Wednesday afternoon by about 3:00 p.m., in time to shower and rest before dinner. I'd fixed a combination of eggplant and squash from my garden, onions, garlic, and Paul Newman's Tomato and Garlic Spaghetti Sauce to serve with whole wheat spaghetti. Great comfort food. Maryada came by to help me.

At about 2:00 p.m., Gene called. Calmly, he said Border Patrol was there in camp and that he'd been read his rights (Later Margo confirmed that this meant he'd been arrested.)

"Oh, really," I answered. "How are you?"

"Just fine. We're just waiting to see what's going to happen."

Border Patrol agents had come to the camp before, but they'd usually waited to be invited before coming in. During 2005-2006, they would ride into camp late at night and do "wheelies" in the parking lot. This time they arrived on horseback and in vehicles encircling the camp. Gene and some others were out on patrol. Just twenty minutes from coming back to camp for lunch, he received a call from Karen, the young Irish woman he'd left in charge, saying that she'd seen Border Patrol agents on horseback on the hills above the camp, and she thought they were coming in. What should she do?

Gene told her Border Patrol agents do have a right to come into our camp (Homeland Security provisions give the government the right to enter private property within 100 miles of the border), and that she should tell the truth in response to any questions they had, including that there were three migrants in camp.

Arrest of Migrants at Byrd Camp (No More Deaths)

Gene tells it best:

About twenty minutes after Karen's call, about 11:30 a.m., I pulled into camp where I saw 15 to 20 Border Patrol officers on horseback, in trucks, and on foot. I got out of my truck and started to pack my camping gear since we planned to leave with the Iliff students right after lunch. I noticed they were questioning Karen, so I walked over to that spot and identified myself as the camp coordinator. The agent in charge replied that Karen had said she was the coordinator. Karen and I explained that she was in charge only for the morning while I was on patrol. He walked me over to another spot and asked me questions. Were there migrants in our camp? I replied yes. How many? Three. He said they had tracked ten migrants to our camp area; had I seen more than the three I indicated? No. He asked me how long migrants had been in camp? I told him. A few minutes later he read me my rights and I said I wanted to invoke my right to a lawyer. He said that was fine. I asked if I could call her. He said I could after he talked to his superior. He assigned Officer Morales to watch me, asked me to stay where I was, and moved back over to continue questioning Karen.

I stood waiting and chatted with Officer Morales about the horses, Border Patrol trucks, and the poor conditions of migrants we both saw often.

Officer Morales said to me, "Gene, we admire the humanitarian work you guys do. I don't know how this is going to turn out, but it's good of you to give water, food, and first aid to the migrants. But you must call us *the moment* a migrant comes into camp." He repeated this advice at least once more during our conversation. I told him I understood what he was saying but disagreed with his interpretation of the law.

He allowed me to sit in the shade. Later, Meg Adams came over with a cell phone saying it was my lawyer; she asked Office Morales if it was okay if I talked to her. He allowed me to take the phone. Margo Cowan asked me a couple of questions, and then advised that I should ask Morales if I could move far enough away so that no one else could over-hear our conversation. He permitted me to move about 20 feet. At some point the supervising officer came back and again read me my rights. At the time I didn't know why, but later heard that the agent had neglected to record the time when he first read them to me. Again, I invoked my right to answer questions when my lawyer was present. Again, he left me alone. Officer Morales told me they had found water bottles like those we put out on the trails, with warnings that *La Migra* (Border Patrol) was ahead on the trail. I told him we did not condone this—usually we write the date and the waypoint on the plastic bottle, and sometimes our volunteers write notes in Spanish like "good luck" and "safe passage."

At some point, Officer Morales told me they found a package with 40 pounds of marijuana at the edge of our camp. I told him we had nothing to do with drugs. Fortunately, John Fife and his group had returned by then, and John was able to photograph the untidy bale oozing with maggots and other bugs. It had been there for some time.

While I was waiting, Officer Morales let people come up and talk with me. I was able to tell Sarah to please inform John Fife that there is only *one* camp coordinator on duty (and it's me!). Only one of us need to take the heat. At some point, Dr. Miguel de la Torre also came over with his tape recorder and interviewed me about my various experiences with Border Patrol, which he planned to include in a book he was writing to help church congregations understand what is happening at the border (Dr. Miguel de la Torre, *Trails of Hope and Tears*, https://www.orbisbooks.com/trails-of-hope-and-terror.html, Ossining: Orbis Books, 2009).

I saw "our" migrants being loaded into a patrol truck where they waited about an hour before being taken away. After I had been in camp about an hour and a half, I saw agents escorting a dark-skinned man from the brush toward one of their vehicles. I did not recognize him.

About two hours after I had returned to camp, the supervising officer came back to me and said: "This is a serious situation. You have been harboring people. They have been staying in your camp with your permission and you did not call us."

I let him know that I heard what he was saying.

He again said this is a serious situation. "This is not over. We will get back in touch with you."

I learned that Margo had been in touch with the U.S. Attorney and requested that there be no "field arrests." We would come in if requested to do so. Thank goodness for Margo. Border Patrol hurried out of camp.

I met briefly with all the volunteers in camp and explained what had been said. As the Iliff group packed up, I also met briefly with the experienced volunteers who were staying in camp to encourage them to take leadership until Steve Johnston arrived on Friday. We left in a hurry with the Iliff group because there was a huge storm cloud upon us. During the monsoon rains, the Papalote Wash next to our camp overflows, allowing no passage along the road into camp. Other washes on the way to the highway would soon flood as well. We learned later the Arivaca area sustained over three inches of rain that afternoon. I think the approaching storm helped Border Patrol make the decision to hurry out of camp. They would not want to be stuck in camp because of flooded washes.

The "Roja" in Papalote Wash Outside Byrd Camp (No More Deaths)

The group arrived "home" in time for dinner. Much discussion and many phone calls ensued as Gene reported what had happened to others. From Tucson, Dr. Norma Price had been directing the care our EMTs give to migrants. She, John Fife, and Gene planned to meet at Margo's office the next day to discuss a "plan." After dinner, some of us watched Bill Clinton's speech at the Democratic National Convention in Denver. Hillary Clinton had just handed over the race to Barack Obama.

On Friday afternoon, after some discussion, Margo fired off two letters—one to Border Patrol asking for a meeting and reiterating that Gene would "come in" if they wanted him to, and one to the United States Attorney. We heard nothing back from either letter.

The Iliff group spent the following two days in Mexico, first at our aid station at the Mariposa port (operated jointly by the Green Valley and Tucson Samaritans, No More Deaths, and the Sonoran

Office to Assist Migrants), then to Magdalena to see the burial site of *Padre Francisco Eusebio Kino*, a Jesuit who traveled widely in this area from the 1690s to 1711.

From there they drove on to Altar, the jumping-off point for many migrants heading for the United States. They come from as far away as Chiapas in southern Mexico and even South America, riding buses and trains to get to Altar where their final *coyote* (or *pollero*, as some call them; there have been many along the way), drives them the 60 miles to Sasabe (a sleepy little town that straddles the border). The *coyote* then helps them hike through the mountains and cross into the United States. The Iliff group stayed at *CCAMYN*, the Catholic migrant center in Altar. There they received dinner and a pad to place under their sleeping bags on the hard cement floor, as well as a talk by the local priest about their work. In the morning they were served breakfast, then walked the couple of blocks to the town square (plaza) to visit with migrants readying themselves for their journey north. Along the way they passed by beautiful homes built in recent years by local drug and people merchants.

After their time in Mexico, they arrived "home" late and came straight to our house for dinner. I had made what I call "stewp" a mixture of black beans, corn, chopped onions, green chilies, squash, chopped tomatoes, garlic, and salsa. Those who were sleeping at the bed and breakfast run by our friends, Kyle and Karen Thompson, headed out after eating. The five women who were staying at our house went to bed.

The following morning, Saturday, both households got up at 5:00 a.m. to go out to the Tohono O'odham Reservation and meet with tribal member, Mike Wilson. Mike and his friend, David Garcia (a former tribal council member), had been putting out water on the reservation for seven years. They had four of Humane Border's water tanks placed where the greatest amount of traffic flows through. By far the most migrant deaths in Southern Arizona occurred on the reservation—some years as many as 40 percent. We suspected that this was the result of the tribal government's refusal to allow outside humanitarian groups to work and place water there.

The group met up with Mike Wilson at one of the water tanks. He had just begun telling them about his work when a tribal officer arrived—a white female. She asked what they were doing there, and Mike told her, "These are my guests and I am telling them about my work to save lives here on the reservation." She told him that he couldn't be there and went to her car.

She came back with word that Mike needed to take down his water stations and that we were all banned from the reservation—*for life*. Mike explained he's been putting water out for seven years and was not about to take the stations down now.

Banned from the reservation. Unbelievable. One of the Iliff students, a man about thirty years of age, said to the officer, "Let me understand this: you mean that here I am, a guest of a member of this tribe, listening to him talk about how he saves lives, and you say I'm banned? Banned for life?"

This was a serious development for John Fife. He's frequently called upon to perform weddings or officiate at funerals, particularly in this part of the reservation since some of these people are members of Southside Presbyterian Church.

As the group stood around waiting, Mike, who had served in the army in the first Gulf War, began preaching on Chapter 25 of Matthew in the New Testament where Jesus separates the sheep and the goats. The sheep represent those who have fed the hungry, clothed the naked, tended the sick, and given water to the thirsty. Even though those people protested their virtue, Christ says they will enter the Kingdom of Heaven.

Mike was preaching to the choir with the group of seminary students, but he was actually preaching over their heads to the tribal officer. She was moved to declare that she was a good person; she didn't want to see people dying, but the migrants chose to come...so it's their responsibility!

The officer was adamant about the tribal district head's position, so the group headed back to Tucson. Some of the Iliff students groused that they didn't get to see the Cultural Center or the special border crossing for the O'odham. Because of their history of traveling back and forth on the section of the reservation that extends into Mexico, Tohono O'odham have been provided with a special gate (or gates) and individual key cards that allow them to go across the border and come back through to visit family or for tribal celebrations. Instead, Gene took them to a little shop along the highway where the Iliff group purchased beautiful Tohono O'odham baskets for Maryann Fife and me to thank us for our hospitality.

The Iliff group came "home" early, ate a makeshift lunch, showered, and rested until dinner. After dinner they had a closing discussion, drank a bit of wine, and went to sleep. The following morning, they headed back to Denver, full of stories. Later, we learned that as a result of their unusual experiences, Iliff Seminary would not permit the December trip that Miguel had been planning.

CHAPTER 36

The Following Week in the Desert

WHEN WE INFORMED THE PASTOR of our sponsor, the Unitarian Universalist Church of Tucson (UUCT), Diane Dowgiert, about the raid on our camp, she felt some urgency to go out into the field and experience firsthand what was happening in the borderlands and to see what No More Deaths actually did each day. So, on Sunday, Diane and her husband, A.J., Gene and I, along with Walt Staton, took our new, bright-blue FJ truck down highway 19, then further along Arivaca and Universal Ranch roads to the No More Deaths camp—about seven miles east of Arivaca.

Five years ago, Gene and I had stood on this same property with a number of clergy and lay people who dedicated the camp as an "Ark of the Covenant," a sacred space for migrants. It looked quite different on this day, having in addition to the original small trailer, several tarps overhead with rows of cots underneath, a designated space for a kitchen, an additional trailer, stacks of both full and empty water bottles, boxes of food, food packs for migrants on the trails, and a couple of tables with chairs all around.

The previous week, Walt served as camp coordinator, and he had made a fresh pot of beans. He heated them up, and we ate a lunch of beans and tortillas, some fruit, and lots of water.

Walt explained the daily schedule of volunteers: get up early, eat a light breakfast, select the trails in need of service, pile into the available vehicles, and head out. Back for lunch and rest. Then a late afternoon patrol on different trails. Dinner and discussion about the results of the day and how people felt about various experiences. Walt also showed Diane and A.J. the book of log sheets where each trip leader describes his or her day, including the number of water jugs placed and where, the number of migrants encountered, and the type of care provided to them. The book was mostly empty as the sheets up to and through the raid were taken into town to copy in case they were needed for "Gene's trial." These logs would support our contention that No More Deaths volunteers frequently call Border Patrol to extract migrants who want to go home. This log book comprised an important piece of documentation for No More Deaths.

As we finished our lunch and sat around the table deliberating the vastness of the desert and the enormity of the migrant problem, someone nodded toward some nearby parked vehicles. There, coming toward us were two young men, probably in their 20s saying "*Tiene agua? Tiene comida?*" "Do you have water and food?" At this point Gene indicated he was leaving, not wanting to be caught again by Border Patrol so soon with migrants in the camp. He headed to Joe and Janet's house (migrant-friendly neighbors who also host No More Deaths volunteers).

We waved the young men over and said, "Of course." They said that they saw the flag printed with the Virgin of Guadalupe at the entrance to our camp. At first, they were shy but soon felt more comfortable once they sat down at the table and drank some water. When they were ready for the second liter, Walt handed them some electrolyte packets. The young man who said he was from Hermosillo put the electrolytes into the bottle right away and started drinking. The man from *Navajoa* asked to taste from his friend's bottle before he put the electrolytes into his own water. He said it tasted okay, added it to his water, and commenced to drink, as well. We offered them soup and other choices, but they preferred the beans and tortillas. While they ate, Walt asked questions about their journey so far, and how long it had taken them to get to our camp from the border (three days). He also asked more personal questions that would indicate their state of health. They didn't appear to be in such bad shape that they needed to receive additional medical care. As was our practice, we warned migrants of conditions that lay ahead if they continued northward and what might happen if they decided to return to Mexico.

They did tell us they had been with a group of nine migrants who left them earlier in the day while they were sleeping, taking their own two backpacks with them. Nothing was left behind—no food, no water, no pack, no money. Walt found used backpacks for them in the trailer and filled them with water and food. As soon as the men finished eating, they left, thanking us profusely.

Shortly thereafter, we packed up lunch, loaded the truck with gallons of water and food packets, and headed out into the hills. Gene chose as our final destination the shrine to Josseline, the 14-year-old El Salvadoran girl who had been found by Dan Millis in February. After bouncing over miles of dirt roads, noting the number of small ranches for sale, appreciating the green mesquite trees (which are skinny black sticks in the winter), and the beautiful hot day (over 100 degrees), Gene pulled into a bare spot and stopped. Since the sun and hiking don't work well for me, I had the book *These is My Words,* which is about life in Douglas, Arizona, during the 1860s written by Nancy Turner ready to read while Diane, A.J., Gene, and Walt headed up the mountain toward the shrine. They carried several gallons of water and food packs to leave along the way. Here's how Diane described it:

> The trek to the shrine is only a quarter mile, but feels farther—up a steep, rocky canyon. I feel the heat of the rocks through the soles of my sturdy shoes. Mountain ranges rim every horizon. The only directions I know for sure are up and down. For all I know, I could be headed south, back toward the border, or maybe north, toward Tucson. How easy it is to become disoriented in this unfamiliar place. How terrifying

to be lost and alone, hungry and exhausted, thousands of miles from home. We pay our respects at the simple wooden cross, inscribed with Joseline's name, marking the place she died. Thoughts of her family and their sorrow—thoughts of the volunteers who found her too late—thoughts of the thousands of others who have died making this perilous passage—these things crowd my mind as we pile into the four-wheel drive SUV to head back to camp. I can't imagine the kind of desperation that would drive someone to embark on such a dangerous journey.

It seemed as though the group had just left when I heard them coming back down the trail—to the place I had moved the car, a better spot to catch the occasional breeze. I had been reading my book and hadn't missed them a bit. With somber demeanors they climbed again into the truck, and we headed over the hills back toward the No More Deaths camp.

As we made a slight turn around a curve, someone yelled, *"Look!"* We all snapped to attention as approximately 30 migrants ran across the road in front of us. A few stayed on the left side of the road fearing we might collide with them.

Walt commanded, "Roll down the window, A.J."

As soon as A.J. began to roll it down, Walt began shouting, *"Tenemos agua!! Tenemos agua!!"*

Reluctantly, a couple of migrants turned back toward the car, then a few more began tentatively to appear. Gene and Walt and A.J. handed each one a gallon of water from the back of the truck. One man asked Gene if he had *comida*, and Gene gave him the one food bag that was left in the truck. The group seemed to be running—not hiking—cross-country. As soon as the migrant received the food bag and a gallon of water, he took off racing to catch up with the others.

Gene cares about his truck and wants it to last, even though he doesn't mind scratches and dents on the sides, he drives slowly to maintain the undercarriage, the brakes, and the tires. He drives between 5 and 15 miles per hour along this bumpy dirt road, mostly at the lower speed. We enjoyed the wild flowers, the hawks, the occasional damp water course—now empty, but it had recently flooded with monsoon rains.

A short time later we encountered another group of migrants— five men and one woman. They stood by the side of the road in a tree-covered watercourse probably trying to dig down to some water. By that time, we were out of water, but Walt showed them a nearby stash that he'd put out on an earlier trip. We left knowing they had plenty of clean water to drink, at least for a while. They still had a long way to go.

Thirty-eight migrants in one trip! Diane received a full dose of borderlands reality. One remarkable thing was that so many migrants were traveling during the day. Although volunteers have seen more migrants during the daytime this year than in past years, one would think they would travel at night in this heat. This area, however, was not well-patrolled on the ground by Border Patrol, so perhaps the migrants and their *coyotes* felt somewhat safe.

After stopping by the camp so Walt could record our activities in the report book and after picking up water from Karl Hoffman's place for the Denver church folks next week, we headed to the little town of Amado for lunch. Along the way we were stopped at the Border Patrol checkpoint of Amado. While one agent was waving us through, another jogged around the back of the car and poked his head in Gene's window. "Are you the folks who put out water? They need you over there. Someone has died." We appreciated his concern.

A little confused at first, we finally figured out he was trying to tell us that we should be taking water over near Elephant Head, across I-19, where migrants go north along established trails.

We drove on into Amado and decided to eat at the Longhorn Cafe. The skull and bull horns (20 feet high) that grace the front door were once located on the Cow Palace across the street (the former highway). We used to enter through them when we stopped for a snack on the way to the border when attending the University of Arizona in the 50s. Shortly after we sat down and ordered, the same agent we'd seen earlier came in to eat. We drew him over and talked more about the migrant situation. He appeared sympathetic to our work and encouraged us once again to go into that heretofore unserved area.

Satisfied with our day, we headed home to Tucson.

As Gene climbed into bed that night, he commented, "I'll never forget the fear and anguish on the face of that man who asked for food. I was just sorry we didn't have more to give him."

The summer flowed along smoothly: No More Deaths had enough money to make it through, and volunteers from all over the country were signing up through the NMD website. Our worst problem was finding enough cars to transport the volunteers to trails in the desert. We had the "Exploder," (an old Ford Explorer), the "*Roja*" (a red Dodge pickup), and a 1997 Nissan Pathfinder. Manny, our friend in Phoenix, sent the Pathfinder down with Gene and me in early June. Prior to that, Manny had sent a very-used Dodge mini-van, but halfway to Tucson, Gene and I had to call AAA to tow us in 105-degree weather, and that darned car never worked once we got it here. Later, Manny and his son towed that vehicle back to Phoenix. Manny's business is in severe trouble from the implementation of the state employer sanctions law in January. Most of his used car business had been with undocumented persons, many of whom left the state for fear that their place of work will be raided, and they'd be deported. At the time, Manny considered taking his business to New Mexico where his brother has moved.

Manny's Nissan helped us make it through the summer, but just barely. Each week Steve Johnston would announce in the Monday night meetings: "We need more vehicles!"

CHAPTER 37

St. Andrew's Delegation–September 12-17, 2008

THE DELEGATION FROM ST. ANDREWS Church, after staying overnight in Tucson, traveled south to the Sonoran town of Magdalena, home of the shrine to Father Eusebio Kino who departed Spain in 1681 and arrived in Northern Sonora in 1687. He came to the new world to establish a mission in the northern frontier of New Spain (today's northern Sonora and Southern Arizona). He traveled throughout the area and established 24 missions. He deduced that the Baja Peninsula was part of the mainland, rather than an island, as had been believed at the time.

Kino was an excellent cartographer, astronomer, and mathematician who drew the first accurate maps of the *Pimeria Alta*. He believed the Indians needed better ways of living. He was important in the economic growth of Sonora at the time. He taught them the basics of farming and brought them farm animals and seeds. His initial herd of 20 imported cattle in Pimeria Alta grew during his lifetime to 70,000.

He remained among his missions until his death. He died from fever on March 15, 1711 in the city known as *Magdalena de Kino*, Sonora, Mexico where his skeletal remains can be viewed today. The history of the area is worthy of a visit, and followers come by the hundreds to view his tomb each spring.[90]

---

90 www.spiritual-temporis.com/eusebio-kino/biography.html.

Following their time in Magdalena, the group traveled on to Altar where they met the staff of *CCAMYN*. Their experiences in Altar included visiting the plaza plus talking with migrants, while eating and sleeping at *CCAMYN*.

Back in Tucson, the St. Andrews folks all attended the Monday night No More Deaths meeting. No doubt some were bored as we worked on the public policy portion of our Working Paper. We usually close our meeting with a few moments of silence remembering all those who cross the desert at night, those who have died, and those who try to prevent the dying. This night, however, Eric from Kansas City, who had come along with the St. Andrews folks, presented a translation of the plaque in front of *CCAMYN* in Altar, Sonora. He read with great feeling the dedication to migrants from the point of view of people in their own country.

To Those Who Have Died in the Desert

In memory of those who went to look for a better life, yet only encountered death.
In memory of those who risked everything and lost everything . . .
Of those who went with hope in their eyes and challenge in their souls . . .
The sun burned them, and the desert devoured them
And the dust erased their names and faces.
In memory of those who never returned . . .
We offer these flowers and say with the deepest respect . . .
Your thirst is our thirst,
Your hunger is our hunger,
Your pain is our pain,
Your anguish, bitterness, and agony
Are also ours.
We are a cry for justice that no one would ever have to leave their land, their beliefs,
　　their dead,

their children,
their parents,
their family,
their roots,
their culture,
their identity.

From out of the silence comes a voice that speaks . . .

So that no one will ever have to look for their dream in other lands,
So that no one would ever have to go to the desert
And be consumed by loneliness.

A voice in the desert cries out . . .

Education for all!
Opportunity for all!
Jobs for all!
Bread for all!
Freedom for all!
Justice for all!

We are a voice that will not be lost on the desert . . .

That insists that the nation give equal opportunity to a dignified and fruitful life to all its children.

Orthon Perez: Summer of 2004
"For the right to live in peace . . ."

CHAPTER 38

Abuse Documentation

*"We must talk about poverty, because people
insulated by their own comfort lose sight of it."*

— DOROTHY DAY

THE FIRST TIME GENE AND I entered Geneva Hall at St. Mark's
Presbyterian Church for a No More Deaths meeting after moving to
Tucson, we saw a small group of people huddled on the floor in a corner. "What's going on there?" we asked. We found out they were the
"abuse doc" people; they're the ones compiling stories of the abuse
of migrants by Border Patrol. "Are they part of No More Deaths?"
Oh, yes, we were told, but there are other volunteers who work in the
border stations at Naco, Agua Prieta, and Nogales that collect stories for us. This group developed a seven-page questionnaire (later
revised to two pages and then to one) to use with migrants who
have been repatriated at the ports of entry in those towns and who
declare they have been abused by Border Patrol.

During the next year and a half, we heard little about the report
except that it was still in process. The key people were Dereka
Rushbrook, Sarah Roberts, Maryada Vallet, Shanti Sellz, Max
Garcia, and later Danielle Alvarado, Hannah Hafter, and Johanna
Allen with many others. Sally Meisenhelder, a nurse and Mariposa

volunteer, provided a great deal of direction. Law professor Andy Silverman from the UA Law School (one of "us") helped the writers steer clear of possible legal issues. Joshua Sutton (Oskar Pawpaw) elegantly formatted the document.

Finally, a date was set for the report's release on August 15, 2008. Over the months, some of us asked to see it, but were put off. We were told to come to the "abuse doc" meetings. That didn't work for me, but I kept my concerns to myself. A draft was presented to the No More Deaths community one Monday evening; I had several problems with it, including the fact that, at that point, not all the data had been compiled. I made a few notes on the report and received a scowl from the writer who proceeded to put it away without looking at what I had written. I know people work in different ways, but I felt that a report as important as this should be well vetted before completion and well understood by the group publishing it—No More Deaths—prior to publication.

Well, then the release date was put off until September 17, 2008. That date was also chosen by our Congressional representative, Raul Grijalva, as a time to present it to Congress. To Congress, and we hadn't even seen it yet?! At the urging of our volunteer, Max Garcia, the printed report should go not only to the congressional committee working on immigration matters, but also to departmental staff (such as ICE and DHS) along with other immigrant-rights groups, and such notable human rights groups as Amnesty International.

The report committee was hard at work. On the one hand, the members of the committee were speaking to our allied organizations in Tucson with copies of the Executive Summary in hand to generate letters of support. They were also setting up meetings in Washington with the help of U.S. Representative Raul Grijalva's office. On the other hand, they were trying to finish the report to meet the September 17th deadline!

They encountered some difficulty completing the report. The person who had the draft kept putting off giving it to the committee for the final edits. Three weeks before the trip to Washington, she admitted that she'd lost the flash drive containing the most recent incarnation of the document. You've never seen such scurrying to redeem the effort. Fortunately, they located hard copies of most of the work from prior meetings and found that none of the actual data was lost. The committee assigned tasks, and everything was retyped into the computer. The report was put together once again.

During the weekend prior to September 17th drafts were sent to those of us who'd agreed to be readers. I took on the Appendix and found—in addition to a few other minor errors—that the numbers, usually of migrants, had been handled inconsistently. I edited the work and sent a marked-up copy to the committee on Sunday afternoon, telling them that it wouldn't be the end of the world if the changes could not be made in time—the hearing was scheduled three days later. The data spoke for itself whether stated in digits or written-out numbers.

Meanwhile, Danielle was finishing a proposal to the national Unitarian Universalist Church for funds to hire a person to do extensive follow-up work on the report over the next few months. She sent me an email asking for the UUCT non-profit letter that Diane Dowgiert had just completed for us. She also requested that a one-page copy of the No More Deaths annual budget, reduced from four pages, be included in the proposal. This had to be sent out by September 15th, Monday.

While I worked on preparing and emailing those documents, I received a call from Walt Staton. He and Maryada needed a ride to the airport on Sunday afternoon for their trip to Washington. So, Sunday at 1:00 p.m. I arrived at Walt's to pick them up.

Walt lived in a small house at the back of a large lot that he owns—well, he paid his mortgage like most of us. After pulling into the circular drive, I traveled a walkway through part of Walt's garden where corn, squash, watermelons, and cantaloupe were growing. I'd just passed by an old school bus out front from where I heard three or four people talking and laughing. They lived in the bus. A short time later these people wandered into the house's kitchen/living room to check out what they could find in the small "fridge."

When I walked in the front door, I saw a clean room with a made-up bed to the left; I believed this was the room our next supported volunteer would inhabit. On a narrow futon in the living room, next to Walt's computer server, a No More Deaths volunteer was sleeping just three steps away. Maryada finished packing her suitcase with clothes and the No More Deaths photographs I'd just printed and mounted for her. The sleeper's cell phone rang off and on. Each time it rang she opened her eyes a slit to read the incoming number, turned it off and went back to sleep. She was there because our summer arrangements for housing for temporary volunteers had just closed down—the owners came home to Tucson separately each thinking the other had sent No More Deaths a message about their arrival date. Meanwhile Walt called from his bedroom to check on last-minute details with Maryada.

While waiting for my passengers, I wandered out the side door of the house. I'd been to some great parties here; the chairs had been organized, the table covered with a cloth or paper, trash picked up. This day it was a mess. An old couch and a variety of cast-off chairs populated the area in obvious disarray. I knew that there had been much to do. More vegetable plants lined the fence. To my left, chickens scratched in an old dog run made of sturdy chain-link fence. Walt started out with a dozen chicks; his makeshift coop now housed about ten almost-full-grown chickens, a variety of types that includes beautiful Rhode Island Reds. He thought only one was a rooster and hoped the rest would lay eggs. A very old mesquite tree and some tarps on the top provided the chickens shade. They clucked softly as I talked with them.

The remainder of Walt's half-acre was covered with a variety of things, large and small cacti, desert trees, a stack of signs saying "Humanitarian Aid is Never a Crime" left over from the campaign to free Daniel and Shanti, and other stuff.

Walt was ready. Maryada was ready, too, and we made an uneventful trip to the airport. They would start the footwork in Washington by preparing for meetings, doing media work, etc. They had the flash drive containing the report and would receive additional edits by email.

Wednesday morning: Washington, D.C. The report was printed, the rest of the committee had arrived, and they headed to Congress. The first meeting was scheduled for 1:00 p.m. Here's what Walt said about it in an email to those of us eagerly standing by in Tucson to hear what happened:

Walt Staton, No More Deaths Volunteer:

Blue skies and pleasant temperatures have welcomed us to the east coast—and of course the gracious staff of Representative Grijalva's office have given us space, copies, and invaluable advice. Our briefing yesterday (in Congress) went very well. Everyone spoke well and just seeing the looks on people's faces, the vivid photos of blistered feet and amputated legs got the point across that something bad is happening down the line.

We printed the report literally minutes before the briefing, thanks to Jennifer at the Kinko's print center who churned out the 55-page (double-sided), spiral-bound document in record time. Aides from Sen. Kennedy, Rep Kucinich, Rep Sanchez, and about 20 other offices, along with representatives from the ACLU, MALDEF (Mexican-American Legal Defense and Educational Fund) and the Latin America Working Group packed a small conference room in the basement of the capital building. The feedback was positive, in that people wanted to learn more and were willing to take action steps as they came up.

...We have one more day of visits, including one to John Conyers' office. It is quite a sight as most of us are sporting our best thrift-store clothing, walking through the halls of lawmakers' offices weaving between the high-flying lobbyists.

Also, we've had great hospitality at the Dorothy Day Catholic Worker house here in DC, which is putting up five of us. Long live the Catholic Worker movement! (Note: Maryada has served as a Catholic worker in Tucson for the past two years.)

Thanks for everyone's support for this trip—we all look forward to getting back into the desert and the border aid stations and do what we do best. See you all soon! Walt

CHAPTER 39

Abuse Documentation Report–2008–
Crossing the Line

*"There is a lack of compassion and concern about
the welfare of migrants who have been in the
custody of the United States Border Patrol."*

— IAN EASTMAN, VOLUNTEER

THE PREVIOUS JULY, NO MORE Deaths volunteers and others began to document abuses by Border Patrol, almost as soon as we'd begun working regularly in Nogales. Soon we learned that the Naco and Douglas/Agua Prieta volunteers were seeing and hearing the same tragic stories that we were experiencing in Nogales, so we began to collaborate with them. By this time, in late 2007, having gathered dozens and dozens of testimonies, we began to think about what we could do with what we were learning. Max Garcia worked with us for several months while he drove back and forth to his job in Florence, Arizona with The Florence Immigrant and Refugee Rights Project.[91]

---

91 Florence Project provides and coordinates free legal services and related social services to indigent men, women and unaccompanied children detained in Arizona for immigration removal proceedings. The Project strives to ensure that detained individuals have access to counsel, understand their rights under immigration law, and are treated fairly and humanely by our judicial system.

Max offered excellent suggestions for reaching relevant committees in Congress as well as various advocacy groups like Amnesty
International. Thus, had begun our plans to go to Washington.

WHAT THE REPORT SAYS

Here is the introduction to the report. See http://forms.nomore-
deaths.org/wp-content/uploads/2014/10/CrossingTheLine-full.
compressed.pdf to read it in its entirety.

Report Findings

The human rights violations identified in this report occur
at all three states of short-term custody: in the field during
apprehension, in the processing centers, and during the
repatriation process. It is the experience of No More Deaths
volunteers that migrants suffer this mistreatment on a daily
basis. The question is not if these practices are intended
outcomes of Department of Homeland Security policy. The
dearth of enforceable custody standards and the lack of
mechanisms for holding Border Patrol agents who commit
abuses to account are directly to blame. Culpability lies with
an internal agency culture that accepts and tolerates abuse,
as well as with the highest levels of DHS administration.

Presented here are the twelve categories of abuse that
constitute the heart of this report:

1. **Failure to respect the basic dignity of migrants:** Repatriation
   of migrants without their clothes or shoes. Migrants being
   denied the right to sleep while in custody. The forced holding of strenuous positions for no apparent reason other than
   to humiliate;

2. **Failure to provide and the denial of water in the field and processing centers:** Inadequate amounts of potable water available. Unsanitary distribution methods. Denial of water when requested, even by vulnerable populations. Refusal to provide water in spite of evidence of kidney damage and other serious ailments;

3. **Failure to provide and the denial of food in the field and processing centers:** Agents throw away migrants' food or feed it to their horses in front of them. Requests for sufficient amounts of food dismissed in processing centers. Children and pregnant women consistently denied access to adequate nutrition. Systematic denial of food exacerbates the implications of dehydration, rhabdomyolysis (kidney failure), and other serious ailments common among migrants;

4. **Failure to provide medical treatment and access to medical professionals:** Medications for preexisting conditions like high blood pressure and diabetes confiscated and not returned. Open wounds, broken bones, and heat stroke go untreated before repatriation. Blisters that cover entire soles of feet and have become infected, requiring amputation due to lack of care. Migrants repatriated from hospital emergency rooms wearing hospital gowns and with unfilled prescriptions;

5. **Inhumane processing center conditions:** Holding cells kept at extreme temperatures. Denial of blankets, or distribution of filthy blankets riddled with cactus spines. Migrants forced to sleep on overcrowded floors of cells;

6. **Verbal abuse:** Migrants abused by agents using derogatory racial and sexual epithets. Yelling and screaming for no apparent reason, both in the field and in processing centers. Often accompanied by physical abuse and threats of violence;

7. **Physical abuse:** Common abuses include agents shoving migrants into cacti, agents striking migrants, the use of chokeholds, sexual assault and the use of standing and sitting positions that are painful—used as a tool to instill fear in the victims and those who witness the abuse—so pervasive that migrants encountered by humanitarian aid workers have been reluctant to have an ambulance called due to a fear of being beaten;

8. **Dangerous transportation practices:** Lack of seat belts in Border Patrol and Wackenhut vehicles. Agents that drive at high speeds over rough terrain. Hazardous overcrowding. Vehicles kept at extreme temperatures;

9. **Separation of family members:** Migrants denied information about the whereabouts of their relatives. Families held in custody separately. Repatriated at different times to different ports of entry, making it nearly impossible to reunite. Border Patrol later repatriation strategy exacerbates these concerns by repatriating migrants to ports of entry other than the closest one to which they have crossed;

10. **Repatriation of vulnerable populations at night.** Repatriation of women and children after dark, in violation of previous Memoranda of Understanding signed by the U.S. and Mexican governments. Migrants repatriated in the middle of the night to unfamiliar cities after shelters and other services are available. Anyone already denied food, water, and medical attention is at a high risk for being a victim of crime or violence;

11. **Failure to return personal belongings:** Common belongings unreturned include clothing, money, contact information, and identification. Identification documents are necessary for migrants to receive social services, to buy bus tickets or to work, and to avoid being detained in their country of origin. Confiscation of personal belongings often means people

lose the few mementos of home brought with them on their journey;

12. **Failure to inform migrants of their rights:** Forms not provided in a language migrant can read. Coercion into signing forms under the threat of further criminal penalty. The failure to inform migrants of their rights to counsel and to their consulate.

This list of abuses is followed by a set of reasonable recommendations for short-term custody regulation that would address each issue followed by the conclusion:

Here are a few of the documented testimonies from migrants that were included in the final report:

Documented Testimonies from *Crossing the Line*

SM 6 92. Nogales 3/13/2007 1:00 p.m. A female, 22, was riding in a vehicle that was being chased by Border Patrol and was pushed out of the vehicle while others jumped. She was picked up on the highway and dropped off at the border without receiving the medical attention she needed for a twisted ankle. She was also deprived of food or water.

SM 19.19 Nogales 7/20/2007, 6:00 p.m. Three males were given insufficient food and inadequate medical care. One of the males had a painful, dislocated knee, blisters on his feet, a red rash, and an unusually strong and bound pulse (a sign of dehydration).

SM 22 100. Nogales. 9/26/2007, 8:00 p.m. A male age 50 reported being detained for nearly two hours while feeling ill. Border Patrol agents confiscated his blood pressure medication and did not return it, even upon repatriation. He was also denied sufficient food and water during this detention.

Also in Nogales. 2007. Alphonso, 27, and Jorge, 34, witnessed an agent kick one man's legs apart so roughly that his pants ripped. When a woman said, "How can you treat us like that; we're not from the streets," an agent said, "You're a piece of shit." Another agent told them, the next time you run we'll kick your butts and leave you in the desert."[92]

Four isolated incidents like these may be overlooked, but when the numbers grow to dozens and hundreds, as they have in our work, it begins to look like systemic abuse.

In addition, the report contains numerous affidavits of testimony from volunteers working with and taking documentation from migrants. For further information, look for the full document at http://forms.nomoredeaths.org/wp-content/uploads/2014/10/CrossingTheLine-ull.compressed.pdf.

---

92 "Crossing the Line," No More Deaths, accessed October 13, 2018, http://forms.nomoredeaths.org/wp-content/uploads/2014/10/CrossingTheLine-full.compressed.pdf.

CHAPTER 40

End of the Summer Program in the Desert–Mid-September–2008

ONE SATURDAY NIGHT IN MID-SEPTEMBER found 30 or so of us sitting around a campfire with people who had worked all summer combing the desert saving lives and reducing the misery of migrants. The sun dropped slowly behind two small hillocks, maybe the very ones from which Border Patrol had watched our camp prior to the raid. The hills turned black as the sky produced gorgeous colors through the atmosphere—gold, salmon, peach, vermillion, magenta. The afterglow finally faded into the night as we finished our meal.

We had dedicated the camp as an "Ark of the Covenant" on June 1st in 2004. At that time, the camp consisted of a small trailer, a shrine, a tent, and some boxes of food. Now, in the fall of 2008, it sprawled over half an acre, with two trailers, several overhead coverings, boxes and boxes of food and socks and medical supplies, dozens of bottles of water, a sculpture made from empty water bottles created by an artist volunteer, tables, chairs, a full-fledged kitchen, an outhouse, and several small tents scattered around in the desert.

Gene and I had left home about 6:45 a.m. this morning, picked up Maryada, and arrived at camp at 9:00 a.m. All the above equipment and supplies had to be dismantled. Some of it needed to be moved to Joe and Janet's house (including the main trailer), some of it taken to the dump, and some of it taken to various storage spots around Tucson. Steve put Maryada in charge of the medical supplies; I was her helper. My first task was to inventory and fill two first-aid bags to be used throughout the winter. Several people worked around me and stepped over me as they followed Steve's orders. About noon, someone began making cheese crisps of whole wheat tortillas and jack cheese. After that it was pretty hot and I sort of pooped out. The others, though, kept right on sorting and boxing and moving items around the camp.

Around 3:30 p.m., I lit the stove and put together a pot-full of "stewp." I cleaned off the two tables we had been using for sorting. The flies disappeared as I wiped clean the spilled Gatorade and Jolt. By 4:30 pm. a number of folks began trickling in bringing a variety of vegetarian food, most of which I couldn't identify. Sun Dog, the King of Ruby, who is always looking for his Queen, brought a pot of mole (sauce that includes chocolate) venison with a side pot of rice. When we got around to eating, I tasted the mole—pretty darned good! Sun Dog lives in Ruby, a former mining town close to the border. Gene thinks that at one time he ran migrants, but now is clean. Maybe. He's the one who tells confused migrants to point their right arm toward the rising sun in the morning and face ahead and they'll be looking north. In the evening if they'll point their left arm toward the setting sun and face ahead, they'll be looking north, as well. Who knows how many lives he's saved? Too often the volunteers run across people who've been wandering in circles near the border for five to ten days—about ten miles. Several months later, Sun Dog, because of some misdeeds, was asked to leave his post.

Gene, Maryada, and I headed home about 9:00 p.m. leaving others to sing around the campfire and enjoy the cool evening. Before we left I finally met Joe and Janet Arachy. They live nearby and have been a wonderful support for the No More Deaths volunteers, letting them take showers, use their generator, help themselves to water, and sometimes watch TV. I talked briefly to Byrd Baylor; she asked if whether we were going to Canada or to Mexico after the election. She didn't place much stock in either candidate or party (McCain or

Obama). She and Gene discussed the raid, and she mentioned that one young volunteer expressed fear that when she mentioned over her cell phone that we had three migrants in camp, that she might have triggered the raid. Byrd cautioned Gene to be careful. But we didn't think the volunteer's phone call had anything to do with it.

CHAPTER 41

Dan Millis' Verdict–September 26, 2008

SIXTY DAYS HAD GONE BY when Dan was finally found GUILTY. No time, no fine, no probation...nothing. What does that say? Our Samaritan friend Kathryn's trial starts next Tuesday, the 30th, in federal court. She's the woman who was stopped by Bureau of Land Management.

Pure Water for Travelers 2008 (No More Deaths)

Regarding Dan, according to the *Arizona Daily Star* dated 9/23/2008:

A federal magistrate judge says a volunteer worker littered when he left full water jugs for illegal immigrants in a national wildlife refuge earlier this year. United States Magistrate Judge Bernardo P. Velasco issued his ruling against No More Deaths volunteer Daniel Millis on Monday. He'd been weighing his decision since the trial July 25.

Millis had been facing up to six months in jail and up to $5,000 in fines if found guilty. But he apparently will not be sentenced for his violation, nor will he have to pay the $175 fine that normally accompanies a littering citation at the Buenos Aires National Wildlife Refuge. The punishment for the federal littering offense amounts to a $150 fine and a $25 processing fee, but Millis had refused to pay that fine, opting for a trial instead.

…Millis had argued that he was punished in the course of offering help. His lawyer, Bill Walker, had argued that a full water jug is not litter.

No More Deaths is a faith-based group that regularly helps illegal immigrants by offering them food, water and medical aid, saying it wants to stop the annual toll of border-crossers who die walking across Arizona's borderlands from Mexico.

Refuge officials think Velasco was clear enough and say they will continue to cite anyone caught littering on the refuge, including people leaving full bottles of water.

"The penalty isn't the point. The point is if you are on the refuge, we don't allow littering. We will continue to enforce that," said Sally Gall, assistant manager at the refuge, which is about 45 miles southwest of Tucson. "I think the decision is the correct one—whether there are immigrant problems or not we are not going to authorize littering."

Officials at the wildlife refuge said they have an enormous problem with trash, much of it caused by the illegal immigrants who regularly travel through, so it's imperative they enforce littering laws.

The refuge has a regular crew of volunteers who clean up trash—thousands of pounds left every year, including plastic water bottles, clothes, plastic food bags, and abandoned vehicles.

The refuge has had as many as 2,000 illegal immigrants a day walking within its desert boundaries.

One of the biggest problems with trash in the refuge is its impact on wildlife, which can end up choking on plastic from the jugs, refuge officials said. Cattle and other animals can ingest the bottles and die. Other animals have cut themselves on lids from tin cans and other pieces of trash left in the refuge, officials said.

Millis was cited as he and three other volunteers with No More Deaths were placing water jugs on a trail in the refuge.

He says he left 22 one-gallon water jugs in the desert. Walker had stressed in the trial that Millis was cooperative with refuge officials, and also that he'd been rattled on the day he was cited because two days earlier he had found the body of a 14-year-old El Salvadoran native who had died of exposure.

Walker said he was disappointed by the ruling. Still, he thinks the suspension of any sentence shows that the court recognizes humanitarian work should not be punished.

"This is a partial victory—it is not your ordinary littering case," Walker said. "It is humanitarian activity."

This story was also posted on the *Arizona Daily Star's* Internet website. Along with the article are ads for stainless steel water bottles and for a chance to advance your career with Border Patrol. Dan's comments follow:

The ruling was delivered as a memo to my lawyer and said only that I had been found guilty of the Class B misdemeanor offense of littering on a National Wildlife Refuge, and that the sentencing was suspended. A suspended sentence means no sentence whatsoever—no fine, no jail, I don't even have to pay the original $175 ticket. Apparently, the U.S. government believes that humanitarian aid is a crime for which no punishment is warranted.

I couldn't disagree more. And I'm not alone. Yard signs and stickers all around Tucson and beyond assert that "Humanitarian Aid is never a Crime" (left there from the Daniel and Shanti case in 2005). Rather, it is an act of compassion and basic decency, like jumping in a pool after a drowning baby. It is a no-brainer. And to say that it shouldn't be punished? Duh! Humanitarian aid should be valued, congratulated, practiced, preached, and most importantly, funded. Even this "guilty" verdict has a conscience and can't quite bring itself to levee a penalty....

We will appeal this guilty verdict. To appeal, we basically have the court type up the manuscript of the trial, and both sides write their arguments, and it all gets sent in to a Federal District Judge to decide. What result might we get? Not sure, but, my lawyer says there's "some chance we might win." And that's "we" as in you and me, not just him and me.... We need your help.

CHAPTER 42

More Reality–Friday, October 3, 2008

WHAT A WEEK!

More reality of the nation: Monday, the House voted down a $700,000,000,000 package to bail us out of the mortgage crisis. The DOW fell by 777.68 points. Wednesday, the Senate passed the bill sweetened by another $110,000,000,000 in earmarks to persuade the House to pass it. Thursday night, Sarah Palin *almost* redeemed herself on national television during her debate with Joe Biden. Friday, the House passed a tweaked package and the totally-discredited President Bush signed it. The Department of Labor announced a job loss of 159,000 for September making a total of 760,000 for the year. After rallying a bit on Tuesday and Wednesday, the markets fell again. Gene, John Fife, and Steve Johnston went on a much-deserved fishing trip.

We had yet to realize the impact of this drop (and further drops later) on the migration of people from Mexico into the United States. But as the bottom dropped out of the housing market, and people were laid off work, the need for manual laborers diminished dramatically. In FY 2000-2001, the number of apprehensions had reached a high of 616,300. In 2007-2008, it was 378,000. However, it dropped to 317,000 in 2008-2009 and 242,000 in 2010-2011. It has continued to drop until, in 2015-2016 it reached only 63,000. No doubt increased enforcement and other factors contributed to the continued reduction in apprehensions. Nevertheless, the rapid drop following 2007-2008 is widely attributed to the recession in the U.S.

Here is one quick snapshot from Mike Hawkes, Chief of the Buenos Aires National Wildlife Refuge, to demonstrate the changes on the Refuge following the recession:

The number of illegal migrants travelling through the Refuge has dropped precipitously from an estimated high of 250,000 per year in 2005 and 2006 to a total of 54,000 in 2008 with a projected 32,000 in 2009. That is an 800 percent decrease in migrants moving through the Refuge for 2009 compared to 2006.

CHAPTER 43

Meeting at Bill Walker's Office

As we entered Bill Walker's office around the first of October, he greeted us with the news that Kathryn Ferguson's case had been dropped by the U.S. Attorney's office. Of course, it was dropped. What would the agents say? That a mouthy woman who looked like someone from *Gone with the Wind* had gotten the best of three burly BLM agents on the open highway near Arivaca? We were all pleased, to say the least.

The purpose of our trip was to discuss what to do next in regard to Buenos Aires National Wildlife Refuge (BANWR). Dan's verdict had just come in. We wondered how aggressive we could be on BANWR while we waited for his appeal. Three of our volunteers continued putting out water on a weekly basis—john heid (sic), Lois Miller, and Jim Marx, as well as others from time to time. Their presence on the refuge was generally accepted by the Fish and Wildlife staff, although there were still reports of water being slashed or taken away by non-migrants.

Since the election was just around the corner, we discussed how things might go if Obama were elected president. He can't know much about the Southwest, but he might be more open to new policies. And, there was speculation that our current governor, Janet Napolitano, might be named to some high office.[93] She might help

---

93 She was named Secretary of Homeland Security by President Obama.

Obama with insight into the Southwest, although many people were disappointed with her migrant-related actions as governor. But we had hope that things might get better.

WALT STATON TICKETED ON BANWR

On December 4, 2008, Walt Staton and three friends were hiking on BANWR, southwest of Arivaca, leaving water for migrants and picking up empty jugs. Federal agents encountered them, and after some discussion about what they were doing and who should be cited, Walt was issued a ticket for littering (later changed to "knowingly littering" by the judge). Like Dan Millis before him, Walt chose not to pay the $175 ticket and instead went to federal court (the following August).

CHAPTER 44

The Working Paper

THE DIVERSITY OF THE No More Deaths volunteers was painfully clear when it came to how we should govern ourselves. Aside from agreeing to use a consensus model to run our meetings, many people had no experience in setting formal goals and objectives.

At my urging, the group agreed to engage in the process of goal setting. We had previously developed a viable mission statement (see Part II), so we needed to start with goals, then flesh out the objectives and activities. Strategies would come later. I listed all the places we sponsor or support programs, for example: the desert; Naco, Agua Prieta, Nogales, etc. It began to look, in a way, like our work had two prongs—serving those traveling north, and serving those being sent south, back to Mexico or parts beyond.

For six weeks, we spent about half of each meeting working on the document. In the process, we educated ourselves about the work other No More Deaths volunteers were engaged in; we affirmed everything that was underway—not one program was cut, even though we knew we had a serious personnel shortage—everything was considered to be important to the mission. Here, I summarize the goals and objectives:

GOAL I. DESERT AID. To **alleviate suffering** by providing water, food, clothing, and medical care to migrants **in the Sonoran Desert**.

Maryada Loading Water for Migrants (No More Deaths)

<u>GOAL II. VOLUNTEERS.</u> To recruit, train, deploy, and support volunteers from the Tucson area, around the country and around the world to work with No More Deaths in the Sonoran Desert and along the border.

Volunteers Erecting Tent at Byrd Camp (No More Deaths)

GOAL III BORDER AID. To **assist migrants being returned by Border Patrol to Mexico** or other countries of origin.

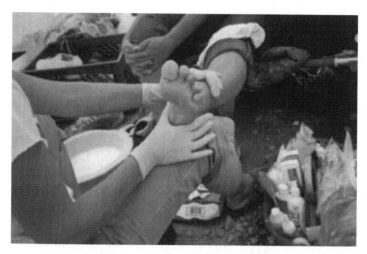

Providing First Aid at Mariposa (No More Deaths)

GOAL IV. PUBLIC POLICY. To bring about **public policy changes** at all levels of government that will fix the systemic problems and improve the lives and status of migrants in this country.

Attorneys Margo Cowan and Bill Walker at a No More Deaths Press Conference (No More Deaths)

GOAL V. INFRASTRUCTURE. To provide such **infrastructure** as needed to support No More Deaths goals.

Tents and Water at Byrd Camp (No More Deaths)

The document also included a fundraising plan, a list of the volunteers who most identified with each goal, and a copy of "Faith Based Principles for Immigration Reform." Copies were made for everyone with a few additional available to hand out to newcomers. To my knowledge they were seldom used or referred to again, but at least by the end point of its development, we were all on the same page and everyone had the document as a resource.

CHAPTER 45

Mariposa Port of Entry

Maryada Vallet:

During 2008, many discussions were held about supplies, security, and other prickly matters. We raised money so that Gilberto, one of the key volunteers at Mariposa, could move back to his home in Guadalajara. Throughout 2008, our presence at Mariposa had become more and more sporadic. In the spring, Johanna Allen and others spent time at the *Comedor,* a feeding program of the Kino Border Initiative (a coalition project of several Catholic organizations), located a couple of blocks from the Mariposa crossing. In the summer of 2009, volunteers (usually two) spent time at the border on behalf of No More Deaths working primarily at the *Comedor* helping with the feeding program and conducting abuse documentation. We also conducted other exploration for the future of our work in Nogales.

At this time, the Nogales working group felt strong support from the larger No More Deaths community. This hadn't always been the case. Now we had plenty of volunteers in the summer to keep the program going; we had people who understood how things worked; we had ties to the community. However, in the No More Deaths and Samaritans training, the border programs at Nogales, Douglas, and

Naco received short shrift. Most, if not all, of the training was focused on the desert aid program. In addition, the Nogales program could have used a vehicle on a regular basis. (These needs were later addressed satisfactorily.)

We faced the uncertainty of when the U.S. government (by way of Wackenhut busses) would drop migrants off at the border. We never knew what the Mexican officials would do—they were constantly threatening to move their operation to the DeConcini port and drop off migrants day or night. We'd lost our spot at the Mariposa border where we could serve hot coffee, soup, and sandwiches, and treat blisters and other complaints.

There was no permanent place on either side of the border where volunteers could eat and sleep for a day or two, or for a week, at a time. For a while Johanna Allen and Sally Meisenhelder, a nurse volunteer from New Mexico, stayed with the nuns in their upstairs "shelter" across from the *Comedor*. We paid a minimal amount for rent and food.

We identified our needs at that point as: 1) become more a part of the Nogales community as is happening in Arivaca, 2) have a greater presence at both Mariposa and DeConcini to get out food, water, and first aid, 3) get a focus—become more self-starting, have more clarity and commitment, 4) get an office, and 5) reestablish our project.

A number of things have changed recently to heighten the sense that we need to address these needs.

* The structure was no longer in place in Mexico—the change of Mexican administration, lack of interest;
* The number of deportees lessened with few people coming through Mariposa;
* Many migrants were being deported at the DeConcini port of entry, many families were separated. Many more were

being deported from raids, or random stops, resulting in people being sent back who have no home in Mexico. For many years, their homes had been in the U.S;

* More people were being criminalized by the justice system, particularly through Project Streamline, and people were being forced into voluntary departures from prisons. The population had changed dramatically;

* The Kino Project (Catholic) started with considerable support;

* The new Mexican government was more consistent (PAN).[94]

David Hill, a young man in his early thirties, graduate of MIT is a No More Deaths volunteer coordinator. He and and Kraig Beyerlein, UA faculty in sociology and No More Deaths volunteer, conducted follow-up surveys with out-of-town volunteers. They reported two to four volunteers in Nogales all 17 weeks of the summer who spent an average of 2.1 weeks there. Of the 18 people, 17 of them were satisfied with their experience there.

Volunteers continued to visit Benjamin Hill and take supplies about once a quarter.

94 Submitted by Maryada Vallet.

CHAPTER 46

Volunteers

**Volunteers Hiking in Streambed with Water
in Springtime (No More Deaths)**

DURING THE YEAR 2008, MANY new volunteers came into our group. I have
mentioned already, Jim Marx. He and his wife, Maureen, retired from
Idaho. Jim was formerly a guidance counselor and then a principal in

public schools. They began coming to meetings with their neighbor, Victor, who had recently retired from the Chicago non-profit arena. Jim worked with the DAWGs and managed to develop successful relationships with those who were antagonistic to the main Tucson group. Maureen, a nurse, worked with the medical team, soliciting free medical supplies from local sources. Later, she was very busy coordinating the assembling of "hydration kits" for the trails. They both sometimes went to Byrd camp with out-of-town volunteers.

When Walt went off to seminary (instead of law school), Jim and Victor took over leadership of the vehicle team. Stephanie and Jim Keenan retired in Tucson from California, he a fisherman and she a kindergarten teacher. They jumped in to help with preparing food boxes and other supplies for camp. Several young adults also tried us out: Veronica, Sebastian Rodriguez, Daniel, Clint Kalan, Jessica Tracy, Craig Metchco and Gabe Shivone (both students at UA), Kevin Riley, August, Annie Swanson, Prabjit and Paseo, Ayala Rahm, and Darby Landy, and many others. I began to lose track. Some of the volunteers preferred their names or last names not be known.

In addition, some people were passing through, mostly on their way to additional schooling: Marie Kessler (former volunteer coordinator) and Stacy Scheff went on to law school, Lane Van Ham finished his doctorate, and so on. Over the next few years, Sarah Launius and Geoffrey Boyce enrolled in graduate school at UA, bought a house, and got married. It became clear that No More Deaths was a stopping point between college and a real life somewhere else out there. However, some people came to volunteer for a few weeks or a summer and ended up moving to Tucson. They began to form a stable force of volunteers for both the border work and in the desert.

INTERPERSONAL RELATIONSHIPS

For the past several weeks, concern had been expressed (usually in meetings designed to debrief desert volunteers, but also in No More

Deaths meetings) about breaks in protocol and improper interpersonal relationships. Several volunteers provided No More Deaths with written statements about their concerns regarding the professionalism of leadership at camp. Therefore, a group was established to deal with these concerns. Called the DAMN (Desert Aid Mediator Network) group, it met and made recommendations. Individual volunteers were contacted personally by the group for further interviews regarding their issues, most of which were mentioned above. Gene and john heid spent many hours listening and talking with two of the No More Deaths long-term volunteers about whom concern had been expressed. In the end, the volunteers continued their commitment, and throughout 2013 and beyond, were still an important part of No More Deaths, even though they could have gone off in a huff. Information collected by the group was kept confidential.

PERSONAL TRAUMA AMONG VOLUNTEERS

Traumatic events take place within No More Deaths in the desert or at the ports. They particularly affect volunteers who come from faraway places and have no concept of border life, although even seasoned volunteers can be severely affected by finding a dead body or remains in the desert, as well. Some volunteers became depressed and withdrawn. When they returned home they weren't sure how to relate to their families and schoolmates who couldn't understand or empathize with their experiences. So, as a starting point for how to address and deal with this concern, No More Deaths asked Sarah Hardin from the Duke Engage groups,[95] to develop some materials for us to discuss and self-educate ourselves about the issue. In the

---

95 DukeEngage, a program of Duke University in North Carolina, empowers students to address critical human needs through immersion in the United States and abroad. Each year since 2007, DukeEngage students have come to Tucson and participated in programs with No More Deaths and other humanitarian groups. With the support of the Duke Foundation Endowment and The Bill @ Melinda

July 6th meeting, we broke into six groups to look at a worksheet that described many symptoms and manifestations that could result from working with No More Deaths. The group members discussed the worksheet and shared personal ideas within the small groups. When the large group came back together, main themes were shared, and ideas lifted up about how to continue exploration in recognizing and effectively dealing with trauma resulting from our work.

Pao San Lucy Zhang came to Tucson in 2008 as part of a delegation from the Duke Engage program. The several college students in the group were placed with various humanitarian organizations--Samaritans, Humane Borders, and so on. Lucy volunteered to spend four weeks with No More Deaths.

Lucy is a first generation American whose father, at age 15, and uncle migrated from their home in China hoping to reach the city of Hong Kong where they planned to find jobs and support their family back home. Lucy's grandfather had been imprisoned by the Communists because of his involvement with the Chinese Nationalist Party. The Communists however, mismanaged her grandfather's farm, and soon the family ran out of resources. The day the young men left on their journey from their rural home, they carried with them a few cups of rice and a steamed chicken. Before they reached the city, the police apprehended them. Lucy's father. unlike his brother, never attempted the trip again. However, eventually her father and other members of his family were able to come to the United States.

When Lucy arrived in Tucson in 2008 from her life as a student at Duke University, at 20 years of age, she attended training and began to learn about border issues and the migration of thousands of people from the south. She soon saw the connection between those migrants and the experiences of her own family many years ago. These stories both:

Gates Foundations, DukeEngage has allowed more than 3,600 students (by 2016) to participate.

. . .allude to universal challenges of political activism, economic freedom, human suffering, and the struggle toward happiness....It is also a common story of a person who seeks to provide for his or her family. Because my story is not a geographically-bound experience, it directly reminds me of the many stories that I heard from migrants crossing the Sonoran Desert. In one way or another, families lost their farms and their ability to sustain themselves. They traveled away from their homes, often selling whatever they could in order to provide for the ones they loved. In this way the story of a man in Oaxaca, Mexico, is also my father's story in Guangdong, China; and it becomes my story in Arizona, United States, as well.[96]

While working on the border, Lucy was traumatized by what she saw there. She was traumatized once again when she returned to Duke and found her friends and other students couldn't relate to her experiences and held very shallow understandings of border issues. As a result, she worked with her advisors and other students to develop several events to help deepen student understandings of border issues. In 2009, she returned to the border and interviewed Gene and other volunteers and then went on to write her senior thesis about her experiences.

---

96 Lucy Zhang, "A Journey Home: Witnessing Trauma and Deconstructing Healing on the U.S. Mexico Border," senior thesis for Duke University, 2010.

PART III
Humanitarians v. Fish and Wildlife (BANWR)
2009-2010

BANWR Terrain 2009 (No More Deaths)

CHAPTER 47

Into What Have We Gotten Ourselves?

*Even someone doing bad will recognize
someone doing good.*

— DR. MIGUEL DE LA TORRE

WHILE THE PREVIOUS SECTIONS OF this book have been written in chron-
ological order, to make sense of the activities and events associated
with Buenos Aires National Wildlife Refuge (BANWR) and the
Southern Arizona humanitarians, this topic is covered primarily in
one section, addressing activities and events that happened between
humanitarian groups and Buenos Aires National Wildlife Refuge
(BANWR) over 2009 and 2010.

NEGOTIATIONS WITH BANWR

Walt Staton's ticket that occurred in December 2008, which was
after Dan Millis had been ticketed in February and found guilty in
September (with no fine or other punishment), led to months of
frustration and conjecture on the part of the No More Deaths community. In meeting after meeting, we discussed how to interact successfully with the federal government in general and the Buenos Aires
National Wildlife Refuge staff. Contrary to direction by BANWR

officials, many volunteers continued to hike specific trails in BANWR leaving water while many of us fretted and planned in meetings.

BANWR lies on approximately 118,000 acres of land in Arizona. Its southern edge is contiguous with the border between the U.S. and Mexico. From the unincorporated border town of Sasabe in the southeast, it extends about 20 miles northward into the state. Established in 1985, the Refuge provides habitat for endangered and threatened plants and animals. Home to 58 mammal species and more than 325 different bird species, it also provides a home for 53 species of reptiles and amphibians. Concerted efforts are being made to restore the sea of grass that used to cover the Altar Valley of which the Refuge is a part. It provides habitat for masked bobwhite quail and pronghorns.[97] Most of the Refuge is open for visiting and research. Guided access is also available with Friends of Buenos Aires.[98]

The following is from the 42 U.S. Code § 4321, title 42—The Public Health and Welfare, chapter 55—National Environmental Policy, section 4321. Congressional Declaration of Purpose.

This law governs U.S. Fish and Wildlife Service, of which BANWR is a part:

> "The purposes of this chapter are: To declare a national policy which will encourage productive and enjoyable harmony between man and his environment; to promote efforts which will prevent or eliminate damage to the environment and biosphere and *stimulate the health and welfare of man* (ed.); to enrich the understanding of the ecological systems and natural resources important to the Nation; and to establish a Council on Environmental Quality."

---

97 The pronghorn is a species unique to the American Southwest. It resembles some antelope species, yet it's one of a kind. Their horns are a cross between horns and antlers. They are the only animals with forked horns and they shed each year.
98 www.FriendsofBANWR.homestead.com.

I believe it is safe to say that most humanitarians believe that the government is meant to serve the people through its laws and policies. As citizens, we generally seek to know these policies and laws and to follow them. However, when people's basic needs come into conflict with government policy, then we have a responsibility to do whatever is necessary to resolve the conflict. Thus, we have asked BANWR to hear our plea for exception to their policy that leads, or potentially leads, to the death and suffering of migrants in the Sonoran Desert.

BANWR PAPER–SPRING 2009

The following paper was written by five No More Deaths volunteers to focus on what's at stake in fighting the prosecutions of our volunteers who are ticketed on BANWR: Danielle Alvarado, Geoff Boyce, Sarah Launius, Joshua Sutton, and Jimmy Wells. It was written in May of 2009, but I want to use this piece to start this section as it lays out the issues we were having with BANWR throughout 2009-2010 and subsequently. This document was not publicly distributed.

WHY DO WE CARE ABOUT THE BUENOS AIRES NATIONAL WILDLIFE REFUGE (BANWR)?

These tickets seem petty (of Dan Millis and Walt Staton), and it might seem like a better use of time and resources to pay the tickets and move forward with direct aid. The reality however, is that the challenge raised is not petty at all. It is significant, and it is one that we must respond to directly.

For more than a decade, the United States has propagated a policy of deterrence that is based on the death and suffering of the poor. Fifteen years and more than 6,000 victims later (7,000 by 2016), the policy continues to undermine basic human rights; migrants are made into criminals, both rhetorically and literally, as they are detained and prosecuted for the crime of trying to feed their families. Criminalization of the humanitarian aid-movement is also a real threat. If we are successfully restricted from BANWR, prosecutions may begin in all the Refuge areas, then the Tucson sector, and then the entire border region. The implications of this enforcement will be more deaths. This is unacceptable.

But this is not about us. Fighting the criminalization of the humanitarian-aid providers is important because it gives us a strong avenue for fighting the militarization of the border and criminalization of human movement, a basic human right. Wherever we are, we can be strong, clear advocates in work and deed for demilitarization, accountability, and justice. Ceding on BANWR would mean ceding on this, our most important task as a community.

U.S. policies are responsible for the human rights crisis playing out in the border region. For over 15 years, the government has refused to respond adequately and most recently has accelerated the strategy of deterrence. Now, through this measure by the Department of the Interior, the government is suggesting that it is illegal for civil society to proactively engage in mitigating the crisis dealt by negligence on the part of the government.

Asserting and maintaining a humanitarian presence on the Refuge has two purposes: to provide immediate, lifesaving assistance and to bring attention to the root cause of the human rights crisis of the borderlands: United States enforcement policy. We must exercise aggressively (and non-violently) our right to do both. The prosecutions on the Refuge do not represent hypothetical challenges. They are real; they have already happened; and they will continue to take place until we build enough public pressure to force them to stop.

HOW DOES ASSERTING OUR RIGHT TO A REFUGE PRESENCE LEAD US TO THE ISSUES WE REALLY CARE ABOUT?

The challenge raised by BANWR is really about the rights of migrants first: the right to a dignified life as they define it, and then of the right to receive humanitarian aid. It is lastly about the right of humanitarians to provide such aid anywhere at any time.

By carefully selecting volunteers to lead such an effort, medical professionals and faith community leaders can take advantage of the opportunity to speak about the real issue: continuance of the failed policy of deterrence. Doctors, nurses, clergy, and humanitarians are the clearest messengers for the moral and ethical imperatives that drive our desert presence. It is possible, as we continue to receive and challenge citations, to build public interest and pressure which we can use to force the root causes of the crisis to which we respond back onto the table.

We should not adopt a campaign whose goal is simply to be able to put out water on the Refuge. Rather, we should use this moment as a tool to reconnect with our supporters and to rearticulate our fundamental message: militarization of the border must end. If we move forward, focusing on the enforcement regime of the past 15 years, we will be able to use the momentum and pressure developed on this specific issue to reignite a local, national, and international movement calling for *no more deaths*.

How do we get others to care about these underlying issues?

We will turn this seemingly petty issue into one worth talking about by turning the focus to the real issues as we see them—the root causes of migration and the failed policy of deterrence. There are four initial steps in the development of this slow-building campaign that is integrated into our current volunteer recruitment, outreach, and direct-aid efforts.

1. Articulate our message:
   * Develop our core principles into talking points so that we are always articulating the absurdity of the tickets in

relation to the catastrophic moral issues surrounding current border policies.

2. Reengage with our base through speaking tours to faith communities:
   * Actively send NMD clergy and lay people to speak with faith communities and sister organizations locally, and eventually nationally, to build public pressure around the ill-conceived policy of deterrence from a moral perspective.

3. Start developing a "list of the willing":
   * Work through our base to enlist clergy and medical professionals willing to get ticketed and use their positions as an opportunity to raise awareness and public pressure about the human rights tragedy playing out in the border region.

4. Actively support current legal battles:
   * We must turn these current legal battles into something "worth noticing" through increased presence, spectacle, and discussions through our base and we hope, through the media.[99]

The following are some of the ways these goals have been addressed:

1. No More Deaths University of Arizona group took a trip across the country in 2009 and met with several schools and other groups telling them about No More Deaths and soliciting monetary gifts. Then in 2013, four other young adults traveled across the country doing the same.

2. A medical tent was erected at Byrd Camp in 2011 with funds from a peace award to Gene Lefebvre and Sarah Roberts from the Freedom from Fear Foundation.

---

99 No More Deaths internal document.

3. In 2010, more than 150 health professionals signed on to a full-page ad in the *Arizona Daily Star* in support of the medical services at Byrd Camp.

4. Following the passage of SB 1070 in 2010, we wrote to Homeland Security requesting the release of individual migrants (as part of the work of We Reject Racism), and this was met with a 95% success rate. By 2017, the tally of migrants released reached 2,000. Media notices were released regarding Dan Millis and Walt Staton and The *Basura* 13.

CHAPTER 48

Millis Interview

Dan Millis' Interview and Samaritan Harassment—April 15, 2009

DAN MILLIS WAS TO BE interviewed in a day or two by Tim Vanderpool of the *Tucson Weekly*. Dan went to the No More Deaths meeting to seek advice on what he could talk about—for example, the camp raid by the Border Patrol last August and banishment from the reservation. Members of the group had several suggestions. Shortly afterward, I offered that he speak with Gene who was out at camp during the time of the raid, and Margo, our attorney, because she had recommended we not go public earlier. Others had different ideas. Dan made those calls to Gene and Margo and received permission, so he was ready to discuss the raid material on the record. Since the incident on the Tohono O'odham Nation when No More Deaths had been banned was previously reported in the paper, it was fair game.

During the meeting, the facilitator asked if there had been other similar problems. Vanessa spoke of a Border Patrol agent trying to take her picture. When asked if she turned her head away, she said, "No, I stepped on the gas and sped off. But he took a photo of my license plate." Then Jim Walsh piped up and spoke about when he and Sarah Roberts had been hemmed in by agents with large guns asking who they were and why they were there. Jim and Sarah were just putting out water for migrants. These incidents were more of the proscription of humanitarian workers—harassment.

WALT'S EMAIL ABOUT SAMARITAN HARASSMENT BY BORDER PATROL–APRIL 22, 2009

Hey, y'all (Desert Aid Working Group—DAWG). I just read an email from Samaritans about how Fish and Wildlife (BANWR), along with Border Patrol and Pima County Sheriff's Office is turning up the heat on them regarding putting out water jugs. I think we need to really start thinking about our plan for water drops as the temperature rises—if you can't stand the heat, then get out of the kitchen!!

Most concerning from Samaritans' email was that they reported how individuals are now getting calls from law enforcement asking about what they are doing, and people are also being asked for ID, phone numbers, and addresses when confronted in the field.

While it may be prudent and good for PR reasons to do some trash pickups in a certain wildlife area, we should also be thinking about reclaiming some humanitarian ground, especially in the context that the death count is now rising again this year, even though arrests are down.

Quick report from Germany—we had an interesting conversation with some church folks and Amnesty International today about the European Union's (EU) very, very, very similar tactics and policies for boundary enforcement. We talked a lot about how they deal with migrants and refugees on the "high seas" where there is no jurisdiction of any nation state, just the obligation of EU nations to comply with human rights protocols when encountering boats of migrants. It is very nearly impossible to have any oversight or observation of activities out in the ocean. So, I'm thinking that if anyone is interested in a nice Mediterranean spring break vacation, we can rent a few sail boats and do some Maritime abuse doc! What say ye? Walt

CHAPTER 49

Walt Staton's Trial in Federal Court–June 1, 2009

*I did not, and I do not believe it is litter. I believe
it is water to save people's lives.*

— *WALT STATON*

Annie Swanson and Walt Staton at Byrd Camp Shrine (No More Deaths)

WALT STATON'S TRIAL BEGAN IN Evo DeConcini Federal Court at Congress and Granada in Tucson on June 1, 2009. He and others had been charged with "knowingly littering or disposing of garbage or other debris on a national wildlife refuge." The other volunteers included in Walt's party were a friend from Chicago, and two UA students of one of our volunteers, Hannah Hafter, who were tagging along for the day to help for a paper they had to write. When none of them paid the fine by the specified date, the U.S. Attorney filed charges against Walt only.

The federal government was represented by prosecuting attorney Lawrence Lee, and defendant Walt Staton by defense attorney William (Bill) Walker. The "state" had to prove beyond a reasonable doubt both the "knowingly" and the "littering" parts of the indictment. Did Staton "know" that he was littering, or did he think that he was providing humanitarian aid? Is a bottle of water considered litter, or is it lifesaving humanitarian aid?

Prior to entering the stately building, a moderate-sized group of us gathered outside to rally on behalf of our friend, Walt. Several people spoke eloquently, Pablo Perigrino sang, and Maria and David Aparicio along with their young son, Ollin, danced and sang to their Aztec drumming in front of the crowd. By the time they finished, we were all pumped up and ready to enter the building. Having been here before, most of us knew to put our purses, wallets, keys, and shoes in the tubs provided by the guards. Cameras and cell phones were not allowed. After we reclaimed our belongings on the other side of the screening area, we studied the sheets on the wall to figure out in which courtroom the trial would be held. We filed onto the elevator and went up to the 5th floor.

Upon entering the courtroom, I was amazed by the number of people it took to prosecute Walt: at least two federal prosecutors, one defense attorney, the judge, the bailiff, two or three officers to keep order, and later, the jurors. Walt thought this might be the first federal trial for Judge Guerin and possibly a first for Lawrence Lee who had previously served as a JAG (Judge Advocate General) lawyer. The trial lasted three days. I couldn't begin to estimate the cost. It hardly seemed worth the effort, yet both Fish and Wildlife and No More Deaths wanted to make a point: putting water on BANWR (and by extension other federal lands) was either legal or illegal.

I attended this trial all three days and took extensive notes. However, I am relying in part on Steve Accardi's dissertation[100] for backup because he took down the details directly from the official court transcript, while mine is from memory and notes. A number of us sat squished together on the left side of the gallery as I scribbled in my notebook. Most everyone just sat and listened intently.

Wearing a dark brown shirt and black-rimmed glasses, a slender Walt Staton sat with Bill Walker at the defence table. After a few preliminaries, jury selection began. More than 30 potential jurors filed into the room. Magistrate Judge Jennifer Guerin asked if any of the possible jurors had strong feelings about providing humanitarian assistance for undocumented migrants. Two responded that they did: a Catholic woman said that her church goes on walks in the desert and provides water to migrants; another woman said she taught bilingual education for years and feels the migrants in the desert could have been her students. Three more spoke up saying they'd have a problem being impartial—all believing that aid should be given. Then one potential juror said he was "personally in support of any human aid" but would be able to follow the instructions of the court. Another spoke, saying he had been a missionary in South America and Mexico and thus believed strongly in providing water to migrants in the desert.

Walker challenged the judge on the form, specifically about her question indicating that the trial is about "knowingly littering"

---

100 Steven Accardi, "Humanitarian Aid is Never a Crime: A Study of One Local Public's Attempt to Negotiate Rhetorical Agency with the State." A dissertation presented in partial fulfillment of the requirement for the degree Doctor of Philosophy (Tempe: Arizona State University, May 2011), 61.

and not about humanitarian aid, per se. Prosecutor Lee said that humanitarian aid is exactly what Walker wants to put on trial. Judge Guerin dismissed all potential jurors who expressed any support of humanitarian aid.

Questioning continued with additional potential jurors being excused, some by Walker, some by Lee, and some by the judge. Accardi says it is clear from one juror's response that this littering trial is not just about littering. It is about humanitarian aid, undocumented migrants, and the crisis on the border.

Later, after the first day of trial, Walt said, "Huh, a jury of my peers; they removed all my peers from the jury."

Following a recess, the trial began. Both Walker and Lee made their opening statements. Walker summarized Walt's life: he's an Arizona boy; he's been one all his life. He attended the Prescott Unitarian Universalist Fellowship and was a Boy Scout who received an Eagle Scout award; he is a certified wilderness first responder; he graduated from high school with a 4.0 grade-point average and graduated from the University of Arizona with an almost perfect-grade point average (3.7) with a degree in Urban Planning. To us in the humanitarian community, Walt is a hero and a model citizen. In addition to that, he is a really nice fellow.

Prosecutor Lee described Walt's egregious indiscretions. He managed to tie Walt to terrorists, illegal aliens, human smugglers, and drug smugglers by getting Border Patrol Agent Thomas Collins to say that those were who he was looking for when he came across Walt and three other volunteers on BANWR. He agreed with Walker that he didn't observe any activities by Walt or the others that had anything to do with border enforcement. He then established that while he sometimes sees full bottles of water on the trails, migrants discard them further north as "garbage."

Lee went back to the litter issue with Collins by characterizing Walt as "catch" in an "illegal alien" hunt narrative. But Border Patrol Agent Blake Baron agreed that when he sees No More Deaths volunteers, they're not doing anything with "aliens." Walker effectively argued that "humanitarians" are not "illegal, are not criminals, nor are they engaging in criminal behavior." He got Baron to agree that water is an extremely valuable, lifesaving commodity, not garbage.

Then Lee went to Fish and Wildlife Officer (FWO) James Casey. Casey explained that parks are for the enjoyment of people while refuges are for the protection of plants and animals. Lee started to show Casey some pictures taken on the Refuge when Walker interrupted: "Sir, it looks as if these photos (#s14-19) were taken in July of 2007 (two-and-a-half years prior)." Casey agreed they were and that he was the one who took the photos—south of the location where Walt was ticketed. Even though the photos seemed highly irrelevant to us as observers, they were entered into evidence over Walker's objection. Later, Walt and others were incensed that the judge allowed these photos to be introduced as if they held any meaning for the trial. Walt pointed out that the water jugs in the photos were not the same as those used by No More Deaths; they had longer tapered necks and came from Mexico. Casey asserted that 60-70 percent of the Refuge (all 118,000 acres of it) is covered with plastic tops and bindings from the jugs.

FWO Casey established that he took a binder from Walt's truck. He read from a section in the binder titled: *Arivaca West Supply Drop Driving and Hiking Route.* "The last three drop points are on BANWR. If you drop (water) here, you risk being ticketed for littering by U.S. Fish and Wildlife, regardless of how much trash you pick up. You can be ticketed for that too." Lee got Casey to agree that Walt obviously knew his water drops were against the law.

Throughout the trial, Walker and the judge had disagreements, and bench conferences ensued. The judge turned on the white noise machine so that trial observers couldn't hear what was said—much to the annoyance of the gallery full of people.

Later, Walker caught Casey in a misrepresentation—or perhaps, a misremembering. In his response to this question from Walker:

"And you, in fact, asked him (Walt), 'Did he usually pick up emp-ties?'" Casey responded, "I do not recall, sir, if I asked him that." As it turned out, Casey had recorded the entire exchange with Staton in the desert without Staton's knowledge. Walker pulled out the tran-script of Casey's recording and pointed to the spot where Casey asks, "Do you guys usually pick up empties when you come out, too?" Casey confirmed that he did ask that question. Later, Casey is recorded as saying, "Well, we appreciate you picking them up on your way out."

Then Walker called Walt to the stand, adding to Walt's list of credits: his knowledge of map making and map reading via his geog-raphy and regional development degree, his volunteer work with the Sonoran Institute (a wildlife preservation not-for-profit agency), his Wilderness First Responder training and certification, and his recent acceptance into seminary (a change from his earlier plan to attend law school). Walker brought up the section about being tick-eted found in the No More Deaths binder and tried to show that Walt, even though he was aware of this, still did not agree that he was in violation of the law. Under cross-examination, Lee asked if Walt notified the Refuge manager that he would be going out there. When Walt answered "No," Lee intimated that Walt was being under-handed in neglecting to notify the Refuge manager.

Under questioning, it was clear that Walt believed empty bot-tles constitute litter, whereas full bottles do not. Then Lee asked if Walt was aware of Dan Millis' conviction. Walt conceded that he was aware. When Lee used this answer to show that Walt knew littering was a punishable offence, Walt countered with the fact that the conviction was still under appeal. To challenge that, Lee pulled out a statement made by Walt to the Presbyterian news ser-vice where he was quoted as saying: "I vow that the organization will continue its humanitarian aid work in the desert regardless of the outcome of the Millis case." It was clear from these exchanges that Walt knew that putting out jugs of water was considered litter-ing by the state.

Walt agreed that littering is wrong and that those who litter should be punished. However, he also stated that this littering law should not be applied to the humanitarian crisis on the border. Humanitarian aid is never considered litter in other contexts, thus a littering law should not be applied to it, should not be enforced, and should not be interpreted this way. "I did not, and I do not believe it is litter. I believe it's water to save people's lives." To the "knowingly" issue, Judge Guerin weighed in with her instructions to the jury by defining "knowingly" as "an act is done knowingly if the defendant is aware of the act and does not act through ignorance, mistake, or accident."

In his summary, Prosecutor Lee said, "He knows the law. He just doesn't want to follow it."

Defense Attorney Walker countered with: "If you have any doubt, a reasonable doubt, that what Walt Staton put out was not garbage, then he should be acquitted."

Additional arguments followed from both sides, and then the case went to the jury.

The third day, the jury came back deadlocked; they wanted to know what Walt had precisely been charged with. The judge agreed with both attorneys Walker and Lee that the jury already had this information and refused to repeat the precise code violation. Instead Judge Guerin wrote back to the jurors that they should use the instructions given to them. After another recess, the jury reconvened and reached a verdict. At that point, the courtroom was filled with volunteers from No More Deaths and Samaritans. The air vibrated with expectant energy. The judge admonished the visitors to maintain decorum, no matter the outcome.

The clerk read the verdict: "We the jury find the defendant, Walter E. Staton, GUILTY of knowingly littering, disposing or dumping in any manner that which he knew to be garbage, refuse, sewage, sludge, earth, rocks or other debris on the Buenos Aires National Wildlife Refuge." Sentencing was to be issued at a later date.

CHAPTER 50

Death in Paradise (Sometime after June 1, 2009)

You will never understand violence or nonviolence until
you understand the violence to the spirit that happens
from watching your children die of malnutrition.

— *EL SALVADORAN COMPASINO*

john heid Marking Water Bottles on BANWR (Paula McPheeters)

A MAN NAMED JOHN HEID (he uses lower case letters for his name) became a part of No More Deaths in 2008. He grew up in the state of Pennsylvania. A very gentle soul, john is usually barefoot with his long, grey hair tied in the back; his demeanor is quiet, but he's always vitally interested in what's going on. He's been an active peacemaker for many years and makes the yearly trek to the School of the Americas to protest the U.S. government's training of Latin American military and police there. He became aware of No More Deaths when our organization contacted the Christian Peacemaker Teams (with whom john was working) and invited them to go to Douglas where a Minuteman militia was active along the border. He joined the team in Douglas, but then stayed behind when they decided to leave Douglas for another venue. Soon after, he joined No More Deaths in Tucson. Since then he's made many trips into BANWR leaving water, food, and medical supplies along migrant trails. Here are some of his observations:

john heid:

> Borders undermine the natural order. They distort our sense and sensibilities. Walls and helicopters. Men with guns. Policies, politics and laws impact everything from living, breathing beings to inert objects. No relationship in the borderlands is left unblemished. No exceptions. No immunity.
>
> Gloria Anzaldua calls the U.S.-Mexico border *una herida abierta*, an open wound. I call it a flashpoint. A place where even benign realities and relationships become volatile, like vapor and spark. Combustible. Who among us can remember those funny mirrors at the amusement park? The ones that warped and contorted our image? We had not changed an *iota* although the mirror presented a clearly different image than the reality.

Situated squarely on the U.S.-Mexico border, the Buenos Aires National Wildlife Refuge seems to live up to its name "pleasant breezes." The Serengeti-esque seas of grass wave to the horizons. Baboquivari Peak presides over the endless savannas of the Altar Valley. Arid cacti-covered hillsides fold into verdant oak-sycamore canyons. The earth here is gradually recovering from generations of cattle grazing along with copper and uranium exploration. One must look carefully beyond the picture-post-card scenery to see that this land is covered with vein-like trails, a lifeline for many passing through *una herida abierta*. Who could imagine that a place of such wide-open beauty would be at the eye of a human rights storm? Who could imagine unnatural death on a wildlife refuge, let alone human death?

"Why do you put gallon jugs of water on BANWR?" we of No More Deaths are often asked. Because there are desperately thirsty people here. Because people die here. Plain and simple. This is not political rhetoric. It's human instinct. It's Gospel. Every human being has the fundamental right to water. For those who require such, surely international law upholds this right and furthermore criminalizes the denial of water.

My initiation into the shrill reality of border politics on BANWR came on June 1, 2009, the first day of the deadliest season of the year. A time when the desert floor becomes a deadly furnace. A lethal time.

That day, I was one of three volunteers placing water bottles along a well-traveled migrant trail when a U.S. Border Patrol agent came running full stride from behind us toting a long rifle. He was respectful and straightforward and slightly out of breath. His message was unequivocal and stark. "If you leave water bottles here you are breaking the littering law and subject to legal consequences." He departed as swiftly as he came. Soon a Border Patrol helicopter appeared and became our shadow until we ceased placing water an hour later.

Some months later, a U.S. Fish and Wildlife law enforcement officer, Jim Casey, approached me on a migrant trail and advised that Border Patrol agents and hunters were retrieving our water bottles and turning them into the Wildlife Refuge office. Mr. Casey added that officials knew our water routes, our schedules, and had cameras situated to observe our activities. In short, he said our efforts were futile. This moment deep in Wilbur Canyon did not seem conducive to reflective dialogue on the inconsistencies of current practice on BANWR and Fish and Wildlife policy, let alone human rights. How is criminalizing access to water consistent with "harmony between man (sic) and his environment?" How does this "stimulate the health and welfare of man (sic)?"

Occasionally, we meet someone walking the trails. Usually we merely see the evidence of people's passing. The stories of their lives are told in what's left behind. Photographs, clothing, empty Red Bull cans, electrolytes and water containers, children's toys. Footprints. Always the footprints. Large and small. Sometimes tiny. Most going north, although not all.

And, from time to time, we've seen water drop sights helter-skelter. Bottles slashed or smashed. Food strewn about. Vandalism by anonymous parties. Who travels these trails besides laborers from the south and humanitarian aid volunteers? Who would do this? Such wanton destruction. It is tempting to blame, speculate, and vilify. That's a dead-end line of query. At the end of the day, we know whether we've been the ones who placed the water bottles. Or, the ones who destroyed them.

One antidote to the anti-human/anti-immigrant attitudes, policies and laws that separate peoples is seeing the faces and hearing the stories of those we encounter in the borderland desert.

José (name changed) had just turned 50, three days before we encountered him on the roadside adjacent the BANWR perimeter. In clear English, José shared that he had been deported from Texas seven years ago after living there much of his life. Now his wife, a Texas resident, was dying of cancer. He produced a carefully folded handwritten love letter from the front pocket of his faded jeans. It was his spouse's plea for him to come home to say good-bye. José had been in the desert five days and believed he was in Texas, not where he was—a 1000 miles away from his beloved. Still he had to continue. With fresh water, food, a prayer and rudimentary directions we sent him on his way. Alone.

Maria was flat-out lost deep in Wilbur Canyon. Two days earlier a Border Patrol helicopter scattered her group in a common practice euphemistically called "dusting." She'd been wandering alone. Maria was barely able to walk when our lives intersected. She was recently widowed with four children. Maria had cousins and work opportunities in South Carolina. This was her only hope for supporting her distant family.

The U.S.-Mexico border is a rich, painful collage of journeys like José's and Maria's. Politics and policies fade into the background with stories like theirs.

Today the borderlands have become an epicenter wherein fundamental humanitarian gestures are criminalized, let alone the right of movement. Questions—that one should never have to say "no" to—arise. Should I offer water and break the law? Water is not the crime here. The forced march is. This human tragedy is.

An insight follows...human rights are not now, nor could they ever be, negotiable. They are not optional. Not open to

public debate or judicial discretion or congressional delib-
eration. They are the *terra firma* of civil society.

Desert borders are caldrons of angst and desperation.
The locus of crisis. The locus of insight. The seedbed of
transformation. Why? Because our options are clearer and
bare-bones here. Life and death are side by side in this fragile, dangerous terrain. While governments produce policies
thousands of miles away that impact life and death in these
Sonoran arroyos, it is our decisions on the ground which etch
out an ethic. It is here that we come closest "to understanding the violence to the spirit that happens when one watches
a loved one die of malnutrition." What will we choose—life
or death?

To add just a bit to john's eloquent comments, we look to historical giants to inform our attitudes about the environment: John
Muir, who discovered and revealed the beauty of the vast terrain in
California, Teddy Roosevelt, who in his position as president, established the National Park System throughout the country, and Loren
Eisley, whose writings help us encounter the minute glories of our
world and derive spiritual meaning from their existence.

CHAPTER 51

Water Sites on BANWR

AN EMAIL FROM MIKE HAWKES dated June 24th notified us that he was sending a letter in response to our email and asked for the name of our spokesperson. We told him to write "No More Deaths" since we are a consensus organization and do not have officers to speak for us!

The day following the press conference, we received a three-page, single-spaced, well-conceived letter from Refuge Manager Michael Hawkes. The letter requested a virtual meeting by email. It went on to spell out Fish and Wildlife law and stated that the National Wildlife Refuge Improvement Act of 1997 requires all refuge management be undertaken with a "wildlife first" doctrine. His letter objected to some of the assertions made at our press conference. We could have challenged a few of their objections but did not formally do so until later. During June and the following months, No More Deaths and BANWR continued to haggle over the number of deaths on the Refuge (we had previously overreported the number) and the number of water sources.

In the letter, Mr. Hawkes wrote:

Buenos Aires NWR has over 30 existing water sites available for migrants, with 14 of those consisting of sources directly tied to drinking water systems. There is more water per acre on the Refuge than on any other comparable landmass on the southern Arizona border. Additionally, we are in the process of redeveloping 4 - 6 new water wells and repairing 10-15 stock tanks that will be available for wildlife and migrant use. Based on this, additional water on the Refuge for migrants is not necessary.

In the next to last paragraph, Hawkes stated:

We have made it consistently and clearly known that this (leaving plastic water jugs on BANWR) is not an authorized activity. If you wish to place water jugs on the Refuge you may submit a detailed proposal with the exact locations, quantity, drop-off dates, pick-up dates, clea- up dates, responsible individual, names of all field workers who would be on the Refuge, and any other pertinent information for our consideration. These are the standard requirements for a Special Use Permit on any National Wildlife Refuge. In support of your application please provide a list of peer reviewed research papers, dissertations, publications or other scientific peer reviewed articles that illustrate the effectiveness, success or benefits of the methods, techniques and practices you propose to use.

He concluded with:

I hope this letter provides your organization's members some insight to the position of the Buenos Aires NWR. I believe we can work together and can facilitate humanitarian efforts without breaking established laws. I look forward to future communication.

At the mention of "research," some of the humanitarian negotiators thought of an alternative approach to the issue.

CHAPTER 52

No More Deaths vs. BANWR

*The thing that does work, after ten years
of research, is water.*

— *THE REV. ROBIN HOOVER*

FOR SEVERAL WEEKS, NO MORE Deaths had been asking the chief at
BANWR, Michael Hawkes, to meet with representatives to plan for
the summer heat. Mr. Hawkes did not respond. So, on June 30th,
we emailed Mr. Hawkes hoping to establish a dialogue that would
lead to cooperation between BANWR and the various humanitarian
groups to save migrant lives:

June 30, 2009

Mr. Hawkes:

Given that the hottest and deadliest time of the year is
already upon us, it is imperative the Buenos Aires NWR representatives make themselves available to meet this week.
We would propose the following agenda for this meeting,
which would include BANWR representatives as well as five
to six people representing humanitarian and environmental
organizations:

- Presentation by BANWR regarding its mission, problems associated with the international border, and concerns regarding humanitarian aid;
- Presentation by environmental and humanitarian organizations regarding their missions, work, and concerns;
- Discussion aimed at resolving differences and concerns, working toward a plan to include collaboration between humanitarian and environmental organizations and BANWR.

We've also updated our materials to clarify migrant death data in the area along Hwy. 286 that you earlier pointed out to us was in error. We had indicated there were eight deaths when there were actually none. The deaths we noted were located east of BANWR.

Sincerely, No More Deaths

We requested that Mr. Hawkes respond by July 4th. When we still had not heard from him by July 6th, we began to plan for an action on BANWR to get his attention.

PLACING WATER ON BANWR. NO MORE DEATHS MONDAY NIGHT MEETING—JULY 6, 2009

Considerable tension and excitement existed at the July 6th No More Deaths meeting as plans were underway for the July 7th press conference and the July 9th action at BANWR. Twelve people had stated they would be willing to place water on BANWR. This would be the first time since winter we had officially gone onto the Refuge. Both the press and Fish and Wildlife personnel would be notified. This water drop was to protest BANWR Land Manager Mike Hawkes' unwillingness to set a mutually agreeable date to develop a plan for distribution of water. No More Deaths had given Hawkes a deadline of July 4th to set a date for a meeting. Instead, Hawkes issued a request for an agenda and list of participants. While this may seem reasonable, No More Deaths viewed this as simply a delaying tactic. Thus, the planned action on July 9th was organized. The group, comprised of volunteers from No More Deaths and Samaritans (Lois Martin represented both No More Deaths and Humane Borders), planned to meet at the BANWR Cienega trailhead a quarter-mile east of the Arivaca Library. Giovanni Conti, Jim Marx and Maryada Vallet would coordinate the activities.

Toward the end of the meeting, the group reviewed the press release that was about to be released. In it we announced our intention to join with other humanitarian groups and prominent members of the community to put out gallon jugs of water on BANWR on Thursday, July 9, 2009.

A letter signed by more than 70 human rights, environmental, and faith-based organizations and individuals had been hand-delivered to Refuge Manager Michael Hawkes on June 16th asking for a meeting by the first of July. A copy of that letter was also hand-delivered to Secretary of the Interior, Ken Salazar. Mr. Hawkes responded on Friday, June 6th requesting a proposed agenda and a list of participants, but no further correspondence had been received.

At the press conference, several people spoke in support of the efforts of No More Deaths and Samaritans. One of those, the Rev. Robin Hoover, pastor of First Christian Church and head of the humanitarian group, Humane Borders, spoke eloquently about the bogus nature of the prosecutions, since BANWR claims that littering and cleanup are one of the main issues. His group had requested permits to pick up trash the last 12 years and was denied. Despite that, Humane Borders volunteers take out "tons and tons" of trash. Robin also mentioned the towers (the federal virtual fence designed to spot migrants) are not well maintained and don't work. "The thing that does work after ten years' research is water."

Successful Trash Pickup (No More Deaths)

Shura Wallin, a founder of Green Valley Samaritans, said that on August 22, 2006, the body of *Alfonso Solis Duran* was found an eighth of a mile off Arivaca Road on BANWR. He had no backpack or food. She said that she stands with Dan and Walt.

Dan Millis (who had been ticketed by BANWR and charged and found guilty by the federal court) now worked for the Sierra Club. He reported that 60 to 70 organizations had signed on to the letter we were sending to the Attorney General and others, including the Center for Biological Diversity. Dan said that this situation is the tragic consequence of our failed immigration policy, and that needed was a wholesale shift in border policy. We need to urge federal land managers to work *with* humanitarian aid volunteers. He went on to say that the main eyesore on the border is not the migrant trash or humanitarian's water but rather the border wall that violates 36 different federal environmental laws. Mike Wilson, a member of the Tohono O'odham Nation, said we should have "good spirit, good heart, clear eyes." He claimed that hundreds of gallons of water that he'd put out on the reservation were slashed by the Tribal Police, Border Patrol, and others. Mike continued: "Despite our romantic notion of native sovereignty, ours are basically federal lands. Border Patrol has been coming after David Garcia and me. These are crimes against humanity. We are all desert peoples; your ancestors were all migrant peoples. They came to America not speaking English. We await our arrest. But we will be back out on the reservation. We are called upon to suffer for those who suffer daily."

CHAPTER 53

Tickets on the Refuge–July 9, 2009

Lois Martin Ticketed on Refuge 2009 (No More Deaths)

FOLLOWING WALT'S CONVICTION AND THE lack of any real response from BANWR, No More Deaths and Samaritans determined to go ahead with their plans and have an event on the Refuge. So, on July 9th a caravan of cars and vans traveled south on Highway 19 toward Nogales where they turned off at Amado and continued southwest toward the Buenos Aires National Wildlife Cienega near Arivaca. Those planning to be ticketed were: Lois Miller, Maureen Marx, John Fife, Gene

309

Lefebvre, Corinne Bancroft, Charlie Rooney, Leesa Jacobson, Jeff Millsap, john heid, Paula McPheeters, Jerry Zawada, and David Hill. By 8:30 a.m. the group hit the road through Arivaca where they turned west, then they drove a short distance and pulled to a stop.

**Basura 13 Gather at Southside Church Before
Action 2009 (No More Deaths)**

Ed McCullough jumped out of the van in which he was riding and quickly marked three spaced-out locations with yellow tape to identify the trails we planned to use. Later in the morning, this earned him a ticket, bringing our total number of offenders to 13 people.

Norma Price was riding with Ed. At one point, an agent went up to her van and asked, "Where's your husband?"

Norma answered, "I think he's home sleeping in bed—naked."

The agent didn't crack a smile. Instead, he clarified that he meant that man who'd been in the van with her. She pointed to Ed up ahead along the road.

For the next hour or so, as we put out water, the Fish and Wildlife people picked up our jugs, and dumped them into their trucks. And, of course, they issued 13 tickets. Ed McCullough gathered up the yellow tape and we headed home. We felt the action had been a success.

We had planned to have additional people go out every week to continue the protest and make it confusing for the court. However, the next day No More Deaths received calls from the offices of both Allen Bursin and Ken Salazar. Bursin has a long history in border affairs and international representation for the United States. I believe at the time we met with him, he was Assistant Secretary for International Affairs and Special Representative for Border Affairs. Salazar was Secretary of the Interior. We met with Bursin within a couple of days. He showed compassion for our cause and seemed to think that the tickets were pretty ridiculous. He tasked his assistants to look into it. We were scheduled to meet with Salazar in Washington and his staff a few days later. Bursin's encouraging attitude combined with our upcoming meeting with Salazar caused us to put off that ongoing strategy.

We received an email from Dan Millis quoting Matthew Hogel of the Sierra Club and member of the Bureau of Land Management's (BLM) Resources Advisory Committee (RAC). Dan wrote that Matthew said: "I don't know how much weight it will pull, but when your group meets with Salazar feel free to say that you have met with me and that your local RAC for the BLM feels that your group's activities and initiatives fall under BLM land management goals based on your efforts to do trash pickups, monitor and re-collect the water jugs; and that if someone were hurt/injured/in need of water in a state or national park, our park managers would give them assistance without thinking twice."

One of our attorneys, Andy Silverman, spoke with our U.S. Representative Raul Grijalva about possibly joining us at the meeting with Salazar. Grijalva declined, reasoning that he could better provide follow-up to the meeting at a later time.

For our meeting with Salazar, The Rev. Robin Hoover of Humane Borders joined the delegation and tried to get us a free ride with prominent farmers who were flying out to Washington—if we could leave on the first date suggested by Salazar. That didn't work out, much to Robin's displeasure. He berated us for our slow decision-making process (using consensus that required us to wait until the Monday meeting for discussion and approval) and resigned from the delegation. For the meeting, finally set for July 21ˢᵗ, our delegation flew to Washington D.C. by commercial carrier.

In addition to our delegation, which was comprised of Danielle Alvarado (former volunteer coordinator for No More Deaths), Ed McCullough, Paula McPheeters (a teacher and a Samaritan), Dr. Norma Price, and Gene Lefebvre, we were joined in Washington by a member of Robins' board of directors and lobbyist in Washington, Dinah Bear. Robin sent a lengthy letter to the those of us who were representatives pointing out how little authority Salazar has as an appointed bureaucrat; but he did believe that Salazar could have some influence on the process.

Gene Lefebvre:

> At the Department of the Interior, a representative met us in the lobby, took us around the screening machine, and led us to Salazar's conference room. We saw Salazar for about ten minutes; he told us he was sympathetic with the problem and had concern for the migrants and respect for us, but we had to follow the law. His assistant, Jane Lyder, chaired the meeting and spent about 45 minutes talking with us after Salazar left. We asked for a directive from Salazar's office to federal land managers stating that humanitarian aid is compatible with the missions of federal lands. We asked that neither a Special Use Permit (SUP) be required, nor onerous conditions imposed that would make the providing of humanitarian aid difficult or impossible to provide.

No promises were made.

CHAPTER 54

Negotiations with BANWR Begin

Gene Lefebvre:

Finally, under pressure from above, we got a meeting scheduled with BANWR for the 5th of August. Samaritans and No More Deaths named a team of five people to meet with their officials: Ed McCullough, former assistant provost at the University of Arizona and mapmaker for Samaritans and No More Deaths; Margo Cowan, our attorney and long-time immigration rights advocate in Southern Arizona; Danielle Alvarado, fluent Spanish-speaker, recent college graduate in education, and former No More Deaths volunteer coordinator; Dr. Norma Price, retired physician who responds to calls for medical assistance from the field for both Samaritans and No More Deaths and conducts our first aid training; and me, a retired Presbyterian minister and immigration activist.

We drove there together in one car. I'd never been to BANWR headquarters before and really enjoyed the ride. The thick mesquite trees were abundantly green from recent monsoons, and the tall grasses swayed in the mild wind. We took Highway 286 south to Three Points where we drove onto BANWR. From there, we drove to about six miles from the border where we turned into the Headquarters compound. As we approached the office we saw several low buildings constructed in a natural style compatible with the habitat.

When we arrived, the agents weren't quite ready for us, so we entertained ourselves in the visitor center with maps, photographs, narratives on the walls, and statuary of birds and other wildlife. We read over the rules on BANWR and discovered how much stricter they are than those for other land-use agencies. Most of the BANWR land was purchased from local owners by the government, and the relatively new refuge was established in 1985. Visitors are barred from taking anything into the Refuge and from taking anything out. Someone in our group had heard of a person being threatened by an agent for trying to remove a rock. We believed these keepers of the Refuge really meant business.

We met in a conference room. Their representatives included two officers from the regional office, Chris Pease and Tom Harvey. In addition, director Michael Hawkes, his assistant, Sally Gall, and two other local officers were in attendance. All were dressed in uniforms. It was obvious from their reaction to us that we didn't conform to their expectations. Mike Hawkes had been presenting us in the media as a shadowy, disorganized, group of radicals. He'd said we didn't have a contact person, we refused to meet with him, and we just cluttered the desert. The local agents were used to seeing No More Deaths folks in the wild. Some of them wear tattoos, many have long hair, and several of the grey-haired hikers tend to look a bit scruffy in the field. We weren't dressed for the opera, but we dressed appropriately for a meeting with government officials. Once they got past all that, they welcomed us cordially.

We saw in the recent letter from Mike that the requirements for their permit would make it impossible for us to comply. It included requirements for peer-reviewed research as well as identification of each trail, dates of trips, who would be taking them, etc. We were also afraid that buying into a permit process might mean that other land managers could also require them with their own limits. Margo told them that our membership had drawn a line at permits; we simply won't accept that requirement. They went into a long explanation of how that is the framework in which they must work. We talked about emergency permits.

Margo presented the Memorandum of Understanding (MOU) which had been carefully crafted by her and approved by Samaritans and No More Deaths. It called for us to put out water and to pick up trash in specific terms. They were quite taken aback; they had never dealt with an MOU, only their permits. They had experiences working with the Tohono O'odham Nation and with other governmental agencies, but always in term of permits, not MOUs. They weren't sure if it was a legitimate approach.

The sticking point for the Fish and Wildlife people remained to be our plastic jugs. In their minds, they were trash; in our view they were precious, life-giving gifts of water. We had suggested an arrangement in which we'd promise to take out at least twice the number of plastic jugs as we'd leave, in addition to other trash. That was not satisfactory to Hawkes and his assistant. They said they wanted to allow more Humane Borders water stations, even though Humane Borders had been asking permission to place more water tanks on the Refuge and had been denied for twelve years. Our reply to this was that it was a great idea to put in more water stations, but they would be fixed units that would have to be accessed by truck and wouldn't even begin to cover the trails used by migrants in the hilly and mountainous areas to the north.

As a secondary idea, they suggested we place five-gallon containers where trails cross dirt roads. Then we could back-pack jugs of water into more inaccessible areas to service the tanks. We pointed out that it would mean 50-plus pound packs. Ed suggested we might place bicycle chain locks around a group of water jugs so that they would stay in place until we picked them up. Hawkes wouldn't accept that. It was left that we would try to think of another method of putting out the water.

Then, they asked how many trails we thought we would put water on, and—after some research—Ed replied six. And how many jugs of water all together? Probably 50 at the most. There were a few minutes of silence. I thought that these regional guys were sharp enough to have been asking themselves— *Is this whole fuss really about only 50 jugs, and the humanitarians agree to pick up at least twice that much in trash?? We think we can work this out.*

The framework we suggested for this whole mess was that we and the government accept that this is an emergency situation requiring exceptional responses. The emergency is that hundreds of migrants are dying crossing deserts, and we must respond with humanitarian efforts that at least offer them water, food, and first aid. This emergency ought to trump ordinary rules.

We talked about the MOU; they talked about their permit process. Nevertheless, the meeting concluded on a positive note. They agreed to take the MOU under advisement and to their attorneys and higher-ups, and we set another meeting date at their headquarters.

CHAPTER 55

In the Meantime

For the past 26 years I've come to know and love many of
our migrant families who have taught me something of the
heart of God. As a Catholic priest and a Franciscan friar, I
feel called to accompany these suffering travelers and work
with others who believe in this journey of compassion.

— Jerry Zawada Franciscan friar

On August 11th, we gathered again in the federal courthouse to learn the sentence Judge Guerin would impose on Walt Staton. Humanitarian representatives filled the section on the left with government representatives including those from Border Patrol and Fish and Wildlife on the right. The judge gave Walt an opportunity to speak. Walt had been an active participant in No More Deaths for three or more years. He handled our website and frequently spoke on behalf of the humanitarian movement. Thus, he was an articulate and accurate spokesperson. He explained that he didn't believe humanitarian aid should be a crime and gave his reasons.

PARTIAL TRANSCRIPT OF PROCEEDINGS

THE COURT: Does the defendant wish to be heard regarding sentencing?

THE DEFENDANT: Yes, please.

Good morning, Your Honor.

THE COURT: Good morning.

THE DEFENDANT: I decided to fight this littering ticket and put the government to its burden of proof because I feel that my actions were responsible.

I feel that the crisis that has unfolded along our border in the last several years warrants an unprecedented response from civil society. Thousands of people have died crossing this desert.

...The very first day I ever volunteered with No More Deaths was July 4th of 2004, and we went out to the Wildlife Refuge looking for people in distress, and we found no one, so we took out two large, black plastic bags and began picking up trash for the entire morning. That was my very first experience with No More Deaths years ago.

Since then, my respect for the desert and the environment has only grown. I grew up in Arizona. I was an Eagle Scout. I've done more trash pickup and more service hours on sides of highways adopted by my Boy Scout troop. I've pulled trash out of the bottom of the Grand Canyon. I've cleaned up wrappers off the top of Baboquivari Peak. I've taken out beer cans and diapers from the Clear Creek wilderness area, not because anyone told me to, but because I don't like seeing our environment trashed.

I feel that the faith that I follow leads me to look at situations that are bigger than I'll even ever understand. I think the border is a situation that falls into that category. It's a situation that many of us will probably never fully understand, the complexities of immigration, of what drives people to come and what drives the United States to enforce the border in such a way as to push people into these remote areas where people who are determined to come anyway are going to come.

...I ask that the Court really disregard the memo filed by the U.S. Attorney's Office. When I read that memo, I didn't know who they were writing about. It didn't reflect anything that I knew of myself. The memo was full of many inaccuracies and, I think, sensationalist language to try and trump up a situation that I really have very little to do with, play a very small role.

...I'm just one person who simply cares and is following in the footsteps of my faith.

In that I don't work much, I don't have any savings. To fine me, I think, would put a huge pressure on my next step, which is to go to seminary school. I plan to move to Los Angeles next week to begin that adventure in my life. I have no savings for that. I'm taking out student loans to go further into debt to follow what I want to do in my life.

I also feel that any kind of probation is completely unnecessary. I've demonstrated that through the entire time before the trial and since. I've checked in with the presentence folks. I'm not out to run away. I'm not going to, you know, continue violating laws.

...We're not here to just challenge what the U.S. laws are. In fact, as I said on the witness stand, I fully agree with the littering laws. Someone who is out picnicking and leaves Styrofoam plates everywhere-- they should get a ticket. But I hope the Court can look to the bigger picture of my actions and the group and the support I get from my colleagues in trying to play a small role in a huge situation here and bring the deaths and suffering to an end, because that's ultimately what we're all trying to do.

And in that case, I also take a huge exception to the part in the sentencing recommendations from the government to ban me from the Wildlife Refuge. I feel that's beyond being mean-spirited, you know. My entire life has been led outdoors in Arizona, all kinds of wilderness and amazing places.

I would like nothing more than to come back to this area on my summer breaks and go out and help pick up trash. I would wake up one...my dream is to wake up one day and hear that immigration reform has passed and people are going to stop crossing the desert, and then I and I know many of my friends would gladly take as many trash bags as needed to clean up the entire Wildlife Refuge and all the areas along the border that we work.

...Our dream is to go home and not continue this work, but by necessity and by our faith and by our conscience, we're going to keep doing humanitarian aid in whatever way, responsible way, we can see that it's to be done.

So, I'd ask the Court to not fine me and place an undue financial hardship on my next moves in life. I'd ask the Court to not give me any kind of supervised or unsupervised release. I don't think that's necessary. I definitely don't want to be banned from any Wildlife Refuge.

So, I hope you can take all these things into consideration and see that the actions that I did take were not malicious, were not in spite of anything, but were taken in a good faith, a responsible way to address a much larger crisis than I think any of us will ever know in our lifetimes.[101]

Two people from California wrote to the judge on Walt's behalf: the president of Claremont College and the president of the Center for Bio-Diversity. Evidently, these were not taken seriously by the judge. Neither was an additional letter and phone calls from jurors in the trial who addressed Bill Walker, saying they felt the discussion in the jury room was unfair.

---

101 Federal Court transcript (Tucson, Arizona, August 11, 2009).

Judge Guerin said that "...while your motives were good and humanitarian assistance is commendable, the more that individuals involve themselves in that community and the issues that we face, the better we can make our community and the world. When you seek to reach those objectives by destroying other objectives and other valid goals, then that does harm, as well."

Then she sentenced Walt to one year of unsupervised probation and 300 hours of community service, specifically directed at trash removal. In addition, based on Walt's comments that he was not committed to nor could he say that he would not engage in this same conduct in the future, she banned him from coming onto BANWR for a year, as well.

Maryada had been at Walt's side throughout this whole ordeal. In late summer, she and Walt headed off to California—Walt to attend Claremont Seminary and Maryada to work for World Vision and finish an advanced degree in Public Health at UCLA. Walt called all around trying to find a place where he could pick up trash under supervision. This was a time of severe budget cuts in California, as elsewhere, and almost every public entity said they had no one to supervise Walt on his trash-pickup forays. He went out two weekends for five hours each. At this rate, it would take him over a year to work off his 300 hours.

The New York Times (August 15, 2009) and *The San Diego Union* (August 18, 2009) both wrote editorials in support of Walt and his predicament. *The Times* pointed out that "Janet Napolitano, gave a speech last week reinforcing her hawkish commitment to border security even as President Obama suggested that he would defer to next year the only real solution to the border problem—immigration reform that gives people an alternative."

As Walt reflected on his "punishment" while picking up trash with work crews on the side of highways around Los Angeles, he worked out a plan to push back against the court-ordered community service.

CHAPTER 56

Second Meeting with BANWR–August 20, 2009

GENE LEFEBVRE:

We arrived at our second meeting with the BANWR officials in an optimistic mood. After the first meeting, we felt good about the way the meeting had gone: the regional officials had taken charge in a conciliatory manner, and our understanding was that they would respond directly to our proposed Memo of Understanding, or they would return with a new proposal of their own. Indeed, we had received a note from Chris Pease saying he was optimistic that we could work things out.

As soon as we arrived in the conference room, it became clear that Fish and Wildlife had no intention of dealing with the Memo of Understanding. The lead negotiator informed us that our memorandum would take years to review, so we should fill out a form and apply for a permit like everyone else. The tone was extremely hostile and much different from our first discussion.

We continued to try to reach agreement on specific language which would permit the placement of water on BANWR. We agreed on the following language—subject to the federal representatives reviewing the language with unknown persons and the BANWR representatives soliciting public review and comment.

1. NMD shall place water on migrant trails to be determined to be active;
2. NMD shall monitor these trails no less than once every 10 days;
3. NMD shall submit to BANWR a list of all known migrant trails with identified sites for potential water deposits;
4. NMD shall communicate to BANWR which sites are no longer serviced;
5. In the event that NMD identifies a trail not listed in paragraph 3 then NMD shall submit the coordinate information to BANWR;
6. NMD agrees that the water left shall not be in containers that can be removed;
7. This agreement shall be renewed annually by the parties;
8. Mike Hawkes shall be the point of contact for BANWR, and Gene Lefebvre and Ed McCullough shall be the points of contact for NMD.

The most meaningful thing that happened was that Hawkes brought out maps and described for us all the water sources on BANWR. We immediately challenged him, so Chris Pease suggested that we take the maps and check out the sources ourselves. Hawkes was reluctant, but Chris prevailed.

EXAMINATION OF BANWR "WATER" SITES

In disbelief and frustration at BANWR's claim that there were 30 potable water sites, Ed and Debbie McCullough immediately drove out to BANWR two weekends in a row and checked out all the water sites identified by BANWR as viable sources of water for migrants.

Ayala Rahm did as well. They drove and hiked all over the Refuge to locate the sites identified by BANWR staff. When they reported back, we were shocked to learn that 22 of the 30 sites were unusable for animals or humans. Another volunteer took photographs of the sites including the one here of a dead squirrel in a full tank of water.

POINT SOURCE WATER FEATURES
BUENOS AIRES NATIONAL WILDLIFE REFUGE

1. **ST-PW**   **Dry tank**
2. **ST-PW**   **Dry tank**
3. **ST-W**   **Dry tank**
4. **ST-SW**   **Dry tank**
5. **ST-SW**   **Has road through tank (breached)**
6. **ST-SW**   **Dry tank**
7. **ST-SW**   **Water is stagnant and dirty**
8. **ST-PW**   **Few inches muddy water in center of tank**
9. **ST-PW**   **Not found**
10. **ST-SW**   **Dry tank**
11. **ST-PW**   **Dry tank**
12. **Spigot**   **Clean water**
13. **ST-PW**   **Stagnant, dirty water**
14. **ST-PW**   **Stagnant, dirty water**
15. **ST-PW**   **No longer a tank: dry**
16. **STPW**   **Stagnant, dirty water**
17. **ST-PW**   **Dry**
18. **ST-PW**   **Dry**
19. **ST-SW**   **Dry**
20. **ST-SW**   **Dry**
21. **Spigot**   **Small trickle water into dirty tank**
22. **Spigot**   **Dry B ST-PW**[102]

---

102 Provided by Ed McCulla.

Dead Squirrel in a BANWR Water Tank 2009 (No More Deaths)

DOJ Staffer Comments on Walt's Trial–September 1, 2009

Margo Cowan sent an email to Alan Bersin to alert him that a comment was posted on a website following an article by our attorney, Bill Walker. It came from a Department of Justice computer (wdc-sun30.usdoj.gov). Margo called it "troubling." The comment read:

> Evidence at trial: A judge had already ruled that plastic water jugs left on the Refuge is litter (ed., in Dan's case). No More Deaths had instructions warning that they could be cited for littering on the Refuge. Yet, Walt did it anyways (sic). One down, 13 more to go.

The 13 were to be arraigned the next day on similar charges.

ARRAIGNMENT OF THE BASURA 13—SEPTEMBER 2, 2009

The 13 offenders from BANWR were arraigned in federal court on September 2, 2009. One by one, the judge called them and announced that they were charged with littering on Buenas Aires National Wildlife Refuge. They each pleaded "Not Guilty," and were bound over for trial on January 13, 2010 (later changed to February).

Following the arraignment, we scheduled a press conference to show the media the results of our investigation of water spots on BANWR. The media representatives who were there were quite interested in the differences between the claims of Michael Hawkes and the reality we found when checking out the sites. It's one thing to sit in an office and look at a map and point out water sources; it's quite another to drive around and hike into each site and check it out.

CHAPTER 57

Third Meeting with BANWR–September 10, 2009

GENE LEFEBVRE:

Four of us from Samaritans and No More Deaths drove from Tucson to the BANWR offices on the Refuge: Margo Cowan, Norma Price, Ed McCullough, and me. There we met four people representing BANWR: Mike Hawkes, Sally Gall, Tom Harvey and an aide.

Tom's opening comments made it clear that they were continuing to say that these issues were mainly to be resolved with Mike Hawkes, as he is the Land Manager for BANWR.

Mike presented a new map that had plotted on it the thirty locations suggested by Ed at the previous meeting. However, Mike had not yet decided the suitability of these sites, as he had agreed to do at the previous meeting.

Mike also announced a new criterion: the water drops would have to be within 100 meters of a road. I thought he was referring to the paved roads, which would have been very limiting and totally unacceptable to us. But when I asked for clarification, he explained that he meant any road open to the public, even the four-wheel drive roads. As we looked at the new map, that restriction seemed to allow for many of the sites Ed McCullough had previously listed. I asked if there could be some flexibility with the 100-meter restriction. For example, if by moving a water jug 200 meters from the road, it allowed us to serve two trails instead of one. They agreed.

We said that we *might* be able to live with putting out five-gallon jugs that were tied down to a tree. We were experimenting to see if much water would be lost in transferring water to a smaller migrant-held bottle. We thought it might work OK with a jug with a spigot.

Mike said other criteria would include endangered plants such as the pineapple yucca. But Sally said those were only found on the flat lands, and the areas we were discussing were in the hills. Mike also said that some sites might be excluded in riparian areas, but the only such area we could think of was Arivaca Creek, and we said that we had no intention of putting water near the creek.

The discussion took an awkward turn when we talked about the request for a permit. Mike said we had to be specific when requesting sites on the permit request. We argued that we had agreed during the last meeting that we would select several trails for him to pre-approve. From that number of about 20, we would select about eight or ten that would become active at any given time. Then, when we needed to shut down one site and move to another, we would notify him and move to another pre-approved site. We said we didn't want to submit a request that was simply going to be rejected by him: please let us know now what was not acceptable and we would leave it out. He agreed.

We asked Mike how long a public hearing would take and where it would happen. He said it would take 30 days and it would be on their website. Could our people respond online? Yes, certainly.

Toward the end of the meeting, we asked if Ed could take a copy of the new map. Mike said no, not if we were going to treat it like the last map he gave us. As he spoke, it was obvious he was angry. What was he talking about? He said he had given us the last map (displaying water sources on BANWR) in good faith, but then we used it in a press conference (after the initial court appearance of 13 people who'd received littering tickets). That had embarrassed them and caused them to lose faith in us. Norma responded that perhaps we could have handled the matter better, but that map showed what Mike had been telling the press, that there was lots of water for migrants on BANWR, was in fact not true.

I then said we did not like the way Mike and the government had accused us before the press and in the prosecution's report at Walt's hearing on the huge amount of trash we were leaving in the desert. In fact, *that* was untrue. And, in these negotiations, we discovered they were not greatly concerned about the trash, after all. They had no response to this.

The meeting ended on a note that Ed would refine our requests in light of the new map and the new criteria that sites must be within 100 meters of roads. And Mike would respond as quickly as possible. In addition, Mike offered to help us complete our permit request. They offered to let Ed take the map, but he declined, saying he could manage without it.

Ed summarized in a statement:

No More Deaths and Samaritans shall:

1. Place water on migrant trails to be determined to be active.
2. Monitor these trails no less than once every ten days.
3. Submit to BANWR a list of all known migrant trails with identified sites for potential water drops.
4. Communicate to BANWR which sites are no longer serviced.
5. In the event that a trail is identified that is not listed in item 3, then coordinate information.

CHAPTER 58

The PR Battle Enjoined

GENE SENT A SHORT NOTE to Jane Lyder in Ken Salazar's office advising her that thousands of emails may be coming her way because of the No More Deaths fall newsletter to our constituency asking them to write to and encourage Ken Salazar to help with BANWR. This was her response:

> Dear Gene,
>
> I remember you from our meeting in D.C. Thank you for the update on the meeting yesterday. I will be in touch with the Regional Director and the Refuge manager to see if there is anything I can do to help the permit review NOT get stuck "in the halls of bureaucracy." I can assure you the folks who get most frustrated with bureaucratic delays tend to be those within the Fish and Wildlife Service—they are the ones often pushing for decisions to be made quickly for on-the-ground action to become a reality.
>
> I don't think I will be able to answer personally all the emails I have already received on this issue. I will answer the letter from the group that Danielle sent to me this week. Please feel free to share my sentiments with others in your group.
>
> Jane Lyder, Deputy Assistant Secretary Fish and Wildlife and Parks

HIKING IN BANWR–OCTOBER 29, 2009

A Migrant Trail on BANWR (No More Deaths)

john heid called Gene to report on their hikes in BANWR during this week, which were conducted despite BANWR's opposition. His group, which included Lois Martin and Kevin Riley, found drop spots where all the bottles had been removed and one where they had all been smashed. The volunteers were now leaving two jugs at a time all along the trails rather than in a bunch, hoping that Fish and Wildlife officers won't go as deep into the desert as the volunteers would.

We have heard of the bottles being taken before. One of the Samaritans was told by a Fish and Wildlife person that he was taking the water home and using it. A Samaritan met another officer who said same thing.

As the Land Manager for BANWR, Mike Hawkes should know where we drop the water, as it can be seen from Border Patrol helicopters that fly overhead. Walt could see them when he did a helicopter trip in an Arizona DPS helicopter. During this particular week, No More Deaths encountered a Fish and Wildlife Officer and a Pima County Deputy Sheriff. In both instances, it would have been obvious that our folks were putting out water, but they didn't try to stop them.

Margo sent a request for a Special Use Permit to BANWR. The conditions she included were:

1. One-gallon sealed jugs containing water will be placed at GPS points on active migrant trails agreed upon by BANWR staff and Ed McCullough, representing the applicant groups (not the five-gallon jugs Mike Hawkes was demanding);

2. Applicant groups will monitor these trails no less than once every ten days;

3. Applicant groups will communicate to BANWR which sites are no longer in service;

4. The number of one-gallon jugs of water left at any particular point will be determined by migrant use and adjusted accordingly;

5. In the event a new, active migrant trail is identified by applicant groups, then that information will be communicated to BANWR staff;

6. Consistent with best practices, the one-gallon sealed jugs will be affixed at each drop site so that they cannot be removed from the site;

7. Applicant groups and BANWR staff will meet quarterly to evaluate the effectiveness of this effort, resolve any issues and/or concerns and make any indicated changes to the description of the work to be performed contained herein;

8. Applicant groups and BANWR staff will meet in the 11th month of this authorized permit period to renew the agreement for a subsequent period of authorization; ADDENDUM

to USDOI U.S. Fish & Wildlife service Form 3-1383 Special Use and Permit;

9. Mike Hawkes shall be the point of contact for BANWR and Ed McCullough and Gene Lefebvre shall be the points of contact for applicant organizations. Particular identifying vehicle information and names of applicant groups volunteers shall be provided periodically by the points of contact;

10. The required Certificate of Liability Insurance shall be submitted upon approval of this permit application.

We awaited his response.

MIKE'S RESPONSE–NOVEMBER 11, 2009

Dear Ms. Cowan:
This letter is in reference to the receipt of a Special Use Application and Permit (Form 3-1383) to permit members of No More Deaths (NMD) to place one-gallon water jugs on Buenos Aires National Wildlife Refuge. As you know we met with you and members of your organization on three separate occasions in order to determine the parameters that would be acceptable to the Refuge for NMD to obtain a permit for this use. During our second meeting we discussed the water container size and you agreed to investigate the use of larger containers (five-gallon) for your activity. During our last meeting I explained to you that the one-gallon minimum requirement was also given to you in a written document which you read and approved. Therefore, I was surprised to receive your application specifying one-gallon containers as the method of delivery to the water drop stations.

The dissemination of one-gallon containers on the Refuge is unacceptable due to the issue of litter created when the containers are removed from the site. One-gallon containers are very easy to remove, even when tied by the handle, and are easy to transport to other areas of the Refuge where they are subsequently discarded and become trash. As I explained, the use of a five-gallon container would eliminate this issue because five-gallon containers cannot be easily carried away and can be cabled to a tree to prevent removal. Your members can easily use the five-gallon containers by carrying in the one-gallon jugs, pouring them into the five-gallon container and carrying the empty one-gallon jugs out with them, thereby eliminating excess litter on the Refuge.

Sincerely, Michael M. Hawkes, Refuge Manager

Possible response to Mike:

Well, we did *not* agree to use five-gallon containers. We did agree to carefully investigate our *use* of the five-gallon jugs. We have conducted such an investigation and discovered problems with such a system. First, two of our people observed over a period of two months that on and near BANWR, migrants were not leaving smaller containers when they picked up new one-gallon bottles. In other geographic areas, migrants exchanged their water containers for the new ones. But, there's no evidence that migrants were coming onto BANWR with their own containers, and we were concerned by that. If it is true, then how would migrants carry any water with them from a five-gallon source? We were inclined to disbelieve the reports of our scouts, so we sent another scout out and he observed the same thing. We need to consider that migrants may not have containers with them.

In addition, the five-gallon containers were expensive and almost impossible to use to fill a migrant's small containers without a spigot. On the most expensive five-gallon containers, the fragile spigots broke easily. The inexpensive ones were made of thin plastic and were as easy to cut as the gallon jugs. The handles that would be used to fasten the five-gallon containers are easily cut on the less expensive models and were only held on by two or three easily-removable screws on the more expensive ones.

Second, we researched biodegradable bottles as a possible solution. There were some options, but they were all too expensive.

We wanted this permit process to move forward quickly as we all had spent a considerable amount of time on this issue. Everyone wanted to establish a system to help migrants survive. No one wanted an idea that would just be sent back.

Paula McPheeters and Others Preparing Water Bottles for the Trail on BANWR (Paula McPheeters)

Frustration Shows–Meeting at Margo's Office to Discuss Responses to Hawkes 9:00 p.m. November 12, 2009

PRESENT: NORMA, MARGO, DEBBIE, GENE, and Sue. This is part of the negotiating team with Debbie in place of Ed, and Sue tagging along with Gene. For this meeting, these were the people who could be gathered on short notice.

Discussion: What to do regarding Mike Hawkes' November 11th reply about the Special Use Permit we requested? Our responses ranged from the sublime to the ridiculous:

<u>Sublime (helpful):</u>   *We want to present this as a win-win cooperative effort (the agreement on BANWR).*
Southern Arizona's Representative Raul Grijalva's committee in Congress is to have an oversight meeting. Maybe that will help.

<u>Moderately helpful:</u>   *The federal agencies are out of control and not responding to the humanitarian crisis.*
We don't want to put out the Special Use Permit for public comment when such a crisis is taking place.
Let's go back to the Memo of Understanding.
This is a crisis—an emergency.

<u>Ridiculous:</u>   *Ask Janet Napolitano to tell Salazar to fix it. This non-*
sense needs to stop!
Let's dump Mike!

By the next morning, everyone had decided the "dump Mike" idea was dead in the water and blamed its conception on a combination of the absurdity of Mike's response, the lateness of the hour, plus the beer from nearby Barrio Brewery. It had seemed like a great idea at the time.

On November 27th, a flyer went out inviting people to BANWR for a Memorial Action to commemorate the deaths of 206 migrants in the desert in Arizona during fiscal year (FY) 2009. People were asked to take rocks and construct a shrine west of the Arivaca Township near Milepost 7, west on Arivaca Road. They were also asked to bring a gallon of water to offer at the Shrine "near an abandoned dry well that BANWR has claimed to be a migrant water source." In addition: "We will be leaving gallons of water (bring as many as you can) and picking up trash on the trails."

A final note stated, "Regrettably, any of these activities (except observance) may be considered illegal by the United States and may be subject to ticketing."

Mike Hawkes wrote a letter back to us stating that many of the activities listed on the flyer are illegal on National Wildlife Refuges. Violations that could be cited included: holding a public assembly without a permit, trespassing, constructing an unlawful structure (shrine) and littering. Mike stated that, "...he was concerned that NMD would knowingly conduct an obviously illegal activity during negotiations to obtain a permit for water stations on the Refuge. Should NMD go forward with this activity on the Refuge as planned it will most certainly jepordize (sic) the chances of obtaining a permit for your activities."

Gene wrote back to Mike and clarified that we would remove the shrine following the service, and we will be hiking just *off* BANWR to drop water and clean up trash. We modified and reissued the flyer. We got the permit.

CHAPTER 60

Support for Walt from Italy–November 30, 2009

*Human rights, the values of our "civilization" (not to
say: Christian) dry out with each and every person
desperately searching for water in the desert--or
drown with all these tiny little boats disappearing
somewhere in the ocean, at the "blue border."*

— ELIAS BIERDEL

WALT SENT AN EMAIL TO the No More Deaths "core group" enclosing
an email he received from Elias Bierdel, a man who was first mate
on the ship *Cap Anamur*. He was arrested in 2004 by the Italians after
trying to take a group of refugees to safe harbor in Sicily. We'd been
following his case and had sent numerous postcards to the judge in
Italy in support.

Walt says:

> He (Elias Bierdel) was finally acquitted at the end of this
> summer—remember those postcards Jim Walsh had us all
> sign? Subsequently, some Tunisian fishermen were just given
> 30-month sentences by the same judge and court in Italy
> after they rescued a group of drowning refugees and took

them to an Italian port. Anyway, I found his letter to be very inspiring personally. But I think his sentiments should be shared with everyone who is participating in our efforts as a reminder of the global nature of borders and migration, and the realities that we face when we stand up for human rights.

Elias email—November 30, 2009:

Dear Walt,

Although we never met personally yet (I hope we will one day!), I follow your "case" as closely as possible. What to say? It has become the common practice in our rich countries to fight migration by use of force; the authorities systematically crack down not only on migrants/refugees, but also on people who speak out loud—and act—against these atrocities. Those who decide not to just accept this inhuman policy risk find themselves in court and jail. Others, who could easily help to save lives, but don't, will never be held responsible.

In the summer of 2004, we (the wonderful master Stefan Schmidt and myself) decided to take a stand against all this with our humanitarian vessel, *Cap Anamur*, in the Mediterranean. We managed to rescue 37 African refugees from a sinking rubber dinghy and brought them to what we mistook as a safe port in Italy. We immediately got arrested for alleged "trafficking of humans." Those rescued were deported, and the ship seized. A complete disaster, as it looked at first sight.

Friends and I were asked to join a group exclusively focusing on that matter—so we became co-founders of "Borderline Europe" in 2007. Ever since, we do our utmost to inform the public about the dramatic facts—just another inconvenient truth!—holding speeches everywhere, taking part in panel discussions, giving interviews, etc. It seems that common people understand more and more that they should not just let run the border patrols and various police (both military and paramilitary units) to solve these problems, as such use of violence affects deeply the heart and soul of society as a whole.

It took more than five years until the court in Sicily found that we were "not guilty," even after the prosecutor had pledged for four years in prison and an additional fine of 400,000 pounds each. It may well be that he decides to appeal, however, through all this time, Stefan and I were absolutely decisive about not accepting even the "lightest" punishment. So, I totally understand your point of view concerning the refusal to do community service.

We found strong supporters inside the Christian churches, but, as always, it depends on certain members to bring things forward—such as Fanny Delthloff, the amazing *fluchtlings-pastorin* in Hamburg. Fanny started a card-writing campaign in our case. It became a big success as thousands of people all around Europe, and even from abroad, expressed their concerns and anger.

Walt, you're acting perfectly the right way. I send you a shipload full of energy and good thoughts! And, in the words of Benjamin Robat (one of the rescued persons onboard of *Cap Anamur*), "Everything is with God."

With love from Austria, Elias Bierdel

CHAPTER 61

Walt Staton Sentencing and Subsequent Strategy

ON AUGUST 11, 2009, WALT Staton, a volunteer with the humanitarian group No More Deaths, was sentenced in federal court to 300 hours of community service and one-year unsupervised probation for leaving one-gallon jugs of clean drinking water along known migrant trails in the Buenos Aires National Wildlife Refuge (BANWR), several miles north of the U.S./Mexico border. He was the second humanitarian convicted on "littering" charges for providing water to migrants in need. He wrote to Judge Jennifer Guerin to inform the court he will not be completing the sentence of 300 hours of community service. In his letter to the judge, he states his belief that the United States is in violation of international human rights law. "The simple truth is that U.S. border enforcement strategy intentionally leads to the suffering and death of migrants—a clear violation of human rights..."

On July 9, 2009, 13 additional humanitarians from a coalition of organizations were cited by U.S. Fish and Wildlife officers for the same act. These groups had attempted for weeks, without success, to arrange a meeting with BANWR officials to develop a cooperative way of addressing the human rights crisis on federal lands. For years, representatives of BANWR have refused to grant permission for any humanitarian efforts on the Refuge. On July 10th, the day after the 13 citations, No More Deaths received an invitation to meet with Secretary of the Interior Ken Salazar in Washington, D.C.

Since meeting with the secretary, No More Deaths and Samaritans have held a series of meetings with BANWR's Land Manager, Mike Hawkes, and Chris Pease, the Regional Director for U.S. Fish and Wildlife.

Talking Points:

The ruling and punishment against Walt Staton are unjust and illegitimate. Humanitarian aid is not a crime, allowing people to die is. Providing lifesaving water is not littering.

The deteriorating situation on the border constitutes a human rights emergency. 2009 was one of the deadliest years on record along the U.S./Mexico border. More than 212 men, women and children perished in Southern Arizona during this fiscal year (2008-2009).

The militarization of the border is directly responsible for these deaths. America's immigration system is broken, and death is an inevitable outcome of an enforcement-only approach that drives unauthorized migrants into more remote and treacherous desert terrain. More than 5,000 people have perished trying to cross the border since the United States began pursuing its "strategy of deterrence" in the mid-1990s. In response, both the United Nations Special Rapporteur on Human Rights and the Organization of American States have ruled that the United States has failed to uphold its obligations to protect the human rights of migrants. The era of immigration enforcement that uses death as a deterrent must come to an end.

Humanitarian aid is never a crime; the U.S. Government is actively violating the law. While it is cynical to declare that one-gallon jugs of clean drinking water constitute "litter," the impact of litter on the environmental integrity of America's borderlands is marginal compared to the environmental damage caused by the border wall and related enforcement infrastructure.

Federal officials and land managers need to support humanitarian efforts to prevent needless death and suffering on our public lands. Many who die along the border succumb to heat-related illness and dehydration. Clean drinking water is one of the most effective means of preventing this death. The ticketing and prosecution of humanitarians for providing water to migrants is a grossly negligent misapplication of federal priorities.

Policy reform is urgent. The most effective way of addressing the crisis on the border is comprehensive immigration reform that provides for safe, legal, orderly, and humane ways for workers and their families to enter, live and work in the United States; respects the human and civil rights of those living in border communities and those in immigration custody, including short-term detention; and restores the rule of law to the borderlands by protecting human rights and repealing Section 102 of the Real ID act.[103]

WALT'S UPCOMING COURT HEARING–DECEMBER 3, 2009

Thanksgiving lay ahead, and along with Walt, many others were obsessing over the upcoming court date that would address Walt's refusal to collect trash. He was expected to have completed 75 hours by November 11th. Walt wrote to the core group to tell them that the court would be holding a hearing for him on December 4th at 3:00

---

103 No More Deaths internal document, truncated, December 2, 2009.

p.m. in the "...federal court we've all gotten to know and love." He reported that Bill Walker (the No More Deaths attorney who had been instrumental in all the "littering" cases) didn't have any clear idea as to what the judge would do to Walt. They both anticipated some amount of jail time—but it was impossible to predict.

Walt pointed out that he saw a strong link between the criminalization of both migrants and humanitarians. Both groups developed due to pressure from the Department of Homeland Security. The cases against Dan, Walt, and The *Basura 13* were all assigned to the very same magistrates that do Operation Streamline. Coincidence? Walt said, "...that those judges are told repeatedly that all of us are criminals." It was quite an experience for him to be arraigned in a room full of shackled migrants (during Streamline) last winter. He wondered if we could renew our pressure on the federal court/ U.S. attorney's office for its continued prosecution of migrants and humanitarians.

Walt wanted our input and wrote the following:

> I've been frustrated through my entire trial at my own reluctance to rally people for my support and for support of the cause in general. We received soooooo many emails before, during, and after my trial with people wanting to know what they could do. Who can they send a letter to? A phone call? Anything? And we never had an answer for them. Perhaps we've been afraid that if we agitate the judges, attorneys, etc., who are part of this, it may further jeopardize our work. That may be so.
>
> At any rate, should NMD decide to engage in something, the energy and support is still there, and we can easily tap into it. NMD just needs a clear vision for our campaign so we can plug people in. I have a bunch of schoolmates here (at seminary) who are wanting to drive out to Tucson for this

upcoming hearing, and I don't know if that's the best use of their resources. Maybe it is....

OK—that's enough from me. Enjoy whatever celebrations you may have this week. I'll be cooking an organic, free-range turkey via the Cajun-injection method. Mmmmmmm
    Peace, Walt

No More Deaths carved out an Action Working Group, and they spent two days refining an announcement to the No More Deaths constituency along with writing a letter to be sent to Interior Secretary Salazar and U.S. Attorney Burke.

The letter to the core group:

Dear Friends:

On Friday, December 4th, a federal judge may sentence a No More Deaths volunteer to jail time. We knew that the criminalization of migrants who risk their lives for the sake of their families was at an extreme when even civilian efforts to prevent deaths in the desert began to be criminalized. Now we have reached a new extreme, but you can make a difference.

The resentencing hearing next Friday comes as a result of Walt Staton's refusal to serve the sentence originally imposed on him when he was found guilty on August 11th of "knowingly littering" in the Buenos Aires National Wildlife Refuge (BANWR). The sentence was 300 hours of community service—trash removal on national public lands. Walt has written a letter to the judge saying that he cannot, as a person of faith and conscience, comply with such a punishment, which would legitimize his conviction: "I will not complete any amount of community service, nor pay any kind of fines."

Amnesty International has already said that if Walt is jailed, they will consider him a "prisoner of conscience."

Here are at least three things you can do right now to defend the work of No More Deaths and the legal space in which we work. There is a fourth: forward this message to everyone you know and ask them to do the same.

1. Write to Ken Salazar, Secretary of the Interior and Dennis Burke, U.S. Attorney for Arizona.
2. Write a letter to the editor of your local paper, or our local paper, or any paper you like, to raise awareness of the absurdity taking place. You can use our talking points as a guide.
3. Plan to attend these events in Tucson next week:
   * Press conference, December 2nd
   * Walt's resentencing at the federal courthouse is at 3:00 p.m. December 4th.

Thank you for your solidarity in this critical time, and for your continued work and support on behalf of human rights in the borderlands.[104]

WALT'S COURT HEARING–DECEMBER 4, 2009 AT 3:00 P.M.

john heid notified us that he had received approval from the city for us to gather in the front plaza of DeConcini U.S. Courthouse from noon to 5:00 p.m. on Friday, December 4th (the day of Walt's hearing). john had described our event as "a small circle of supporters (30-50) for the resentencing of Walt Staton, with speaking, singing, silence." The approval included a few modest conditions like no bullhorns or loudspeakers.

We began gathering about 12:30 p.m. with Maryada Vallet serving as the mistress of ceremonies. Musician Ted Warmbrand led us

---

104 Steve Johnson email.

in singing several songs including: "Who's the Criminal Here," which is one of his own compositions. This was followed with meaningful speeches by: Isabel Garcia, Pima County Legal Defender and a representative from *Derechos Humanos*; Alison Harrington, pastor of Southside Presbyterian Church; Margo Cowan, Pima County Public Defender; and Sarah Roberts, RN and volunteer for both No More Deaths and Samaritans. Then we watched an Aztec dance being performed in the plaza by Maria and David Aparicio and their young son, Ollin. At 1:30 p.m., a silent vigil was held to bring our focus of attention to Operation Streamline victims.

At 2:00 p.m., Jim Marx (a volunteer for No More Deaths), took over as MC and introduced The Rev. Diane Dowgiert, the pastor of the Unitarian Universalist Church of Tucson—Walt's church. She spoke of Walt's activities in the church as well as his extensive advocacy experience. Additional speakers included Dan Millis, Borderlands Campaign Organizer for the Sierra Club, and Alessandra Soler-Meetze, Executive Director of the Arizona ACLU. Additional singing was led by Pablo Peregrina and Pat Morrison. The closing was done by Seth Pauley who was from the Episcopal Border Ministry in Bisbee.

Those of us who wanted to go into the courtroom left to do so. Others stayed in the plaza to continue the vigil and maintain a supportive presence.

Attorney Bill Walker addressed the court by stating that Walt's circumstances had changed. He was now in seminary and found it difficult to identify appropriate sites for cleanup. Bill appealed to the judge that it was obvious that Walt complies in an unusual way by the nature of what he does in society. "This is not a necessary condition." He said that Walt feels strongly about the work of No More Deaths, of doing it in contact with others. "Humanitarians do what they do—and must do so without fear of prosecution." He invited the judge as a "citizen of the planet" to see that Walt had good intentions.

The judge told Walt that what he'd been found guilty of was littering by the jury. She quoted the flyer that had been prepared for the event the following day by saying that if he went to jail, he would be a "prisoner of conscience" as declared by Amnesty International.

In the end, the judge said she could not accept Walt's noncompliance and stated that if he defies the court order, he must complete the 300 hours of community service or spend twice that amount of time in federal prison (25 days). She stated she would hear Walt's response on Monday, December 21st at 9 a.m.

On that date, Walt re-agreed to his community service. During the same time his attorney, Bill Walker, was giving oral arguments in Dan Millis' appeal to the Ninth Circuit Court of Appeals, so Walt's community service paused until that ruling could come down—probably during the following year.

After the court hearing, folks were invited to go to Mariposa House or to the Rose of the Desert Catholic Worker House. Gene and I stopped by *El Minuto* Restaurant and bought a few cheese crisps that we took with us to Mariposa House to share.

Later, Gene drove to BANWR and got a permit for the Saturday memorial event on BANWR.

CHAPTER 62

Memorial Shrine on BANWR–December 5, 2009

Shrine at Chavez Crossing (No More Deaths)

ON DECEMBER 5TH, A GROUP of us caravanned to Arivaca and proceeded to the appointed spot which, as it turned out, had also been a stop for the historical Butterfield Express. Directly below the site lay one of the empty "water tanks"—a 30x40-foot-wide depression in the earth totally devoid of water. We were met by Officer Dennis from the Department of Fish and Wildlife. He helped some of us climb through the fence. Gene showed him our permit which, of course, he already knew we had obtained. People brought rocks and piled them up for the shrine. A banner of Our Lady of Guadalupe hung as a backdrop to the proceedings. A number of water jugs defined the speaker's area. Messages written on the bottles said such things as *Valle con Dios* (Go with God). We stood in a semicircle as The Rev. Alison Harrington from Southside Presbyterian Church and a few others spoke words to memorialize the 206 migrants who had perished in the Arizona desert during the previous year.

When we finished, we gathered up our scattered the items, mostly rocks, from the shrine and collected the jugs. We made certain the area looked pristine. Together we drove down the road to a location off BANWR land, took jugs of water from the backs of our vehicles, and walked to the entrance to a trail up a hill. Officer Dennis and other Wildlife personnel followed us to the entrance. On our return from the hike, we picked up several bags of trash and dropped them into the back of Gene's truck. Six of us squeezed into the vehicle, throwing extra things into the back as we added to our number from earlier.

On the way home, we stopped at a lunch wagon owned by Virginia (*Ver-heen-ia*), but a crowd had gathered there, so we went down the road to a pizza place. While we waited for our lunch in a nearby, screened-in building, Gene took the trash to the dump. When he returned, Noel Andersen ran to the truck and then came back quickly, saying, "Where's my backpack?" We soon realized that his backpack, having been tossed into the rear of Gene's truck, had been thrown into the trash receptacles along with all the trash we'd picked up along the trail.

As soon as we finished eating, we drove back to the Arivaca town dump, Noel chomping at the bit the whole way. The dump consisted of about 25 oversized trash receptacles lined up in a row with a large van parked off to the right. Gene went straight to the green container where he'd dumped our stuff. It was empty! The collection truck had been there during the time we had eaten our lunch and returned to the site. We all stood around dismayed—not believing what we were seeing and wondering what we could do next.

Shortly, a person emerged from behind the receptacle to our far left. Dressed like the street person she was, with baggy pants and sweater and gloves with the fingers removed and a knitted hat, she slowly approached us pushing a small, wire belongings cart. As she drew near, she called, "Are you looking for something?"

Gene and Noel explained about the backpack and described it to her. At first, she said, "They came and picked up everything." Then, she headed toward the van and motioned for us to follow. Inside, we could see it was stuffed with items that she must have fished out from the trash containers. She located the backpack, and piece by piece, came forward with its contents. She had stashed each item in a different location in her van—a sorting of sorts, we thought.

Noel practically swooned with relief. Someone gave the woman ten dollars, and we went on our way. We learned later that she was a well-known Arivaca town character.

The following evening at the No More Deaths meeting, we were told that upon examination of the trail we'd hiked that day, all the jugs had been slashed or removed.

CHAPTER 63

BANWR Coalition Formed

A COALITION OF REPRESENTATIVES FROM Humane Borders, Samaritans and No More Deaths was formed to address BANWR issues since all three humanitarian organizations were involved in putting out water for migrants. The named representatives included: Jeff Milsap (S), Bob Kee (S), Lois Martin (HB, NMD), Steve Johnston (NMD) Leslie Carlson (S), Gene Lefebvre (NMD), John Fife, (S, NMD), Dr. Norma Price, M.D. (S, NMD), Michael Hyatt (S), Maureen Marx (NMD), Sarah Roberts (S, NMD), Felipe Lundine, (HB), Executive Director Sophia Gomez (HB). At the August 23rd meeting, guests included Jim Marx (NMD), Jean Boucher, the current NMD volunteer coordinator, and me—Sue Lefebvre.

At our first meeting, we agreed that our goal was to provide a united front on behalf of the humanitarians to BANWR. As we talked about what this meant and what the current issues before us were, it became clear that Humane Borders was in a better position with BANWR than No More Deaths or Samaritans. They were currently negotiating for three more water tanks, in addition to the three already in place. With their presence at the meeting, we hoped they would be able to support No More Deaths and Samaritans with the effort to place water bottles in areas higher up on the mountain slopes. The Humane Border water tanks could serve in the flat areas where they were accessible by water trucks, while the one-gallon jugs could be hiked into the foothills, canyons, and more mountainous areas.

In years past, there had been some friction between the leadership of Humane Borders and that of No More Deaths. Humane Borders now had a new executive director, Sophia Gomez, so at this meeting, No More Deaths took the opportunity to publicly state that No More Deaths held no ill will against Humane Borders and looked forward to working with them on this and other projects. We hoped that this cleared the air.

THE MEMORANDUM OF UNDERSTANDING—DECEMBER 7, 2009

Margo sent this letter to BANWR via certified mail on November 12, 2009:

Dear Mr. Hawkes:

Please be informed that the No More Deaths/Samaritan negotiating group has met and reviewed your comments contained in your letter of November 11, 2009.

We take issue with several conclusions you draw in your letter. First, we do not view the purpose of the meetings with you and other representatives of the Department of the Interior as limited to "determine the parameters that would be acceptable to the Refuge for NMD to obtain a permit." Secondly, we did not agree to any particular water-container size.

We find your argument on the issue of litter to be disingenuous. We offered to remove no less than twice the aggregate amount of food and water left on public lands through an organized trash removal plan we would coordinate; all we requested from the Interior was that a receptacle be placed at a designated location and trash bags be provided. You and other Interior representatives rejected our offer outright. It is, therefore, a flawed position for you to base your position with regard to our proposal as unacceptable on litter when you refused our offer of trash removal. We are left with the obvious conclusion that the issue of litter is a thinly-veiled excuse to keep lifesaving water from those who need it.

I have enclosed for your consideration and review the Memorandum of Understanding we proposed at our first meeting on August 20th. We submit this Memorandum in lieu of any revised application for a Special Use Permit and we expect a formal response as was promised at the August 20th meeting. As you know, it has always been our position that it is not appropriate to apply for a "permit" to intervene in an emergency situation. I urge that you agree to work together with the humanitarian community to save lives and care for our environment.

As always, your kind assistance in this matter is most appreciated.

Sincerely, Mary Margaret Cowan

MEETING WITH REPRESENTATIVE GRIJALVA–DECEMBER 12, 2009

Gene Lefebvre:

One of our lawyers, Andy Silverman, received a call from Ruben Reyes, an aide to our Congressional Representative, Raul Grijalva. He and Grijalva had met with U.S. Fish and Wildlife officials in Washington, D.C. Now they wanted to meet with No More Deaths to hear our side of the story. The team we assembled to meet with them included Andy Silverman, Margo Cowan, Lois Martin, John Fife, and me. We five representatives met beforehand and developed a presentation for the meeting which was to be held on Saturday, December 12th, at Grijalva's office in south Tucson.

Most everyone was on a first name basis since Raul knew Margo, Andy, and John very well from years past. There was light-hearted conversation for five minutes or so, then the meeting began in earnest. I said we had reached a critical stage with our humanitarian work on the border, and we were here to tell them why this was a crisis. Grijalva interrupted. He said he had met with Fish and Wildlife about our issue with BANWR, and he had some questions about our negotiations with them. I asked Margo to spell out how those negotiations had gone.

Margo quickly sketched out the history and gist of our negotiations. The main point she made was that we wanted to go back to the beginning. During the first meeting, we had produced a Memorandum of Understanding (MOU). The Fish and Wildlife people said they would take it up the chain of command and get back to us. But, at the second meeting they reported that they would not consider the MOU. Instead we would have to go through their normal permit process. It was our position that the deaths of thousands of migrants constituted an emergency. An emergency requires special handling and an MOU would expedite the process. But Fish and Wildlife refused to budge, especially Mike Hawkes, the Land Manager of BANWR, who, we were told, had the authority to deal with this matter. That meeting had almost ended at that point, but Margo said we brought them back to the negotiating table, and that we agreed to try to work within the bounds of a permit. At the third meeting, we made some progress. Then, Mike Hawkes informed us by mail that no more face-to-face meetings were required—we just needed to file a permit request.

Since that time several things have happened: First, we came to the realization that trash was not the issue for the BANWR people, but a disguise for the real issue, which (presumably) is that they do not want migrants coming across their land, and they do not want us helping those who do. Second, Mike and his people would use regulations, including his interpretation of a public hearing, to shut us out. Third, Fish and Wildlife officers had been telling our volunteers that we were not allowed to put water on *any* federal land, which was not accurate. In fact, Border Patrol officers had also been threatening to cite our people for littering, and they had no authority to do so. Fourth, we believe law enforcement officers are the ones who are slashing and confiscating our water jugs on BANWR and in other areas. Fifth, and more to the heart of the matter, Mike Hawkes trivializes the life and death of migrants, as evidenced by a recent *Washington Times* article (which Grijalva acknowledged he had read).

So, Margo concluded by asking Raul to encourage Secretary of the Interior Ken Salazar to tell his people to work with us through the MOU. Raul asked if we were willing to negotiate details of the MOU with Fish and Wildlife. We replied that we absolutely would negotiate.

John then asked Raul to make another request of Salazar, that he issue a "finding" that humanitarian aid is compatible with the mission of the Department of the Interior. Raul agreed to do that.

He told us the basic problem for the Obama administration is that there were far too many holdovers from the previous Bush administration. These holdovers have a much different agenda from Obama, and the new administration needed to replace them. Raul thought that Salazar could help with this changeover by issuing the directions we requested (the finding and the MOU).

We left the meeting with the sense that Raul Grijalva would approach Ken Salazar soon with these two requests.

CHAPTER 64

A Smoking Gun–December 2009

AFTER THE MEETING WITH RAUL, Margo *strongly* urged that we get photos of federal officials slashing or dumping or removing our water. So, Daniel, Kevin, and some others purchased some outdoor motion-activated cameras (trail cams) that Gene found at Sportsman's Warehouse and prepared their plans for the placement and monitoring of the cameras. Daniel bought another one somewhere else, and they put them all out in strategic locations.

Kevin Riley sent an email to the Desert Aid Working Group (DAWG) on Saturday the 19th about the current status of traffic along the trails:

> It's true that migrant traffic has slowed since summer. But there still is traffic. Numerous people in and around Arivaca have said there is always a slowdown right before Christmas, and a significant upsurge right after New Year's—a "deluge" as one resident said.
>
> There are still folks out there, and just because there are fewer, does not mean they are any less important or in need of less attention than when there are many. It only takes one large group to pass through and exhaust an entire water drop. What's the feeling you get when you arrive at a drop to find nothing there, not knowing how many people have passed through without water? A drop off near Ruby Road is a perfect example. There were 61 gallons there three weeks

ago. We began a process of removing some bottles because none had moved in two or three weeks. The following week, 41 gallons and all the food and Gatorade had been taken.

In addition, (though we are the group that's in the least amount of danger), yes, it is dangerous. But we've always known that, and it is not a reason to reduce the already minimal presence we have out there at this time of year. I'd argue, with fewer people passing we should increase our presence. People are freezing at night, and because the desert is abnormally dry, if they do not come across our water drops, they are finding no water anywhere. Also, if lost, left, or both, folks stand much less a chance of finding another group, or anyone to help them out.

**Agent Kermis Pouring out Water for Migrants
(from video) 2009, (No More Deaths)**

Slashings are nothing new either. More slashings shouldn't mean that we put out less water, but that we become more inventive in our water placements and adapt to the situation. When things become difficult, it makes no sense to ease up. It makes sense to work harder and figure it out. The route adoption system ensures there is no overlap in water drop placement and allows for the route "bottom-liners" to decide how often and how much water to place. I doubt too that there is any trail-walking overlap, given the limited amount of hiking that's taking place. Kevin

CHAPTER 65

Walt's Dilemma—Hearing December 21, 2009

ON THE TUESDAY BEFORE HIS December 21st hearing for probation violation, Walt saw two tracks: Track A would send him to jail for the 25 days; track B would give him no jail time but meant that he would have to complete his 300 hours. Over a period of a few days, he talked with his attorney, Bill Walker, Margo Cowan, John Fife, Maryada, as well as some student friends and teachers at Claremont.

By 4:00 p.m. on Monday, December 14th, he was on a conference call with Gene and John Fife. His plan was *not* to go to jail. He felt the issue was becoming more about him and less about No More Deaths. He wanted a lower profile. Gene and John supported his decision and talked about everyone going out to do community service along with him.

Gene wrote to Gabe: "As of yesterday afternoon, Walt has decided to take community service after all. I asked him to email our core group today with his reasoning. We have had too much of hearing his thinking either second or thirdhand. For me, the key thing he said over the phone was, 'Don't make this about me.' I think we ought to forge ahead with whatever we decide NMD needs to do. I heard you were writing an op-ed, and I wanted you to know the latest developments. At least, I think this is the latest development."

At 6:00 p.m. on Monday evening, the 14th, during a No More Deaths pre-meeting, both Sarah Launius and Vanessa said Walt *wanted* to go to jail, and that he felt doing so would revitalize the group. Vanessa seemed so positive about this that Gene and John didn't bring up that just two hours prior, Walt told them that he *didn't* want to go to jail.

By Monday morning (the day he was to appear in court), he had decided to tell the judge he would do the 300 hours. He did not want to go to jail. Margo and others had pointed out that it could have life-long implications, and they convinced him that it wasn't worth going to jail to make a point.

Walt's court appearance was uneventful. After he explained his position, Judge Jennifer Guerin restated his sentence of 300 hours of trash pickup. However, she said she would work with him and his schedule to maybe let him have a longer period than a year (from that date) to accomplish the task.

When I spoke with Walt after the first of the year, he said he had been miserable and felt let down since the latest court appearance. He and Maryada had spent a few days, including Christmas, with her parents (who had been very supportive through it all), and he could hardly engage in meaningful discussions with them. Later, when they visited his folks in Prescott Valley, it was even worse. His parents had also been very positive through all the trauma, but he just couldn't get over how "down" he felt. He closed in on himself and had no energy for anyone. Then they returned home to Mariposa House[105] where he rested and began to feel like himself again. He said he could finally smile. The several residents of Mariposa House were very understanding and supportive. Soon, he headed back to seminary and would be looking again for a non-profit organization with whom he could work by picking up trash in his "spare" time.

---

105 Mariposa House was constructed during the heyday of the railroad-building era as a place for railroad workers to live in Tucson. It has about six rooms on each side of a wide hall and a large screened porch to the rear. One side also houses a kitchen and the other a gathering room. The current residents named it "Mariposa" (butterfly) House. They developed a close community by sharing meals, meeting together, and publishing a newspaper. Later, the community moved to a different location in Tucson, but maintained their ideals.

CHAPTER 66

2009–Summary of Migrant Deaths

UNDER THE TITLE: "NO SIGNS of Letup in Entrant Deaths," Brady McCombs wrote in the *Arizona Daily Star* that during the final fiscal year 2010 (October 1-September 30) tally of border deaths confirms a lethal trend: illegal border crossers face a deadlier trek than ever across Arizona's desert. The 241,673 apprehensions made in Border Patrol's Tucson Sector in 2009-2010 marked a 10-year low, Border Patrol figures show. These figures, along with the declining remittances (monies sent back to the country of origin from those working in the U.S.) from the U.S. to Mexico and anecdotal reports that the economic recession had slowed illegal immigration, pointed to a dramatic slowdown in illegal border crossings. The chart below runs from federal FY1994 through FY2018, with latest data incomplete at this writing. You'll notice that as the number of Border Patrol apprehensions decreases, generally speaking, the number of remains found per 10,000 apprehensions goes up. The highest number of Arizona apprehensions took place in 2000-2001 (616,347), while the number of remains found was only 1.2 per 10,000 apprehensions. In the period of 2016-2017, 38,657 remains were found, while 39.0 remains were found per 10,000 apprehensions. Even though the number of crossers is down, crossing the border is still a deadly activity.

RECOVERED HUMAN REMAINS IN THE ARIZONA DESERT

Data for "BP Arizona Apprehensions" comes from Border Patrol. Data for "RHR in Arizona" comes from the Pima County Forensic Science Center. It represents Pima and Santa Cruz Counties primarily but may contain data from Pinal, Gila and Graham counties from time to time. As of May 2012, Pima County is under contract to process RHR for Pinal and Cochise Counties. The RHR data is from the area primarily patrolled by the Tucson, Green Valley and Ajo Samaritans, as well as No More Deaths. The data represents much but not all the Tucson Sector.[106] **This chart includes the number of RHRs per 10,000 for each year the information is available.**

Federal Year	BP Arizona[107] Apprehensions	Number of RHR in Arizona[108]	RHR per 10,000 Apprehensions
1994-1995	139,473		
1995-1996	227,529		
1996-1997	305,348		
1997-1998	272,397		
1998-1999	387,406	11	0.3
1999-2000	470,449	29	0.6
2000-2001	616,346	74	1.2
2001-2002	445,675	80	1.7
2002-2003	333,648	134	4.0
2003-2004	347,263	137	4.0
2004-2005	491,771	142	2.9
2005-2006	539,079	219	4.1
2006-2007	392,074	169	4.3
2007-2008	378,239	202	5.3

---

106 Edgar McCullough, Professor Emeritis, University of Arizona, modified by author. He compiles this data for Southern Arizona humanitarians.

107 www.cpb.gov/newsroom/stats/ofo-sw-border-inadmissables-fy (x)

108 Op.Cit. McCullough

2008-2009	317,696	171	5.4
2009-2010	241,673	212	8.8
2010-2011	212,202	251	11.9
2011-2012	123,285	177	14.3
2012-2013	120,000	194	16.2
2013-2014	120,939	121	10.0
2014-2015	87,915	133	15.3
2015-2016	63,397	145	23.0
2016-2017	38,657	151	39.0
2017-2018	NA[109]	123	NA
2018-2019	NA	NA	NA

---

109 Border Patrol data not available at publication date.

CHAPTER 67

Dan Millis' Appeal

EMAIL RE: NINTH CIRCUIT COURT OF APPEALS SELECTS MILLIS' CASE–JANUARY 20, 2010

Hi Dan,

The Ninth Circuit Court of Appeal has selected your case, together with two others, for oral argument to be held at the Thomas & Mack Auditorium at the William S. Bond School of Law in Las Vegas, Nevada, on March 2, 2010 at 10:00 a.m.

The court is allowing each side (the government and Bill) only ten minutes for oral argument. Your attendance is not necessary. Most appellants do not attend the oral arguments, but you are welcome to do so.

If you DO wish to go, I need to know by the end of this week as the Court requires that the attorneys give them notice of how many people are coming (i.e., attorneys and clients).

I know this is short notice, but that's how the Appellate Courts operate. Let me know if you have any questions. Again, I need to know by the end of the week if you want to attend.

Thanks, Dan

Sharon (Bill Walker's assistant)

OMG! What should I do? Should I go!?! Anyone want to come? Dan

WORD FROM MICHAEL HAWKES, BANWR LAND MANAGER—JANUARY 20, 2010

The same day Dan received notification of his pending appeal, BANWR wrote to Margo, Ed McCullough and Gene to press for a meeting date within the next couple of weeks, considering that the "summer season is fast approaching."

CHAPTER 68

Mike Hawkes Replaced; Special Use Permit Signed

AT THE TURN OF THE new year, 2010, No More Deaths and Samaritans were still hopeful that an agreement could be worked out with BANWR. However, during January, Mike Hawkes spoke disparagingly and intemperately about the humanitarian work to the *Arizona Daily Star* newspaper upsetting officials all the way to Washington, D.C. and back. As a result, we could look forward to a very confusing year.

On February 10, 2010, No More Deaths, via Margo Cowan, received a letter from Fish and Wildlife's Regional Director, Benjamin Tuggle, expressing his commitment to finding a solution to serve both parties. He noted that we (BANWR and the humanitarians) would be meeting February 18, 2010, for a negotiation session facilitated by an affiliate of the Udall Foundation's U.S. Institute for Environmental Conflict Resolution. Tuggle continued:

> In anticipation of that meeting, I wish to take his opportunity to assure you that I and my staff at the regional headquarters for the Southwest Region are fully engaged in this issue. Moreover, we are fully committed to resolve this issue cooperatively and within the latitude allowed by the laws governing management of national wildlife refuge lands. We are encouraged by the progress that has been made thus far and are hopeful that the cooperation that has been forged will continue to grow.

To that end, I have asked Chris Pease, Regional Chief of the National Wildlife Refuge System, to represent the service during future negotiations with No More Death.

Thus, Mike Hawkes was relieved of his negotiating responsibility. We heard that one of his sins had been to print signs saying, "Humanitarian Aid is *Always* a Crime." In June, he retired.

SPECIAL USE PERMIT SIGNED

In the meantime, No More Deaths and Samaritans received a draft Special Use Permit from BANWR with a start date of March 10, 2010. Gene thought it would be good to frame the group discussion around No More Death's mission (to save lives and relieve suffering) and Civil Initiative, especially regarding the role of the community. After talking with Margo, they decided that she and Gene and Ed should meet Saturday to discuss strategy for the Monday meeting. Gene and (hopefully), john heid, would drive back from camp—it was the first week of spring break and both Gene and john were camp coordinators—Monday afternoon to be on hand for the meeting. john indicated that he wasn't indispensable, but Gene wanted him to be there. Margo planned to be her strongest self.

We took copies of the Mission Statement and Civil Initiative to help support the agreement

Some members of No More Deaths did not want to sign the permit because it limited access to the Refuge. The following evening, the Samaritans agreed to sign it. Eventually No More Deaths did as well, offering BANWR some new stipulations. It did allow for the use of one-gallon, as well as five-gallon containers.[110] The Special Use Permit says:

---

110 Note: Humane Borders was negotiating a separate agreement with BANWR for additional sites for 55-gallon tanks.

No More Deaths (NMD) will establish stationary drinking water stations on Buenos Aires NWR for use by migrants traveling on the Refuge. Up to 30 humane watering location sites will be pre-approved by the Refuge Manager. The Permittee will provide water stations at no more than eight of these pre-approved sites at any one time. Water station locations may be subject to change by the Permittee on an as-needed basis in consultation with the Refuge Manager. Stations will be located within 100 meters of existing public use roads, unless otherwise approved by the Refuge Manager. <u>Each water station will consist of a minimum of a single-use gallon container or larger</u> (emphasis added, ed), tethered to the site so as to be non-removable by person or persons on foot. NMD will monitor all water stations on a weekly basis and remove all related trash and other accumulated debris at each site resulting from their activity. Green Valley Samaritans and Tucson Samaritans may also assist NMD with activities under this permit.

Attached were ten provisions, some of which further clarified those in the description above.

CHAPTER 69

More Tension–February 2010

THIS AND OTHER SIMILAR CONFRONTATIONS between law enforcement and No More Deaths could be very intimidating to our volunteers. Nevertheless, there was no hint that anyone wanted to stop their efforts to place water on BANWR. On their way back to Tucson, driving in their car, they debriefed their experience. Sometimes, as in this case, they wrote about their experiences. This would serve as john's formal account should he be asked to testify in court. Border Patrol would have quite a large dossier if they kept all their reports and photos together.

john heid:

> Affidavit re: February 24, 2010—Buenos Aires National Wildlife Refuge
>
> Around noon on Wednesday, February 24, 2010, No More Deaths volunteers, john heid, Lois Martin, and Jessica Tracy, accompanied by a friend of No More Deaths and artist from Northern Mexico, Raechel Running, arrived at the Buenos Aires National Wildlife Refuge. We observed two BANWR vehicles, including a canine unit, at the Wilbur Canyon entrance on Arivaca Road.
>
> The four of us proceeded into the Refuge and stopped a mile or so in for a comfort break. The two BANWR vehicles

stopped where we were parked. BANWR Fish and Wildlife Officers (FWO) James Casey and Brian Elliott, along with a U.S. Forest Service officer, Chad (dk last name), from Nogales, Arizona, approached us and advised that there have been reports of mountain lion incidents on the Refuge including visitors being stalked. They warned us to be careful and added they were going up Wilbur Canyon with their "police dog" to follow up on these cat reports. They proceeded up the trail.

We next encountered their vehicles parked near a migrant trail proximate to Rock Tank. No one was present. We drove on to the edge of BANWR property to investigate the use of trails that we had previously served. At these off-Refuge sites, we noted minimal trail use, so we left only seven gallons of water and equivalent food in light of the forecast weekend winter storm. Upon our return to the Rock Tank vicinity, we observed Casey, Elliott and Chad entering the 4-wheel drive road on foot, carrying long strings of empty, crushed new water bottles. Rachael, a photographer, asked Casey if she could photograph the FWOs carrying these bottles. He replied: "I'd prefer you not." She did not photograph this incident. The officers entered their vehicles and departed the vicinity.

We volunteers and Raechel decided to investigate trails on the opposite side of the road from where the officers came. We observed evidence of moderate migrant travel and agreed to put out four gallons of water, socks and canned food. We four then agreed to investigate the trail where we'd seen the agents emerge to determine the extent and nature of their activities. On the main trail, all the gallons of water we knew to be there previously were gone and many sites gave evidence of fresh water spills. We found only one food can, which had been punctured.

On a side trail we found two unused gallons of water. It was at this point that Raechel and I were encountered by two Border Patrol agents. I did not get their names. They asked our citizenship and where we were parked. They said they'd walked in from Arivaca Road looking for people based on a report from BANWR officials.

No More Deaths volunteers Jessica and Lois were also encountered by these two Border Patrol agents. After the agents left the vicinity, we placed our remaining four gallons of water, socks, and food at this trail intersection rest area. When we returned to our vehicle, we discovered these same agents looking in the Jeep windows. No substantive conversation here. They walked up the wash.

The four of us drove off BANWR. We took a break at camp site 66 to repack the vehicle. At this point, Agent Michael St. John drove by and then stopped. I was in the driver's seat. St. John asked me to come out of the vehicle. I complied. He asked if we were putting water gallons out and demanded my ID. I identified myself as a U.S. citizen, declined to answer his question and replied that I was not required to produce ID, under my lawyer's advice. This led to a protracted back and forth: "I want to see your ID" and "I am not required to produce it." St. John then demanded the vehicle keys. I refused to turn them over and passed them into the vehicle to Lois who did relinquish the keys on St. John's demand. He placed the keys on the hood of our vehicle. He entered our vehicle on the vacant driver's side and took photographs of the contents of the back seat. I repeatedly asked if I was under arrest to which St. John replied:" You are being detained."

The stalemate between St. John and me was defused by Raechel who began a line of calming conversation. The tension was substantially reduced. Raechel agreed to produce her ID upon request. Martin and Tracy declined a similar request.

St. John said BANWR officials had been called and would be arriving directly. Approximately 40 minutes later, FWOs Casey, Elliot, and Chad arrived. Lois, Jessica, and I produced our IDs upon Casey's request. We also provided our current phone numbers on request. Elliot read the Miranda rights to us. All but Raechel chose to accept the rights and thus was not interviewed by Casey. Raechel was questioned privately.

While we were detained another half-hour awaiting the Border Patrol agents who'd encountered us earlier in Wilbur Canyon, I asked Mr. Casey if he had in fact poured out water from the gallon bottles we had seen him carry earlier in the day. He acknowledged that he had.

The four of us were photographed individually and as a group. When the two Border Patrol agents arrived, they identified us as the individuals they had met on the trail. They took photographs of the soles of our shoes. Jim Casey then advised that no citation was being issued at this point. He asked if we would be willing to come to any meetings that might occur relative to this incident. We agreed. We were told we were free to go, and we left the Refuge in near darkness with the silhouette of Baboquiveri (the sacred Tohono O'odham mountain) behind us.

CHAPTER 70

Dan's Court Hearing

March 2, 2010: We received an email from Dan saying he had been sick and unable to travel to Las Vegas for the ten-minute presentation by his attorney, Bill Walker.

Dan said,"...our lawyer says he thought it went pretty well. The three-judge panel asked rough questions of the prosecution and defense in front of a crowded auditorium in the law school in Las Vegas."

Bill said, "There is some hope here."

It may still be possible for you, the reader, to listen to the hearing by going to the Ninth Circuit Court on the Internet. Clearly, some judges thought that a ticket for littering was pretty foolish.

CHAPTER 71

Finally, the "Alternative Approach" Emerges

ONE OF THE PROVISIONS FOR a BANWR Special Use Permit called for a research project. It occurred to some in the joint humanitarian group to consider developing a research project that might meet the current needs. So, despite progress on the Special Use Permit, when the joint humanitarian group met on February 18th, it decided to develop a research project for BANWR to determine the better of two sizes of water containers—one-gallon jugs or five-gallon containers. We, of course, wanted the one-gallon while BANWR was still pushing for the five-gallon. Jim Marx had pointed out that, "The constantly changing migrant trails across BANWR and the Arizona desert over the past decade must have a multipronged approach by humanitarian groups to provide aid in the form of lifesaving water, food and medical assistance. No More Deaths, Samaritans, Humane Borders and BANWR complement each other in our efforts for this complex geographically challenging region. Stationary water sources and large fixed tanks work best in flat country. Smaller, one-gallon jugs work best on trails far off the roadways on trails in rugged, mountainous areas. NO SINGLE APPROACH ALONE IS SUFFICIENT TO PREVENT MIGRANT DEATHS. ALL ARE NECESSARY."

A couple of weeks later, March 3rd, the newly-formed BANWR research group (including the Udall Institute) gathered in Tucson. Margo had previously made this arrangement with the foundation to assist the coalition in designing the research project, with Hawkes' concurrence. When the meeting started, Tom, from Fish and Wildlife in Albuquerque (Mike Hawkes' boss), took the group to task for the incident with John and Lois and the others a couple of weeks ago.

We hadn't been ticketed in eight months. Perhaps there was a moratorium on ticketing until an agreement was in place. Margo didn't bring this up, however; she simply said that once the agreement is in place we will ask everyone to comply with its provisions.

Tom said they had hidden cameras in place and had photos of our folks dropping water that could be used in court, if necessary. Additionally, according to John Heid's affidavit, Fish and Wildlife personnel had taken pictures of the volunteers individually and as a group, including photos of the soles of their shoes. But, we were not intimidated.

Those present that day included Margo, Debbi and Ed McCullough and Gene for No More Deaths; Tom for Fish and Wildlife; Mike and Sally for BANWR; and an observer and a researcher, both from the Udall Institute for Environmental Negotiations.

It was announced that the research study would take place on BANWR over a period of one year, not six months as discussed previously. There would need to be a group of people assembled to oversee the monitoring of the sites—a group that could be fair—made up from No More Deaths, Tucson Sams and Green Valley Sams. People would be selected based on their lack of extreme positions either for or against the agreement, and they wouldn't be the same people who would be servicing the sites and recording data regarding usage, footprints, etc.

Maybe cameras could be placed on two or more sites. Infrared cameras, or even sensors placed in the ground that could measure the foot traffic might work. They were talking about eight sites near the back roads.

Gene brought up the issue of how the Special Use Permit was written—in the name of No More Deaths, with Samaritans permitted to work under it. Gene pointed out there are three groups—No More Deaths, Tucson Samaritans, and Green Valley Samaritans. Mike Hawkes said three permits would be needed then. Tom overruled him and said there could be one permit with the names of all three entities. Each, through its sponsor, would have its own insurance covering the Department of the Interior—No More Death under Unitarian Universalist Church of Tucson, Tucson Samaritans under Southside Presbyterian Church, and Green Valley Samaritans under Sahuarita United Church of Christ.

The research group met regularly throughout the spring.

By summer, the troops were restless. The "troops," of course, were those volunteers who had been putting water on BANWR for years, and whose work had been curtailed since the Department of the Interior and the Fish and Wildlife Service began their engagement with No More Deaths and Samaritans slightly over a year before. As the temperature had been running in the 90s and 100s for weeks, and the monsoons had failed to materialize—we'd had no rain for more than 70 days—volunteers were chomping at the bit to get out onto BANWR to place water. They succeeded in locating trails exiting the Refuge and met the challenge of very rough, hilly terrain to place water where it could be found by migrants as they leave BANWR. However, the most heavily traveled trail runs the length of the Refuge south to north and presents a serious challenge to traveling migrants. Our volunteers were hiking that trail regularly, not dropping water jugs, but carrying water to provide for people they may encounter.

For weeks these volunteers begged the DAWGS and the Monday night circle to permit them to place water on the Refuge. One pair of volunteers took it upon themselves to do so but was severely chastised by members of the Monday-night group. The action of these volunteers demonstrated the level of frustration of those who had a special commitment to BANWR. That we are all committed to the migrants goes without saying, but some folks have hiked BANWR trails for years, during which 20 migrant remains have been found, and they feel the threat of action by the government is unconscionable and unsupportable in the law. BANWR represents only 10% of the area we serve, but it became symbolic of all the work we do. We all felt that the bogus charges for littering that placed us in conflict with the departments of Fish and Wildlife, Forest Service, Border Patrol, Arizona Fish and Game, State Trust Land officials, and others represented a death knell to many migrants all over Southern Arizona.

A meeting scheduled for June 14th with regional Fish and Wildlife staff and researchers from the University of Arizona—at which we hoped to get the go-ahead to start placing water on the Refuge—was cancelled in a letter to Margo Cowan. Tom Harvey wrote in this email dated June 13, 2010:

> I apologize for not contacting you sooner but as you may have surmised we need to cancel the meeting planned for tomorrow to discuss the cooperative study. As you know, we are in the midst of developing our agency position on placement of water stations on Buenos Aires NWR. Due to the level of attention and complexity that permitting this activity has taken on and the many other border-related demands we are fielding, we continue to need more time to establish an approach for this potential use. It will require close coordination among the various parts of our organization. *I have also been directed that given the uncertain outcome of this process, we should refrain from engaging in any further discussions regarding planning for the cooperative study.* (Emphasis by author).
>
> Please be assured that we are proceeding as expeditiously as possible with developing a final position for the Service on this matter and we will keep you informed of its outcome. We appreciate your patience and please contact me or Chris Pease if you need further information.

There are so many things to say about this email, it's hard to know where to start. First, the process of issuing the permit had taken so long that, surely, at this meeting, the permit issue would have been addressed as well as the finalization of the study. Fish and Wildlife had requested an extension of time on issuing the permit to further analyze the many responses received during the public comment period. We had originally hoped to hear within a month of the end of the comment period.

"Agency position"—we thought that Fish and Wildlife *had* an agency position, developed after almost a year of negotiation in good faith and coming back to the table time after time. We had correspondence saying their people had reviewed and approved the terms of the Special Use Permit. In addition, we had correspondence from Mr. Benjamin Tuggle of the Department of Interior, which oversees Fish and Wildlife, stating they "are doing everything possible to resolve this issue in a way that meets everyone's needs."

Next, after the terms of the Special Use Permit were agreed upon by all parties, including mediators from the Udall Institute, Fish and Wildlife staff, and No More Deaths and Samaritans representatives, how is it that in this letter from Tom Harvey there is the implication that the Special Use Permit might now NOT be approved? "Given the uncertain outcome of this process, we should refrain from engaging in any further discussions regarding planning for the cooperative study."

Meanwhile, it seemed there was considerable benefit to delaying this process. Dan Millis' case in the Ninth Circuit Court of Appeals was still under advisement. Again, we thought we'd have an answer within 90 days of the oral argument held on March 2nd, and now, more than four months had gone by with no result. So, with the hope that the Ninth Circuit would throw out Dan's littering case, any delay in a formal agreement with Fish and Wildlife could be positive—in that if Dan's case was thrown out, we couldn't be ticketed for littering for putting out water on BANWR, and by extension, probably not on the other federal and state lands as well. The downside was that we had heard BANWR officials had identified other bases for ticketing us and put out a new brochure listing a variety of things people can't do on the Refuge, including "abandoning property." No doubt Margo had all this in the back of her mind when she responded to Tom: "I have no problem with rescheduling the meeting but NMD cannot continue to refrain from placing water on these trails with temperatures in excess of 100 degrees every day and no rain. I will notify the U.S. Attorney of our decision."

At our Monday night meeting two weeks prior, volunteers gritted their teeth as John Fife and others urged volunteers to stay the course another two weeks until this meeting. We agreed that if no resolution occurred at that meeting, we would meet Thursday night to plan the next steps and make recommendations to the Monday night group.

So, No More Deaths scheduled a meeting the next night at Southside Presbyterian Church to decide what action to take next. Our guiding principle is Civil Initiative. Shall we consider the further step of civil disobedience? If so what form would it take?

CHAPTER 72

Compatibility Determination

WHILE THE COALITION AND THE Udall Center worked week after week on the research study, BANWR developed a Compatibility Determination to determine the compatibility of the No More Deaths and Samaritan water program with the goals of BANWR. Its stated purpose was to "...evaluate potential establishment of additional drinking waters on Buenos Aires NWR that would consist of a minimum of one-gallon containers and up to a maximum of two 55-gallon water containers."

Dale Quinn of the *Arizona Daily Star* reported on April 4, 2010, that BANWR was asking for public input on the proposal to establish and maintain drinking water stations on BANWR to prevent migrant deaths in the rugged terrain southwest of Tucson. Comments could be faxed or emailed to BANWR within a one-month period.

At this point, humanitarians were optimistic that an agreement could be reached. Quinn quoted the draft Compatibility Determination written by BANWR as saying, "drinking water stations would be strategically placed on or near existing trails. Refuge management would ensure that water stations would not be placed in areas that may impact threatened or endangered species, sensitive habitat areas, or frequently used visitor areas such as designated camping sites and recreational trails."[111]

---

111 Quinn, Dale, *Arizona Daily Star,* Sunday, April 4, 2010.

The Compatibility Determination stated also that "The Refuge, as well as other lands along the United States/Mexico border, experienced a tremendous increase in illegal border traffic moving through the area; reaching a peak in 2006-2007 when an estimated 250,000-300,000 people traveled through the Refuge annually. In recent years, largely due to erection of a seven-mile pedestrian border fence, these numbers have declined significantly to approximately 31,500 in 2008 and 20,700 in 2009. It is still common to have 50-60 immigrants traveling through the Refuge each night..." The Compatibility Determination goes on to say: "CBP (Customs and Border Patrol) has steadily increased its patrol of the Refuge and surrounding lands."

The Compatibility Determination also indicated that 25 migrants had died on the Refuge between 2002 and 2009, not to mention those who were never found. Our statistician, Ed McCullough, noted that 15-20 migrants have also died north of BANWR during that same period, most likely having traveled through the Refuge on their way to the location of their demise.

The comment period would end May 4th, however, Refuge officials asked for additional time to assess responses. We understood the more than 800 responses were split about 50-50, half in favor of the water stations, half against.

Following a meeting of the Desert Aid Working Group (DAWG) when we still had not heard from BANWR by early June, Gene Lefebvre emailed Margo Cowan:

Since our meeting with Secretary Salazar last July, No More Deaths and Samaritans have worked to reach an agreement on the availability of water on BANWR for migrants crossing the Refuge. After many months of negotiations, we reached agreement on a plan that would allow us to place containers of water on a limited number of sites on the Refuge under certain conditions. BANWR officials and No More Deaths representatives agreed on the plan and it was put forth for public comment for an agreed period of up to 30 days. By the end of the 30 days, Fish and Wildlife asked our attorney, Margo Cowan, for extended time to evaluate public comment. She agreed, with the understanding that between the time the 30 days had expired and when the evaluation was completed, BANWR staff would not ticket No More Deaths and Samaritan volunteers for placing water on the Refuge.

Time went by and we heard nothing from BANWR despite our attempts to reach them. This past week, we discovered that Mike Hawkes has left his post on the Refuge. Perhaps this is the reason we have received no communication from BANWR. Whatever the reason, we feel that BANWR has not held up its end of our agreement. We are now fully into the summer when people die crossing the desert in the heat. We are compelled to respond to the prospect of human tragedy. So, we plan to again place water at strategic points on the Refuge pending completion of their study. Fish and Wildlife officials will move forward with us in the spirit of cooperation until our permit is issued.

BANWR postponed any further meetings and on July 27th notified No More Deaths and Samaritans that there was no longer any point in meeting, as "there is no guarantee the deliberations of Fish and Wildlife Service will lead to the issuance of a permit." *Really?*

What about the Compatibility Determination? Part of its conclusion, in the draft dated March 23rd that was signed by Mike Hawkes and Chris Pease, stated:

Stipulation 1: All water stations must be accessible from established roads and placed no further than 100 meters from a road. No new roads of any length may be established to access any site and sites must be accessed by foot from the established road without the use of any mechanical or wheeled device.

Stipulation 3: The water stations would consist of a minimum of a one-gallon tethered container up to a maximum of two 55-gallon containers that are placed on a site

in a manner that prevents their removal by a person or persons traveling on foot.

Stipulation 1 would disallow the placement of one-gallon jugs in the northern and/or mountainous reaches of the Refuge that cannot be accessed by roads. Stipulation 3 requires that the one-gallon jugs be tethered, a condition to which we had *not* agreed—since many migrants had previously lost or discarded their own personal containers and needed a way to carry water with them northward. Other stipulations required additional limitations on the humanitarians.

Since this Compatibility Determination was dated March 23rd, it seemed likely that it was the one posted on April 3rd to the Fish and Wildlife website.

Dr. Norma Price wrote to the humanitarians negotiating team saying, "There is nothing in the Compatibility Determination that would save the lives of migrants crossing the Refuge. Just the opposite. This plan would increase the deaths. It is unclear why FWS changed positions after months of negotiations working together to arrive at a mutually acceptable conclusion."

John Fife drafted talking points: "BANWR issued a press release recently titled 'Service to Continue to Allow Humane Water Stations on Border Refuge.' We wish it were true. But after ten years of denying repeated requests to place lifesaving water on BANWR, a careful reading of the documents reveals only a bureaucratic bait and switch. The bait is the commendable but lamentably late announcement 'that placement of water for use by those in need in the desert will help save lives and is compatible with the purpose of the Refuge.' The switch is the bureaucratic maze of regulations and restrictions which will put major sections of the Refuge off-limits for water sites and even impose new restrictions on three existing sites (operated by Humane Borders). The most egregious switch was the cancelling of an agreement with No More Deaths (the Special Use Permit) which would have allowed water to be placed on critical trails where too many deaths have already occurred."

It appeared that 18 months of work was down the drain. No More Deaths and Samaritans had good cause to feel dejected. However, on second thought, we realized that the government failed to change our behavior. We had continued to put water on the Refuge for virtually the entire time negotiations had been underway. Margo contacted the Udall Institute and thanked them for their time and effort in helping develop a research study that might've provided a solution to at least one of the issues at hand. Instead it was all left hanging. BANWR, for its part, stopped ticketing our volunteers. Much later, in 2013, newer agents ticketed Jim Marx and his small group from No More Deaths, but no prosecution ever took place. Since then, there has been no ticketing by BANWR officers—nor by Border Patrol.[112]

Questions hung in the air. Who left us with no definitive response? Who decided not to ticket us any longer? Some people wondered if it all dated back to the time in 2009 when Interior Secretary Salazar summoned us to Washington and listened for about ten minutes while we pleaded our case. He was sympathetic but admonished that we must follow the law. He then turned over the conversation to his aides, including Jane Lyder. It seemed obvious that behind the scenes something was going on. In cancelling the July meeting to discuss the research study, Tom Harvey (regional Fish and Wildlife officer) had said, "due to the level of attention and complexity permitting this activity has taken on...we continue to need more time to establish an approach for this potential use. Needless to say, it will require close coordination among various parts of our organization."

---

112 Until the ticketing of Scott Warren and eight others in 2017 and 2018 (see Part V).

Who pulled the plug—who decided it wasn't worthwhile continuing to argue with these humanitarian groups for just six, seven, or eight water sites and possibly 50-60 gallons of water at a time on the 118,000-acre refuge? Perhaps it was Benjamin Tuggle, from the Regional Fish and Wildlife office; perhaps it was Allen Bersin, the border czar; perhaps it was Representative Raul Grijalva. Perhaps it was one or more of those "various parts" of BANWR mentioned by Tom Harvey. Who figured out a way so that BANWR (Fish and Wildlife) wouldn't lose, and the humanitarians wouldn't win? We'd never know.

Interestingly, On August 23rd, BANWR issued a "final" Compatibility Determination signed by Sally Gall, Acting Refuge Manager, and Donna Stanek, Acting Regional Chief. This document was significantly different from the one given to the public. The Compatibility Determination (CD) states:

One-Gallon Jugs Stored at Mobile Camp, 2009 (No More Deaths)

The purpose of this Compatibility Determination is to evaluate whether or not the Refuge should continue to permit establishment and maintenance of drinking water stations on Buenos Aires NWR. The types of water station strategies under consideration include placement of small containers tethered to trees along active illegal immigrant trails or the placement of large, semi-permanent stationary containers.

The document discusses the pros and cons of both small one-gallon and large 55-gallon containers. Regarding the small containers, the Compatibility Document states:

Under consideration is the "tethering" of one-gallon containers to trees along foot trails used by illegal immigrants. This is intended to provide easier access to water since it could be laced on trails that are less visible and more discrete than along public roads. The smaller containers would allow humanitarian groups to more easily transport water to the tethered sites which would be located away from roads and along actively-used trails.... The Refuge has concerns that if an illegal immigrant is not carrying his or her own container, there is a possibility that tethered containers could be cut from the tether, carried along the trail and later discarded on the Refuge. *This small container approach may not be consistent with DOI guidelines regarding placement of water stations since the proposal is to place the stations away from roads, on trails actively used by illegal immigrants. As a result, use of small containers could potentially result in negative resource impacts due to increased litter and continued use of illegal trails that the Refuge plans to restore to natural conditions. In addition, monitoring these containers for compliance with applicable government water quality standards may be difficult, if not impossible. (ed. emphasis added)*

However, the conclusion of the Compatibility Determination states:

Based on sound professional judgment, and in adherence to all applicable Federal laws and Service policies, the proposed placement of large (i.e., 55-gallon) semi-permanent containers—subject to conservation stipulations—is found to be compatible. This water station strategy ensures the Refuge has the capacity and resources to effectively administer the activity.

How Many More? 55-Gallon Water Tank (Michael Hyatt)

Thus, in the end, Humane Borders could move forward with their 55-gallon containers (upon further approval by BANWR), but small containers were not mentioned. Not allowed, or just ignored?

In the book entitled, *Faithful Resistance* (2016), Rick Ufford-Chase discusses how the United States has become an "Empire." It's not the way we want to think of our country, but his points (and those of the contributing authors) are valid. The evidence is there.

Rick:

Nowhere is the real cost of the "Empire project" as clear as it on the border where the Empire claims to be defending itself as it defines who is "in" and who is "out." The greater the economic power and political hegemony of the Empire, the more it must defend its border (including BANWR, and against the humanitarians as well as the migrants) with automatic weapons, tens of thousands Border Patrol agents, steel walls, and a sophisticated high-tech security system that can determine in an instant whom it deems should be a threat.

The United States has stimulated the movement of people from the south to the north, yet it refuses to take responsibility for the result of that stimulus. To date (2019), more than 7,000 people have died crossing the Southern U.S. deserts.

WAITING: TUESDAY JULY 27, 2010

It's been 78 days without rain, and finally, it rained. Not long, not enough, not really satisfying, but at least the air had that wet-dirt smell that's unique to the time when the first drops fall. But...we couldn't really call it the beginning of the monsoon. It was just a false start that left us waiting for the real thing. Day after day, the clouds would gather, and the wind would blow the wind chimes my daughter gave me for Mother's Day, but we were still waiting.

Fortunately, there were probably no deaths on BANWR as we waited, but 48 of 60 deaths in July occurred on the Tohono O'odham Nation. Why are migrants shying away from BANWR and from the Santa Cruz Valley where Arivaca is located?

We were also still waiting to hear about Dan's verdict from the Ninth Circuit Court of Appeals. They heard oral arguments March 2nd and that was almost five months past. Margo was worried that this was a bad sign.

We were waiting for approval of the Special Use Permit from the Fish and Wildlife Service, when that letter came last week from Tom Harvey saying there wasn't any point in meeting any longer about the study, as there was no guarantee the deliberations of the Fish and Wildlife Service would result in a Special Use Permit for us to put out water on BANWR. All our work and all our hopes down the drain. We left things open, if they wanted to get back to us, but we weren't going to initiate any further discussion.

Since 2004 No More Deaths had maintained its strategy of non-violent, responsible behavior, simply by placing water for desperate migrants and removing trash. It appeared that the government found it difficult to adapt to the introduction of migrant deaths into a geographic area their officers were charged to protect. How could they adjust to these new challenges without seeming to be inhumane? Just when we seemed to have come to mutually agreeable plans, the government pulled out the rug.

We discussed, for the third time in two weeks, whether to send a letter to Ken Salazar, director of the Department of the Interior, Dennis Burke, U.S. Attorney, Raul Grijalva, representative in Congress, and/or others to let them know that the Fish and Wildlife Service has halted the process that would give us access to BANWR (and possibly the other federal lands). Members of the negotiating team, Steve Johnston, and I all voted not to send a letter, thus, in our method of consensus, blocking any further action. It was very stressful. Last Tuesday some people went onto the Refuge and left water; then another group went out on Thursday. The Thursday volunteers found the Tuesday water (20 gallons of it) had all been taken, not by migrants, but most likely by Border Patrol. We thought this battle was almost over, but it continued, and we were still awaiting a final resolution. Or maybe there wouldn't be one, and we'd just be left waiting. Each patrol that went out to deliver water on BANWR—or any other state or federal land—would have to wonder if they might receive a ticket, or worse, be arrested, as had been threatened.

CHAPTER 73

The Courts Weigh In

In September 2010, at a No More Deaths meeting, attorney Andy Silverman quietly announced the Ninth Circuit Court of Appeals had vacated the ruling against Dan Millis for littering on BANWR. He could be re-prosecuted under different parts of the Refuge regulations, but prosecutor Lawrence Lee chose not to pursue it. We all cheered.

As Andy had predicted, this was followed on December 8th by Walt Staton's verdict of guilty being remanded back to the District Court by the Ninth Circuit. You will remember that Walt was found guilty for "knowingly littering" on BANWR. Subsequently, the District Court dropped all charges against Walt Staton—and the 13 volunteers (The *Basura 13*) who had been ticketed June 9, 2009, on BANWR.

Humanitarians 19;[113] the Empire 0.

Wow!

I was reminded by jon heid that still hovering in the background was the statement by the attorney general—that he would not prosecute these tickets, as he had much more important cases to handle. That left BANWR without any teeth—at least for now.

---

113 Shanti Sellz and Daniel Strauss taking sick migrants for medical care along Arivaca Road in 2005, Kathryn Ferguson along the highway near Arivaca in 2008, Gene Lefebvre at Byrd Camp in 2008, Dan Millis on BANWR in 2008, Walt Staton on BANWR in 2009, and the Thirteen ticketed on BANWR in 2009.

In 2018, one-gallon jugs of water were still being placed on BANWR; however, for a variety of reasons, the number of migrants crossing the Refuge had diminished considerably. The relationship between the Refuge and the humanitarians had resolved into an amicable one. jon heid reminded the acting chief, Sally Gall, and the Refuge staff that the humanitarians are the only ones who know where every rock had been placed and where every shrub resided. No More Deaths loves the Refuge and works very hard to keep it clear of trash and as pristine as it was meant to be, all the while trying to save lives.

PART IV
SB 1070 and More
2010

Brother David Buel at a Migrant Shrine (No More Deaths)

CHAPTER 74

2010–SB 1070–What Kind of People Are We?

Since 1995, Maricopa County Sheriff Joe Arpaio
institutionalized racial profiling against LATINOS; GOP
Governor Jan Brewer signed the "show me your papers"
law SB 1070; and Republicans swept every state office.

— LINDA VALDEZ, ARIZONA REPUBLIC, 6-5-2016

Walt and Maryada Leaving Water in the Desert, Baboquiviri
in the Distant Background (No More Deaths)

In August last year (2009), Walt's case seemed settled, so Walt Staton and Maryada Vallet left for school and work in California leaving two enormous gaps in the No More Deaths volunteer corps. Maryada had been the leader in the Mariposa working group and Walt had handled media, vehicle repairs, computer work, and other tasks within the organization. Their departure meant a significant reshuffling of responsibilities.

Then, with the passage of SB 1070 in the Spring of 2010 and subsequent legislative actions, Arizona became the focus of significant national attention. Who could imagine a more punitive, racist piece of legislation? Following its being signed into law by our governor, Jan Brewer, every major effort that happened in the state regarding immigration was colored by this drastic law! Because of that, and because of our divided focus between SB 1070 and BANWR, and because of some restlessness within No More Death, new strategies for the use of volunteer time began to emerge, while at the same time the desert and border work continued. This chapter follows both the old and the new (*sans* BANWR, of course—previous chapter).

DEATH IN THE DESERT—FEBRUARY 9, 2010

On February 9th, a group of five No More Deaths volunteers including Annie Swanson, Molly Little, Kevin Riley plus two others were hiking in a remote canyon near the border south of Ruby. They came across the remains of someone who had been hiking on his way north. The remains had been placed with care in a shallow grave and marked with a handmade cross. When the volunteers found them, the remains had been rudely uncovered and mauled by animals.

Upon their discovery, a couple of the volunteers hiked out to Ruby Road to call for help.

After some time, two overweight, out-of-shape sheriff's deputies responded. When they reached the location, they placed the remains in a body bag. The deputies hiked out of the canyon (with our volunteers doing most of the carrying of the bag). Dark descended quickly, and before long, the group stopped to rest because the deputies were exhausted.

The volunteers called for help again—this time to ask Border Patrol to bring a helicopter. They explained that the trip was becoming very difficult in the steep and rocky canyon. Still, the group continued hiking while waiting two hours for Border Patrol to arrive. Our volunteers turned on their headlamps to assist with their progress, but the deputies instructed them to turn off the lights because they were afraid of smugglers hiding in the hills waiting to shoot them. Annie and the others refused to comply. They wouldn't be able to see the treacherous trail in darkness. And waiting overnight wasn't an option.

Finally, they met up with Border Patrol agents who wanted them to exit the area using a different route from the one that the volunteers had used to enter. The No More Deaths folks objected, but the agents prevailed. After some time, the agents concluded they were lost, so Annie and the others used their maps and GPS to lead the way back to where they had previously left "their" trail and guided everyone out to the vehicles. *Que frustrante!* From there, Border Patrol agents took the remains to the Medical Examiner's office in Tucson. The individual was never identified, in spite of a valiant effort by the Pima County Medical Examiner's office.

Annie and other members of her group were greatly affected by this frustrating, lengthy, and distressing experience. It's hard enough to hike into rocky, mountainous areas for the first time in daylight; but to do so at night while carrying an awkward, heavy bag—and being unsettled by its contents—along with arguing with your "helpers;" it was too much.

A week or so later, Dr. Norma Price and her husband hiked into the same area and found a human femur. Upon taking it to the Medical Examiner's office, they learned it was from a second person. Norma and her husband scoured the area but found no additional evidence of human remains. The elements and the animals often leave nothing behind.

VIGIL AT TIRADITO SHRINE—FEBRUARY 11, 2010

That night we participated in the regular Thursday-night vigil at the Tiradito Shrine across from the Convention Center in downtown Tucson, led by Father Ricardo.[114] But that night was anything but regular. Father Ricardo stated, "Five young adults found the remains of a migrant on Tuesday night (February 9th) two miles east of the little town of Ruby. They discovered the body in a shallow grave covered with rocks and adorned with a handmade cross in a narrow canyon."[115]

Following the service, Annie and Molly and a few others moved toward the altar. Some of us tried to comfort them, but they seemed to prefer consoling one another. Those of us who haven't had their experience couldn't begin to empathize with them adequately.

Later Kevin Riley sent an email to local volunteers: "We really appreciate the care and concern many of you have expressed to us. While this is very difficult for each of us (the five who were on site), we hope that the process for the group is one that keeps our thoughts and prayers with this person, and his or her family and friends. We also hope it focuses even more on the reasons that the work we do is necessary, the humanitarian crisis that is happening every day on the border, and the inhumane border policies we are all working to end."

A short while later, Annie was involved in another recovery.

---

114 No More Deaths, *Press Release*, (February 11, 2010).

115 The Tiradito shrine, also known as the Wishing Shrine, is a small site on dirt ground, featuring a shrine dedicated to star-crossed lovers. An adobe wall with niches provide space where people place small *mandas* (promises) or pray for successful ventures. The shrine holds a votive candle stand. El Tiradito is the site of small weddings and is frequently used for candlelight ceremonies. It is on the Historic Register and is a unique part of Tucson history._https://www.tucsonaz.gov/parks/special-places#ElTiradito.

CHAPTER 75

Spring Break 2010

BEFORE SPRING BREAK, WE HIRED Jean Boucher to be our volunteer coordinator. He came from El Paso, Texas, where he had been working in a halfway house for migrants. He knew of No More Deaths and had previously met Maryada and others during his time in El Paso. He came highly recommended from those who knew him. At 45, he was somewhat older than the other coordinators we had employed in the past. He had good sense and lots of skills; we felt lucky to have him. Later, some of the volunteers complained that he was too exacting with regards to money and other administrative duties, but his work ethic was excellent. Perhaps the volunteers needed some supervision and direction.

When he first arrived, he stayed in our home for about five days until he settled into Casa Mariposa. He cooked for us and taught me to make a one-dish meal in the frying pan—starting with onions, adding veggies, cooked rice, and green chilis. Delicious!

Jean (pronounced like the French Jhan) wasn't sure what he wanted to do for the rest of his life; he intended to work that out while spending time with No More Deaths. Right away he went back to El Paso for a week of Capacitar International Programs training, which he believed would help him with his interactions with volunteers and migrants in Southern Arizona. Later he duplicated that training for some of us in Tucson to make us more sensitive to others and better able to interact with migrants.

THINGS COMING TO A HEAD FOR SPRING BREAK

It seemed as if everything was happening at once:

Forty young adults from Notre Dame, University of Veritas Montas in Vermont, and North Carolina University all arrived to start training for the first week of spring break. Annie Swanson experienced her first big task coordinating the training and making things work. Of course, they didn't all work, but she handled them very well. One evening, part of the dinner was late, so one of the cooks asked Gene if he could "vamp" for a few minutes while they decided what to do—order Mexican food and pick it up, or order pizza and have it delivered. The planned food arrived before they could decide. Also, the history instructor failed to show up for training. Then the law instructor failed to show up—although maybe they pulled Andy Silverman in at the last minute for the legal class; I don't know. Turns out Margo was out of town and Annie hadn't been notified.

Someone had the idea to increase the number of college and university young adults over the three-week period during spring break from the 109 we had last year to 160. So, following our "rule" of 15 non-local volunteers per camp, three camps were needed for each of the three weeks. For months Gene had been running around like a crazy person locating picnic tables, potty seats, rebar (to hold down the tents), fire starters (those things about 10 inches long that are used to light barbeques and church candles), tarps, tents, more tableware, and everything else needed in addition to what was already there from last year. This allowed us to conduct three camps—one at Byrd Baylor's place, one at Chavez Siding, and one outside the town of Ruby. I asked Gene what they planned to do if the Forest Service kicked them off the Ruby site. He said they could move to Karl Hoffman's camp, even though they'd been trying to wean themselves from his place. It was still being used to store water and other supplies until they could make the final break. Karl seemed to have a love-hate relationship with No More Deaths, being helpful to our faces and hurtful behind our backs (in blogs and such), so it seemed prudent to cut ties.

GETTING READY FOR THE GERMANS

Before leaving for the desert with his group, Gene reminded me of my tasks for Monday: run copies of the Special Use Permit (SUP) for BANWR and its supplemental provisions, front and back; run copies of the No More Deaths Mission Statement and Civil Initiative, front and back, all needed for the Monday night No More Deaths meeting when we'd decide on BANWR's SUP; check with Sarah Roberts about plans for the Germans coming the following week; and to "… remember, Sue, we're having them and the No More Deaths folks who went to Germany last year over for dinner on Friday night."

We were anxious to meet with the Germans. They were Lutheran Church pastors and teachers giving safe harbor to migrants who had traveled by boat in the Mediterranean Sea and had found their way into Germany. They had also dealt with people migrating from eastern Europe. The Germans saw themselves as part of the continuing Confessing Church in Germany dating back to World War II. They felt motivated by their history of resistance since the rise of Hitler, and by their academic interest in the church-state relationship, to work for the migrants.

CHAPTER 76

Abuse Documentation Interim Report to the Unitarian Universalist Association Funding Program

THE NEXT DAY I STARTED on the abuse documentation group's proposal for second year funding from the Unitarian Universalist Association (UUA), their national body. Even though many members of the committee were doing all the work, I was the one putting it together. I'm so proud of their work I'm including part of the report here.

Those who had been working on abuse documentation included Molly Little and Danielle Alvarado, to whom we paid a small stipend from the Unitarian Universalist Association Funding Program. In addition, there was Hannah Hafter, Jessica Tracy, attorney Andy Silverman, and Cesar (a community organizer for TYLO). It was challenging to work with these committed college graduates whose energy far surpassed mine.

Below is the progress completed since beginning of the grant period July 2009, including updates since sending our interim report in February 2010:

Communication and collaboration with resource centers in Naco, Agua Prieta, and Nogales, Sonora, and participation in documentation efforts:

* The "stipended" volunteer spent time in Naco, Arizona and Naco, Sonora and in Douglas/Agua Prieta learning about their migrant programs' documentation systems and

discussing collaboration in filing reports. Another NMD volunteer spent two weeks with those programs following up on the collaboration;

* Between November 2009 and June 2010, a group of four to six local No More Deaths volunteers maintained a presence in Nogales two to four days a week, building collaborative relationships with community partners and conducting interviews with recently deported migrants. They documented over 88 cases of abuse in Nogales over the course of the last eight months. These will be included in an upcoming publication;

* For two weeks in March 2010, No More Deaths hosted its first Nogales Alternative Spring Break Project, bringing in between six and ten national volunteers each week to expand and deepen the scope of our work in Nogales, and to conduct interviews with recently deported migrants. No More Deaths volunteers participated in the formation of a new, binational Human Rights team in Nogales, Sonora to collaborate around documentation of Human Rights abuses in Mexico and the United States. We attended regular meetings with the team, helped coordinate fundraising to obtain an office, and shared No More Deaths documentation tools.

Improving logistics of documentation system:

* We established a volunteer log at the Nogales aid station to monitor volunteer presence, numbers of interviews conducted, and medical care provided. We also supplied the Nogales aid station with copies of the latest documentation form, long-term detention form, and third-party complaint forms;

* We cooperated with Arizona ACLU to adopt use of their questionnaire specific to long-term custody; we worked collaboratively with them to pass on cases of abuses in long-term

detention and detention in Maricopa county that they can use in their own documentation efforts; and we participated in meetings with the New Mexico ACLU to strategize around the planning of a border-wide online documentation system;

* We began collaboration with the Kino Border Initiative around use of their intake form to gather more comprehensive demographic information about people who have recently been deported and are seeking resources in Nogales;

* We created a new questionnaire, as a supplement to the abuse documentation questionnaire, that seeks to more accurately and accountably reflect the realities of people deported after living for many years in the United States to be used to document the familial, psychological, and public health consequences of these deportations. The phenomenon of deporting long-time U.S. non-citizen residents increases daily.

Establishment of three-tiered process for following up on reports of abuse:

* We collaborated with the Naco aid station to develop a No More Deaths-specific system for follow up on reports of abuse, including producing a No More Deaths-specific third-party complaint form used to submit cases to the Office of Civil Rights and Civil Liberties of the Department of Homeland Security;

* We compiled and filed over 80 reports of Border Patrol, ICE, and Maricopa County Sheriff's Department abuse to the Department of Homeland Security between January and May 2010, and we filed copies of some of these reports with Arizona congressmen, Border Patrol, the Mexican Consulate, and others;

* In coordination with aid stations in Naco and Agua Prieta, we initiated and maintained communication with Moreen

Murphy, a representative of the Office of Civil Rights and Civil Liberties in the Department of Homeland Security, about establishing a system of accountability and follow-up on the part of her agency;

* We prepared for the visit of Moreen Murphy to the Naco aid station in February, the first visit from her office to officially investigate short-term custody abuses documented by our partners in Naco; and we prepared for the visit of Ms. Murphy to Arizona in July of 2010, when she will undertake to investigate reports No More Deaths has filed with her office;

* We participated in a conference call with the Office of Civil Rights and Civil Liberties regarding improvement of their complaint process and submitted written recommendations to the Office;

* We established an organized system in the No More Deaths office to maintain copies and records of communication with Department of Homeland Security and the complaint forms that we have filed;

* We distributed abuse interview summaries to local email lists and to family, friends, and organizing partners in other parts of the United States and began the process of working to incorporate these narratives into our website in order to provide resources anyone can use and share;

* We conducted ongoing strategy conversations with documentation partners and legal resources around framing our demands and requests in our communication with Department of Homeland Security and other targets.

Coordinating abuse documentation volunteers:

* Our stipended volunteer collaborated with the No More Deaths volunteer coordinator to discuss placement of volunteers doing documentation work in Nogales, Agua Prieta, and Naco;

* Our stipended volunteer communicated with, interviewed, oriented, and served as mentor and supervisor for two No More Deaths interns through the Earlham Border Studies Institute throughout Spring 2010 and began outreach to a local volunteer base in Tucson and Nogales;
* We planned and implemented an intensive documentation project during a two-week alternative spring break program in Nogales in March, which brought in volunteers from around the country;
* We planned and implemented the opening of the Nogales summer volunteer program, the preparation for which included facilitating a training for volunteers, maintaining a calendar of on-site No More Deaths volunteer coordinators, facilitating daily volunteer debriefings and evaluations, facilitating daily and weekly work structure and schedule, communicating with community partners in Nogales, and the writing and distribution of a Nogales field manual for volunteers;
* We continued ongoing work to seek human rights observer status for international documentation volunteers and provided guidance to interns who worked on the project in the spring.

Development of training specifically for abuse documentation volunteers:

* We prepared a training for the alternative spring break program in March, which included the following elements: introduction to No More Deaths' documentation project and presence in Nogales, logistics of documentation, and introduction to working with people who have experienced trauma;
* We incorporated feedback in the March trainings in order to improve and coordinate training for summer volunteers, which now also includes the political and strategic framing

of the documentation project and an introduction to the outreach conversation that continues at the end of the week; we established a training schedule, list of available trainers, list of necessary resources, and a more thorough training outline, in preparation for the remainder of the summer volunteer program.

Collaboration with members of the Tohono O'odham Nation:

* We formed a new collaboration between No More Deaths and O'odham VOICE Against the WALL, an organization of Tohono O'odham tribal members;
* We designed an abuse documentation questionnaire and complaint form specific to Border Patrol abuses on Tohono O'odham Traditional Land and indigenous rights;
* No More Deaths volunteers conducted four interviews on the Tohono O'odham Nation and worked to connect people through this project with legal representation;
* We facilitated sending a group of No More Deaths documentation volunteers to the Tohono O'odham Nation in March for a preliminary O'odham VOICE Against the WALL training;
* We filed two cases of abuse of Tohono O'odham tribal members with Moreen Murphy at the Office of Civil Rights and Civil Liberties;
* We worked collaboratively with O'odham VOICE Against the WALL to create Know Your Rights cards and pamphlets specific to the context of tribal members and yard signs instructing Border Patrol to not enter the property without a search warrant and facilitated the printing of these materials;
* We attended a community meeting on the Tohono O'odham Nation in June, presented alongside O'odham VOICE Against the WALL about the documentation project and distributed

questionnaires, Know Your Rights materials, yard signs, and complaint forms to community members.

Outreach:

* In addition to the outreach identified above, over the past year we have collaborated with policy-making partners to expand our recommendations for short-term custody standards and to distribute them to key legislators and advocacy organizations. We have developed a strong relationship with the National Immigration Forum and the Border Stakeholders, a coalition of community organizations from across the Southwest; as a result, we have developed legislative and administrative language which has become incorporated into three pieces of proposed legislation (H.R. 4321, S. 1150, H.R. 4470) as well as into unprecedented ongoing dialogues with national staff from the Department of Homeland Security Office of Civil Rights and Civil Liberties and Customs and Border Protection. We have spoken on the issue at numerous meetings of policymakers and at three public conferences, and there is now a working Policy Table of D.C. organizations with whom we are continuing to collaborate in the absence of a staff person based there;

* It is a major accomplishment of our policy efforts that short-term custody is now a recognized piece of both detention and border policy conversations, and that No More Deaths is looked to as a national leader on the issue. While we remain central on short-term custody continuing to be a priority for advocates, it is also carried by several organizations with additional capacity and resources to devote to it. Another significant victory for us was that some of our recommendations were included in detention reform and comprehensive immigration reform legislation in the 111th Congress.

Preparation for supplementary report to 2011's **Crossing the Line:**

1. We wrote the structure for a report to be worked on through-out Summer 2010, which will include reflections and testi-mony from all summer documentation volunteers and an appendix of summaries of the interviews conducted by these volunteers;

    * After nearly a year's hiatus from meeting with Border Patrol sector chief, a meeting was held the last week in July in which short-term custody standards were again discussed—we requested that the chief implement his own standards for the Tucson Sector of Border Patrol, absent national standards. No promises, but the new Sector Chief agreed to look into the problem;

    * As you know, Immigration Reform is coming to the forefront of the national discussion. We will continue to contribute to the discussion as an on-the-ground grass roots organization that understands the issues. We can also continue to make progress on two fronts. First, our online toolkit does not have as many resources as we'd like at this point. We are currently working with volun-teers to develop additional tools over the rest of the sum-mer in order to address this shortcoming. We also did not have a committee hearing on short-term custody as we had planned; it did not seem to be an appropriate time given the other topics taken up by Congress in the first half of 2010, and we held a Senate staff briefing that included short-term custody instead.[116]

The project was refunded for the following year.

---

116 Molly Little, et.al., *Abuse Documentation Interim Report to Unitarian Universalist Association Funding Program* (Arizona: No More Deaths, 2010).

CHAPTER 77

A Culture of Cruelty–Abuse and Impunity in Short-Term U.S. Border Patrol Custody–2011

INTRODUCTION:

In 2006, in the midst of humanitarian work with people recently deported from the United States to Nogales, Sonora, No More Deaths began to document abuses endured by individuals in the custody of U.S. immigration authorities, and in particular U.S. Border Patrol. In September 2008, No More Deaths published *Crossing the Line* in collaboration with partners in Naco and Agua Prieta, Sonora. The report included hundreds of individual accounts of Border Patrol abuse, as well as recommendations for clear, enforceable custody standards with community oversight to ensure compliance. Almost three years later, *A Culture of Cruelty* is a follow-up to that report—now with 12 times as many interviews detailing more than 30,000 incidents of abuse and mistreatment, newly obtained information on Border Patrol's existing custody standards and more specific recommendations to stop the abuse of individuals in Border Patrol custody.

The abuses individuals report have remained alarmingly consistent for years, from interviewer to interviewer and across interview sites: individuals suffering severe dehydration are deprived of water; people with life-threatening medical conditions are denied treatment; children and adults are beaten during apprehensions and in custody; family members are separated, their belongings confiscated and not returned; many are crammed into cells and subjected to extreme temperatures, deprived of sleep, and threatened with death by Border Patrol agents. By this point, the overwhelming weight of the corroborated evidence should eliminate any doubt that Border Patrol abuse is widespread. Still the Border Patrol's consistent response has been flat denial and calls for reform have been ignored.

We entitled our report *A Culture of Cruelty* because we believe our findings demonstrate that the abuse, neglect, and dehumanization of migrants is part of the institutional culture of the Border Patrol, reinforced by an absence of meaningful accountability mechanisms. This systemic abuse must be confronted aggressively at the institutional level, not denied or dismissed as a series of aberrational incidents attributable to a few rogue agents. Until then we can expect this culture of cruelty to continue to deprive individuals in Border Patrol custody of their most fundamental human rights.

BORDER PATROL SHORT-TERM CUSTODY CONDITIONS

Our documentation from Fall 2008 to Spring 2011 includes 4,130 interviews with 12,895 individuals who were in Border Patrol custody, including 9,562 men, 2,147 women, 533 teenagers (ages 13-18), and 268 children (ages 0-12). Most interviews were conducted in Naco (3,201), followed by Nogales (834), and Agua Prieta (62). Based on these interviews we have identified 12 areas of concern, and in the full report provide prevalence statistics and case examples for each denial of or insufficient water, denial of or insufficient food, failure to provide medical treatment or access to medical professionals, inhumane processing-center conditions, verbal abuse, physical abuse, psychological abuse, dangerous transportation practices, separation of family members, dangerous repatriation practices, failure to return personal belongings, and due process concerns.

Our findings included the following:

* Border Patrol agents denied food to 2,981 people and gave insufficient food to 11,384 people. Only 20 percent of people in custody for more than two days received a meal;

* Agents denied water to 863 people and gave insufficient access to water to 1,402 additional people. Children were more likely than adults to be denied water or given insufficient water. Many of those denied water by Border Patrol were already suffering from moderate to severe dehydration at the time they were apprehended;

* Physical abuse was reported by 10 percent of interviewees, including teens and children. The longer people were held in custody, the more likely they were to experience physical abuse;

* Of the 433 incidents in which emergency medical treatment or medications were needed, Border Patrol provided access to care in only 59 cases—86 percent were deported without necessary medical treatment;

* The most commonly reported forms of inhumane processing center conditions were overcrowding (5,763 reports), followed by unsanitary conditions (3,107), extreme cold (2,922), and extreme heat (2,349);

* We recorded 2,926 incidents of failure to return personal belongings: 398 cases of failure to return shoes or shoelaces,

211 cases of failure to return money, 201 cases of failure to return identification, 191 cases of failure to return important documents, and 125 cases where no personal belongings were returned at all. People deported without money or key personal belongings are at heightened risk of exploitation and physical harm;

* Border Patrol deported 869 family members separately, including 17 children and 41 teens. Family separation frequently involved "lateral repatriation," or deportation through ports of entry that are distant from the location of apprehension. It is a costly practice that increases the risk of physical harm to those who are repatriated to unfamiliar or dangerous locations;

* 1,051 women, 190 teens, and 94 children were repatriated after dark in violation of the Memorandum of Understanding between the Mexican Consulate and U.S. Customs and Border Protection and, in the case of children, the Trafficking Victims Protection Reauthorization Act (TVPRA) of 2008;

* Increasing reports of psychological abuse included threatening detainees with death; depriving them of sleep; keeping vehicles and cells at extremely hot or cold temperatures; playing traumatizing songs about people dying in the desert (*migracorridos*) loudly and continuously; and forced holding of strenuous or painful positions for no apparent reason other than to humiliate.

Clearly, instances of mistreatment and abuse while in Border Patrol custody are not aberrational. Rather, they reflect common practice for an agency that is part of the largest federal law enforcement body in the country. Many of them plainly meet the definition of torture under international law.

For Example:

June 14, 2010 with Gerardo, 47, from Nayarit, Mexico:

His feet were severely blistered and were being treated by a volunteer EMT during the interview. He was detained for two days at a Border Patrol detention center near Why, Arizona after walking through the desert for three days. At the detention center, agents went through his belongings and those of others and threw away identification, cell phones and lists of phone numbers. He recovered his cell phone from the trash and had it in his possession during the interview. Gerardo requested medical treatment for his feet, but was only told, "Later." He never received any care. Migra corridos *(migrant songs) played over the loudspeakers 24 hours a day at high volume. Every two hours, guards would come in shouting at the detainees and required them to line up for inspection. These measures prevented the detainees from sleeping and Gerardo regarded them as forms of psychological torture. He reported substandard conditions that included inadequate food, overcrowding and excessive cold.*

The report continues with (1) Documentation of Findings and Methodology, (2) Existing Standards and Policies for Border Control Custody, (3) The Political and Context of Border Patrol Abuse, and (4) Recommendations and Conclusion. To read the entire report, go to *www.cultureofcruelty.org.*

**Margo Cowan, Isabel Garcia, Lois Martin and Sarah Roberts
Deliver *A Culture of Cruelty* to Border Patrol (Michael Hyatt)**

CHAPTER 78

Mariposa Stories

In Nogales, Sonora, No More Deaths works with the *Comedor, Grupo Beta* and other local organizations to assist migrants. The *Comedor* is one of the first stops after crossing the border. Its mission is to feed migrants traveling through or staying in Nogales. It is run by the Kino Border Initiative (KBI), a Catholic organization comprised of three cross-border parishes. Its director, Father Sean Carroll, SJ, helps No More Deaths with abuse documentation and keeps the food coming and migrants fed seven days a week. Below Rosemary Milazzo tells about her experiences in Nogales.

Rosemary Milazzo, Volunteer:

> I spent two weeks in Nogales, Mexico. While there, I worked closely with the Mexican Sisters at their reception center. I met many migrants who had been deported. I heard their stories of hope crushed, of travails in the desert, and so on. There were many that moved me, but the one I will recount was perhaps the worst scenario I experienced.
>
> I met a young man who was all swollen. He had been in Tucson working at a car shop when Border Patrol came in and took him because he had no papers. All the other workers had already fled, but he was too slow, so he was taken.
>
> When he arrived at the *Comedor,* he couldn't eat because he needed dialysis three times a week, which he had been

receiving in Tucson. Now, it was Monday and he had missed dialysis since his capture on Friday of the week before. His body was swollen, his hands were red, he felt badly; he had not urinated for a while and therefore was afraid to eat or drink.

We got him to *Grupo Beta* and they helped us get him to the hospital. When we arrived, we were informed that they had no dialysis machine there and that we would have to take him to a hospital about four hours away. In the meantime, the nurse took his blood pressure and it was 190 over 120—extremely high. He was given a bed and we were sent away to get transportation to get him to the other hospital. The nurse promised to keep him until we returned. By this time, his arm was so swollen with fluid that it looked like a camel's back with humps.

We spent the day trying to get transportation but were unable to do so. We called the embassy, the government offices, and so on. We returned to the hospital and, happily, found that he had already been moved to the hospital where he could be helped.

However, we never heard again what happened to this young man. If he stayed in Mexico, would he be able to get dialysis treatment? We were very concerned about his family back in Tucson and sent a note to them. However, by the time I left, we had no word. So now, we hope and pray that he isn't another of the "lost" people trying to find a place in U.S. Why should anyone be "lost" trying to find a job or trying to be reunited with family?

As I reflect on my time in Nogales, I am very grateful that the Sisters were there full-time helping make life more endurable by providing food, first aid, telephone service, clothing. This was the first sense of hospitality for many of the migrants for quite a while. I remember the Jesuit priest who welcomed the migrants to the morning meal always beginning with something like, "Don't give up...life is precious, although sometimes more difficult to achieve. But, you are important, never forget that."

I am grateful that I could share life with them for two weeks. I saw how the human spirit can enable us to keep moving towards our goal even in the face of tremendous adversity. I hope I shall be able to return sometime this year.

Blessings of peace to you.

CHAPTER 79

Volunteer Casualty

THE FIRST SERIOUS CASUALTY OF AN OUT-OF-TOWN VOLUNTEER–SPRING BREAK (MARCH 2010)

GENE LEFT SUNDAY WITH ALL the young adults from Guilford College, about 12 young men and women, who had come to work in the desert during spring break. He and Christa Sadler from Flagstaff, along with Ayala and Darby were running the camp. The next day, Monday, Gene came back to participate in the Monday night meeting to decide whether No More Deaths would approve the proffered Special Use Permit (SUP) for BANWR. Just before we left home for that meeting, we received a call saying that one of the students, Alice Harty, had fallen on rain-drenched rocks and injured her head so much that it was bleeding over her eyes. Christa called for an evacuation. One helicopter showed up and circled overhead. Then two Border Patrol cars arrived with the agents knowing nothing about first aid. Fortunately, Christa and Darby are well-trained and could adequately assess Alice's condition to provide her with first aid. Finally, BORSTAR (Border Patrol's search and rescue unit) arrived fully prepared to deal with just about any medical crisis. They immediately immobilized Alice's head and neck, loaded her onto a stretcher and put her into their helicopter.

Meanwhile, one of the Border Patrol agents yelled at Christa that she shouldn't be out there, blah, blah, blah. Fortunately, the accident happened close enough to Ruby camp that volunteers could gather up most of Alice's belongings and send them along with her in a large garbage bag in the huge Blackhawk helicopter. Later she told me she couldn't remember anything about the helicopter ride (to Tucson Medical Center, a Trauma One hospital); she just remembered a loud noise—from the rotors on the helicopter. It seemed as if she were suddenly dropped in the hospital, with no travel time. It probably took about 20-25 minutes from the scene of the accident.

Because of her head injury and some stiffness in her neck, they cut off all her clothes in the emergency room (just like Danilo earlier). This protocol was new to me, but no doubt hospital personnel didn't want to take a chance of injuring her further while removing her clothes.

"They could at least have pulled down my pants!" Alice said later.

She had been wearing two pairs of long underwear—one pink silk and the other the usual cotton kind—and some black pants. She lamented the loss of these, plus a new running top and sports bra that were definitely goners.

Our son, Mark, went to pray for her in the hospital's chapel along with Gene, Maureen Marx (one of our nurses), and some other No More Deaths people. By 12:30 a.m. or so, she'd had a CAT scan and other diagnostics, and she was discharged to come to our house. She and two of her friends from Guilford who, along with Christa Sadler (from Flagstaff), had driven from Tucson all came over.

When Christa went to Walgreens to fill prescriptions for super-ibuprofen and Percocet, I set about making toasted cheese sandwiches for everyone who hadn't eaten dinner. By a little after one in the morning, everyone had found a place to sleep. We all crashed and slept until about 9:30 a.m. the next day. Then it was decided that Christa would take one of the girls back to camp and leave Jasmine (yazmín) at our house with Alice. Each day we made tentative arrangements for Alice to go back out to camp, but each day she continued to have a headache and nausea, sometimes not-so-bad and sometimes severe.

Nurse Maureen called Dr. Norma and asked her to visit Alice to check her out. On Wednesday morning, Norma came by to give Alice some neurological tests and interviewed her. She thought Alice should continue to rest for at least another day. She'd call again in the morning. When she called, she told us she had consulted with a neurologist friend who said that even if Alice went back into the ER, she wouldn't be rescanned because CAT scans these days are so efficient that one would've caught any serious problem the first time. So, we continued with the regimen of sleeping, eating, watching TV, napping, and then eating some more. Norma also recommended some walking around, as Alice was not yet steady on her feet. Alice called her mother in New York who assured her it would just take some time for her to heal.

I called Alice's father in New York—Gene had talked to him previously from the hospital. We both assured him that Alice was receiving good care both in the hospital and at our home. I let him know that she appeared to be on the mend. I also told him that Alice was our first volunteer casualty during the past six years of running desert camps. He was very supportive and thanked us for taking such good care of his daughter. Additionally, I enjoyed having her for company throughout the week while Gene was at camp.

Alice ended up staying at our house until late Friday night when I took her to meet her friends at St. Mark's church. They were all spending the night on cots and in sleeping bags on the floor in the Kino Room. Everyone laughed and hugged her when she arrived and wanted to know how she was feeling. Still a little rocky, I think, but she seemed glad to be with her schoolmates. After the debriefing on Saturday morning, they planned to head up to Phoenix where Jasmine's family would feed them all dinner and put them up for the night. From there, they'd fly back to North Carolina with plenty of stories to tell.

But let's not have that kind of trauma again. I felt very conscious of the liability of taking young adults into the desert, especially with all the possible dangers we might encounter. Not the least of which were rattlesnakes emerging from their winter hibernation, the Minute Men, drug runners, or unpredictable weather.

REPORT FROM MARIPOSA: SPRING BREAK, WEEK TWO

Email from David Hill to No More Deaths Volunteers:

Hi everybody,

Just taking a few moments, while I'm at the apartment recharging the cell phones, to give you an update from week two of spring break Nogales 2010. This is an AMAZING group of people—thank you, Annie, for lining them up. We include two native Spanish speakers, one nursing assistant, a human rights law specialist—nobody hasn't found a function, not even me. One of us left Guatemala as a political refugee in the 1980s, got to know how police/military terror works pretty well there, and is finding her time here both disturbingly reminiscent and empowering because she can do something about it and isn't afraid for herself. She's a teacher at a Quaker school and is journaling her experience to present to her students.

All of us have been kept thoroughly busy with abuse documentation, first, and phone calls. The last few days have re-convinced me that every day of the year here, No More Deaths volunteers are critically needed. In the last couple of days, volunteers have accompanied multiple people to the hospital for serious injuries, either inflicted by or left untreated by United States officials. Even an ill volunteer's trip to the hospital in Nogales, Arizona (she arrived with food poisoning and needed rehydration—is recovering steadily now) turned up a horrendous story of Border Patrol abuse. The nurse asked Holly (the ill volunteer) why she was in Nogales and she explained that we were here to document Border Patrol abuses. The nurse said they document abuses at the hospital too; for instance, a man was recently brought to the hospital by Border Patrol with severe injuries all around his head. The nurse asked him what happened, and he explained that they told him not to move, and he moved, so they clubbed him. She was so angry about this she called the police. They came and told the man that basically he deserved it; he shouldn't have been in this country anyway, and they walked away. Is there a possibility of establishing a relationship or contacts with that hospital? Well, experiences like that have helped us recognize that we are truly in the midst of a war zone, with violence all around.

Some of our work in the desert didn't change much. The following account from Kat Bucciantini will remind you of a similar event two years ago that told the story of Danilo and the No More Deaths volunteers experiences with Border Patrol, ambulances, and repatriation. It's all the more frustrating because we believed things were happening (both behind the scenes and in public agreements) to ease our relationships with other desert denizens—like BANWR, Forest Service or Border Patrol. However, it appeared to be difficult for the government to translate high-level policy decisions down to the boots on the ground. We were determined to stay within the law and were working hard to do so, but I'm afraid we couldn't do much about the snakes, neither the figurative ones nor the actual rattlesnakes.

CHAPTER 80

Spring Break Report to Family and Friends–March 2010

THE FOLLOWING TESTIMONY IS FROM Kat Bucciantini, a young nursing instructor from Chicago, who first came to Tucson by herself and later brought several students with her to experience the desert and help migrants:

> For spring break this year, I camped in the Arizona desert south of Tucson and volunteered with an organization called No More Deaths. No More Deaths volunteers hike the migrant trails in the desert between the Mexico-U.S. border and Tucson and leave water and food for people who may need it
>
> Migration is absolutely in no way an issue of law enforcement. Crime is NOT the root cause of migration and thus criminalizing it is NOT a solution. Starving children, sick relatives, violence, separated families, lack of work, no hope for a future. *These* are the reasons that people are willing to leave their country and their culture to travel through the deadly desert and arrive in a country that considers them criminals and thieves. Migration is an issue of LABOR RIGHTS and HUMAN RIGHTS. Migration is an issue of LOVE and FAMILY. Migration is an issue of SOCIAL and ECONOMIC JUSTICE.

Preach it sister.

Kat continues:

Being one of two in a camp of 20 with a medical background, I soon became known as "Nurse Kat." Besides toting food and water out along the trails, I also carried the Med Pack and was sought out for medical advice from other volunteers and migrants—as well as for the occasional identification of remains (meaning I had to determine if the bone we were looking at was animal or human). Although the bones were always completely clean, it was still horrifying.

Moving on—about half-way down the first migrant trail, my group had come across multiple pairs of pants discarded in various places alongside the trail. We had learned that in a state of dehydration delirium, a migrant will often discard his hat, bag, or shirt. But it is unusual for them to take off their pants and even more unusual to see multiple pairs. Migrants often only have the one pair they are wearing. Questions that came into my mind were: *What were they wearing when they took these off? OR What drove them to do it?*

One pair had an especially large, dark stain. I was asked by another volunteer if I thought it was blood. I honestly had no idea. This question, like many others, went unanswered, but it was hard not to imagine the worst. I walked off the trail and searched around in the ditches and underbrush for any sign that someone had stopped there and never gotten up. I saw nothing, so our group hiked on.

The second day we were driving to a trailhead and turned a corner only to see a Border Patrol agent handcuffing a migrant. Migrants often travel in groups, led by a "coyote." But this guy was alone, so we immediately wondered about the rest of his group. We got out and explained to the agent that we had food and water for the migrant if he needed it.

The agent said they didn't need it because there was some in their truck. From past No More Deaths experiences, there was reason to believe this was unlikely. I understand that it's their job to arrest anyone who is undocumented, but the people they pick up are usually dehydrated and not to even offer water is inhumane.

When we finally got going on the trail, we had a good hike ahead of us, mostly uphill (the desert is not flat, my friends!). We finally got to the top only to come across a variety of women's underwear strewn about. Some of it was still hanging on or near a tree called a "victory tree" (or sometimes a rape tree). This is a place where women are raped, and their clothing hung up to announce it. Rape is such a startling reality for women trying to cross the border that they often take birth control before beginning their journey. They are usually raped by the *coyotes* leading the group or by the men in the group. Sometimes women who believed they were crossing with their boyfriends learn they're going to be used as a sex slave in the US. For anyone who thinks that slavery in the US ended with the Civil War, I'm afraid you are mistaken. The sex slave trade is so common that the Salvation Army has an entire department dedicated to working against it.[117] It was shocking to see the tree, and have it explained for the first time. It was almost more than I could bear. I gently removed the clothing from the tree and paused for a second to let it sink in. Overwhelming emotions caused me to stop, double over, and let tears slip down my cheeks.

---

117 The Salvation Army firmly believes that the abuse and exploitation of human beings through any form of human trafficking is an offense against humankind and against God. This belief, combined with our mission to preach the gospel of Jesus Christ and to meet human needs in His name without discrimination, motivates us to work vigilantly for the prevention of human trafficking and for the restoration of survivors. salvationarmy.usa.org.

From that point on, I became numb to the things I witnessed, mainly so that I'd get through each workweek. Since I got back, not a day has gone by that I've cried that hard. I was shaking out of anger, sorrow, guilt, shame, horror....

As we left the site of the rape tree, another volunteer came across a bone. It was completely clean, and I thought it must have been out there a long time. But our leader, Gene, said that bones get cleaned quickly out in the desert. Everyone stopped as I looked at the bone. For a few horrifying moments, I was unsure if it was human or animal. Finally, we decided it belonged to an animal. I put it aside, and we continued back down the trail to our car.

Water for Migrants (No More Deaths)

The next day we conducted water drops in a few areas close to the road. This meant less hiking with the gallon jugs. As we prepared to do a water drop near a ghost town called Ruby, a migrant was brought to us needing first aid. This was the first migrant I had run across, and I was a little nervous that I wouldn't know what to do for him. Diego had a very deep cut between his thumb and finger, at least an inch deep. After hiking for five days (three before the border and two after he crossed), he had fallen on a rock. The cut was still pretty clean, and I found no sign of infection. I explained what I was doing and what he would need to do to keep the wound clean. I explained the signs of infection and told him that he would need to get help immediately if any of these signs occurred.

We talked to him a little and learned that he had no one to greet him once he made it to Tucson or Phoenix. He 'd been traveling alone the entire time and was concerned that his cut was so severe it might prevent him from getting work once he did make it. We explained that if he needed help before he reached Tucson or Phoenix, he should simply go to the main road and wait for someone to pass by. Possibly Border Patrol would arrest him, but he might receive medical care.

After dressing Diego's wound and ensuring he had enough food and water, we parted ways with him. I can only hope he made it all the way. Later that day, as we made our way down a treacherous river bed that started at the top of a mountain saddle and worked its way down to the foot, we came across some more bones. After I determined they were animal bones, we buried them with reverence.

When we returned to camp that night, we greeted other volunteers who had been on patrol in other areas of the desert. One of the patrols had run into three migrants hiking together. One was a 16-year-old girl named Crystal who had been living in the U.S. since she was three and was recently sent back to Mexico by her parents. She was crossing for the third time—all she wanted to do was to get back to her family in California. Crystal was traveling with her boyfriend,

Carlos, along with another man, Javier. They had been separated from a larger group when dogs were sic'd on them by Border Patrol. This was the first time No More Deaths volunteers had heard of the use of dogs. The dogs bit some members of the group. This was confirmed later when some of the volunteers at the migrant resource center in Nogales reported treating dog bites on migrants who had just been dropped off by Border Patrol. When the dogs went after their group, these three had run. Crystal fell at some point (she has asthma and her inhaler had been taken from her by Border Patrol during her second attempt at crossing), and her left knee was banged up. She also had the beginnings of blisters.

In the desert, for migrants, blisters can be fatal.

On each corpse that had been found so far, large blisters covered the feet. Some of the blisters that have been treated by No More Deaths volunteers spread over nearly half the foot. When this happens, the pain is so intense that the migrant can't keep up with his *coyote* and is left behind. This greatly increases the chance of never making it out of the desert alive.

It was our last day at camp, Friday. That night, we got to take showers for the first time that week—best five minutes of my life! Then, we went to a nearby cafe to eat really good pizza and listen to the locals play music. Saturday, we had a debriefing session and then I started my way back home via Southwest Airlines. Since then, I have been processing the week in small increments; it is all I can bear most of the time, and crying—a lot. Many emotions welled up in me as I wrote this—anger, sorrow, inspiration, disgust, despair, hope—the list could go on.

At this point, you may be wondering if No More Deaths is breaking the law by not calling Border Patrol every time we run into an undocumented migrant. No More Deaths has a whole slew of lawyers who ensure that we are operating within legal limits. We are not required to turn people in. We do not ask their status. We offer food and water to everyone we run across, including U.S. citizens who are simply hiking, undocumented migrants, and even Border Patrol. We have the right to provide medical treatment to anyone we run into and are, in fact, ethically responsible to do so. We do not hide our camps or pretend we are doing something else to avoid detection. That isn't the point. Only when humanitarian aid becomes illegal, will we become outlaws.

I want others to know what is going on at our border.

Peace and goodness, Kat.

CHAPTER 81

The Passage of SB 1070 (Support our Law Enforcement and Safe Neighborhoods Act)

The law signed today by Arizona Gov. Brewer is a social and racial sin and should be denounced as such by people of faith and conscience across the nation. It is not just about Arizona, but about all of us, and about what kind of country we want to be. It is not only mean-spirited—it will be ineffective and will only serve to further divide communities in Arizona, making everyone more fearful and less safe. This radical new measure, which crosses many moral and legal lines, is a clear demonstration of the fundamental mistake of separating enforcement from comprehensive immigration reform. Enforcement without reform of the system is merely cruel. Enforcement without compassion is immoral. Enforcement that breaks up families is unacceptable. This law will make it illegal to love your neighbor in Arizona and will force us to disobey Jesus and his gospel. We will not comply.

— *JIM WALLIS, SOJOURNERS MAGAZINE*

THE FOLLOWING DESCRIPTION OF SB 1070, its impetus and implementation, is taken from Wikipedia and is supported fully by Wikipedia's documentation, plus local news reporting (*Arizona Daily Star*):

U.S. federal law requires all aliens over the age of 14 who remain in the United States for longer than 30 days to register with the U.S. government, and to have registration documents in their possession at all times; violation of this requirement is federal misdemeanor crime.

The Arizona act (SB 1070) additionally made it a state misdemeanor crime for an alien to be in Arizona without carrying the required documents, required that state law enforcement officers attempt to determine an individual's immigration status during a "lawful stop, detention or arrest," when there is reasonable suspicion that the individual is an illegal immigrant. The law barred state or local officials or agencies from restricting enforcement of federal immigration laws, and imposed penalties on those sheltering, hiring, and transporting unregistered aliens. The paragraph on intent in the legislation says it embodies an "attrition through enforcement" doctrine.[118]

A first offense required a minimum fine of $500, and a second violation a minimum of $1,000 fine, and a minimum of 6 months in jail. A person is presumed not to be an alien who is unlawfully present in the United States if he or she presents any of the following four forms of identification: a valid Arizona driver's license; a valid Arizona non-operating identification license; a valid tribal enrollment card or other tribal identification; or any valid federal, state, or local government-issued identification, if the issuer requires proof of legal presence in the U.S. as a condition of issuance.

The Act also prohibits state, county, and local officials from limiting or restricting "the enforcement of federal immigration laws to less than the full extent permitted by federal law" and provides that any legal Arizona resident can sue the agencies or officials in question to compel such full enforcement. If the person who brings the suit prevails, that

---

118 https://en.wickipedia.org/wiki/Arizona_SB_1070, accessed October 12, 2012.

person may be entitled to reimbursement of court costs and reasonable attorney fees.

In addition, the Act makes it a crime for anyone, regardless of citizenship or immigration status, to hire or to be hired from a vehicle which "blocks or impedes the normal movement of traffic." Vehicles used in such manner are subject to mandatory immobilization or impoundment. Moreover, for a person in violation of a criminal law, it is an additional offense to transport an alien "in furtherance" of the alien's unauthorized presence in the U.S., to "conceal, harbor or shield" an alien or to encourage or induce an alien to immigrate to the state if the person "knows or recklessly disregards the fact" that the alien is in the U.S. without authorization or that immigration would be illegal....The transportation provision includes exceptions for child protective services workers, and ambulance attendants and emergency medical technicians.

Unite to Resist SB 1070—Isabel Garcia at the Microphone (No More Deaths)

On Thursday, April 23, 2010, the law was passed and signed by Governor Jan Brewer.

Loud, continuing criticism of SB 1070 erupted in Tucson, Phoenix, and other communities across the country. Just one week later, one consequence to the objections resulted in passage by the Arizona legislature of HB 2162 which Governor Brewer signed. The amended text stated that "Prosecutors will not investigate complaints based on race, color, or national origin." The new text also stated that "Police may only investigate immigration status incident to a 'lawful stop, detention, or arrest.'" It also lowered the original fine from a minimum of $500 to a maximum of $100. Additionally, it changed the incarceration limits for first-time offenders from 6 months to 20 days. A modest modification. Soon, lawsuits were filed, and later other changes were made.

CHAPTER 82

No More Deaths Strategy Changes– We Reject Racism

As most of you know, I now regularly file asylum applications on behalf of Mexicans in Removal Proceedings. Lately I have, by chance, encountered several people who report relatives being kidnapped and killed in Nogales, Sonora. I would like to suggest the following project for the WRR campaign: I would like to designate a day at a community location and place ads on the Spanish-language radio stations calling people who have first-hand knowledge of kidnappings, extortions, and murders to come forward and execute affidavits--just based on my casual encounters, I suspect several hundred people would respond. Is this a project the campaign could assist with?

— *EMAIL TO WE REJECT RACISM FROM ATTORNEY MARGO COWAN*

THE PASSAGE OF THESE BILLS helped initiate a virtual diaspora of No More Deaths volunteers into the community to meet the challenges that had been created by the legislation. It also instigated a climate in which cooperation among humanitarian agencies could grow and flourish. In the religious sector, ministers and other clergy came together and created an interfaith clergy group that set about to meet the growing needs in the community. Among other actions, the clergy group encouraged South Tucson to become a "sanctuary city."

On the 22nd of April, a group convened at the Public Defender's office called by No More Deaths volunteer coordinator, Jean Boucher, and volunteer Lois Martin. Both attorneys, Margo Cowan and Andy Silverman, were there, as were others, to begin talking about what could possibly be done to stop Operation Streamline. They also discussed types of resistance to SB 1070 that could be employed, and what would be appropriate assistance for families whose members had been caught up in the Operation Streamline process.

Activity planning moved quickly. On Friday, April 24th, another group met at Casa Mariposa, which included the Reverend Alison Harrington from Southside Presbyterian Church, the Reverend John Fife, and the Reverend Carol Bradson along with Maryada Vallet, Jim Marx, Gene Lefebvre, and me. The premise of the meeting was as follows: The governor has signed SB 1070; how can we resist? Alison noted her frustration that De Cristo Presbytery (a regional, Presbyterian group encompassing Tucson, Southern Arizona and Southern New Mexico) had not agreed to resist the law. We all met for a couple of hours discussing ideas for resistance. We agreed to meet again early the next morning. That meeting included Gene Lefebvre, Randy Meyer (pastor of the UCC church in Green Valley), Noel Andersen (Randy's assistant), John Fife, Brandon Wert, Reverend Carol Bradson, Maryada Vallet, two Episcopal priests, and some other pastors. Other groups convened around the city to hold meetings as well.

Our group decided to hold a press conference on April 29th to present objections to SB 1070. We decided that our theme would be: "We Resist Racism." In no time, buttons and posters stating the theme were available to distribute throughout the community. Soon after that, a campaign was initiated in which volunteers went from door to door to businesses in Tucson asking them to sign a pledge that they would not discriminate against anyone coming to their doors based on race. The businesses signed the statement saying that they were welcoming to anyone. They were given *Resiste* posters to put in their store windows. The response was overwhelmingly positive.

We wanted more Hispanic pastors to get involved and reached out to invite them to join in the process. There were stories of families being torn apart in Nogales, and we also knew of families being torn apart in Tucson. Southside Presbyterian Church ministered to families whose members were caught up in the raids on small bus and van companies providing transportation for migrants. Our people met with neighborhood groups, told them their rights, gave information about helpful resources, and encouraged them to call upon one another when tragedy struck.

No More Deaths volunteer, Jimmy Wells, became involved with a group of families who were organizing to protect themselves post SB 1070. This group met in community assemblies and wanted to make sure all families could participate. With Jimmy's help, they arranged for the children to be cared for by volunteers while the mothers organized as part of the group *Corazon de Tucson*. In 2014, the mothers started taking turns watching the children since the number of families and children increased. At that time, three volunteers and one mom worked with the children.

Margo Cowan met with day laborers at Southside Church to reassure them and talk with them about their issues. One aspect of SB 1070 was directly related to the Southside Work Center—the act made it a crime for anyone, regardless of citizenship or immigration status, to hire or to be hired from a vehicle which "blocks or impedes the normal movement of traffic." Vehicles used in such manner were subject to mandatory immobilization or impoundment. After coping with thousands of migrants during the Sanctuary Movement in the 1980's, Southside had built a new sanctuary and education space. It included showers and sleeping spaces on hand when a new wave of migrants began to arrive. Each day migrants staying at the church, or nearby, would gather at the church to be picked by people looking for workers. Their previous habit had been to stop in the street. However, this strategy changed to comply with the law and pickup took place in the parking lot.

Margo emphasized that our churches are communities of faith and open to all people—all children of God. She explained that the ethics of the situation calls for people of faith to resist this bad law. She assured the workers that we were standing in solidarity with the Latino community but not speaking for them.

Sarah Launius one of No More Deaths key volunteers, writes about some of the collaborative efforts that took place during this time:

> In the fall of 2009, members of to Tucson-based organizations—Tierra Y Libertad Organization (TYLO), a barrio-based *Chicanx* youth collective on the south side of Tucson that focused on livelihood struggles to promote sustainability and self-determination, and No More Deaths had begun conversations with one another to strategize on how to collectively respond to HB 2008, the Arizona law that forced state-funded health and social service providers to report anybody they suspect to be unlawfully present to federal immigration authorities, under penalty of criminal prosecution. By the spring of 2010, activists had surveyed and met with area clinics, agencies and other service providers to assemble a list of those who were privately funded and therefore exempt from the law, and who agreed they would not contact immigration officials under any circumstances. This organizing effort provided the immediate basis for a coordinated organizing campaign almost as soon as SB 1070 passed into law.[119]

---

119 Geoffrey Boyce, Sarah Launius, and Adam O. Aguirre, "Drawing the Line: Spatial Strategies of Community and Resistance in Post-SB 1070 Arizona," School

The "We Reject Racism" (WRR) campaign was launched to forge relationships and disseminate strategies whereby Tucson residents could practically resist SB 1070. . . The campaign's strategy targeting a diverse cross-section of the city's population generated a tremendous response. Between June and July 2010 more than 3,000 Tucson residents joined the WRR campaign, including at least 200 businesses comprised of restaurants, laundromats, car mechanic shops, bars, and grocers, among others. On July 27, 2010, an entire southside Tucson business district, "Plaza Azteca," held a press conference where business owners declared the district an anti-racist zone and announced that every shop in the plaza had agreed to join WRR. The control of business owners over semi-public space, and the proliferation of stores and services declaring noncompliance with SB 1070, gave residents safer locations where they could travel and take care of everyday needs. It also gave all Tucson residents a constructive way to channel their economic activity in sympathy with the national boycott campaign.[120]

We Reject Racism planted the seeds for "Keep Tucson Together (KTT)," a volunteer-run free community immigration clinic; and the KTT clinic in turn helped launch a wave of churches across the United State providing Sanctuary to protect individuals from immigration authorities and prevent their deportation. One of the early No More Deaths volunteers, Jennifer Hill, became a leader in that effort.

---

of Geography and Development, University of Arizona, published in ACME, An International Journal for Critical Geographies, 2017, p. 12.
120 Op. Cit., pp. 14-15.

CHAPTER 83

Keep Tucson Together (KTT)

**Margo Cowan Explains Migrant Rights and the Keep Tucson
Together Program to a Rapt Audience (No More Deaths)**

As VOLUNTEERS MOVED THROUGHOUT THE barrios of Tucson and South
Tucson, they learned how much the residents needed advice about
their legal status, and how much help they needed with completing paperwork for DACA, asylum, and other legal matters. DACA

is Obama's 2012 program called Deferred Action for Childhood Arrivals and applies to children who came to the United States before the age of 16, have lived here continuously since June 15, 2007, and were under the age of 31 on June 15, 2012. DACA was created at the urging of DACA-aged students who felt they belonged in the U.S. By June 30, 2016, more than 740,000 young people had received DACA status. The number of people affected when counting the young people's parents amounts to more than 1.6 million individuals. The Arizona Board of Regents granted DACA recipients, "DREAMers," the right to pay in-state tuition to public colleges.

DREAMers (No More Deaths)

Growing out of We Reject Racism, the Keep Tucson Together established a free clinic that would meet the needs of the immigrant community. Sarah Launius, UA graduate student, and Kat Sinclair, UA teaching assistant, supported by attorney Margo Cowan, initiated the program for three hours each Saturday at Southside Presbyterian Church. Later clinics were held in the Pueblo Magnet High School gym and other locations.

Sarah Launius said, "We need to keep communities together. People need to know that if they resist deportation, we (the advocates and humanitarians) will have their backs."

No More Deaths collaborated with Tierra y Libertad (TYLO) at their invitation and the National Dreamer Coalition. Together these two organizations developed the capacity to help individuals. Then, they trained others who had already been helped by the program to assist in helping others.

The volunteers helped individuals gather the information needed to pursue their cases. These could include documents showing their ties to the community, documents showing ties to their family in the U.S., and evidence of no criminal history.

A $495 application fee was required for the DACA application which, interestingly, mostly paid for the program. In June 2011, John Morton, director of Immigration and Customs Enforcement (ICE) issued a memo calling for ICE attorneys and employees to refrain from pursuing noncitizens with close family, educational, military or other ties in the U.S. Instead, they should spend the agency's limited resources on persons who pose a serious threat to public safety or national security.[121] The concept of "prosecutorial discretion" was applied to gain administrative closure of each DACA case (and others). This allowed people to go back to their regular lives.

Initially, Launius and Cowan developed a prosecutorial discretion request packet that would provide information about mitigating circumstances and completed it for 69 individuals. They delivered these requests to the ICE office and invited the media. They wanted ICE to know the community was watching.

In the first few months, KTT achieved a 95-percent success rate, second highest in the nation. They continue to lead the nation in case closures. In some cases, members of the community were asked

---

121 Shoba Sivapradad Wadhia, Esq., "The Morton Memo and Prosecutorial Discretion: An Overview. July 20, 2011" (www.american immigration council.org), accessed May 20, 2018.

to provide letters of support or to call well-placed individuals to offer their verbal support.

By 2019, Margo Cowan reported to the No More Deaths spokes-meeting that KTT now has several distinct areas of work: asylum, family unification, cancellation of removal for non-lawful and lawful permanent residents, U.S. citizenship, community office, volunteer lawyers, DACA, work permits, bonds and detention visitation. Each working group has one or two group leaders and several regular volunteers who perform the work. At the moment, more than 150 people volunteer in various capacities. Cowan says that KTT now represents more than 400 people and families in removal proceedings and our lawyers see an average of 40 new people seeking legal representation every Thursday at the Pueblo High School clinic. No one is turned away. Recently KTT has represented Nicaraguan asylum applicants detained in Pima County and our lawyers have been winning their cases. Currently, the demand for representation is overwhelming.

Cowan says that the role of the clinics is to "...demystify the law. It's sharing information with everybody, getting people accurate information so they know how to take care of themselves and keep their families together."[122]

At this writing, the DACA program has been halted (September 5, 2017) by President Donald Trump. Several court actions that would continue DACA are awaiting completion. Check the Internet for the latest information. From Trump's action, Margo Cowan was heard to say, "This is the day DACA died."

Let's hope this isn't true.

---

122 Linda Ray, "Keep Tucson Together" (Arizona: Tuscon Weekly, December 17, 2015), available at www.Tucson Weekly.com/Tucson/keep-tucson-together/Content?oid=5995069, accessed April 20, 2017.

CHAPTER 84

Doing the Work 2010

GENE AND I BECAME IMMERSED in both the issues and work surrounding illegal immigration. Monday night meetings, while essential to our work, could be very challenging; our method of government, while democratic and consensus-based, can drive one bonkers. Some people were still complaining they weren't kept informed about the decisions around BANWR.

The budget process had been a nightmare. The UUCT had integrated our budget into theirs for some reason—I guess it was a sign of ownership—a good thing. But they needed our input by March 1st. We'd been so busy with the BANWR negotiations for the past few months that the budget was the last thing anyone wanted to address. Not to mention getting ready for spring break in the desert and at Mariposa. Then, as the institutional memory of planning and creating a budget a year ago faded, one of the groups spent $4,700 on T-shirts, buttons, and stickers to sell without checking with the finance committee, the fundraising committee, or their brains. We had an agreement that any proposed expenditure over $500 went before the whole group ("circle," as Steve calls it); surely someone had to have known that when the decision was made in DAWGS. Especially since we'd never had an order greater than $1,000 before. Institutional memory again—or thoughtlessness, maybe. I do recall some issues around the same time last year that seemed to arise when people's actions were so at odds with the budgeting process that it seemed like they forgot we even had a budget.

Then, there are the folks who say, "We can't have the budget driving our work!" Our budget was over $125,000 this year (2010); we must pay attention to whether the money is coming in and what is going out besides the one important thing wanting to be funded!! All this told me that we needed to provide reports more regularly to the working groups and write an operations manual—and insist that people read it. ACK, I knew that everyone would resist becoming more institutionalized, though (*didn't happen—until much later*).

Some things never change, and we often fail to learn from past experiences. It can be frustrating, as many people tell me.

The weather here in Tucson had just been gorgeous. The mercury hit 90 degrees a couple of days ago, but it dropped back down into the lower 80s. In the backyard we had a cactus that we got from our neighbor in Phoenix. It bloomed with seven bright red flowers, making my day a very happy one. Our artichokes were producing like crazy—I picked about a dozen and cooked them up. When I woke from my nap, my son, Mark, was eating one. Gene had just finished one, so of course I had to have one too. They have a few aphids but not enough to fuss about. But, when I picked them, I found a ladybug. I haven't seen a ladybug in years. How in the world do ladybugs know to show up to eat the aphids? Last year I planted marigolds around the artichokes to keep the aphids away and I think that helped. I'm glad, however, that I didn't get to that this year. It was worth it just to see the one tenacious ladybug—bright red with tiny black dots—busily eating aphids.

Gene's involvement with No More Deaths had been growing each week. He was still on the BANWR negotiating team, although that team no longer seemed to be negotiating with BANWR now that the Special Use Permit process was in place. However, now a group led by the University of Arizona's Udall Institute to develop the research project had had several meetings during the past few weeks and were now putting off any more work on the project until mid- or late-June. Perhaps they wanted to gauge public response to the Special Use Permit posting. Then there was the ministers' group planning its response to Arizona's SB 1070.

Meanwhile, the personnel committee for No More Deaths had hired two new stipended volunteers (at a whopping $1,000 per month). The first, Hannah Hafter, who had been working hard with the abuse documentation working group, was just finishing up her degree in public health and accepted the position of outreach/ mobilizer to help us involve more people in understanding why a humane immigration reform is essential through using the unique perspective of No More Deaths to speak to the issue. It looked like we'd be calling for an end to border militarization plus a hold on all raids and removals until immigration reform was passed and SB 1070 was banished.

Shaw Drake, a former No More Deaths volunteer at the end his college career, would arrive in a couple of weeks to start the logistics-coordinator position. This job entailed getting volunteers from the airport to their temporary housing in Tucson (actually, first finding that temporary housing), making sure they are fed, arranging full-day training sessions each Saturday, deploying our four vehicles, and ensuring that all cell phones were in place and working. It was a huge job, but fortunately for both new staff people, delegation was the key. We had lots of people helping: my group would be guiding Hannah's work. Several others would be helping Shaw. And in addition to the Desert Aid Working Group and the Mariposa group, Gene and I did the in-town phones, Victor Ceballos and a few others were on the vehicles. Some Tucson residents who leave for the summer make their condos available for volunteer R&R. Paul Barby provided financial reimbursements whenever volunteers had to use their own money to pay for camp or border essentials.

Jean Boucher prepared and issued the invitation to volunteers around the country. It wasn't long before he was responding daily to questions and applications. He made the field placements by week for the couple hundred volunteers who came during the 17 weeks that the camp was open as well as for the fewer number of weeks at Mariposa. Naco and Agua Prieta would also receive their share of volunteers from this group. I worked with Paul and our newly-added statistician, Kat Sinclair, on the bills, budget, and bookkeeping. During that spring, we spent a great deal of time with the UUCT making certain we were following all the protocols recommended by the Unitarian Universalist Association (national) and the local Unitarian Universalist Church of Tucson. Before she returned to Wisconsin for the summer, Unitarian and attorney, Leila Pine, carried the heavy load of negotiating a few minefields in that process. We appeared to be on a sound footing at that time, thanks to her and to the UUCT pastor, The Rev. Diane Dowgiert.

In addition, I worked with the fundraising working group, which included Jim (and sometimes, Maureen) Marx, Victor Ceballos, Eldonna Fisher, Sarah Launius, and others. That spring, we hosted a Charlie King Concert at the UUCT venue with the guidance and help of No More Deaths friend, Ted Warmbrand. We made just under $3,000. Not too much, but a local restaurant and another program Ted works with benefitted as well. We sent out an email appealing to folks for funds and had a newsletter that informed them about our summer activities. We needed money, water, migrant packs, white socks, and medical supplies. We were hoping for an excellent response—not only were we conducting our usual summer activities, but we'd also added an outreach on the political front to our efforts.

As a result of SB 1070, a lot of people contacted our media group wanting information about No More Deaths position on the bill. They were from all over and asked if they could come to Arizona and check things out for themselves. Sarah Launius and Geoff Boyce manned phones day and night. Gene spent a day speaking with a group of Quaker tax resisters who wanted more information about what was going on at the border. Other groups planned to arrive, as well—folks who fell outside of the scope of our volunteer program. It seemed that Gene and John Fife would be carrying the brunt of talking with these groups along with Sarah and Geoff.

On Wednesday, Gene was going to take a group from Michigan on a desert patrol. They'd just spent the past week with BorderLinks and would be joined by a group of 20 high school students from Tucson. Gene planned to involve them in helping to get Byrd Camp ready to start in just two weeks. Six clergy members from Rhode Island had arrived in time to participate with the local ministers to help them prepare their local church's response to SB 1070. Some Lutherans were rumored to be in Phoenix in hopes of coming to Tucson, but we never heard anything further. Our volunteers had to be prepared for any type of request that came our way.

Fourth of July: Gene went out to Byrd camp to brief everyone about some changes in our approach to the desert and its various inhabitants—we wanted to keep confrontations to a minimum. Darby had been back in town for a week or so after spending time in Guatemala and Mexico. Ayala and Lydia Delphia (a young woman who was spending her senior year in high school with us) had just come in, and there were a few others who had been at camp for a couple of weeks that were also new to No More Deaths. Gene felt they should know the latest information.

He returned home about 1:30 p.m. and we went to my cousin Linda and Sam's to celebrate the Fourth of July. Gene mentioned he'd like to get a bell for camp—Sam knows where to get everything you need at swap meets. Sam took Gene out to his shop and they returned with an oxygen tank made into a bell, with a hook already attached to a chain at the top. It had a great sound, if a bit loud. After we visited with them for a while, we returned home, with the bell. Gene was tired, so he napped on the couch for an hour or more. Then we went to Southside Church to watch the fireworks on "A" Mountain. The city of Tucson, in its cost-cutting mode, had cut out the fireworks, but some local business people came up with the money to put them on. Southside's parking lot has a perfect view; people were parked in every lot in the neighborhood, with lots of little kids running around the cars and having a great time. Later, the bell was hung at Byrd Camp.

July 11th: Gene and I drove to Phoenix with John and Maryann Fife for a fundraising event sponsored by Phoenix No More Deaths. This event was being held to raise money for the purchase of water that we'd place on the trails and use in Nogales. The fundraiser was being promoted by the Hispanic Chamber of Commerce and many Hispanic entrepreneurs; both men and women, were in attendance. Music was played throughout the night, starting with *Mariachis* in the foyer where everyone could examine the auction items. Speakers included former state representative, Alfredo Gutierrez, current federal representative, Kyrsten Sinema, John and, of course, Gene. The event raised over $7,500, enough to purchase 15,000 gallons of water from our favorite grocery stores in Tucson and Green Valley.

July 14th: Gene attended a DAWGS meeting to work out leadership for camp; it had been difficult since several of our camp coordinators had retired or were out of town. Afterward he attended a meeting to plan activities for July 29th.

All the while, we were wondering what would happen if there were an injunction against the law going into effect in just two weeks.

CHAPTER 85

WAITING—Tuesday July 27, 2010

IT HAD BEEN MORE THAN 70 days without rain up until this day. Unfortunately, it didn't last long enough, not really satisfying, but at least the air had that unique wet-dirt smell as the first drops fall. The monsoon season was late, and it seemed like a false start that left us waiting for the real thing. As July rolled into August, the clouds gathered day after day, and the wind chimes my daughter had given me for Mother's Day pealed, but we were still waiting.

Fortunately, there probably weren't any deaths on BANWR as we waited. Migrants were shying away from BANWR and from the Santa Cruz Valley where Arivaca is located. We were concerned because 48 of the 60 deaths that had occurred this month last year were on Tohono O'odham Nation's land.

As we waited to hear Judge Susan Bolton's decision about SB 1070, we wondered: Would she issue an injunction to prevent the law from going into effect in two days, on Thursday? Would she declare outright that it was unconstitutional? Would she let it stand? Sheriff Joe Arpaio raided a small restaurant in west Phoenix and netted four hapless migrants on Tuesday, July 27th. A petty gesture, with promises of more to come. The local and national news media ran stories about families leaving Arizona for safer places to work and live. Manuel, a friend in Phoenix, reported a significant loss at his used car dealership because his clientele was leaving the state.

Food, Water and Trash (No More Deaths)

For the third time in two weeks, we discussed whether to send letters to the director of the Department of the Interior, Ken Salazar, U.S. Attorney, Dennis Burke, and our representative in Congress, Raul Grijalva, to let them know that the Fish and Wildlife Service had halted the process that was supposed to give us access to BANWR (and possibly the other federal lands). Steve Johnston, and I voted NOT to send the letter, thus, in our method of consensus, blocking any further action from our core group. It was very stressful. The Tuesday prior, some people went onto the Refuge and left water. Then another group went out Thursday. The Thursday volunteers discovered that the Tuesday water (twenty gallons of it) were all gone. Most likely taken by Border Patrol, not the migrants it was intended for. We thought this battle was almost over, but it continued, and we were still waiting for a final resolution. Or maybe there wouldn't be one, and we'd just be left waiting. Each of our patrols that went out to deliver water on BANWR or on any other state or federal land would always have to wonder if they'd receive a ticket for doing so, or worse, get arrested, which had been threatened.

July 29th was the day SB 1070 would go into effect, barring intervening action. Many, many people and groups had generated energy around this issue. It caught fire nationwide—celebrations, vigils, religious services, rallies, marches, and protests had been planned across the country. Some people left Tucson for Phoenix to join in with their activities. Gene and I planned to stay and support the Tucson effort. Many of our out-of-town volunteers who'd normally be sent out to Byrd Camp, Agua Prieta, or Nogales to work directly with migrants were reassigned back in Tucson to work with families during the SB 1070 campaign.

It seemed to me that this was becoming more of a young person's fight. The young he's and she's simply could not stand the injustices. The pressure from the youth weighed heavily on most of us in No More Deaths as well as other humanitarian organizations. It affected everyone differently. For me, it brought a sense of depression from all the unfinished things in which I had no control. It made me strive for greater control over smaller things within my life.

STILL WAITING—WEDNESDAY, JULY 28, 2010

The meeting with Border Patrol sector chief that afternoon had gone well, and the attendees reported it was positive. However, no promises from the chief. Our representatives tried to show the video of Agent Kermes dumping No More Deaths water, but the equipment wouldn't work. The video was left with the chief to review later. The group would meet again in three weeks. All the waiting was taking its toll. Gene came in from a DAWG meeting. He had stopped at Walgreen's on the way home and bought a fresh bottle of Tums—the 1000 mg size. We were coping every way we could.

SB 1070 Injunction and Protests–July 28, 2010

The day before SB 1070 was to go into effect, Judge Bolton came through with an injunction on controversial sections:

> In her decision, Bolton accepted the Justice Department's argument that the law—which empowers police to question people who they have a "reasonable suspicion" are illegal immigrants—intrudes into federal immigration enforcement. She granted much of an injunction the administration had sought, blocking portions of the law from taking effect while the federal lawsuit proceeds.

> The judge put on hold provisions that would require police to check immigration status if they stop someone while enforcing other laws, allow for warrantless arrests of suspected illegal immigrants, and criminalize the failure of immigrants to carry registration papers. Civil rights groups and federal lawyers had objected to those provisions, while Arizona officials defended them as necessary to fight a tide of illegal immigration.

> Requiring Arizona law enforcement officials and agencies to determine the immigration status of every person who is arrested burdens lawfully present aliens because their liberty will be restricted while their status is checked," wrote Bolton, a Democratic appointee, who allowed other, less-controversial portions of the law to take effect Thursday as scheduled.[123]

On the night of July 29th, Gene and I met Jim and Maureen Marx at the corner of Alameda and Granada not long after the start of

---

123 http://www.*washingtonpost*.wp-dyn/content/article/2010/07/28/AR2010072801794.html.

a vigil taking place at the northwest corner. There were 80 to 100 people standing around with signs protesting SB 1070. A purification ceremony was being held on the grass, several people spoke—starting with Isabel Garcia of *Derechos Humanos*. Around 9:00 p.m., poets, artists, singers, and the like contributed to the emotion of the evening and helped bring people together.

After a while the four of us left to get a beer at *Enoteca* (a wine shop). As we finished visiting and were about to rejoin the crowd outside, the owner/manager offered to buy us another round; he had seen our posters with *Resiste* written on them. However, we were ready to leave and just expressed our appreciation. He asked for one of the posters for his window. Another woman, an employee of El Charro, wanted one for the restaurant, and her husband Ricky (a cousin of Representative Raul Grijalva) took one for his truck. After distributing posters, we stood around chatting with them for a while and afterward, decided that it had been a very productive experience.

Later, Gene went back downtown to Presidio Park where an all-night vigil started at 11:30 p.m. John Fife opened the service with recognition of the victory gained by the injunction which had just come through—especially for the many people who would otherwise be afraid to leave their homes on Thursday.

Thursday: This morning Gene left early for a worship service concluding the all-night vigil at 7:00 a.m. Both this service and the all-night vigil were sponsored by the group of religious leaders who had been working together since the bill passed.

Gene then drove over to Southside Presbyterian Church to march downtown with about 20 people who populate the Day Labor Center housed at the Southside Church. The 80 or so marchers arrived downtown about 9:45 a.m. and joined the other protestors and celebrants in front of the federal and state buildings at Granada and Congress. Southside's pastor, Alison Harrington, and the day laborers (mostly migrants) were very grateful for all the support.

Activities continued throughout the day. At some point Gene came home. At 5:00 p.m. we turned on the TV and watched as demonstrators moved into the intersection at Granada and Congress. The police had blocked off traffic close to the I-10 freeway to the west, and at Stone to the east, and both south and north on Granada. About 5:15 p.m., the crowd was asked to disperse by the police. When they did not disperse, several people carrying large banners were arrested, and the banners removed. The police asked again for the crowd to disperse. When they were slow to do so, a group of cops with bikes formed a barrier and began moving the crowd toward the sidewalks. It was gracefully done.

At one point, a group of activist cyclists came driving through the intersection, turned around, then came back toward the police. They were asked to disperse, and shortly later, they did. They did come back through the intersection again sometime later with no incident.

Once again, the crowd was asked to move back and the police with bicycles moved right up to the edge of the sidewalk. Then everyone was out of the intersection. By six o'clock many people had left; we watched as Kat Rodriguez of *Derechos Humanos* told Barbara Grijalva from Channel 13 that she was packing up materials from the vigil and leaving also. The demonstration went on for some time after that but with diminished fervor.

No doubt the demonstration planners (from many organizations) felt the 24-hour effort had been successful. This peaceful event received a great deal of press coverage; many people driving by honked and waved in support; no one had been hurt; there was a lot of joy over the injunction against parts of SB 1070. We saw No More Deaths, Humane Borders, and Samaritan volunteers at all the events.

PHOENIX PROTEST

Later we learned that Daniele Alvarado (former volunteer coordinator and a significant participant in our work with BANWR), Kat

Sinclair, and Asa Duffee of No More deaths were among the 80 or so people arrested in Phoenix, along with the former state senator, Alfredo Gutierrez, in addition to those arrested in Tucson

Several people from the Unitarian-Universalist Church denominational (UUs) office in Boston went to Phoenix to participate in the July 29, 2010, reaction to the implementation of SB 1070. So, while many folks were demonstrating in downtown Tucson streets, others were also demonstrating in downtown Phoenix. A number of people from Tucson drove up to Phoenix to join the UUs there, including Asa Duffey, Kat and others from local UU churches.

Asa and Kat Sinclair were arrested along with the president of the Unitarian Universalists, Peter Morales, and about 100 others—50 at the jail and about 50 more in the street. Forty-seven of those arrested were UUs.

The word was that Sheriff Joe Arpaio was planning to raid some barrios on the Phoenix west side. As an alternative to the raid, some of the protesters tried to keep the sheriff's officers busy in front of the Wells Fargo Building while others chained themselves in front of the jail. The Maricopa County vehicles couldn't get out of the bay area where they had been parked because the opening was blocked by protesters. This effectively prevented them from going on their raid. The sheriff locked down the jail.

In the street 1,000 cops tried to manage the throngs of people. About half of them were in front of the jail. The organizer of the protestors was kicked and beaten up. Kat was taken into the jail and eventually arraigned. She and two others went before the judge at the same time. When they returned to jail, the corrections officer (CO) shoved a girl. She called her a "fuckin' bitch" and the CO shoved her head into a glass window and then the floor until she was unconscious. An orderly mopped up the blood after the girl was moved; then she used the bloody water to mop the cells.

From Asa Duffee:

Well, for starters, I want people to get a glimpse of my perspective on the issue of immigration, and I don't think it's enough to just know that I went to jail for this issue. I want people to know everything that happened at that jail. I want people to feel like they were there themselves, so they can begin to understand the importance of what this experience means to me.

The fact is that I learned much more about the American penal system than I had anticipated, and this introduction of a new social justice issue is just as important as immigration, even if I was only involved for 26 hours. I'd like people to keep that in mind as they read this, though I don't think it would be appropriate to separate the two issues entirely. They are very much connected outside of my own experience, in which they clearly attach.

The second topic, giving to others, further illuminates my egotism (in my mind). It's that one can give to others and only give to others, or one can give to others through a communal sharing. In the way my friend put it, it can be a one-way road or a two-way road—the two-way road being preferable. On this two-way path, all parties grow from the experience, but on the one-way path, one party thinks it grows from the experience, when there is still much left in the experience to discover.

I'm sure one could write a book on the subject, but I'll just leave my explanation to one paragraph, since it was so recently introduced to my mind.

But I think application of the idea in this jail experience is appropriate. Was this only giving, or was it sharing? Further, how does the idea apply to my whole summer working with

No More Deaths? I still haven't reached a concrete conclusion, so I'll leave that up to you.

4 p.m. I walk through the doorway, eager to escape the room after having been there for about two hours. "I just thought you could use a break," the guard says when I look at him expectantly. I'm not sure what his true motivations were—the fact that he had placed an accused murderer in my cell, that I was the very last prisoner of conscience for the Phoenix police to process, or that in fact he just thought I could use a break. Either way, we stand outside the cell for a minute or two until he takes me to medical processing.

I'm taken to a long, wide hallway of sorts, in which a row of benches parallels one long desk with dozens of computers and deputies behind it. The benches are almost filled with a mix of inmates and prisoners of conscience. This is the last time I'll see the women until tomorrow morning, though Kat must have already been processed, since I don't see her here.

Someone calls my name and I go up to feature myself for my mug shot. When she reads out my physical characteristics, the deputy behind the camera says "hair color--red." I do a slight double take but assure myself that she must have been talking about someone else. Unfortunately, I was mistaken – by the time I departed jail, I discovered that my hair is apparently red, and my name is actually spelled "Ase Duffe."

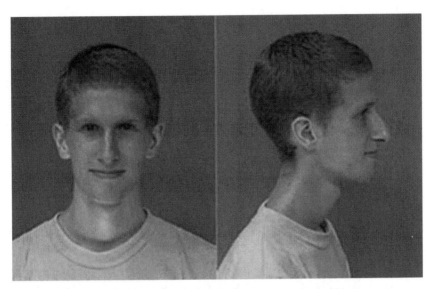

The Notorious and Red-Haired Ase Duffe (Asa Duffee)

Once I'm done with the hallway processing, I'm treated to the wonder of removing my shoelaces and thus converting my shoes into something like decrepit flip-flops. After this is done, the deputy in charge glances down at the blue charm resting on my left ankle. It's a Brazilian charm that my friend Stephanie bestowed upon me when I left school in the spring. The story goes that you must tie the charm in three knots, and you make a wish when the third knot is tied. Then, when the charm breaks, your wish comes true. Anyway, the deputy glances at the charm and asks if it can be untied. I tell him it cannot, and I recite to him what it is. As he uses a pair of scissors to cut the charm away, he says he hopes I made the wish to get out of jail. I tell him it was a much more important wish than that.

CHAPTER 86

A Tohono O'odham Perspective

MIKE WILSON ATTENDED OUR NO More Deaths meeting on September 20, 2010. Mike is a member of the Tohono O'odham Nation located west of BANWR. He is big and strong and during one of our recent wars, he was a member of the U.S. Army Special Forces. At the No More Deaths meeting he expressed deep disappointment at the lack of support from his own people for water stations on the reservation.

He stated, "God's children die in the desert and we remain silent."

He said that he was fed up with the deaths on the reservation. In July of the previous year, 44 of the 59 deaths in the Tucson Sector occurred there. "No one holds the tribal council accountable for these deaths," Mike said. "We rail against Border Patrol (for tearing up our land and building the wall), but where is the moral outrage for 44 deaths in one month?"

As he was driving out to resupply his water drops on the Mexican side, he saw a brand-new water tanker filling tanks for cattle and horses. He learned that the tribe had purchased two new 4,000-gallon tanks at a cost of one million dollars ($.5m each). Plenty of water for the horses and cows but none for the migrants.

Mike asked us to join in a boycott of the Desert Diamond Casinos located on the reservation because they're the source of funds for the tribe. The following is what Mike Wilson told us about his cause:

"I have my battle against the tribal government—the tribal government has migrant blood on their hands. They take down my water stations on the Nation and remove the gallon jugs of life-saving water. The Presbyterian Church at Sells *(Mike was a supply pastor for the church)* fired me because I put out water and would not stop when they told me to. I asked my friend David Garcia, a former member of the tribal council, how the tribe makes its budget. David said that they get a forecast of the profits expected to come in from the casinos during the upcoming year. They use that forecast to make their coming year's budget. We must hit the tribe where it hurts—in their pocketbooks. We will threaten to boycott the casinos and if there is no action to help the migrants, then we will boycott the casinos."

A couple of weeks later, Mike returned to No More Deaths to plead his case once more, but we explained that our focus was on the border and the desert south of Tucson. We suggested that his fight would have to be fought by members of the Nation.

Earlier, some of our abuse documentation folks secured funding to help tribal member Ofelia Rivas and her group, VOICES Against the WALL, document Border Patrol abuses of migrants on the "res," and file those forms with the appropriate agency.

MONDAY, NOVEMBER 1, 2010

Many things happened during this week—Hallowe'en, Day of the Dead, and recognition of migrants.

We attended the Day of the Dead celebration at Evergreen Cemetery, which was also the seven-year anniversary of Rick Ufford-Chase's idea for No More Deaths. The Day of the Dead event had changed—it no longer started at First Christian Church where Humane Borders was based. The pastor, the Rev. Robin Hoover, had been asked to step down from Humane Borders and their office moved further south. They no longer sponsored the march. This year it was sponsored by the clergy who had been meeting regarding

SB 1070, etc. It was a wonderful program with excellent turnout from the churches. Most moving: the reading of the names of those 252 persons (and one fetus) who had died during the past year.

Lois Martin reported on Naco. There had been no migrants through Naco or Agua Prieta since July. All were sent by bus to Nogales. The shelter cared for people coming from Nogales. Some people felt Naco was safer.

Cecile Lumer, the coordinator in Naco, was concerned about receiving monthly hard-won funding from No More Deaths. However, she wanted to keep the shelter open because at any point, Border Patrol could start sending folks there again. She'd been speaking around the country asking people to contribute to No More Deaths. A donation was expected from Albany, New York, in the amount of $700, which she planned to send to us.

There was the possibility of getting an arrangement for people from Nogales to go to Naco. Maybe *Grupo Beta* would facilitate this. *Keep families together.* Could we turn that idea over to the Mariposa working group? There was no rhyme or reason to us for the shift in traffic. Douglas sisters said Nogales did it better; although, Naco and Agua Prieta interviewed all migrants going through. Cecile had been keeping the Naco center open for four-hour days a week for the prior four months.

CHAPTER 87

No More Deaths Strategy 2011

IN FEBRUARY 2011, THE MONDAY night group reviewed and reestablished its goals and set out a new plan based on current needs and resources. Two of their goals reflected items from our Mission Statement verbatim: to end death and suffering in the desert, and to build global movements in solidarity with other groups opposed to border militarism.

Additional goals included:

* Change the national narrative surrounding border issues;
* Abolish private prisons; end militarization of the border;
* Stop deportations, end discriminatory and racist legislation in Arizona;
* Pass comprehensive immigration reform at the federal level;
* Promote clear, humane, and enforced custody standards for Border Patrol and ICE;
* Abolish private prisons;
* End militarization of the border.

The final set addressed the need to work with others to accomplish our goals. We needed to build community within Tucson, Arizona, the United States, and organizations in Mexico.

All these goals were fleshed out in subsequent meetings with certain goals assigned to existing working groups. New working groups had to be formed to address specific goals. Some goals became or continued to be the responsibility of the entire membership.

CHAPTER 88

More Deaths in the Desert

DURING THIS PERIOD, MATT JOHNSON and fellow volunteers came across another set of migrant remains. Gene and I happened to be attending a party at the home of several volunteers, including Matt, and I asked him if he would talk with me about what happened. He said flat-out, "no." Unlike Anna, who had been willing to talk with Gene and me over lunch at *El Minuto* about her experience, Matt was part of a new crew of young adults (mostly anarchists) who distrusted those of us who made up the greater part of the Monday night group. It seemed like Matt might not trust me with his feelings. He didn't understand I would hold them dear.

It's common for young adults to think they're invincible and are often dealt a heavy blow when faced with the death of another young person—as are most of the migrant remains we encounter. Professional counseling can sometimes help, but many volunteers don't take advantage of that opportunity. The *Capacitar* training that Jean Boucher had provided enabled more of our people to be of assistance to one another.

As I think about this a few years later, I'm struck by the fullness of Kathryn Ferguson's vivid description of the death of a migrant. It seems we must have respect for this process, give words to its discovery, and then consciously allow ourselves to grieve. Kathryn writes:

Each year the number of desert deaths in Arizona equals the number of people on an airplane. As the local saying goes, it is as if an airplane crashes in the desert every year and all the passengers are killed. Unlike in a plane crash, nothing is done about these deaths. Unlike in a plane crash, these people die as a result of dehydration under a white-hot sun.

Death is at the beginning, the enemy. He is a shy shape-shifter. And quiet. You barely notice when he first takes your tongue. It becomes heavy and rough, like a dead dog. You mistake the feeling as a familiar thirst you have known before.

Next, he takes your throat as it shrivels, then pricks like cactus spines. With his sleight of hand, you become so thirsty you suck on anything—your tooth, a rock—to find saliva. You rage at your thirst, then at the thought that he is near. If you are loud enough, and say the right prayer, he will go away, as do all spooks.

He whispers to you that he can wait, that in time you will learn to love him. He will become your only friend. Then he torques the muscles in your legs. As cramps grab you like a vise, you bend over to dig thumbs into calves to stop the pain. You beat the calf with a rock. As you lie on the ground rubbing muscles, you think of those you love. You are afraid here alone. Death takes your tears, so your sobs are deep and dry.

Sitting on the desert floor, you begin talking to your wife. You forgot she was here. Then she speaks. You look up to her face, but it is not hers; it is the face of your new companion. You are confused. Death nudges you, like a cat with a lizard under paw.

Then he takes your belly. Cramps. You roll in the sand, arms clutching your abdomen. You hear the drumming. It is your heart. It will not stay in its cage. It wants out and it will come out. It will explode. Death sits close, to toss you to his other paw.

You go unconscious. When you awaken, you see that you are lying next to a pond of water. With joy, you roll over to lick the glistening sand. It tastes so good. You swallow it. Your mouth fills with dry dirt and teensy hot rocks. You choke. Your heart pounds. Your body spasms. Death licks at your head. He is no longer your enemy. He is your only friend. You want him to take you. You beg. He tosses you to the other paw, then puts you between his teeth and carries you away.

No one is interested...[124]

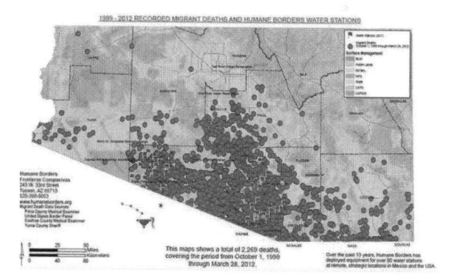

1999-2012 Recorded Migrant Deaths (Prepared by Ed McCullough for Humane Borders and Other Humanitarian Organizations)

---

124 Kathryn Ferguson, *The Haunting of the Mexican Border* (Albuquerque: University of New Mexico Press, 2015).

CHAPTER 89

Border Patrol–José Elena Antonio Rodriguez

I DO NOT BELIEVE THAT I'm overstating when I say that a pall fell over the general population of Southern Arizona, especially the humanitarian community, when it learned that 16-year-old José Elena Antonio Rodriguez had been shot to death in Nogales, Sonora from the American side by a Border Patrol agent on October 10, 2012.

At the time, it was reported that José's body was found on a sidewalk across *Calle Internacional* about 40 feet from the U.S./Mexico border. He'd been shot from two locations from the top of a 25-foot embankment where there's a bollard-style border fence (vertical posts with spaces between) approximately 20 feet high.

**Looking Through the Bollard-Type Fence to Spot Where Jose
Elena Antonio Rodriguez was Shot (No More Deaths)**

Border Patrol claims they were responding to a report that there were people carrying drugs across the fence into Mexico who were throwing rocks up toward the agents. Some spectators said they saw four people running away. However, Nogales resident, Isidro Alvarado, stated that he was walking about 20 feet behind José when the other two men ran past him onto a side street. Then he heard the shots.

Agent Lonnie Swartz was charged with firing the shots that hit José. Swartz said that he aimed his .40 caliber pistol through an opening in the fence. He emptied his pistol, reloaded, and then continued firing. He hit José a total of ten times in his arm, back, and head. José was found with a Blackberry and a plastic lighter in his pockets—no rocks. His mother is reported to have said that she couldn't understand why they shot him so many times.

Swartz's trial was postponed many times. In 2018, he was finally acquitted, although there is talk of retrying him.

During the years between the shooting and the trial, No More Deaths volunteers and others provided support to his family as they drove from Tucson to Nogales for each hearing.

A tension seems to exist between the humanitarians and the law enforcement community of Southern Arizona. Our country is built upon trust and support of the police and Border Patrol (the largest law enforcement agency in the country). People seem to understand that Border Patrol's responsibilities are to protect the citizenry and guard our borders. In some ways both our missions are similar— to save lives. In 1998, Border Patrol established a program called BORSTAR—a search, trauma, and rescue arm whose explicit purpose is to aid the agents and migrants who are in trouble. It deploys helicopters to areas where their help is needed. Nevertheless, as you have read in this book, humanitarian groups have experienced numerous times where Border Patrol and other enforcement agencies have held volunteers at gunpoint, treated migrants inhumanely, destroyed life-saving water placed on trails for migrants, and/or conducted themselves at odds with life-supporting and life-saving ways.

The public has the responsibility to speak out when constitutional rights are abrogated, and No More Deaths has done that through several reports of aberrant Border Patrol behavior.

As an early childhood professional, I've long been interested in child and adult development. From the field of psychology, we learn that law and order is not the highest form of justice. It's considered a four in a one to six scale. That's why we ask police to identify potential perpetrators of crimes, but then turn them over to our justice system. Punishment should come from many factors that need to be considered before such justice is applied.

Lawrence Kohlberg is just one of the many people who has studied how people find justice, but he was one of the first to identify several levels of it. Above law and order, he identifies social-contract orientation and universal ethical principles—the things we all can agree on in a democratic society. That is "principled conscience." I don't plan to belabor these concepts—you can look them up. I just want to point out that as a democratic society, we do not permit the police agencies to act as accuser, judge, and jury. We respect *due process* for adjudication of perceived crimes. Therefore, we expect law enforcement officers on the street and in the field to refrain from taking another person's life unless it becomes absolutely necessary. Shooting an unarmed young man through the bars and into another country? Questionable at best!

José Elena Antonio Rodriguez' Memorial Service (No More Deaths)

CHAPTER 90

Pertenencias (Migrant Belongings)

AFTER A STINT AS THE volunteer coordinator for No More Deaths from 2009 to 2010 while living in Tucson, David Hill moved to Nogales to be part of the action there. At first, he lived in the house rented by No More Deaths for border volunteers, but he soon moved into his own apartment. David has a degree in Literature from Massachusetts Institute of Technology and makes a living editing manuscripts.

Very soon after his move, David learned of the problems that occurred to migrants while being sent from Tucson back across the border into Nogales, Sonora, without their personal belongings. David responded by developing a program for returning *pertenencias,* the Spanish word for "belongings," to individuals. This involved going to the court in Tucson and requesting the belongings. After receiving them, David, or in many cases, Antonio Zapien or other Samaritan volunteers, returned to Nogales and began the tedious job of locating the individual migrants. In some cases, they were right there in Nogales; however, many had returned to their original homes somewhere else in Mexico, or they had made it to their family or friends in the United States. No More Deaths paid for the packaging and postage. The work was very successful. As you will see below, volunteers helped 469 people recover a total of $54,134 from the Arizona Department of Corrections after they were deported, just in 2016.

After a while, the abuse documentation working group, some of whose reports I have addressed earlier, turned its attention to the issue of immigrants being denied their own money and other belongings—their *pertenencias*—after being deported to Nogales. Below are parts of the executive summary of the report entitled "Shakedown." You can see the full document and the entire report at www.nomoredeaths.org.

Shakedown—How Deportation Deprives Immigrants of their Money and Belongings
Executive Summary

As of 2013, the Obama Administration had deported 1.9 million people from the United States, many of whom did not get back their personal property—including money—that they were detained with or that they were allowed to receive while in detention. 34 percent of deportees interviewed by the University of Arizona reported that they did not get back at least one item of their belongings. This mass failure to return money and belongings affects both people detained by Border Patrol while crossing the US/Mexico Border and undocumented individuals detained by Immigration and Customs Enforcement (ICE) anywhere in the U.S.

Though the indicated scale of dispossession is shocking, no large figure can illustrate the daily impacts of this abusive practice. The failure to return money and belongings is a dangerous human rights violation that is not acceptable on any level.

Dispossession by deportation, and the scope of the suffering it creates, is largely invisible inside the United States. It affects a marginalized, hyper-criminalized population, and its consequences are felt mainly after deportation to another country.

As our documentation shows, the property lost is at once humble and substantial. For the most part, the money lost was under $100 USD per person. These are the personal effects of ordinary working people, however, for whom $80 in their pocket, or no longer in their pocket, may represent both a week's pay and a ticket to safety in the country to which they are deported. The impact is not only monetary: largescale loss of IDs, clothing, cell phones, and personal tokens such as wedding rings and family photos also takes a heavy toll on people's safety and psyche. Being deported without money and belongings makes people vulnerable to further exploitation and abuse. Recovery of the withheld property is sometimes belatedly possible through the assistance of a humanitarian organization or one's consulate but never without effort, time, and much uncertainty. As you will see below, volunteers helped 469 people recover a total of $54,134 from the Arizona Department of Corrections after they were deported.

DISPOSSESSION THROUGH DEPORTATION

"Shakedown" provides a detailed account of why and how immigrants' belongings and money are not returned upon deportation and advocates for specific remedies. We present data based on 1,481 cases handled by No More Deaths Property Recovery Assistance Project, which helps people recover personal property after being detained in Arizona, from 2011 to 2014 and with 165 interviews with immigrants deported without some or all their money from 2013 to 2014. We recount stories of money that disappeared from belongings or that was stolen by U.S. agents in plain sight, money deposited into prison accounts that never arrived or from prison labor that was never paid, and money that was returned in forms unusable after deportation such as money orders, prepaid debit cards, and personal checks.

We found that dispossession occurred through three main mechanisms:

> *"When I was detained, Border Patrol threw my necklaces and belt in the trash yelling* 'esto va a la basura.' *They put my cell phone and birth certificate in a bag and said they'd hold on to it for me. I asked for it from ICE when I was being deported and they told me, 'You don't have anything!' I showed them a slip with the items listed and they said, 'Border Patrol has that, not us,' and told me there was nothing they could do." – Yolanda, April 2014, Tijuana, Mexico*

Complete failure to return money and belongings;
Cash returned in forms difficult or impossible to use internationally;
Money directly stolen by agents.

Our key findings include:

- From 2013 to 2014, No More Deaths documented intervention for 165 money-specific cases in which 59% were helped to recover some or all of their lost funds. Out of the $37,025 that was reported lost or unusable, $12,851 was recovered, while $24,174 was lost for good;
- From 2011 to 2014, No More Deaths responded to 1,481 requests for property-recovery help from people who had been deported or were awaiting deportation. We physically handled 884 deportees' personal effects recovered from U.S. Border Patrol alone;
- For property subject to the Border Patrol's standard policy of destruction after 30 days, our Property Recovery Assistance Project (PRAP) rate of successful recovery is only 22%; the rate falls to 12% if the person was subject to criminal prosecution and then initiated their property-recovery effort after deportation;

- Based on a sample of personal effects recovered from Border Patrol, detainees have on average the equivalent of $38.14 in Mexican currency; 60% have one or more foreign-government-issued IDs; and 52% have a cell phone. These are the items that make a crucial difference for their safety and wellbeing at the moment of deportation and afterwards;

- As a result of being deported without access to their money, 81% of those asked reported that they could not afford to travel home, 77% could not afford food, 69% could not afford shelter, 64% lost time, and 53% were exposed to danger.

CATASTROPHIC CONSEQUENCES

No More Deaths chose to highlight the issue of dispossession because, in addition to suffering and trauma, powerful stories of strength and courage are embedded within it. Migrants put their most precious possessions into one backpack to traverse a deadly desert, only for that backpack to be taken by authorities and not returned. In addition to money and identification documents, people travel with medication, cellphones with family phone numbers, irreplaceable keepsakes, spiritual items, and heirlooms. These cherished items represent peoples' histories and their connections to loved ones, which are necessary for their psychological, spiritual and physical well-being.

Similarly, money in this context not only means value in dollars, but frequently represents borrowed sums of money that may take years to repay, whose loss means the impoverishment of loved ones or the forfeiture of homes, land, or other mortgaged assets. Sums of money must be measured against the wages of a Southern Mexican or Central American farmer and how long it may have taken to save or borrow enough to go north, only to have money returned as a non-cashable check or, if the amount is large enough, for it to be confiscated as evidence of "illegal activity." Money also represents the sacrifices that peoples' families made to send them money in immigration detention or that people earned at $1 a day while in a prison or detention center labor and painstakingly saved, only to find themselves penniless on the streets of Mexico because they cannot use the prepaid debit card given to them.

Finally, identification documents may be the only way people can prove their identities. When these documents are seized by U.S. agents and not returned, people are left on the border without the basic documents needed to receive a money transfer or have any recourse when harassed or extorted by the local police. With ID that proves Mexican citizenship, deported individuals gain some access to assistance from the Mexican government. Without ID, the risk of extortion, kidnapping, and sexual assault drastically increases. Without ID, individuals are unable to apply for legitimate work in the border towns where they are deported. With few or no options available to earn money or to leave town, some individuals are recruited into smuggling cartels or otherwise convinced to try crossing the border again as quickly as possible by guides who may take advantage of them. The psychological damage of being stripped away, not only from one's home, but also from resources and autonomy may be felt for a lifetime.

CASE EXAMPLE

Carlos, April 2014, Tijuana, Mexico: "After I was deported in Mexico, police picked me up and took me to jail for not having an ID. I went to Grupo Beta [the Mexican federal agency for migrants] to find out how to replace my birth certificate. They sent me to another government office where I was told that someone from

Jalisco has to pay 430 pesos to get it from where I was born, which I didn't have. I got a job that told me I have 20 days to show them my birth certificate. Once I get my first paycheck, I will have to take the day or maybe days off work to get the replacement, losing even more money."

The vulnerabilities associated with dispossession are especially severe for individuals already at a greater risk due to their gender identity, sexual orientation, age, ethnicity and geographical origin. The United States has a responsibility to ensure the well-being of individuals in its custody and must not engage in practices that needlessly put people in additional harm's way as soon as they are deported.

GOVERNMENT LACK OF ACCOUNTABILITY

When No More Deaths brought concerns related to lost money and belongings to the attention of Border Patrol and ICE, they have responded by saying returning these belongings is not part of their responsibility, and that migrants are not automatically entitled to get their belongings back. According to the U.S. Constitution, property can be seized only for use as evidence or in the event that it is identified as the illicit proceeds of a crime. The comments made by both low-level officers and higher-level officials suggest a willingness at all levels of CBP to use power to seize belongings at will rather than in accordance with the law.

The United States government, specifically the Department of Homeland Security (DHS), is responsible for the direct and collateral damage of dispossession through deportation since they are ultimately responsible for all removals. "Shakedown" includes six clear recommendations that could be implemented today, without congressional action, and that would significantly ameliorate the issue.

RECOMMENDATIONS ARE AS FOLLOWS:

* Immigrant detainees must always have access to vital belongings while in custody, such as medications necessary for their health and phone numbers necessary to contact loved ones;
* Immigrant detainees who will eventually be deported by ICE should have their belongings, including money, follow them to the end of their chain of custody and should be reunited with these items, including money in its original form, immediately upon their release;
* ICE ERO (Enforcement and Removal Operations) must ensure that every individual has the opportunity to convert his or her commissary funds to cash before deportation;
* CBP should retain prosecuted individuals' belongings for a minimum of 30 days past the end of their prison sentence, or until ICE picks up the belongings. Belongings should never be destroyed while their owner is still serving a sentence;
* CBP property management practices must be brought into conformity with law-enforcement norms and CBP's own written policies;
* DHS must create an accessible and transparent mechanism for accepting complaints filed by immigrant detainees and

ensure adequate oversight to remedy the problems identified by the complaints;

    * The failure to return peoples' belongings upon deportation represents one more way that ICE and CBP have failed to uphold basic law enforcement standards and human rights norms in their rush to expand the United States' detention and deportation apparatus. The most appropriate short- and long-term solution to these problems is to enact a more reasonable and humane approach to immigration policy. During its five-and-a-half years in office, the Obama administration has accomplished an unprecedented volume of deportations from the United States. Systemic abuse and neglect, including the practices documented in this report, are an unavoidable consequence to detention and deportation, especially of this volume.[125]

---

125 No More Deaths, "SHAKEDOWN, How Deportation Robs Immigrants of their Money and Belongings," https://tucson.com/shakedown-how-deportation-robs-immigrants-of-their-money-and-belongings/pdf_69708962-8092-11e4-bd41-af90c03e3b33.html, accessed October 23, 2018.

CHAPTER 91

No More Deaths 10th Anniversary–April 2014

In the blink of an eye, ten years had passed us by. The greater wisdom had expressed optimism that Immigration Reform would have passed Congress by 2010, and we could all go home. Here we were, ten years after the beginning of the humanitarian response, with no change in status of the immigration debate. No More Deaths marked this passage of time by holding a celebration first at Nancy Myers' home in downtown Tucson, then at a larger event at *Mercado San Augustin*. Dozens of photos of all past events in the desert and along the border ran in a continuous loop. Several people spoke to the large assembled group, some reflected dismay that we were still at work, Walt Staton reminisced about his unwanted experience with the government through his BANWR rap:

Walt Staton

BANWR Rap

A ticket, a citation
a manifestation of a government bent
on enforcing a policy of deterrence
that requires adherence from all agencies
    on the line
a literal line in the sand
that is now a 2000-mile band of unmarked graves.

Fish and Wildlife—this is not your battle
to fight. But hold tight, we won't lose sight
of what's right. Watch out; we kick and bite.

Bring it to the court to sort it out.
But even in the marbled halls and 30-foot
high ceilings of justice, a jury—not of <u>my</u>
peers—sits and jeers while the attorneys try
to steer their perception of wrong and right.

I did it. It was nothing to hide or shy
away from. Yes, I put that water there,
and everywhere else. Hundreds of gallon jugs
with dates and messages and good intention.
Chugged by thirsty bodies, or
slashed and kicked by green uniformed thugs.

A bottle costs less than a dollar but
it got the government so worked up in frenzy.
so now they got my fingerprints
and mug, but didn't expect the tug on the heartstrings
of people who see right through it all.

From ticket to trial, there's no denial
that while we try to negotiate all we do
is wait. Arizona, it's a dry hate.
A judge reads the jury's paper
"guilty" of premeditated littering—yeah,
        that's a real thing, in the first degree
United States of America vs. me.

Community service, 300 hours, ready, set, go
to LA to start grad school. 300 hours, I'm no fool,

A letter back, thanking the court for
the State-sanctioned opportunity to clean
up my community.

I reject the sentence, not agreeing to this
penance for a crime that is so narrowly defined.

The hours doubled, 600 in prison—or keep the
original offer, it would be my decision.
Was I radical enough, made of the right stuff
to serve time for my own vision? What point did
I want to prove; whose hearts would I move?

Back and forth, struggle with my conscience,
My own soul fighting with itself. No clarity,
Just flip a coin, tails, I choose—the 300.

A few more moons and we win the circuit appeal.
Dan Millis, how do you feel? Keepin' it real, water
bottles are not garbage. Webster and the judges agree,
charges overturned, a glimpse of humanity.

A reflection of our actions,
questions about our decisions.
Learning from mistakes, because the stakes
are so high.
Transforming from charity to solidarity.
Collaboration between privilege and poverty
instigates creativity.
The invitation is always there.
Will you RSVP?

CHAPTER 92

En Requiem–Joe and Janet Arachy

STEVE JOHNSTON WROTE ABOUT JANET and Joe Arachy because, of all the No More Deaths volunteers, Steve has known them the longest and most intimately.

Steve Johnston:

JANET AND JOE ARACHY (AND MAXIE AND MYRNA)–BYRD CAMP'S GODPARENTS

He came riding into camp on a big, bay horse, followed by his best friend on a Paint. He wore a ten-gallon cowboy hat, leather full chaps, with holstered rifle and six-shooter at his side. He looked to be back from another century, or even further, with long handlebar mustache and his own Sancho Panza riding beside. For those who didn't know them, their arrival was alarming. This was Joe and Maxie's way of introducing themselves to the new No More Deaths volunteers at the Arivaca desert aid Byrd Camp.

Joe and Janet Arachy were a study in contrasts. Joe was as gruff and scary, with a booming voice and prominent Vietnam War "dancing skeletons" tattoos on his arms (symbols of his two tours there as a Marine), as Janet was sweet, gentle and, obviously, caring. But Joe was a sweetheart, too.

His heart reached out to all the many migrants who came knocking on their door at any hour of the day or night at the Sands of Time Ranch, just up the hill from Byrd Camp. For at least a decade before Byrd Camp was founded in 2004, the Arachys, along with Byrd Baylor and Maxie's family (and many, many others), had been giving lifesaving assistance to the hundreds of travelers who arrived at their doors, exhausted and sick from dehydration. The migrants knew they were welcome by the gallons of water left by their gates.

Janet's motives seemed obvious—she showed her kindness in every smiling glance. She was a gentle soul who, all at one time, had 33 pets: four dogs, nine cats, three mules, two cows and a calf, three horses and a foal, and assorted chickens and guinea fowl. The greatest grief I ever saw her express was for the loss of her 35-year-old mule, "High-Stepping." Childless, Janet and Joe welcomed their new neighbors at Byrd Camp as fellow humanitarians and extremely good company. Janet was quick to wash any and everyone's dirty laundry, including the camp towels, and, if need be, clothing donated for (and, occasionally, by) the passing travelers. Her care for others really knew no bounds.

Joe, on the other hand, looked like the kind of guy who might not be a natural ally. A big man, gun-toting and loud talking, he might have been a member of a vigilante militia or even a racist minuteman. As ever, appearances can deceive. Joe had been born in France during World War II to Hungarian parents. His father and grandfathers (and, probably, many great-greats) had fought in the incessant European wars of the 19th and the first half of the 20th centuries. Joe's parents were doubly immigrants, having fled Hungary to France, then moving to Connecticut when Joe was a young kid, where he grew up. After Vietnam, of which he loathed to speak about, he became a long-haul truck driver, finding and uniting with Janet on his travels. They retired to the Sands of Time in the mid-1990s, at the very beginning of the NAFTA-induced Great Migration to El Norte.

The Arachys and Maxie (Maximiliano) Gonzalez had been out there in the desert wilderness—more than seven miles down a dusty, ungraded and unkempt, potholed dirt road—long before NMD got there. Maxie's self-built home was about two miles further east of Byrd Camp and about ten miles north of Mexico. His was the last house for many miles distance before the Tumacacori Mountains to the east, and the first sign of humanity since crossing the border for those passing north through this vast, torturous, and uninhabited stretch of the Sonoran Desert. As traveling folks crested the innumerable ridges on their journey north, they could see his solar-powered porch light from many miles away. Those who were sick, injured, hungry, thirsty (and who among them wasn't) or just lost, could make their way down the eroded fire roads (really, just double tracks) that led to his home. Many a morning Maxie and his family would feed 20 or more travelers. When No More Deaths arrived in the Altar Valley, we made a point of bringing 50-lb. bags of beans and 40-lb. bags of rice to Maxie every few weeks. Maxie's wife, Margarita (she and he were both Mexican citizens with U.S. green cards), made corn tortillas and spoke fluent Spanish, with calming assurances for the many frightened people who passed their way that they were through the worst of the mountains.

Joe and Janet welcomed the mostly young No More Deaths volunteers to the desert. The Sands of Time Ranch was 80 acres of scrubby grassland perched on the highest hill in the area (save for Twin Peaks), where Joe and Janet lived in a double-wide just a couple of hundred yards up the hill from Byrd Camp. In their kindness, in the early days of camp, they allowed us to keep a freezer in a very hot shed, where we froze two-liter water jugs, which we daily retrieved to keep our food coolers cool. They also supplied hot showers and clean towels to all-comers from camp *and* from the desert. Most importantly, we took tens of thousands of gallons of water from their windmill-powered well, cleaning and re-filling the empty jugs we found on our daily trips into the far desert. We diligently placed these on the trails, hopeful that the literally tens of thousands of those who passed by each year would find them.

Wednesday (or whichever night was most convenient for the desert work) was "Movie Night" up at the Sands of Time. Janet would cook a huge pot of spaghetti and meatballs and Joe would make popcorn. He would often play—always (prompted by him) by request—his favorite movie on the VCR, the super-violent war epic, "300," about Sparta and the Persian Wars of antiquity. But there were gentler romcoms and the like in their video collection, most certainly acquired by Janet. Laughter was an easy part of camp life, and Joe and Janet supplied much more than their share.

Joe and Janet died within little more than a year of each other in 2011-2012. Janet passed in a freak winter accident of carbon-monoxide poisoning in her new and much-cherished Chevy Cruiser. Her loss was devastating to all who knew her but, of course, most especially to Joe. Her funeral took place at the Sands of Time, and her many No More Deaths and Arivaca friends scattered her ashes literally to the four corners of the land she loved so much. Byrd Camp would never be the same after losing her gay and tender spirit.

Joe had suffered from diabetes and Agent Orange poisoning for many years. His $60,000 settlement with the War Department came 35 years too late, but it paid for Janet's Cruiser and a lot of other purchases that the newly-flush couple had never before considered possible—like a very fancy telescope for Joe's birthday. The service-induced illnesses from which he suffered resulted in the painful and complicated replacement of arteries in both of his legs from his thighs to his ankles. This kept him in a wheelchair for most of the last two years of his life. After Janet's passing, Maxie's daughter, the lovely and capable Myrna Quintanar, diligently gave Joe around-the-clock care till the end. Her son and her husband, both named Julio, took care of the animals—Janet's pets—and the homestead, and Maxie and the Byrd Campers provided humor and encouragement. A rugged outdoorsman and hunter, Joe's friends made his final months of virtual immobility more bearable, if still miserable from his multiple losses.

A personal side note: the day Joe died, I visited him at the Sands of Time, collecting the frozen jugs for the camp coolers. He was sitting in his bedroom in his wheelchair, "cleaning"—sorting out the stems and seeds—the last of his stash of marijuana, which he used to ease the pain of his medical and emotional conditions. "Joe," I said, as I was leaving, "You better be careful. That stuff can cure your glaucoma." He gave that big, hearty, Arachy-laugh—the last that I ever heard. That night he died in his sleep.

The very next day, when a brace of an unfriendly niece and nephew came to claim Joe's worldly goods, Myrna was armed with all the previously-prepared legal documents that made her the executor of Joe's will, and which made her and Maxie total beneficiaries of the land, the home, and all the guns, swords, and military hats—some worn by his European forebearers—in Joe's collection. When the greedy relatives called the law to enforce their claim and evict Myrna, the sheriff arrested one of them for an outstanding warrant and told the other to clear off Myrna and Maxie's property. Joe got the last laugh.

Joe's death was especially hard on Byrd Camp. From its inception, most everyone who had volunteered there—and there were many, many hundreds of us—had met Joe and had chortled or been appalled by his coarse wisecracks. He and Janet left a legacy of caring.

The Arachys will live in the hearts of those who volunteered at Byrd Camp in the first eight years of its existence, reminding us of the generosity and good-heartedness of our neighbors and the humanity of all those who are unafraid (or, perhaps, just a little fearful) of taking risks for the well-being of the strangers in our midst. REST IN PEACE, *DESCANSE EN PAZ*, Joe and Janet.

PART V
MORE No More Deaths Stories
(including Phoenix and Ajo)
Through Early 2019

Hanging Fruit (Michael Hyatt)

CHAPTER 93

Why am I Shaking?

SOME OF THIS SECTION WILL look backward to provide information about No More Deaths work in Phoenix and in Ajo not previously addressed, while some of this section will look to the future. It will also see how the government continues to keep No More Deaths in its sights.

Gene and I moved back to Phoenix from Tucson in 2013 for reasons I describe below. But before we left, I wanted to interview Carlotta Wray. Carlotta lives on a 28-acre spread southwest of Arivaca very close to the Mexican border. Earlier, during a training event for local volunteers Gene had conducted in Arivaca, Carlotta shared two stories that she'd previously kept to herself. She had decided she was ready to tell about her experiences with migrants and Border Patrol, and she chose to do it with this supportive group of neighbors and friends.

Gene and I arranged to meet Carlotta at a restaurant near Amado where her sister worked. It was almost empty. We sat in a booth, ordered drinks, and Carlotta began to retell her stories.

She had come across the border from Mexico many years before. She met and married her husband, a member of the Tohono O'odham Nation, and moved into his desert home. A few years prior he died, leaving her alone to manage their land.

In the recent past, Carlotta was walking home from shopping in Arivaca when she came upon a group of Border Patrol agents stopped on the side of the road with several migrants in custody.

She spoke with them for a little bit and then asked if she could go home and bring back some food for the migrants. The Border Patrol agents agreed that she could. She walked a little further along to her home and made a pile of ham sandwiches. She brought the sandwiches back to the men. Border Patrol had provided water, which the men were drinking eagerly.

Carlotta said she was impressed that Border Patrol appeared to be gracious and supportive of the migrants, unlike the tales she had heard in the past. After the migrants were loaded into the trucks and taken away, she reflected on the fact that at least these people not only received some food on this day, but they also received humane treatment from their captors.

Another time, Carlotta saw a man staggering down the dirt road toward her house. She went out to greet him and could immediately see he was in bad shape. He had blood on his clothes and was haggard and tired. He was so exhausted that he couldn't speak. She invited him to sit on her porch and rest. She gave him water and talked to him in soothing tones. Finally, he was able to answer her questions.

He told her that he and his wife crossed the border with a group of people a couple of days earlier, led by a *coyote*. His wife became sick as they hiked along and finally had to rest. She was in pain. The group sat down with them and discussed what to do. Over time, it had become obvious—she wasn't recovering. The *coyote* said they needed to move on to avoid capture. The man and his wife would stay behind. The *coyote* assured them that he would notify someone along the way that they needed help. "Just stay here," he told them.

They waited and waited; she became sicker and sicker as the day went on. Soon, she became feverish. All the while, no help arrived.

As nighttime drew near, both the man and his wife fell asleep. In the morning when he awoke, he found her dead. He was beside himself with grief. He felt as though he could not go on without her. He looked around and saw shards of glass on the trail and decided to kill himself. Although it was very painful, he used the glass to cut across his wrists. The blood drained out, and he fell asleep again. When he woke up, he was surprised to discover he was still alive. He took that as a sign he should go on to find someone who would take his wife's body for a proper burial. So, he pulled himself together and started walking until he came upon Carlotta.

Carlotta called Border Patrol to come and help. Meanwhile, she continued to give the man food and water. When Border Patrol arrived, they immediately wanted to take him away. The man balked and refused to go until they retrieved his wife. He couldn't bear leaving her alone in the desert. Finally, the agents agreed to go with the man to his wife's body. He guided them back to the place where she had rested. They bagged her up and carried her out to the road and ultimately to the Medical Examiner's office in Tucson.

When Carlotta told this story initially in the training group, she'd pondered why—since Border Patrol had behaved so humanely— why was she shaking so hard and feeling so very upset. She asked the group: "Why am I shaking? Why am I so affected about this?"

People in the group responded with comments like: "This is where we live—under constant tension and fear. Border Patrol comes through and ruins our land with its bulldozers. Then, they tear up our roads with noisy trucks and scatter our wild and domestic animals. Border Patrol cuts our fences, chases people who are running for their lives, and people who have nothing to do with us are injured and killed. The drug people come through and threaten our way of life. We are a quiet, peaceful people, why do we have to see people with guns? Why do we constantly hear helicopters overhead? We never have a chance to live in harmony with our surroundings. It's no wonder you are disturbed."

The answers weren't enough, but they satisfied Carlotta for the moment.

Border Patrol has access to land and people in the area extending 100 miles north of the border. Everyone living in that area is subject to Border Patrol intervention, which has made some areas of Southern Arizona a virtual war zone. Checkpoints stand at major highways where brown-skinned people are constantly stopped and searched. It's a far cry from "normal." A significant portion of the American population has been relegated to this hostile, confrontational life—even when their own personal safety is not being challenged. Surely comprehensive immigration reform could help transform this scene from one of anxiety and fear to one of a simply "normal" existence—with "normal" drama and "normal" life and death circumstances.

Here is No More Death's statement regarding immigration reform that was written in 2005. It still stands today, and its implementation might give hope to Carlotta and others like her.

Faith-Based Principles of Immigration Reform

Preamble: We come together as communities of faith and people of conscience to express our indignation and sadness over the continued death of hundreds of migrants attempting to cross the U.S./Mexico border each year. We believe that such death and suffering diminish us all. We share a faith and a moral imperative that transcends borders, celebrates the contributions immigrant peoples bring, and compels us to build relationships that are grounded in justice and love. As religious leaders from numerous and diverse faith traditions, we set forth the following principles by which immigration policy is to be comprehensively reformed. We believe that using these principles—listed from the most imminent threat to life to the deepest systemic policy problems—will significantly reduce, if not eliminate, deaths in the desert borderlands.

1. **Recognize that the current Militarized Border Enforcement Strategy is an ill-conceived policy.** Since 1998 more than 7,000 (2018)[126] migrants—men, women, and children—have

---

126 U. S. Border Patrol (accessed December 13, 2017).

lost their lives in the deserts of the U.S./Mexico borderlands trying to make their way into the United States. These
tragic and unnecessary deaths must stop. The border blockade strategy has militarized the U.S./Mexico border drives
migrants into remote desert regions yet has failed to stem
the flow of immigrants into the United States. Further, the
fragile desert environment has sustained severe damage as
a result of both the migrants moving through remote desert
regions and the responding enforcement patrols. Indeed,
a militarized border control strategy has never in United
States history successfully stemmed the flow of immigrants.
We recognize the right of a nation to control its borders,
but enforcement measures must be applied proportionately,
humanely, and with a conscious effort to protect the people
and the land.

2. **Address the status of undocumented persons currently living in the U.S.** Workers and their families currently living
   in the U.S. must have access to a program of legalization
   that offers equity-building paths to permanent residency
   and eventual citizenship for workers and their families.
   Legalizing the undocumented workforce helps stabilize
   that workforce as well as their families. A stable workforce
   strengthens the country.

3. **Make family unity and reunification the cornerstone of the
   U.S. immigration system.** Migrants enter the United States
   either to find work or to reunite with family members, yet the
   arduous and lengthy process forces families to make potentially deadly choices. *Families must be allowed to legally and timely
   re-unify as well as to immigrate together as a unit._(author's accent).*

4. **Allow workers and their families to enter the U.S. to live
   and work in a safe, legal, orderly, and humane manner
   through an Employment-Focused immigration program.**
   International workers' rights must be recognized and hon-
   ored in ways that protect: the basic right to organize and

collectively bargain, individual workers' religious freedoms, job portability, easy and safe travel between the U.S. and homelands, achievable and verifiable paths to residency, and a basic human right of mobility.

5. **Recognize that the root causes of migration lie in environmental, economic, and trade inequities.** Experiences in Mexico and countries further south demonstrate that current trade and aid strategies that are based on greed and lack of basic respect deeply and negatively impact workers, their families, and the environments in migrants' homelands. This is forcing a quest for survival-based migration of unparalleled proportions. International agreements must be negotiated in ways that build mutual and just relationships. Such agreements must be designed to meet the needs of the present without compromising future generations' abilities to meet their needs. New strategies must include incentives for the public and private sectors to invest in economic and environmental repair and sustainable development in the sending communities.

Carlotta Wray also provided the following story to No More Deaths for its Spring 2017 *Newsletter.*

Carlotta Wray

REMEMBERING MIGUEL

I had a painful but powerful experience on February 20, 2016. My daughter and grandchildren and I were returning home. It was after sunset on the Arivaca-Sasabe road. We saw something up ahead. When we got closer, we saw a man lying by the side of the road. My daughter slowed and drove past him. The man stood up and staggered a few steps toward the car, then fell down again. I shouted to her to stop. She had locked the doors. She told me later that she was worried it might be a trap. I was certain it was just a man who desperately needed our help.

We all rushed out and I sat on the ground next to the man and held his head in my lap. I asked him what had happened, but all he could whisper was, "I'm dying." He told us he hadn't eaten in three days, and the last water he had drunk, a day and a half before, was dirty. His chest and back hurt and he couldn't move his legs because of spasms. My daughter, who knows first aid, took his pulse. She realized he needed medical assistance immediately. We had no cellphone reception there, but some miles back we had seen a Border Patrol truck parked. My granddaughter drove back to ask them to call for help.

While we waited, we gave the man a little to drink and eat, but he immediately vomited. We knew we shouldn't give him anything else even though he begged for water. I just held him close and my grandson brought him a blanket because he only wore a T-shirt and was very cold.

The Border Patrol agent arrived and stood over the man and asked him, "What's your name?" The man said his name softly and we could hardly hear him. I will call him Miguel. The agent went to his truck and made a radio call. Miguel's eyes kept rolling back in his head, so I kept telling him he was going to be all right and praying it was the truth.

About twenty minutes later, the Arivaca Fire Department van drove by, going west. My granddaughter went after them in our truck. They returned in a few minutes. The paramedics checked Miguel's heart and gave him oxygen, and tried to put in an IV, but couldn't because he was dehydrated. They finally put Miguel in the van and the Border Patrol agent followed them toward Arivaca.

I picked up his T-shirt that lay on the ground—it had been ripped open when they had checked his heart. I bunched it up and held it and cried. My grandchildren came to comfort me, and I told them they should never forget what they had experienced. They should never hesitate to help someone. Somehow people have to work together to make this a world where young men don't have to risk their lives to find a better life.

CHAPTER 94

Phoenix No More Deaths—The First Ten Years

LAURA ILARDO—

In the late fall of 2003, I was approached by Gene Lefebvre to accompany him and a few others from Phoenix as they traveled to Tucson for a gathering of people to discuss the increasing number of deaths occurring in the Southern Arizona desert. Those gatherings eventually led to the creation of No More Deaths (in Tucson) in January 2004. Each week, Gene, Liana Rowe, and I would make the two-hour drive after work to the weekly meetings as we helped shape No More Deaths in those early years. After many weeks of driving back and forth and talking to everyone I knew here in Phoenix about the work happening in Tucson, I was encouraged to start a group in Phoenix. The purpose of Phoenix No More Deaths was to assist Tucson with its broader mission of consciousness raising, witnessing and responding, global movement building, and finally, direct action.

Initially, we met in my home until we found a more suitable location that could accommodate all the new people wanting to come and assist. Central United Methodist Church of Phoenix has been our home ever since. One of our first tasks was to gather as many faith leaders as we could in Maricopa County who would listen. We encouraged their participation and their congregation's participation in our work. We held a breakfast with over 50 faith leaders from the community in attendance. Slowly, we built a network of folks willing and able to donate needed funds to Tucson. We created a database of volunteers who spent part of their summers and weekends in Arivaca. After the first year, Phoenix No More Deaths had well over 500 members signed up.

Over the next ten years, Phoenix No More Deaths shared stories of thousands of migrants who were lost or who have died along the U.S./Mexico border. We gave countless presentations to colleges and universities that encouraged many students and faculty to get involved, volunteer in the desert, and start No More Deaths clubs on campus. We organized and presented at teach-ins, recruiting new volunteers every year. Many students were out-of-state residents, so they took the news of the deaths and suffering back to their home communities who were equally willing and interested in offering assistance.

We held monthly screenings of relevant films. We facilitated discussion forums on topics related to migration. We were invited as guests to national movie screenings and conferences. We participated in No More Deaths benefit concerts and tabled at monthly art walks in downtown Phoenix. We shared stories of the tragedies as well as the hopes and dreams of the migrants. Every summer for ten years we walked with others on the Migrant Trail Walk—a 75-mile, weeklong journey from the border in *Sásabe, Sonora* to Tucson, Arizona to bear witness to and call for an end of the deadly and inhumane policies of the U.S. government against migrants and border communities.

We assisted with the Humanitarian Aid Is Never A Crime campaign when two of our Tucson volunteers, Shanti Sellz and Daniel Strauss, were arrested for assisting immigrants who were in need in 2005. We sent out thousands of post-cards and yard signs in support of them and helped start the national conversation regarding humanitarian aid and the plight of immigrants.

We worked with the Jesuit Volunteer Corps (JVC) in Phoenix who assigned volunteers to work alongside us in the desert. This collaboration with the Jesuits has created a long-lasting relationship that has continued for more than ten years. We organized two immersion trips with the JVC volunteers and other No More Deaths volunteers to Southern Mexico to get a firsthand account of the migration story and to facilitate a partnership with organizations in Mexico doing similar work with migrants. We visited coffee farms in Southern Mexico that have been negatively impacted by NAFTA trade agreements. We met with community leaders who spoke of the loss of jobs, loss of communal farming practices, and the inability to feed their families which has forced many to leave their homes. We visited sisters with the *Misioneras de la Eucaristía*, some of whom were living in Veracruz, helping Central American migrants with shelter, food and other aid as they made their way north on trains. We were able to see firsthand the destruction and impact of U.S. policies on these communities.

**Volunteers Serving as Legal Observers of
Minutemen in Douglas (Laura Ilardo)**

Most importantly, we developed relationships with immigrant communities in Phoenix through our work by fighting Prop 200, organizing against the Minutemen through assisting as legal observers in Douglas, walking side by side with the hundreds of thousands who came out for the Big March of 2006, organizing against Sheriff Arpaio's illegal raids and policies, and finally, organizing against SB 1070 in 2010.

I have been so thankful for the involvement that immigrants have had with No More Deaths. For three summers, committed immigrant volunteers helped organize "Aguathons" (water drives) and have successfully gathered more than 10,000 gallons of water to take to Arivaca each summer. Additionally, they were instrumental in raising well over $40,000 over the years to help with the costs of running the Arivaca camp. They've held galas, art auctions, music festivals, or they've sold tamales and other goods…all to support the work of No More Deaths. Without their invaluable hard work, we would not have lasted long.

Phoenix No More Deaths Group in Arivaca (Laura Ilardo)

On the weekend of October 16, 2010, a group of volunteers from Phoenix and I went to Arivaca for a weekend patrol of the area. During this trip, we came across the body of a young man who had recently died. At first, it appeared that he was simply asleep, escaping the heat of the Arizona sun. Unfortunately, his body was just a few hundred yards from our water drop. We stayed with him while waiting for Border Patrol to come and take him. That weekend left quite an impact on me and the other volunteers. I haven't returned to that desert, nor done a patrol with No More Deaths since then. One year later, after burying my stillborn son of 32 weeks, I realized I needed a break from actively facilitating the Phoenix group.

For the next three years, I took a backseat role away from my leadership position with the group. Volunteers continued to raise money, spend weekends in the desert and network with other organizations doing local activism in Maricopa County. During this time, a new group of volunteers, along with some core members, decided they wanted to take Phoenix No More Deaths in a new direction—one that was different from the original focus of our work. My absence left a void that others were happy to fill. The agenda of this new group forged ahead. After much discussion with my community and family, I decided to part ways with the group I'd helped found in Phoenix and focus my energy on No More Deaths in Tucson in order to start a community collective of volunteers to assist immigrants with deportation support, asylum relief, and DACA applications.

I owe everything that I've learned about immigrants— their stories, their courage, their hope, their faith and determination to define their own futures—to the ones in my community. I take this knowledge with me as I continue to work alongside them to fight for justice and an end to the border walls that continue to kill and separate communities. I am so grateful to them all.

CHAPTER 95

MORE Phoenix No More Deaths

GENE AND I MOVED BACK to Phoenix on July 30, 2013, and it was one of the hottest days of the summer. Gene had turned 80 in June. We decided that it made sense for us to move closer to our daughter and her family, and for me to have access in a retirement center to medical services, massages, haircuts, and regular meals. There were also built-in friends in Phoenix from before we left. It was heart-wrenching to leave Tucson and our community of friends, ones that were forged in adversity...in a low-intensity war. We remain bonded forever.

Gene discovered the Phoenix No More Deaths group in some disarray. Their one vehicle kept breaking down, and few funds were in the bank account. Laura had done a terrific job networking with Latino groups and other people interested in improving the conditions of immigration. The Phoenix No More Deaths meeting had grown in size with many of its volunteers Hispanic—unlike Tucson. But now there was only a tiny group in attendance with one or two people attending the bimonthly meetings. Because Laura had married, had a beautiful child, and still had her full-time social work job, she had turned over some of the work to others. She did not attend the meetings, but kept things moving from home.

What suffered most was the desert work. Phoenix No More Deaths had responded to the increasing number of migrant deaths in the corridor from Organ Pipe National Park to the area north toward

Phoenix and Gila Bend with new desert patrols. Chris Fleischman, a bright young engineer and committed activist, and others had left town not long after Laura's withdrawal from the meetings, and the desert patrols finally came to a halt. Gene went on one patrol with a couple of others, but the well-worn Ford Explorer had lost its capacity to four-wheel drive over the rough terrain during those trips. The remainder of the group limped along and slowly grew to include Gene, Carmen and her husband Ricky Ramirez, Suzanna Quitana, Susanne Congress, Chelsea Di Pasquale, Silverio and Susan Ontiveras, and some others. After a stint working in another state, Chris returned and provides consistent, competent leadership to the group.

Gene approached a friend, John Micheaels, for help. John and his wife, Marylou, donated money to buy a Ford four-wheel drive truck for us. Later they donated funds to help us buy another truck. Then one evening eight guests showed up to our meeting with their leader, Juan Guevara, saying they had heard of us and wanted to sit in on our meeting. We welcomed them. At the end of the meeting, they explained they were part of a personal development and leadership training organization for young adult Latinos called *Espacio Vital*. One of their assignments was to choose a charity and raise money to give to that group. They chose us and wanted to know what was on our "wish list." We didn't have a wish list per se but said we'd let them know what we needed. We gave their leader such a list three days later. It totaled $5,000. "No," the leader said, "you don't understand. We have $15,000 dollars to give you now, as you need it." We gratefully accepted that amount and bought another truck![127]

In 2014, students from ASU instructor Scott Warren's human geography class and others from ASU participating in a border-focused club program joined our group. The number of volunteers from those sources varied over the next few years, but they proved to be a good addition. Scott brought students from his classes to some

---

127 In 2018, this group donated an additional $7,500 to Phoenix No More Deaths to sustain desert patrols.

of our meetings and they conducted desert patrols. Over the course of two years, Scott and his students joined No More Deaths volunteers from Phoenix and Tucson along with Samaritans from Ajo (where Scott lived) forming a strong task force to help the increasing number of refugees crossing the desert in the corridor from Organ Pipe to the Gila Bend and Interstate 8.

Our group decided that Phoenix No More Deaths needed a stand-alone storage unit that could serve as a "camp-in-a-trailer." The group purchased a 6'x8' enclosed utility trailer. Gene approached his old friend from many other work projects, Lee Case, to customize the trailer to hold sleeping bags, cooking stoves, tents, cooking equipment, work table, and much more. Even though it was built for Phoenix, the trailer has spent several spring breaks in Southern Arizona. It now resides in Ajo. It has been very handy and a well-coveted resource to use in the desert at many of our locations.

**Guilford College Volunteers at Chavez Crossing
(Camp in a Box in the Rear) (No More Deaths)**

A man named John Dailey appeared one night at a No More Deaths meeting. He lived part-time in the little town of Maricopa, Arizona and the remainder of the year in California and Alaska. He offered the use of his house and garage in Maricopa (south of Phoenix). With this offer, No More Deaths vehicles could be parked in the garage, and volunteers could use the house for meetings or to house groups coming from Flagstaff and other locations.

This work continues today.

CHAPTER 96

Water for the Bombing Range

GENE MCWHORTER AND GENE LEFEBVRE

Raul said to Cheryl, "I need help! I don't want people dying on my farm."

Raul Puente was a leader at Phoenix Botanical Gardens. Cheryl Duvault was a volunteer there, and she knew where to take Raul's plea—to her church: Shadow Rock UCC in Phoenix. Shadow Rock was already involved in the New Sanctuary Movement, helping Central Americans fleeing violence and poverty in their homelands and going north to the United States. Raul owned desert farmland, where he grew needleless prickly pear cactus (prized for its juice) on a route used by refugees. Toward the end of the first part of their journey into the U.S., they crossed his fields, and some of them died a horrible death while there.

Cheryl told us (Gene Lefebvre and Gene McWhorter) the story at church one Sunday. We were moved by what she had to say and went to scout the farm southwest of Gila Bend, about an hour-and-half from Phoenix, and a short distance south of Interstate 8. The farm was part of a section of land poking south into the Barry Goldwater Bombing Range. That's right, the final part of a migrant's dangerous journey crossing about seventy-five miles on trails—with virtually no water while hiking under the burning sun and stumbling through cactus forests at night without light—was across an active bombing range!

We located the southeast corner of Raul's farm. We could see a trail coming down from the mountains and across the corner of his property into the fields. If migrants made it this far then the interstate (where they hoped to catch a ride) was within view. But pavement was about ten miles away, and some would not make it.

Shadow Rock Water Station: Sonya Scott, Howard Tigerman-Green, Eldon Wick, Gene Lefebvre, Sheryl Devault, Alex Scott (Gene McWhorter)

We bought a small trailer for sale on craigslist, and our Tucson friend, Steve Johnston, brought two fifty-five-gallon barrels. Gene Mc organized a team of people from the church, and on December 6, 2015, nine of us set off to install the lifesaving water station. We met Raul at a community water supply where Gene Mc supervised the filling of the two barrels from an overhead pipe, then we drove to a point near our site at the southeast corner of Raul's land. We managed to tip over the trailer *(Oh no!)* and lose the barrels on our way off the main road into the desert. We worked to right the trailer, put the barrels back, and proudly put the portable water station in place with a large *AGUA* (water) sign—only a few yards from the Bombing Range.

Over time, people were using the water; we could tell from the water levels in the barrels. We continued to serve the station monthly and learned a lot: the two barrels of water provided more than enough for demand, but we also needed to put out gallon water jugs because the migrants did not have containers with them to fill for the rest of their journey.

On March 5, 2016, Cheryl and Gene L were headed for home after one of our patrols. We were traveling west on I-8 when we passed two men walking in the desert brush alongside the highway. Cheryl parked the truck and we walked back to talk to the hikers. The hikers spoke a little English and Cheryl spoke a little Spanish. They had crossed the border fence into the U.S. in Organ Pipe National Monument and had been walking for two weeks, about 75 miles, with very little water and food, at night, dodging cactus, and hiding from view. Now they had reached their goal of this highway. From there they had no plan; somehow, they would get a ride to a place where they could get a job.

Cheryl tells the story: Ricardo said, "Maybe Gene and I could give them a ride." We shook our heads. "But they could work for me, didn't I have yard work they could do? They're hard workers." I was feeling real compassion for them now.

Ricardo's companion joined in, "Please give us a ride," he said, "Just take us with you into Phoenix and we would be very grateful."

It was clear to me that Cheryl was ready to give them a ride, so I stepped in, "We can't do that. Here's what would happen if we did: If Border Patrol stopped us, we two would be arrested for smuggling, a major crime. You would also be arrested for a lesser crime, but at least one of you would be held in jail as a witness against us. The last time this happened, the migrant was held for many months. He could not support his family or even see them. Our friends were declared innocent more than a year later, but they confiscated her truck and charged her a lot of money before finally giving it back." Cheryl was crushed. She wanted so much to help, but the risks were too high for all of us. We left them, praying for their safety.

On April 30, 2016, we (the two Genes) happened upon a truck coming down the road toward our water site. It turned out to be the new owner of the farm, Mike Paskett. That surprised us, and we thought, *Oh no! This may end our project.* But Mike knew all about us and approved of our efforts.

On the next trip on May 28, 2016, we discovered the trailer was gone—nowhere in sight. We asked a farm worker who agreed it was gone.

Who would have done this?

We drove west to the ranch house to discover that another worker had driven it to the backyard where it was hidden from the road. Our relief at this news disappeared as we talked to Mike. Someone had stolen a pickup truck, an all-terrain vehicle (ATV), and a rifle. The house had been broken into and many things were trashed. Mike and his partner had spent hundreds of thousands of dollars to buy this land and plant the new crops on the property. He had talked to Border Patrol, asking if they could help defend them against this new threat that had simply materialized out of the hills west of Mike's farm. The authorities said that these bandits belonged to the drug cartels, which are infamous for their violence. The main tool Border Patrol had to confront them was a highly-trained special unit called BORTEC. BORTEC could handle these criminals. However, they couldn't promise help would be here anytime soon, nor could they be expected to stay for any length of time. So, Mike seriously considered hiring a private security force. It might be his only option to save his investment and his home.

Mike suggested we place our water just south of the farm on the Bombing Range. We followed him down a dirt road to a light beacon. Mike said that sometimes people will come to this beacon if they were lost. We left several gallons of water there. By that time, we weren't sure where we were. Probably on the Bombing Range. We felt badly about Mike's dilemma.

As we left the farm, we discussed how these developments might spell the end of our water program. Our water station worked for migrants who were unarmed and exhausted from their long desperate hike. But we were not capable of dealing with violent drug runners. In fact, the migrants would change their routes to stay away from the criminals and, subsequently, our site. Humanitarians have experienced almost no threat when they've come across drug runners while putting out water and food. But this was an area where the cartel gang was running up against land owners and potentially armed security guards hired by the farmers. It was no place for us.

Filling Water Tanks from the Community Station (Gene McWhorter)

Upon reflection, we decided that we would continue our good work at another area where it was needed. One such place was a short distance from the farm, an inactive part of the Bombing Range for which we could gain permits to access. And, indeed, we did move to that area where water was also desperately needed. We conducted three patrols there and left water.

Meanwhile, Shadow Rock Church had become more deeply involved with refugees and migrants. Not only were they providing sanctuary, but they took on duty one night a week to care for people who were who were dropped by ICE at night at the Greyhound station, with instructions to go by bus from Phoenix to another city to appear at an office to be processed by a court. Now here they were, in a strange city with no idea how to find a place to sleep and eat. Volunteers at Shadow Rock and other churches were willing to extend hospitality. Soon Shadow Rock was taking in even more migrants and refugees for extended stays.

Considering the resources and energy the church was expending on these programs, we decided it was time to fold up our water program. Thank God and the migrants for all we learned and experienced.

**Shadow Rock Group Places Supplies Under a Very
Old Mesquite Tree (Gene McWhorter)**

CHAPTER 97

When is a Ticket not a Ticket?

CHRIS FLEISCHMAN RETURNED FROM HIS work in other states shortly after Gene and I returned to Phoenix from Tucson. Chris and Gene organized water patrols along desert routes Chris and Laura had established earlier along Highway 8, and in the Table-Top area. In addition, Chris coordinated Phoenix work with ASU's Scott Warren and his students in the same desert areas and in Ajo. He also worked with David Alaniz, Maria de la Castro, and other volunteers who conduct Kermes fundraising activities from time to time that generates approximately $3,000 per event. Chris has been a faithful, steadfast individual who has kept the Phoenix No More Deaths functioning since 2013—in addition to the efforts by Laura Ilardo and her team mentioned above. His Catholic faith sustains him whether working on behalf of migrants, supporting socially-responsible political campaigns, or participating in other activist pursuits.

Chris Fleischman Second from Left –Ticket Day (Chris Fleischman)

Chris Fleischman

Around 2010, migrant remains were discovered north of the Tohono O'odham Nation in BLM territory known as the Sonoran Desert National Monument. Clearly beaten-down migrant trails on both sides of the mountain in the area called "Tabletop" were near the recovery site. A few years later, some petroglyphs were discovered on the trail and were estimated to be from 1,000 to 1,400 years old by archaeologists at Arizona State University. They concluded that the petroglyphs marked a trail of equal age, which reminds us that the border crossed the people as opposed to the other way around.

Over time, volunteers from Tucson and Phoenix scouted the area to determine locations for water drops. At the beginning, they established only one location, known as the "Bike Drop," (because a non-functional, rusty bicycle was abandoned along the trail) on the west side of Tabletop not far from Interstate Highway 8. The spot was easy to find, a short hike from the parking spot, but unfortunately it was prone to vandalism by anti-immigrants who sometimes slashed the bottles. We never let this malicious expression of hate deter us from putting more lifesaving water along the trail. Rather it motivated us to explore additional water drop locations that would be easy for a migrant to find, yet not easily spotted by rangers, hunters or militia members.

Several volunteers reported run-ins with militiamen in the early years of our Tabletop mission. A friendly encounter took place with a man who was sympathetic (or indifferent) to our cause and was only there to report drug-smuggling operations to law enforcement. Another confrontation was a little scary, with the man threatening two of our women by showing his holstered gun when asked for his ID. Our de-escalation training came in handy and became part of the protocol when dealing with any law enforcement personnel, legitimate or otherwise.

The main protocol instituted for Tabletop trips states that one person (generally the driver or the most experienced person on board) does all the talking with law enforcement. This prevents multiple stories from being played against each other, and newbies will learn before speaking out—enthusiastic as they might be to stand up for human rights on behalf of migrants. As a newcomer myself, I learned this in February 2008 when I joined Dan Millis on the trip when he earned the first littering ticket in No More Deaths history and was able to take all the blame for the team. One ticket is better than four!

No More Deaths earned several littering tickets after Dan's, and we always refused to pay the fines. I ended up testifying in federal court in Tucson in Dan's defense, and although we lost the case, eventually we prevailed on appeal in the United States Ninth Circuit Court of Appeals While it would have been cheaper and easier to pay a $175 littering fine, the stand we continued to take against littering prosecutions made each one seem like a merit badge, and we never backed down from the guiding principle, "Humanitarian Aid is Never a Crime."

I earned my badge on December 10, 2011, on the east side of Tabletop. My girlfriend at the time wanted to celebrate her birthday by making her inaugural water drop with me. We organized a crew, rented an off-road vehicle, and set out that morning with several gallons of water and other provisions.

This was only my second or third time in the area, so we only had a few locations of water drops scouted. We were eager to explore and possibly find lost souls wandering in the arid wilderness. As luck would have it, we noticed a man walking up a ridge away from our vehicle, and one of our volunteers jumped out of the car with a couple gallons of water to see if help was needed. It turned out he was a park ranger, and soon his crew and vehicle were parked behind our vehicle blocking its exit, and I was up to bat for our team.

My understanding at that time was that No More Deaths operates with transparency and when asked, I divulged that we were placing water on trails. Later, our lawyers explained to me that we do not have to be quite so transparent—just our names and citizenship will do! My girlfriend's birthday trip ended in tears for her and a citation for me with the description of my offense: "Litter—Water Bottles."

At the time of the incident, I was temporarily working as a contract engineer in Savannah, Georgia, so taking a principled stand looked like an expensive and inconvenient process. The ticket indicated a $75 forfeiture amount plus a $25 processing fee, which is not cheap when combined with the round-trip ticket needed for the court appearance. The officer did not indicate how much time I had to pay the fine (not that it would have mattered) but in the *YOUR COURT DATE* section he simply wrote *YOU WILL BE NOTIFIED.*

Chris Fleischman's Littering Ticket (Chris Fleischman)

A couple of months later, my notification arrived as a summons to appear in U.S. Magistrate Court, Sandra Day O'Connor Courthouse in Phoenix, at 9:30 a.m. on February 16, 2012. By this time in No More Deaths history, we all knew the drill—don't pay the ticket, stand up, lose in federal court, and win on appeals. My concern was missing work and spending money on airfare, but our lawyer advised me to let someone from his office appear and plead innocent on my behalf. I thought this was a great option, giving me time to finish my contract in Savannah and then return later to fight for humanitarians in court.

What I hadn't anticipated was that the federal government was sick of us—they were fatigued by our stubbornness and from our victories in appeals court. Plus, they had bigger fish to fry, and my follow-up court date never happened. I was deprived of my day to be heroic like Dan Millis and others! For a few years, I bragged that I was a fugitive from justice...hiding in plain sight...waiting for that next summons. After several years now, I don't use that tired joke anymore because we've all realized that law enforcement is not interested in pursuing littering charges against humanitarian aid in the Sonoran Desert (ed. until Scott et.al. in 2017).

While it wasn't fun at the time of the incident, it is a fond memory when I recall the support that we have given each other in times of conflict. I have made subsequent trips to the same area and had one or two additional encounters with Border Patrol or rangers, but the only attempts made to push back on our group have been slashed water bottles. As I've previously said, this has not and will not deter us, and if anything, it is a reminder to us to drive out more frequently to take water and food to people who desperately need it.

**Water and Food for Hungry Migrants in the
Altar Valley 2009 (Michael Hyatt)**

CHAPTER 98

The Ajo Story

GENE SAYS THAT ED MCCULLOUGH (our data tracker) for many years had been warning Samaritans and No More Deaths volunteers (both in Phoenix and Tucson) that many migrants were again dying in the Ajo Corridor, west of the town of Ajo. This area was the 1991 scene of many tragic deaths in Luis Urrea's book, *The Devil's Highway*. The humanitarians already had their hands full and were slow to respond.

In this chapter, Scott Warren describes this unusual territory, its danger to migrants, and the eventual humanitarian response.

Scott Warren, Adjunct Faculty, ASU

Ajo is located in far western Pima County and separated from Tucson by 130 miles of Sonoran Desert and the Tohono O'odham Nation. The population of Ajo is about 3,000 and is clustered into a relatively dense, settled area that encompasses the townsite. Unlike other rural border communities such as Arivaca, Ajo has no outlying ranches or private properties. Instead, the town is surrounded by federal and public lands, such as Organ Pipe Cactus National Monument (Organ Pipe), Cabeza Prieta National Wildlife Refuge (Cabeza Prieta), and the Barry M. Goldwater Bombing Range (Goldwater Range). Ajo sits at the center of the "Ajo

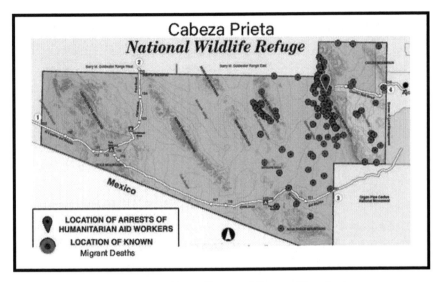

**Black Dots Indicate Recent Migrant Deaths in
the Ajo Corridor (No More Deaths)**

corridor"—as it is known by Border Patrol—which stretches 70 miles in a straight line from the border to Interstate 8 and the town of Gila Bend. The combination of federal lands, distance, and concentrated settlement makes the crossing of the Ajo corridor one of the longest, remotest, and deadliest for migrants anywhere along the border.

Tucson-based humanitarian aid groups have long recognized the need to provide water and other lifesaving supplies to migrants in the Ajo corridor. The deaths of 14 people from a single migrant group in the summer of 2001 proved to be a catalyst. In May of that year, a group of 26 migrants set off from Sonoyta, Sonora; but after becoming lost, disoriented, and scattered, 14 of the group died. Humanitarian aid groups petitioned land managers to do more to prevent death and suffering. As a result, the group Humane Borders was allowed to site a handful of stationary water tanks in Organ Pipe. In subsequent years volunteers from Tucson Samaritans and No More Deaths made forays into the Ajo corridor to map migrant trails and create experimental water drops. However, the distance from Tucson and the vastness of the desert in Southwestern Arizona stretched the capacity of these groups and challenged their ability to maintain a regular presence in the area.

In 2012 Tucson Samaritan and Franciscan Brother David Buer traveled to Ajo and made a call for recruitment within the local Catholic Church. Subsequently, several residents formed the Ajo Samaritans who aligned with the mission of the Tucson Samaritans to end death and suffering in the deserts of far western Pima County. Ajo Samaritans established several water drops in adjacent areas on public lands and sponsored a series of educational events to inform the local community about border and humanitarian issues.

In early 2014, Ajo Samaritans connected with No More Deaths and began collaboration to expand water drops and patrols into even remoter areas of the Ajo corridor. Beginning in March of that year, No More Deaths volunteers from Byrd Camp, Tucson, and Phoenix began servicing water drops in areas adjacent to Ajo, on Bureau of Land Management (BLM) land, and also on public access areas in the Goldwater Range. Volunteers either camped in the desert or stayed with residents during these trips. Resources were shared among the various groups. The need to put water out in the Ajo corridor was great, and it was not uncommon for volunteers to distribute up to 500 gallons of water over a few days on the dozen or so drop sites that had been established in the Ajo corridor.

Samaritans, Humane Borders, and No More Deaths responded to the enormous need for water in the Ajo corridor. However, it should be noted that residents had long

provided humanitarian assistance to undocumented border crossers in the area. Families living there were known
to have offered food, water, and shelter to migrants who
arrived at their doors. Additionally, hikers and cowboys have
offered what help they could to the migrants they encountered out on the desert trails. In 1980, for instance, when
14 El Salvadoran refugees died while crossing Organ Pipe,
residents responded by helping the survivors of that group
in a number of ways. In this regard, Samaritans, No More
Deaths, and Humane Borders are continuing a long tradition in Ajo by providing aid to those in need.

The work of Samaritans and No More Deaths raised the
profile and visibility of humanitarian aid in the community.
This immediately caught the attention of local (federal) land
managers. Initially, members of Ajo Samaritans were warned
not to leave water on federal lands during a meeting with
the representatives of Organ Pipe and Cabeza Prieta. While
disconcerting from a rhetorical standpoint, the warning
was mostly a non-issue from a practical standpoint. Most of
Organ Pipe was closed to the public and therefore inaccessible to humanitarian aid volunteers, and the remoteness of
Cabeza Prieta along with the limited capacity of volunteers
made it practically inaccessible as well.

This began to change in 2015 when Organ Pipe was
gradually reopened to the public and the capacity of the
various groups began to increase. No More Deaths volunteers established several water drops in Organ Pipe, and
exploration began in Cabeza Prieta—volunteers sometimes carrying as many as eight gallons of water at a time.
Spring break programs, summer volunteer programs, and
month-long volunteer programs all served to increase the
capacity of humanitarian aid volunteers and expand the
work farther west into the areas near Ajo. Furthermore,

a local resident allowed his property to be used as a staging area for No More Deaths and other humanitarian aid groups, providing an essential base from which to do patrols in the Ajo area. Both Tucson and Phoenix No More Deaths provided vehicles and other resources to support the work in Ajo.

Search and rescue/recovery was an essential part of this collaboration from its beginning in 2014 and corresponded with an effort within No More Deaths to cultivate a more formal search and rescue/recovery capability. In fact, one of the first trips that Ajo Samaritans and No More Deaths did together was a search for a missing migrant in 2014. The search involved a dozen volunteers, spanned four days, required special permission to access areas of the Hickiwan District of the Tohono O'odham Nation, and resulted in some six flat tires from the rugged roads.

The ability to respond to search and rescue/recovery calls in the Ajo area has since grown. Yet another organization, *Águilas Del Desierto* (Eagles in the Desert) or simply *"Águilas"*[128] had begun to work in close collaboration with No More Deaths and Ajo Samaritans. *Águilas* is a San Diego-based, volunteer search and rescue/recovery group. Many of their cases originate in the Ajo corridor, and so for that reason, they spend a lot of time searching in the desert areas surrounding Ajo. All these various groups support each another in numerous ways: sharing information, resources, and often directly collaborating on searches.

Perhaps the most troubling aspect of the work in Ajo has been the increasing frequency of human remains recoveries. These recoveries spiked as No More Deaths expanded their range of patrols, water drops, and searches into the

---

128 A California-based humanitarian organization.

Growler Valley some 15 miles west of Ajo. The Growler Valley is a wide valley that includes parts of Organ Pipe, Cabeza Prieta, and the Goldwater Range. It stretches some 40 miles north and south. The Growler Valley is a major travel corridor for migrants, but due to its remoteness and lack of public roads, it has been largely inaccessible to humanitarian aid volunteers.

This changed during a month-long volunteer program in December 2016. With a contingent of volunteers based in Ajo for the entire month, No More Deaths finally had the capacity to begin systematic exploration of the Growler Valley. Before exploration of the Growler Valley began, human remains discoveries by humanitarian aid volunteers in the Ajo corridor occurred about once every other month. In the six-month period from December 2016 to May 2017, volunteers discovered about 18 sets of human remains in the Growler Valley alone. *Águilas* had a similar experience with its recoveries in the Growler Valley, finding eight sets of human remains during a single day of searching in June 2017.

> **December 2016 to May 2017: No More Deaths volunteers discovered about 18 sets of human remains in the Growler Valley.**

No More Deaths developed protocols and best practices for dealing with human remains recoveries, both in terms of the logistical work in making sure that sheriff's deputies do a thorough and complete recovery with the hope of identification and family notification, as well as in terms of volunteer wellness and mental health. Recently, No More Deaths volunteers have realized that mental health and wellness providers should be considered just as integral as medics, nurses, and medical doctors. They've become an essential resource for volunteers as the weight of this type of work (human remains recoveries) increases.

In April 2017, Ajo Samaritans drafted a new mission statement that made explicit the need to support all groups and individuals who provide humanitarian aid in the Ajo corridor. Arguably, the strength of the humanitarian aid response in the Ajo corridor had been the collaboration of many different groups to address the needs of migrants. Especially important has been the increasing presence and support of Phoenix No More Deaths. Both Tucson and Phoenix groups have forged strong connections to the community in Ajo and have worked in partnership with residents to build capacity.

Perhaps most important has been the budding relationship between humanitarian aid workers in Ajo and the organizers of the migrant shelter in Sonoyta, Sonora. In June 2017, aid workers in Ajo were put in contact with organizers in Sonoyta who were trying desperately to get Border Patrol to respond to a case concerning lost and injured migrants in Organ Pipe. Thankfully, those migrants were eventually found alive. Subsequently, aid workers in Ajo, No More Deaths, and Sonoyta have organized joint searches for missing migrants and for migrants who have perished in the desert. Volunteers from No More Deaths have also provided support to the shelter in the form of food, water, and clothing. Increasing collaboration with organizers in Sonoyta is a logical next step for humanitarian aid workers, since nearly all migrants who cross through the Ajo corridor originate from Sonoyta.

Local aid workers and No More Deaths volunteers continue to push for humanitarian aid in new ways. Recently, for instance, No More Deaths volunteers have begun driving the roads into the Growler Valley that are normally closed to the public. These roads are well traveled by Border Patrol for law enforcement purposes and by Cabeza Prieta personnel for refuge management purposes. These roads would also provide necessary access to remote areas for volunteer search and rescue/recovery groups as well as humanitarian aid volunteers.

Ajo is a small and intimate town where aid workers and their families regularly associate with Border Patrol agents, land managers, and other law enforcement officers and their families. As No More Deaths volunteers and local advocates push for greater humanitarian aid access, the residents of Ajo also recognize the need to remain in dialog with both individuals and the agencies they represent in the Ajo corridor.

CHAPTER 99

The Camp Raid 2017

Border Patrol Helicopter Hovers over Byrd Camp (No More Deaths)

WITH ONE HELICOPTER, 15 TRUCKS, and 30 armed agents, Border Patrol officers raided Byrd Camp on June 15, 2017. The camp, as described earlier, is just outside of the rural town, Arivaca, and is staffed 24/7 to provide humanitarian aid services for migrants crossing the desert. For several years, No More Deaths has offered first aid, water, food, clothing and protection from the elements to those facing the extreme conditions of heat and dryness in the Arizona desert.

During the June 2017 raid, Border Patrol officers detained four migrants. The last raid of this type at Byrd Camp was ten years ago (2008) when Gene Lefebvre was detained and promised further action (that never came to be), and several migrants were taken away.

"No More Deaths has documented the deaths and disappearances of hundreds of migrants in the Arivaca corridor of the border. Today's raid on the medical aid station is unacceptable and a break in our good faith agreements with Border Patrol to respect the critical work of No More Deaths," said Kate Morgan, Abuse Documentation & Advocacy Coordinator for No More Deaths.

> Migrants who have died from extreme desert conditions are found on an average of once every three days in the Southern Arizona desert. Climate change seems to have exacerbated the crisis, and advocates argue that we must recognize the intersection between environmental and migrant justice.[129]

In an interview on NPR/KJZZ two weeks after the raid, host Kirk Siegler said, "One thing is clear. The Border Patrol is beefing up its public presence here in Southern Arizona. The Tucson sector alone is hiring 4,000 new agents. A few miles from the No More Deaths humanitarian camp, the county highway is packed with green and white Border Patrol pickups."

No More Deaths volunteer Geena Jackson said, "Our clinic space being compromised will lead directly to more suffering and more deaths in this desert."[130]

---

129 "No More Deaths Raid, U.S. Border Patrol Detains Migrants at a Humanitarian Aid Camp and Breach International Law, *Everyday Embellishments*, June-21,2017
130 Siegler, Kirk, *NPR/JKZZ*, "Desert Aid Camp Turning Away Migrants Following Border Patrol Raid," June 28, 2017

**Border Patrol at the Entrance to Byrd Camp
During 2017 Raid (No More Deaths)**

CHAPTER 100

Disappeared

Disappeared 2018 (No More Deaths)

INTRODUCTION TO THE THREE-PART REPORT

"The reality is you're looking at 114-degree temperatures, this very rugged terrain that you see behind us, and once they cross the border, many times they're abandoned there and left vulnerable to the elements."

MANUEL PADILLA, JR., BORDER PATROL SECTION CHIEF, 2013-2015

APPROXIMATELY EVERY TWO YEARS SINCE 2008, No More Deaths has produced a report describing the actions of the U.S. Border Patrol. The most current reports are a three-part series that explain how U.S. Border Patrol enforcement agencies are fueling a missing persons crisis. For this three-part series No More Deaths, with its 12 years of 24-hour direct medical and humanitarian aid and presence in Arizona backcountry, joined with *La Coalicion de Derechos Humanos*— whose staff and volunteers have more than 20 years of witnessing and listening to thousands of stories of border crossings throughout Southern Arizona. Their combined research goals are transformative: to expose and combat those U.S. government policing tactics that cause the crisis of death and mass disappearance in the borderlands.

The report focuses on those who attempt to enter the U.S. on foot between ports of entry located in wilderness regions (as opposed to other unauthorized crossing methods in urban areas). It refers to those individuals who travel through the U.S./Mexico border region without official permission as border crossers (ed., rather than migrants, undocumented immigrants, aliens, or other term).

Over the past 20 years, the U.S, has armored border cities with walls, cameras, sensors, personnel, and military-style infrastructure from all the way from San Diego, California to Brownsville, Texas. As a result, border crossers now enter the U.S. through remote rural areas, fanning out across the backcountry region north of the border and carving a complex web of trail systems through mountain passes, rolling hills, desolate plains, and dense brushlands.[131]

In their 1994 strategy document, Border Patrol lists "indicators of success" for Prevention Through Deterrence. These indicators would be used to measure the efficacy of the strategy once implemented. In addition to shifting the geographical flow of migration into the Sonoran Desert, other indicators of success would include:

---

131 La Coalicion de Derechos Humanos and No More Deaths, *Disappeared,* "How the U.S. Border Enforcement Agencies are Fueling a Missing Persons Crisis", 2014.

* Fee increases by smugglers
* Increased incidences of more sophisticated methods of smuggling at checkpoints
* More documentation fraud
* More violence at attempted entries
* Possible increase in complaints (Mexico, interest groups, etc.)
* Potential for more protests against immigration policy."[132]

If functioning as intended, Prevention Through Deterrence would reshape migration to become more treacherous, more criminalized, more cartel-driven, and more politically fraught.

> The magnitude of this tragedy is disputed, as there is no consensus on how to count the death toll on the border. . . Border Patrol claims that at least 6,029 border crossers have died crossing into the United States since the 1990s. However, audits suggest that the agency underestimates the number of border deaths by as much as 43 percent,[133] which yields a death count of over 8,600 people in the U.S. borderlands.

Part I of this report shows how border enforcement personnel routinely scatter people by using low-flying helicopters, chasing them over cliffs and into dangerous waters, and by tackling non-resisting people to the ground.

I am not planning to review Part I of the report within this book. You can find it at www.nomoredeaths.org. I choose, rather, to move on to Part II which has direct implications for No More Deaths.

---

132 U.S. Border Patrol, "Border Crossing Strategic Plan: 1994 and Beyond", July 1994, http://ewrutledge.com/text-books/9780415996945/gov-docs/1994.pdf.
133 Op.cit., No More Deaths, *Disappeared*, Introduction, p.7

Interference with Humanitarian Aid—Death and Disappearance on the U.S./Mexico Border (Part II)[134]

Miguel, a 37-year-old man from Sinaloa, tried to cross the US/Mexico border on four separate occasions, each time walking from seven to eight days. On each of these trips he saw food and water gallons left out on trails. On the third day of one of his trips, he came across water gallons that had been vandalized:

"Yes. I saw the water bottles stabbed. They break the bottles so you can't even use them to fill up in the tanks. I needed water, some of the other people in the group needed water, but we found them destroyed. [I felt] helplessness, rage. They [US Border Patrol] must hate us. It's their work to capture us, but we are humans. And they don't treat us like humans. It's hate is what it is. They break the bottles out of hate."[135]

In the desert of the Arizona-Mexico borderlands, where thousands of people die from dehydration and heat-related illness, Border Patrol agents are destroying gallons of water intended for border crossers. Border Patrol agents stab, stomp, kick, drain, and confiscate the bottles of water that humanitarian aid volunteers leave along known migrant routes in the Arizona desert.[136] These actions condemn border crossers to suffering, death, and disappearance.

In data collected by No More Deaths from 2012 to 2015, we found that at least 3,586 one-gallon jugs of water had been

---

134 Op.cit., No More Deaths, *Disappeared*, Paart II, p. 5.
135 Personal interview, September 20, 2016, Nogales, Sonora, Mexico.
136 The report includes four videos documenting such destruction by Border Patrol.

destroyed in an approximately 800-square mile desert corridor near Arivaca, Arizona.

Furthermore, Border Patrol agents in the Arizona borderlands routinely intimidate, harass, and surveil humanitarian aid volunteers thus impeding the administration of humanitarian aid. These actions call into question Border Patrol's own claims to be humanitarian. The practice of the destruction of and interference with aid is not deviant behavior of a few rogue agents, it is a systemic feature of enforcement practices in the borderlands and a logical extension of the broader strategy of Prevention Through Deterrence. According to the logic of Prevention Through Deterrence[137], anything that makes the journey more dangerous or difficult for border crossers could be considered a reasonable tactic for enforcement, including the vandalization of safe drinking water. While humanitarian aid volunteers attempt to mitigate the crisis of death and disappearance, Border Patrol agents routinely sabotage this work and maximize the suffering of border crossers.

Part II of this three-part report series documents the interference with and obstruction of humanitarian aid efforts in the Arivaca migration corridor in the Arizona borderlands. *Interference with Humanitarian Aid: Death and Disappearance on the US/Mexico Border* is divided into four sections.

The first section establishes the critical role that the provision of humanitarian aid plays in mitigating death and suffering for those crossing the US/Mexico border. An understanding of the perils of the border crossing, the deadly logic of Prevention Through Deterrence, and the medical consequences of dehydration plus exposure to the elements

---

137 US Border Patrol, Border Patrol Strategic Plan: 1994 and Beyond, July 1994, http://cw.routledge.com/textbooks/9780415996945/gov-docs/1994.pdf.

are all necessary to understand why people are dying and disappearing along the border.

The second section explores the vandalization of the water drops established by No More Deaths volunteers in the remote borderlands of Arizona. Drawing on data collected by volunteers over a three-year period, we use a Geographic Information Systems (GIS) analysis to provide evidence that Border Patrol agents are the most likely actor responsible for the destruction of water provisions. No More Deaths uses GIS analyses to establish the potential consequences of these actions for border crossers.

The third section documents the obstruction of humanitarian aid efforts. Testimonies offered by No More Deaths volunteers reveal the extent to which law enforcement agencies have targeted humanitarian volunteers, preventing border crossers from accessing lifesaving resources and medical aid in the remote regions of the borderlands.

Finally, we demonstrate the need for a non-enforcement related response to the crisis of deaths and disappearances along the US/Mexico border. We demand the dismantling of the border enforcement agencies and an end to the policies responsible for this human-made crisis. We also call for an end to interference with humanitarian aid.[138]

From here, I plan to focus on section two of the report: the vandalization of water drops. Section three addresses the raid of the No More Deaths humanitarian aid camp (Byrd Camp) near Arivaca and it is addressed separately.

(Vandalism) Findings
During the 46-month period covered in this study, No More Deaths recorded 5,187 events—separate incidents of

---

138 Ibid.

volunteers servicing a particular water drop site—during which volunteers placed a total of 31,558 water gallons along migrant trails in remote stretches of the Sonoran Desert. Of the distributed 31,558 gallons, records indicate that 27,439 gallons were used by those in need of water. On average, 5.4 gallons were found to have been used by border crossers on each visit to each site.

Occasionally, unused gallons of water were destroyed by birds, cattle, and other animals. A total of 533 gallons of water showed telltale signs of animal damage. The vast majority of destroyed gallons, however, were destroyed by people. We refer to this human-caused destruction as *vandalism*.

Vandalized Water Gallons
No More Deaths volunteers found water gallons vandalized a total of 415 times during our study period, or more than twice a week on average. In all, 3,586 gallons of water had been vandalized during this time period.

Vandalized Water Jugs (No More Deaths)

Who Is Likely Responsible for Vandalizing Humanitarian Aid?

Hunters, hikers, birders, members of militia groups, ranchers, forest service personnel, and wildlife refuge personnel—as well as residents—are all present in the area where No More Deaths works. There is limited reliable data that could catalogue the activities of all these different actors. Although it is likely that multiple actors are responsible for the destruction of humanitarian aid at our water drop sites, the results of our GIS data analysis indicate that Border Patrol agents are likely the most consistent actors. We arrived at this conclusion by using a series of statistical tests combining the logbook data with information about land jurisdiction and hunting seasons. Each geographical variable we looked at was keyed to the locations of the vandalized water drop sites and the time of visits to those sites. These tests have clearly identified patterns of vandalism that are extensive across space and time.

. . . it is not our claim that Border Patrol is exclusively responsible for the vandalism of water supplies. In addition to hunters, we know that other actors in the area are periodically involved in destroying water. For instance, there is a small, right-wing militia group with occasional presence near Arivaca who publicized the destroying of humanitarian aid during the time period in which this data was collected. However, this militia presence was sporadic and generally confined to a small geographical area. Given the scope of destruction, we concluded that the only actors with a large and consistent presence across a wide area of the desert (periods when hunting is both authorized and prohibited) are agents of the U.S. Border Patrol.

**U.S. Border Patrol Agents Heading Toward No More
Deaths Volunteers on BANWR (No More Deaths)**

This report reached Border Patrol offices on January 17, 2018.

CHAPTER 101

Dr. Scott Warren and Eight Others Arrested

"The U.S. Fish and Wildlife service itself describes Cabeza Prieta as 'big and wild' and 'incredibly hostile' to those that need water to survive... Thirty-three sets of human remains were found on the refuge last year alone."

— RYAN DEVEREAUX

Scott Warren (Scott Warren)

LITTLE DID SCOTT KNOW WHEN he wrote the earlier section about humanitarian aid in Ajo that he and eight other humanitarian volunteers would soon be facing charges for helping migrants in the Ajo area. Obviously, something had changed. According to *The Guardian*, "Hours after a humanitarian group released videos with the report above showing Border Patrol agents kicking over water bottles left for migrants in the Arizona desert, a volunteer was arrested and charged with harboring undocumented immigrants."[139] Scott Daniel Warren, 35, is an instructor at Arizona State University and a No More Deaths volunteer. A connection had been made between Scott (and his students) and Phoenix No More Deaths a few years before. He combined that connection with his doctoral studies of migrants in the Ajo area and involved his students in providing humanitarian aid. He and his partner Emily Saunders live in Ajo.

On January 17, 2018, Scott was providing water, food, beds and clean clothes to two migrants who had stopped at "the Barn" in Ajo seeking respite. The timing of Scott's arrest was suspicious to some, coming as it did a few hours after No More Deaths released part two of a three-part report *The Disappeared*; however, volunteer Parker Deighan stopped short of calling the arrest an act of retaliation. "We see it as an escalation and criminalization of humanitarian aid workers."

Border Patrol, for its part, says that Scott's arrest came after several days of Border Patrol surveillance of the Barn and was simply part of a routine "knock and talk" event. Text messages released in the case show that at least eight different officers surrounded and surveilled the barn for hours before they approached. Bill Walker, who initially represented Scott, said his client's actions were not criminal. "This is a humanitarian aid worker trying to save lives."[140] "We have always had an understanding here with both the U.S.

---

139 *Associated Press, The Guardian*, "Group accusing US border patrol of water sabotage sees member arrested," January 22, 2018 (accessed August 20, 2018).
140 Ibid.

Attorney's Office and Border Patrol and also the wilderness area managers that we are a neutral party. We don't smuggle people, we don't violate the law—what we do is we help to save lives—and they've recognized that for years."[141]

In pretrial motion hearings, Scott testified that, to him, "providing humanitarian aid is a sacred act." He also described how spiritually devastated he had been when he had come upon human remains in the desert. "The work that we do in discovering, working to identify and recover the people who have died is one of the most sacred things that we can do as humanitarian aid workers in Southern Arizona and in the desert. . . we witness, and we are present for people and for their families ..." When asked why he risked violating the law by providing water, food and clothing to migrants in the desert, he testified," Based on my spiritual beliefs, I am compelled to act. I am drawn to act. I have to act when someone is in need."

In 1993, Congress passed the Religious Freedom Restoration Act (RFRA) that was designed to protect the exercise of religious beliefs, especially those of religious minorities. It provided narrow exceptions to neutral laws that apply to everyone. The law has been cited in such recent recognizable cases as Hobby Lobby and a much earlier case allowing the use of peyote by certain religious groups.

Citing the RFRA, Scott is using his strongly-held beliefs as one basis for his legal defense.[142] According to Ryan Lucas of NPR, the "legal team's decision to stake out part of his defense on religious liberty grounds has made the case a clash between two of (former) Attorney General Jeff Sessions' top priorities: cracking down on

---

141 Daniella Silva, Volunteer arrested after giving food, water to undocumented immigrants in Arizona, January 23, 2018 ((accessed August 1, 2018 at www.nbcnews.com/news/latino/volunteer-arrested-after-giving-food-water-undocumented-immigrants-arizona-n840386)

142 Currently, Scott's legal team consists of Greg Kuykendall and Amy Knight.

illegal immigration and defending religious liberty."[143] According to Lucas, Sessions called religious liberty America's "first freedom" in a July speech and vowed to aggressively protect it. He announced the creation of a task force to help the Justice Department accomplish that goal.[144]

The U.S Attorney's office in Arizona and Border Patrol have declined to comment on the motion to seal certain exhibits revealing animus toward No More Deaths. Motions filed the week of September 16, 2018, provide evidence that law enforcement actions taken against No More Deaths are part of a campaign targeting the organization.

> In a sworn declaration, Robin Reineke, a cultural anthropologist and director of the Colibri Center for Human Rights, an internationally renewed organization that repatriates the remains of migrants who die in the desert, described a meeting last summer in which a senior Border Patrol agent angrily told her that because of the bad press No More Deaths stirred up for his employer, the agency's plan was to "shut them down."[145]
>
> Recently she explained, she has observed a marked change in the Border Patrol's treatment of the organization. On June 12, 2017, Border Patrol raided a camp that No More Deaths has used to provide medical aid for migrants for more than a decade, following a tense three-day standoff and leaving with five undocumented men it had tracked to the location.

---

143 Ryan Lucas, *NPR*, "Deep in the Desert, A Case Pits Immigration Crackdown Against Religious Freedom," October 18, 2018, (accessed October 23, 2018).

144 Ibid.

145 Ryan Devereaux, "Justice Department Attempts to Suppress Evidence that the Border Patrol Targeted Humanitarian Volunteers," *The Intercept*, September 16, 2018, pp. 3-4. (http://theintercept.com/2018/09/16/border-patrol-no-more-deaths-prosecution-arizona-immigrants) (accessed October 15, 2018)

Reineke happened to have an appointment with BORSTAR representative Agundez and Alonzo. At that meeting she expressed her anger and dismay that agents would raid a humanitarian aid station in the desert during a heatwave. Agundez's response was angry and defensive, and he referred to the negative press (the recent *"Abandoned"* report), saying they had gone too far.

Eight additional volunteers are facing multiple misdemeanor charges for actions taken in the Cabeza Prieta National Wildlife Refuge near Ajo on August 13, 2017: Natalie Renee Hoffman, Oona Meagan Holocomb, Madeline Abbe Huse, Zaachila I. Orozco-McCormick, Caitlin Persis Deighan (Parker), Zoe E. Anderson, Logan Thomas Hollarsmith, and Rebecca Katie Grossman-Richeimer. Charges include: Abandonment of Personal Property, Entering a Wilderness Area Without a Permit, and Driving in a Wilderness Area. Each of these volunteers faces a $5,000 fine and up to six months in prison.[146]

Last July (2018) four of these defendants responded to a distress call from a woman who reported that two family members and a friend were without water in one of the deadliest sections of the U.S.-Mexico border. For hours, the volunteers' messages to Border Patrol went unanswered. Finally, they set off in a pickup truck toward the peak where the migrants were said to be located.

Once on the Cabeza Prieta Wildlife Refuge, the volunteers were tracked by federal agents and intercepted. Five months later they were charged. In court, both sides acknowledged that the No More Deaths volunteers explained on site that they were on the Refuge in search of three people in distress, that they lacked permits, and that they "did not see the signs labeling the road as an administrative road because they were in a hurry to search for the three distressed individuals."

---

146 *No More Deaths Update*: #DropTheCharges!. August 2, 2018 (accessed August 2, 2018)

Ultimately, two of the migrants were found by Border Patrol agents stationed in Ajo and a CBP helicopter crew out of Yuma that had established communications with the No More Deaths volunteers. The third individual was never found.

Exhibits introduced in court include text messages between Fish and Wildlife and Border Patrol which Fish and Wildlife say, "Love it!" in regard to the prosecution of the volunteers, calling them "bean droppers" In addition, Fish and Wildlife refused to issue permits to some No More Deaths Volunteers and modified permit applications requiring applicants to specifically agree to not leave food, water, or clothing on the refuge. All this information is being used by the defense in court. "By seeking to imprison a group of humanitarian volunteers over their efforts to save three people in the desert, the state has entered into dark territory reserved for the worst regimes," the attorneys said.[147]

The attorneys argued in court:

> Common decency requires that a government do what it can to prevent unnecessary death and suffering inside its borders. To actively thwart efforts of its citizens to assist those in need through the provision of the most basic necessities—emergency food and water—is cruel and shameful behavior. And to threaten to imprison citizens for searching for distressed migrants stranded in highly dangerous locations—generous, humane actions the government should encourage and applaud—is unconscionable. It violates the universal sense of justice.[148]

Prosecution of these volunteers will likely take place in 2019.

---

147 Op.Cit., Ryan Devereaux, pp. 2-3.
148 Op.Cit., Ryan Devereaux, p. 12.

CHAPTER 102

The Morning After

August 5, 2018: Gene and I spent an extraordinary weekend in Ajo. We joined 75 pastors and local volunteers to flood the desert (*inundar el desierto*) "to call attention to the criminalization of humanitarian aid and the crisis of death and disappearance in the west desert. These faith leaders came from all over the country to stand in solidarity with humanitarian aid workers and residents who assert their right to provide humanitarian aid in the borderlands."[149]

The effort was a collaboration between No More Deaths, the Unitarian Universalist Service Committee (UUSC), and the Unitarian Universalist Association involving leaders and members of many faiths from around the country.

We left Phoenix about 9:00 a.m. and arrived in Ajo just in time for lunch. We met many old friends. john heid, who had moved from Tucson to Ajo, served us a lunch of delicious spinach and cheese pie with a filo crust. In addition to him, John Fife, Jim Marx, Jean and Charles Rooney, Lois Martin, Janie Foy, and others. It was wonderful to reconnect personally with these old friends.

Program leaders included Catherine Gaffney, Sebastian, Scott Warren and his partner, Emily Saunders. Hannah Hafter, a former stipended volunteer for No More Deaths, did much of the organizing for the UUSCs. Geena Jackson had gone to great lengths to

---

149 No More Deaths press release, August 1, 2018 (accessed August 2, 2018 at www.nomoredeaths.org)

make our participation possible since it was created to involve out-of-town pastors.

Following lunch, speakers gave the lay of the land, including an explanation of the long history of migrant travel through the area known as The Devil's Highway (an area that crosses the U.S./Mexico border and travels through the Cabeza Prieta Wildlife Refuge). Almost half of the recovered remains of border crossers found in 2017 in Arizona (128 total) were found in the West Desert (57 total or 44%). Both raw numbers and percentages have increased steadily since 2012 when more border crossers moved west toward California.

Also addressed were the recent charges against Scott Warren and eight other volunteers. Scott faces two counts of felony harboring and one count of felony conspiracy under U.S.C. 1324. If convicted of all three charges and issued a consecutive sentence, Scott faces up to 20 years in prison.

Mentioned also were the recent national awards given to attorney Margo Cowan and Dr. Norma Price. Margo is one of the co-founders of No More Deaths and the pro bono attorney for both No More Deaths and Samaritans. She was recognized in June at the annual conference of the American Immigration Lawyers Association and given the Arizona Chapter Pro Bono Champion Award, honoring her years of pro bono service.[150]

Norma Price, MD, volunteer with No More Deaths, Tucson Samaritans, and other humanitarian organizations in Tucson, was recognized by Physicians for Human Rights at their annual gala in New York in May. The gala honors health professionals working on the front lines to defend human rights. Norma was one of three people to receive the Heroes of Health and Human Rights Award, which honors American Health professionals who have taken courageous stands in extraordinary times, resisting government policies that threaten their patients' health and rights and ensuring that the

---

150 *No More Deaths Update*: Two Volunteers Recognized, August 1, 2018 (accessed August 2, 2018)

needs of their patients and the ethical demands of their professions come first.[151]

Margo Cowan Receiving Award (No More Deaths)

Toward the end of the afternoon, Emily told the group that a body had been found that morning just outside Ajo. She spoke his name, Saul Salazar, several times in acknowledgement of the need to give names to the dead whenever we can. Ironically, Sr. Salazar's nephew, Fidel Moreno, had drummed during a portion of this event. Emily asked Gene to pray after she made the announcement, which he did. This was followed by a collection of donations to assist in Sr. Salazar's burial and for additional family needs. The collection amounted to $840.

Gene and I were a bit surprised at the spiritual tone of the event, given the frequent disdain expressed previously by some of our younger volunteers. However, something must have happened—after

---

151 *No More Deaths Update*: Two Volunteers Recognized, August 1, 2018 (accessed August 2, 2018)

all, spiritual leaders had been invited to this event from all over the country. During the explanation of Sunday's event, people had been encouraged to express their faith in a variety of ways—meditating, praying, singing, reading poetry—however they wished. After we returned to Phoenix, Jim Marx told Gene in a phone conversation that he thought the planning group had been greatly influenced by Scott's recent declaration in court—that his work with migrants is motivated by the depth of his spiritual life. Scott is well-admired and respected within the group.

Following the afternoon briefing, the group gathered in the grass at Ajo Town Square for more passionate remarks and participation by some of the religious folks who'd traveled all this way from their homes around the country. The "flood the desert" event was dedicated and blessed.

After that, the group moved slowly into the Under the Arches art studio for dinner and to take in some local art, much of which depicts the anguish and loss of life in the nearby desert. It was delicious and powerful.

Most of the people stayed overnight either in residents' homes or in a local defunct school. Gene and I checked in to the nearby La Siesta motel. Gene was up at 4:30 a.m. to get dressed for the desert (the day's weather was expected to be 107 degrees).

The group gathered for breakfast at 5:15 a.m. and then moved out to drop water on two major areas in the nearby desert—Cabeza de Prieta National Wildlife Refuge (three vans with 15 people each) and the Devil's Highway (two vans with 15 people each—also on the Refuge).

Amazingly, there were no major incidents during the hike. Fish and Wildlife and Border Patrol agents who are responsible for the area were very helpful and cooperative. It was as if they had decided or been briefed beforehand not to take the bait to arrest out-of-towners for putting water on the Refuge. However, there was some concern among volunteers that tickets would be issued later by mail. *A ver* (we'll see).

Several young adult volunteers guided the groups. Kind volunteers were very solicitous of Gene in the heat, acknowledging his senior status (now 85). His only complaint about the hike was that it was too slow. No doubt the presence of both John Fife and Gene Lefebvre hiking was a motivation to others.

Gene returned to the motel at two, flushed red and exhausted. I had booked the motel for a second night, so he could nap before heading back to Phoenix around 4:30 that afternoon.

Organizers (of the event) were calling for all current charges against humanitarian aid workers to be dropped and for land managers in the West Desert to ensure that civil humanitarian response be allowed on public land without fear of harassment or prosecution.[152]

---

152 No More Deaths press release, August 1, 2018 (accessed August 2, 2018 at www.nomoredeaths.org)

CHAPTER 103

The Trials–2019

**Signs Throughout Tucson Saying, "Drop
the Charges" (No More Deaths)**

*Members of our organization are being criminally
prosecuted for placing water in areas where hundreds
of people have died of thirst. Anybody who has visited
the refuge understands the harshness of the terrain
and the need for a humanitarian response."*

— *PAIGE CORICH-KLEIM, NO MORE DEATHS VOLUNTEER*

THE FIRST FOUR VOLUNTEERS FACING federal misdemeanor charges for their humanitarian work on the Cabeza Prieta National Wildlife Refuge began January 15, 2019. Hoffman was charged with operating a vehicle in a wilderness area and entering a national refuge without a permit. Holcomb, Huse, and Orozco-McCormick were charged with entering without a permit and abandonment of property, each a class "B" misdemeanor. According to Paul Ingram of the *Arizona Daily Star* in Tucson,

Four Ajo Defendants 2018 (No More Deaths)

Prosecutors argued in court (this week) that the four women violated federal law when they drove a Dodge Ram pickup truck into the wilderness on an administrative road to Charlie Bell Well on August 13, 2017, and left milk crates containing one-gallon jugs of water, along with cans of beans. A remote camera captured images of the Dodge truck as U.S. Federal and Wildlife Service officer Michael West intercepted the women after they returned from a water drop. West ordered the volunteers to head back out of the wilderness, and they headed back. He collected the supplies they left.

Attorney for the defense, Louis Fidel, argued that in Cabeza Prieta there was a "trail of death" that flowed along the west face of the Growler Mountains. Showing a map of the corridor spattered with red dots marking where human remains have been found in Cabeza, Fidel said, "This map is shocking, and the women were compelled to act." Fidel also argued that this was a selective prosecution, because for months, No More Deaths told the Fish and Wildlife people they were doing water drops in Cabeza Prieta, but no one was cited.

According to Ed McCullough, almost half of the recovered human remains of border crossers found in 2017 in Arizona (128 total) were found in the west desert (57 total or 44%). Altogether, more than 387 known deaths have occurred on these land areas since 2001: 209 in Organ Pipe Cactus National Monument, *130 on Cabeza Prieta National Wildlife Refuge,* and 48 on the Barry M. Goldwater Bombing Range. Others cite 155 deaths on Cabeza since 2001.

The second group of four defendants, including Parker Deighan, Rebecca Richeimer, Zoe Anderson and Logan Hollarsmith, faced criminal prosecution in February 2019. On Thursday, February 21st, criminal charges were dropped and they accepted civil responsibility for their actions. They were each fined $250. A ninth defendant, Scott Warren, faces misdemeanor charges for is work on Cabeza Prieta as well as three federal felony charges for other humanitarian work. Both trials are scheduled for May 2019. Please check the Internet to learn the disposition of these charges against Scott.

**No More Deaths Defendant Parker Deighan
on Cabeza Prieta (No More Deaths)**

More than 10,000 individuals and 500 organization signed a statement of support asserting that faced with the same crisis of death and disappearance, they too would choose to put water in the desert. The statement was published on the March 1 sentencing date for the first four defendants, in the *Arizona Daily Star*. These young women were sentenced by U.S. Magistrate Judge Bernardo P. Velasco to 15 months unsupervised probation, fined $250, and banned from the Cabeza Prieta National Wildlife Refuge. As it happened, Judge Velasco presided over the case against No More Deaths volunteers, Shanti Sellz and Daniel Strauss in 2006. District judge Raner Collins took over the case and the charges were subsequently dismissed. The case against Dan Millis in 2008 was dismissed in the 9th Circuit Court.

"The border crisis in this country is a matter of life and death. History will not favor those on the wrong side of it," Huse said in a news release following the sentencing hearing. "Our border policy continues to push people into remote and dangerous parts of the desert."

In October 2018, Curt Prendergast in the *Arizona Daily Star* asked: At what point does humanitarian aid become human smuggling? Does religious freedom protect leaving food and water on federal land without a permit? Is aid work protected by international treaties on migrants' rights? After these trials, do we have any answers?

CHAPTER 104

Spiritual Influence in Humanitarian Efforts

To love mercy is to love those who have never had a break,
where the cards are always stacked against them. It's to
love—to open our hearts and our arms to embrace those who
have been treated harshly, ignored, forgotten, discounted,
abused—the immigrant, the Muslim, the Jew, the African
American, the Latino, the Asian, the poor and the hungry. It's
about honoring all people no matter their circumstance.

— *THE REV. DR. JAMES L. McDONALD*

THE MAJOR THRUST OF ACTIVISM in current migrant issues in Southern Arizona emanates from individuals who have come from or are still active in the Judeo-Christian tradition. During the 1980s, when the Sanctuary movement was at its height, the Tucson Ecumenical Council (comprised on faith-based groups, including Jewish congregations) spun off from the Tucson Refugee Support Group (TRSG), which was made up of individuals from several churches and synagogues. They took the lead in helping the hundreds of refugees who had flooded into Southern Arizona.

Members of these groups were already primed to respond to needs in the community and stepped up when it became clear that migrants were dying in the desert around year 2000. These people were unwilling to simply teach Sunday School, feed the homeless, participate in worship services, and attend to their own buildings and grounds. Being the Church meant far more to them than that. Usually through intentional study, they heeded the admonition in Chapter 25 of Matthew and responded to the crisis facing their own communities that increasingly consisted of people of color from the south whom they recognized and loved.

You may remember from earlier in the book when Gene Lefebvre, John Fife, and Miguel de la Torre along with his students from Iliff Seminary had been spotted on Tohono O'odham Nation land and summarily directed to leave (ironically, by a white female officer). Mike Wilson, a tribal member, had invited the group to see how he and his friend and fellow tribal member, David Garcia, made water available to migrants traveling north through the Nation. Mike, who'd previously served as a lay minister for the Presbyterian Church in Sells, Arizona (on the Nation) began preaching the Gospel to the assembled group, including the officer who had interdicted them. Mike was urgently preaching from the Matthew text above, identifying the imperative to feed the hungry and give water to the thirsty.

Churches that had been involved from the very beginning of the current crisis included Southside Presbyterian Church under the leadership of The Rev. John Fife and later The Rev. Alison Harrington. It provided volunteers, physical space, and emotional and spiritual support to those in need. Showers for migrants had become more important than a library. Facilities for day laborers took precedence over adult Sunday School classes. Some years earlier, under the leadership of Fife, the entire church had entered into a covenant with the hungry, and the thirsty, and the sick as well as those headed to prison. It hasn't always been easy but, in the face of the crisis arising around 2000, they renewed this covenant.

The humanitarian group Samaritans currently operates out of Southside Presbyterian Church and enjoys its full support. No More Deaths had started out there and then moved on, first to St. Mark's

Presbyterian Church, and finally to Tucson Unitarian Universalist Church (although still using St. Mark's physical space and volunteer support), with other churches contributing volunteers, space, and energy to the movement. Various Catholic Churches and their adherents have also contributed significantly to the work.

The first humanitarian group to form up after the crisis in the desert was identified was Humane Borders. Originally under the leadership of the Rev. Robin Hoover and located in the First Christian Church, it's comprised of many folks who are committed to going into the blazing desert to set up 55-gallon tanks of water for migrants. It takes strong motivation to do that week after week.

I should also say the humanitarian groups have historically been joined by all types of "people of conscience" in their efforts. Volunteers for No More Deaths often refer to themselves as people of faith and conscience. Restrictive religious dogma has no part in the work. The motivation and goal for them is justice.

Let me broaden this out to recognize and include others involved in the humanitarian efforts in Tucson. The existence of these groups in no way diminishes what has been said about Christian-based groups. In fact, their work has also been informed by the basic support and philosophy of Christianity, however secular the mission. These groups include The Asylum Project, *Derechos Humanos*, Border Action Network, BorderLinks, *Tierra y Libertad Organizacion (TYLO)*, Humane Border Solutions (Bisbee), and others. All are infused with the values and personnel similar to those of the three humanitarian groups mentioned above. Some of them also look to the statements of "Civil Initiative," written during the Sanctuary Movement by the Quaker, Jim Corbett, as guiding principles.

Then, what about the anarchists who keep the desert work of No More Deaths functioning from day to day and have recently taken significant leadership roles in the organization as well? I suspect many of the early No More Deaths folks were already borderline anarchists themselves. Discouraged with the organized church or synagogue or mosque, they brought their basic values of honesty, fairness, and care for the downtrodden into No More Deaths to work along with others on current justice issues. When, around 2009-2010, many avowed anarchists came from all over the country to volunteer in the desert, their philosophy was subtly identified with by many in the core group. Some desert workers, Like Scott Walker, point to a spiritual base that is not necessarily of a main-line church origin for their motivation.

Seasoned volunteers found resonance with the newcomers' disdain for hierarchy. They also shared in their frustration about the excesses (or failures) rampant in the U.S. government. Fortunately for the anarchists, the existence and support of the main No More Deaths community along with our strong value base has allowed these "churchless" volunteers to spend weeks in the desert (along with many others) identifying trails, providing water and food, and enjoying their own style of community. If they have felt the need to avoid core group meetings or reject established No More Deaths protocols forged over time, so be it. They did the work in the field and did it with skill and diligence. Early on in this process, some in the core group who were frustrated with the anarchists thought to tell them if they didn't like our group and our rules, they should just go out on their own and do their own thing. This was never a real possibility. What would they do for vehicles? What about gas? How about food and water? How about tents and cots? Most practically and importantly, how would they cope if they were arrested and didn't have the No More Deaths legal team to cover their backs? Over the years (and with some difficult work on the part of both sides), a new working relationship has been forged, broken apart and forged again. Although the anarchists may feel independent, a part of the Church that is sometimes called "the faithful remnant" still provides a sturdy foundation to No More Deaths.

This Judeo-Christian heritage provides many Americans with a unifying attitude toward justice, including the quest for individual rights (present administration not withstanding). As effective as this approach may be, Miguel de la Torre, in the following section, shows us how our firmly held attitudes and styles may well get in our way when seeking justice for Hispanics.[153]

---

153 This section has been informed by Rick Ufford Chase's 2017 book, *Faithful Resistance*.

CHAPTER 105

A New Ethical Imperative

*Tricksters are rule breakers, and thus employ a praxis
that is needed if the marginalized are to break free from
the rules that hold them in a subordinated space.*

— MIGUEL DE LA TORRE, LATINA/O SOCIAL ETHICS

KUDOS TO THE VALIANT VOLUNTEERS who have worked with the humanitarian aid programs in Southern Arizona. Their motivations vary, but all are hardworking, dedicated individuals with a deep-seated sense of right and wrong and a strong desire to make things better. The beginnings of No More Deaths, Humane Borders, and Samaritans, among others as described above, are rooted in religious communities. Ministers, rabbis, imams, and lay people responded to the deaths in the desert after learning about them and invented significant responses to those disturbing facts. Since then (2000), additional people of conscience have joined this work and have added to its success.

Volunteers work side by side with little need to identify the affiliations or non-affiliations of their coworkers. However, some of the religious leaders' affiliations are obvious and some of the volunteers are acknowledged anarchists. If author Miguel de la Torre is correct, all come from an ethical, Christian, Euro-American background even if they've discarded—or have tried to discard—their adherence to a specific faith expression.

No More Deaths training for new volunteers tries to help them understand that their views, biases and behaviors are those of the dominant Euro-American culture. In order to be successful working with migrants, volunteers must suspend their own biases and views, and be open to the thoughts, feelings, and priorities that migrants have developed within their own Hispanic cultures. No More Deaths most successful volunteers know to ask permission before administering first aid, which conveys to the individual that he or she has control. Volunteers also request permission before taking photos of migrants and explain how any photos might be used. These are basic examples of ways volunteers can express their understanding and respect of others.

De la Torre says:
If ethics is the construct of a particular type of culture, then those born into and/or raised within the Euro-American culture are a product of a society where white supremacy and class privilege are interwoven with how Americans have been conditioned to normalize and legitimize how they see and organize the world around them.[154]

De la Torre cites Ismael Garcia as characterizing Eurocentric values as based on "a culture that is dominantly rights-oriented, impersonal, individualistic, and radically private. (2009a, 631). De la Torre says that, generally speaking, Hispanic values, by contrast, are based on a culture that is dominantly justice-oriented, relational, liberationist, and radically communal.

Even if volunteers have shrugged off Christianity—one young woman staying at our home told us that if only you'd get rid of that

---

154 Miguel de la Torre, *Latina/o Social Ethics, Moving Beyond Eurocentric Moral Thinking*, Baylor University, 2010.

God stuff, No More Deaths would be OK—[155] they're still saddled with other culture-based attitudes de la Torre identifies. Many of the desert volunteers have left their families "to do their own thing," while many young migrants leave their own families to actually help *them.*

De la Torre (who is Hispanic) calls for Hispanics to move away from Euro-American ethics that stand in opposition against the Latino/a community. He says, "Euro-Americans who wish to do Christian ethics must move away from white ethics and, in solidarity with marginalized communities, participate in liberative practice that is rooted within the Hispanic culture."

De la Torre explains that borders are where the brokenness of Hispanic life is most evident and that these Latino/as are disjointed from their culture of their heritage and the cultures in which they reside. Thus, for any ethical analysis to be called "Hispanic" it must originate with the goal of seeking justice-based alternatives to the struggles for communal survival.

De la Torre also cautions Latino/as to be wary of the Euro-American culture due to the fact that the domination of non-whites abroad is mirrored domestically in the disproportionate disenfranchisement of Hispanics from the political benefits of society. Hispanics are usually not even invited to the table where decisions are made. This is evident in U.S. government policies that have established "zero-tolerance" for refugees coming from Guatemala, El Salvador and Honduras in 2018, which took just shy of 3000 children from their parents.

A solution proposed by de la Torre includes the use of *jodiendo* (to screw with—in polite terms, that is). This expression connotes an individual who is purposely a pain in the rear, who is purposely causing trouble, who constantly disrupts the established norm... someone who refuses to stay in his or her place. De la Torre suggests

---

155 The main expressions of "God stuff" that happens, like desert memorials, are organized by volunteers.

that Hispanics have little hope of vanquishing the empire's impact on their lives and they continue the struggle—if not for themselves, then for their children.

If it is true that Christian ethics as practiced is the ethics of an empire whose supreme goal is to maintain social order, then those claiming faithfulness to the biblical call for justice (such as feeding the poor, caring for the sick, and visiting the orphans) may be the ones needed to bring about social disorder.

Miguel de la Torre:

Ironically, when those in power have their power threatened, they call the disrupting of the status quo patriotic. When they kill, arrest, detain in internment camps, kidnap, torture, disappear, assassinate, spread propaganda, or engage in military conflict against whoever is labeled an enemy of democracy and "our way of life," they herald these actions as "our fight for freedom," which, of course, is never free. Thus, they make terms like justice, patriotism, equality, and law and order meaningless.[156]

When thousands die in the desert attempting to cross artificially constructed borders, when a Latina must provide sexual favors to obtain legal immigration status or a job to feed her children, then the abuse that overtly targets one "offending" Hispanic is symbolically directed at all potential Latino/as who might dare to step out of line and request *dignidad* and *justiciar*. For this reason, the display of abuse or punishment must be seen or known by all within the targeted community, while masked and hidden within the dominant culture.

An ethics *para joder* relies on the trickster figure to challenge external oppression and uncover its

---

156 Ibid, pp. 77-78.

internalized manifestation. Tricksters allow us to suspend strict Eurocentric paradigms and definitions of morality, what is right and what is wrong, to provide us the opportunity to study and comprehend how social structures are constructed to the detriment of our people. Generally speaking, tricksters are characterized by ambiguity, transformative power, and razor-sharp wit.[157]

De la Torre provides many examples of *jodiendo.* One of my favorites is the story of "Pepito" visiting the doctor. Through his innocence, Pepito uses his wit to unmask the shortcomings of those who perceive themselves as better or of higher social value.

Miguel de la Torre:
As can be imagined, some of the Pepito stories are a bit racy. For example, Pepito walks into the crowded doctor's office and tells the receptionist that there is something wrong with his penis (of course, a more vulgar word is usually used when recounting this story). Shocked, the receptionist states that such words should not be used in polite company lest he embarrass the ladies or gentlemen who might be present. She tells Pepito that he should have said something was wrong with another part of his body, like his eye or ear, and then discussed the real problem in the privacy of the doctor's office. She then sends Pepito outside and asks him to try again. Pepito leaves, only to return saying that there is something wrong with his ear. Feeling satisfied that Pepito has been put in his place, the receptionist smugly thanks him for the information and asks what is wrong with his ear. Pepito responds that he can't urinate out of it. In this story, the

---

157 Ibid, pp. 103.

hypocrisy of those who consider themselves better is humor-ously unmasked.[158]

De la Torre points to the people's saint, *Jesus Juarez Mazo*, who is also known as *Jesus Malverde*. He has been revered throughout Northern Mexico for nearly a century and has become a popular icon in the United States since the start of the 21st century, particularly in California and the Southwest. On the trails in Southern Arizona, we see shrines dedicated to Jesus Malverde with many tokens placed there to appease him. According to folklore, Jesus Malverde was a Robin Hood-type bandit who stole from the rich and gave to the poor. He was killed in 1909 by the police. With time, people began to believe that his image offered protection from the law. Many migrants venerate the image of Jesus Malverde, praying he will pro-vide either safe passage into the United States or money once they arrive.[159]

> For ethics to be authentic, for ethics to be closest to the bib-lical mandate, it must arise from disenfranchised commu-nities that are reflecting on the praxis they are employing in order to survive. To that end, an ethics *para joder* incor-porates civil initiative—a concept developed by the inner religious circle for ethics, specifically as it is presently being integrated along the U.S. southern border as a methodology that brings to light the human rights violations taking place against the undocumented.[160]

During the Sanctuary Movement, the goal was not to do away with bad laws but to force the government to follow good laws that existed. The Movement had been using the term "civil disobedience," until

---

158 Ibid. Page111
159 Ibid, pages 117-118
160 Ibid, page 118

John Fife received a call from an attorney in New York who told John he wasn't performing civil disobedience. So? John asked him what *they* were doing. The attorney told him that that was for John to figure out! Thus, a new term and strategy were required. Jim Corbett, a Quaker activist and one of the co-founders of the Sanctuary Movement, reflected upon the work of the movement and developed the term, "civil initiative" in order to put into words the practice that participants in the Movement were carrying out. Civil initiative derives from international law developed during the Nuremberg trial of Nazi officials who used the excuse that they "were just following orders." The court concluded that international duties transcend individual obligations to obey national states. [161]

However, the U.S. government, rather than acknowledge its complicity in causing undocumented immigration and rather than working toward a comprehensive and compassionate immigration reform, responded to the predicted increase in immigration by implementing Operation Gatekeeper the same year NAFTA was ratified.

Until then, most migrants crossed into the U.S. through urban centers like San Diego, Nogales, and El Paso. Operation Gatekeeper sealed the border at these traditional entry points, pushing the trails through inhospitable mountain ranges and deserts. Operation Gatekeeper was based on the assumption that migrants would die crossing the desert. Thousands did die. These "collateral damages," it was believed, would deter others from thinking about the dangerous crossing. What we do know is that no one was deterred. The Mexican economy in shambles, to which we contributed, forced desperate people to face any obstacle in

---

161 Ibid, page120

the hopes of being able to send money back home to feed their hungry children.[162]

Civil initiative becomes a Hispanic-centric ethical response developed by those doing feet-on-the-ground ethics. Not to sound trite, but, as one of the posters of the organization No More Deaths succinctly states, humanitarian aid is not a crime. While No More Deaths plays a cat and mouse game with the Border Patrol in order to place water and food on the trails, as well as provide medical aid, they are *jodiendo*—they are "screwing" with the officials.[163]

When volunteers at Byrd Camp go up on the hill behind the camp to take food to Border Patrol and then stay a while to chat, they are *jodiendo*. When BANWR claimed they had 30 working water sites and volunteer Ed McCullough checked out each site and found many defunct...when we presented those results to the media, we were *jodiendo*. There was the time Kevin Riley captured pictures and video of a Border Patrol agent dumping out water meant for migrants while the agent kept saying, derisively "You're out of video!" Kevin knew his camera included lots of video space—and so he kept filming. He was *jodiendo*, and the video not only still gets played from time to time on the national media but is included in the latest No More Deaths report. When the government had failed over and over again to return migrant belongings upon their release, No More Deaths (David Hill) developed a system to retrieve the belongings from court and unite them with their owners—returning more than $54,000 in cash during 2016 alone. Just *para joder!*

---

162 Ibid, "Introduction"
163 Ibid, pages 119-120

CHAPTER 106

What's Left Out

THIS BOOK COVERS A LOT of ground, but I have not adequately covered the time since the tenth anniversary of No More Deaths in 2014. During that period, two or three generations of highly competent volunteers have joined the work. When Gene and I moved back to Phoenix, we lost track of the day-to-day work of No More Deaths, except what we could learn from meeting minutes and conversations with friends. I know, for example, that the volunteers have restructured the No More Deaths organization and have focused their efforts to greater effect. I also know that the work of No More Deaths has been extended into Northern Mexico. I've been told that, while improved, tensions continue to flare from time between the young people and the elders. I sincerely challenge the many competent writers to take up the story where I left off. I believe the work of humanitarians in Arizona needs to be recorded as a significant part of history in the 21st Century.

In addition, I have barely touched on the important emerging issue of the New Sanctuary Movement. In this movement, churches once again provide housing, food, and emotional support to migrants and asylum seekers who face imminent deportation, often without due process. Leaders in this movement in Arizona include Southside Presbyterian Church and Rincon United Church of Christ in Tucson, Shadow Rock United Church of Christ and First Christian Church, in Phoenix, as well as many Hispanic churches.

In 2014, a wave of Central American children arrived at the border of Texas along the Rio Grande River. I have not addressed this migration, although some of the children ended up in institutions and churches in both Tucson and Phoenix. According to former Homeland Security Director Jeh Johnson (from the Obama administration) speaking on Rachel Maddow's MSNBC show in June 2018, thousands of people from Honduras, El Salvador, and Guatemala continued coming throughout 2015, 2016, and 2017. Those coming in 2018 are a continuation of those others who started fleeing gangs and violence in Guatemala, El Salvador, and Honduras in 2014. Although the policy of separating children from parents is not new, the fact that the media jumped on it as proof of Trump's lack of compassion catapulted this "crisis" into new possibilities for the reform of Immigration and Customs Enforcement (ICE), Customs and Border Patrol (CBP), and Border Patrol (BP). No More Deaths has important information to contribute to that effort. Our reports about Border Patrol include many recommendations.

It was challenging enough working with the Obama administration, given the lack of progress on immigration reform—hindered, of course, by the opposition party. Shortly after the 2016 election, a conference of humanitarians convened in Tucson and people discussed their sense of the future and planned for their ongoing work. A recommitment was made to fight for justice for migrants and humane practices for those who enter country seeking relief from their trauma back home. Weeks later, Border Patrol invited humanitarians to a meeting where they outlined the new crackdown on migrants and humanitarians. Again, we saw the implementation of these new policies in the raiding of the No More Deaths camp and the arrest of Dr. Scott Warren and eight others in the Ajo area in 2017 and 2018.

This new administration is ruination for the immigration reform that has been called for by the public since the early 2000s.[164] A model

---

164 Include percentages of support

piece of legislation, HB 4321, was put forth by Illinois Representative Luis Gutierrez in 2009. Later, a gang of eight senators including Dick Durbin (D-IL), Michael Bennet (D-CO), Jeff Flake (R-AZ), Lindsey Graham (R-SC), John McCain (R-AZ), Robert Menendez (D-NJ), Marco Rubio (R-FL), and Chuck Schumer (D-NY) made a significant effort to address the need. Since then any immigration reform bills, like these, have been DOA.

As this book itself becomes history, it will be interesting to see how these issues will have played out. No More Deaths will continue its work with migrants and advocate for immigration reform in the belief that ultimately greater justice will prevail. When my husband and I moved to Tucson in 2007, there was strong anticipation that comprehensive immigration would become a reality soon. Perhaps one day it will.

CHAPTER 107

What Does Recovering Human Remains Mean?

"You can't call somebody dead who struggles for life."

— ANONYMOUS JOHN HEID—

There is no easy way to write about this. The words when put side by side are shrill. A keen.

Recovering. Human. Remains.

How does one "recover" another who is dead? Another whose body parts are strewn about, blanched, clotted with dirt, or even intact, sun seared and gray?

"Humans," even in death, shouldn't look like this.

"Remains": a euphemism. This is what's left. What wasn't eaten, or dragged off by coyotes or ravens, or buried in monsoon mud.

A being is reduced to a statistic. A what, rather than a who....

Who lived inside this skull anyway? What were their last thoughts? Who is their mother? Lover? Did they have children? Does anyone who loved them know their fate? Why did they come this way? Will I ever get used to this part of the work? Do I want to?

And yet, can I stop? When I encounter some-body, I re-encounter myself. The living meets the dead. And stops me. Cold. Even at 115 degrees.

Sometimes I go into work mode. I become methodical. Set up a grid search...to look for more body parts, more of who this Juan or Juanita Doe was. Mark a GPS waypoint. Take photos. Call the sheriff's office. Mark the area with bright tape and...and, and, and....

And yet here or nearby is where someone took their last choking, sun-racked breath.

Sometimes I just sit down in the deep stillness. Paralyzed in the moment. Looking death in the face, or more accurately, in the eyeless skull. Looking into the maw of needless death. Premeditated death. Death by policy. Murder.

My intellect and my emotions collide. And I'm pushed deeper into that dark, dank internal cavern where the query "why" bangs off the walls. And shatters the stillness.

There is no easy way to write about this. How can you call somebody dead who struggled for life?[165]

---

165 heid, john, *No More Deaths Newsletter,* June 20, 2018.

CHAPTER 108

From the Beginning into the Future

MANY ORGANIZATIONS EXIST TO DEFEND immigrant rights, yet the Southern Arizona humanitarians and those in nearby states are the ones who interface with the raw humanity of fleeing individuals at their most desperate times. No More Deaths volunteers know that civil initiative's mandate for direct action leads to an understanding of the causes of pain and injustice felt by individuals entering this country. They also understand that "screwing the system" can provide some measure of satisfaction when they are working in the midst of incomprehensible policies, actions, and failure to act

While effective, *jodiendo* is not the only approach taken by No More Deaths and other Southern Arizona humanitarians. Let me remind you of some of the conditions during the early years (2000-2007), where we are now (2018), and the role of No More Deaths during that journey as our lives were oddly disordered. Then let's look to the future.

In the 1940s and 1950s, people traveled back and forth across the border through a hole in the fence to get immediate necessities (like groceries) or to move further into the U.S. to find jobs. In the 1980s, this existing "system" was still comfortable for U.S. residents—we were getting the workers we needed through the Bracero Program, or later, through the underground railroad. Mexico in turn was receiving significant economic remittances from their countrymen working in the U.S. There appeared to be little motivation for change and little accountability of who came in and who was sent back. During a visit crossing the border back into the U.S. in the 80s, Gene asked an agent at the border checkpoint, "How many times can a migrant cross the border and you "catch and release" him?" His response was, "I've seen them come back as many as 27 times."

In 1994, U.S. policy changed significantly with the implementation of NAFTA. The government predicted more migrants would come in. Sylvestre Reyes in Texas implemented "deterrence by death" when it was decided to close the border ports of entry of migrants that forced people into hostile mountains and deserts. Now our entire country is aware of immigration issues. People are angry, frustrated, and/or of a punitive mind—depending on their point of view. Now each person who enters at a port of entry is processed and jailed or immediately returned to Mexico or to another country of origin. A small percentage are granted asylum.

Ignorance and malaise existed among the general population regarding immigration when No More Deaths was formed in 2004. Lack of resources, little research, few articles, books, TV and newspaper coverage, nascent Internet sources, and minimum data from governmental organizations and private agencies made it difficult not only to know the extent of growing immigration issues, but also to affect sentiment around the country or to develop interdiction strategies.

This began to change over time as people began to study the issue and write articles and books and develop TV coverage. Reporters traveled to originating countries bringing back stories to help them develop series of articles about root causes of the migration. Through on-the-ground interviews with migrants who had been returned to Mexico, No More Deaths gradually became aware of the abuses our government was perpetrating on vulnerable migrants. Thus, No More Deaths contributed to the literature through individual articles in magazines, book chapters, and intense abuse-documentation research which resulted in six separate reports. Several No More

Deaths volunteers have based their doctoral studies and/or dissertations upon the issues surrounding migration in the Southwest. Data is now available on such issues as: migrants taking our jobs, migrants murdering our citizens, the failure of migrants to contribute to the wealth of our country, or migrants overusing our services without paying for them. It has been clearly shown that perceptions such as these are not rooted in reality.

If they even thought about it, most people in immigrant-rich areas exhibited a general sense that Border Patrol, police, and other government agencies were just doing their job, but didn't usually have any specific biases against migrants (although documentation exists that Border Patrol has a long history of bias and persecution of people in its care.). They seemed to perceive the enforcement as perfunctory police action, with a minimum of over-heightened emotion. This notion, however, is contrary to evidence that has surfaced in recent years.

Now, shootings of migrants and other abuses have created a gradual awareness among people of conscience of the questionable behavior of law enforcement toward migrants. The deep anger and hostility toward migrants seen on our southern border seems too widespread to be contained to a small percentage of Border Patrol and other enforcement agents, as shown in our most recent abuse-documentation report--*Disappeared*. Their actions reflect on the entire border apparatus. This appears to mirror what we see in the relationship between law enforcement and black folks in many American communities. Humanitarian volunteers have seen first-hand numerous acts of deprivation and overt brutality, and they've documented hundreds more through the stories of migrants. The separation of parents from their children at the border in 2018 raised this national awareness to a new level, a condition that will likely stain our political life for some time to come.

No More Deaths and other humanitarian volunteers. while experienced from their years working in Sanctuary during the 1980s, still had much to learn about the challenges in the desert, along the border, working together, and working with several government agencies. When Gene and I arrived in Tucson in 2007, Ed McCullough was busy mapping more than 2000 miles of trails in Southern Arizona—many close to the border. The several humanitarian groups were working independently and spent some energy guarding their own territory. Those organizations working in the desert had yet to test the boundaries of Border Patrol, Fish and Wildlife, Bureau of Land Management, Forest Service, and state-owned jurisdictions.

Humanitarian organizations now know the Sonoran Desert very well after years of exploring its washes, mountains, saddles, and valleys. More than 2000 miles of trails are programmed into GPS units carried by volunteers, and paper copies of maps of all the areas are available as well. Logs are kept of patrols into desert areas documenting everything from all water drops to any migrants encountered—and any unusual incidents. Some of the newer volunteers know the trails "like the back of their hands."

Kathryn Ferguson's encounter with Bureau of Land Management was testy. However, our encounters with the Forest Service for permits have been mostly benign. Overall, humanitarians have a level of understanding of the challenges associated with each governmental agency that was lacking in the early years. Always, we seek mutual understanding of our common goals and strive to work together in productive ways.

For years, assisting migrants was a part-time, family business. A man in Agua Prieta told Gene he would lead a migrant (or migrants) to a hole in the fence, maybe walk with them a short distance into the U.S., then leave them on their own for the remainder of their journey. The migrant's guide received a small amount of money in return. Big bucks were not involved. By 2004, when Gene and I were in Altar, Mexico, the past mayor of Altar explained that the Mexican mafia had already established a formal route from Southern Mexico up through Hermosillo and Altar and on to the border. Soon the cartels had organized their activities into several major groups that worked throughout Mexico and cornered the migrant trade and making it a very lucrative business.

In 2005, the government established Operation Streamline, a court procedure for charging "illegal immigrants" with the crime of crossing the border. Since then, No More Deaths and other humanitarian organizations in Southern Arizona have monitored daily proceedings for up to 70 individuals each afternoon. More recently, the newer influx of Central Americans has been added to the mix causing extreme pressure on the capacity of the court to manage the flow of people in courts all across the border.

When No More Deaths moved into Byrd Camp in 2006, with its tentacles into the town of Arivaca, volunteers encountered a great deal of pushback from the locals. Overt hostility, name-calling, and cold shoulders at Arivaca Mercantile were commonplace.

Within a few years, this began to turn around: Some Tucson humanitarians moved to Arivaca; long-time residents began to join the work; volunteers established People Helping People, a local effort initiated in a rented building in town to help migrants passing through the area. No More Deaths was invited to provide training on resident rights, how to deal with Border Patrol, and what they legally could do to help migrants. Now most locals are friendly to No More Deaths and not too happy with Border Patrol whose policy is to stay aloof from local involvement. Members of the community work together to gain closer access to and monitor the check-point outside of town. Then, following the 2017 raid of Byrd Camp, volunteers established the temporary *Jalisco* camp in the backyard of an Arivaca town resident.

During the first two years we were so focused on the deaths in the desert, we paid little heed to the plight of those migrants who were captured and returned to Nogales. It slowly began to dawn on us (most especially, to Maryada Vallet and Antonio Zapien), that a tremendous humanitarian crisis existed among those returnees.

Thus, in 2006 we not only began to work with other Nogales organizations like the *Comedor* and *Grupo Beta* and the various shelters, but we established a station at the border to greet returnees and offer them food and first aid, along with information about other local services. We even toyed with the notion of setting up our own water-processing system.

In 2008, when No More Deaths found it required a new nonprofit home, little was known about the Unitarian Universalist faith. Only a few UUs were part of the group and its tenets eluded the group's focus. Probably the UUs knew little about us.

However, once we took Walt Staton's suggestion to consider approaching his church, the Unitarian Universalist Church of Tucson (UUCT), we learned their inclusive philosophy was consistent with No More Deaths "Civil Initiative" and with our mission. Subsequently No More Deaths became a UUCT mission and more UUCT members became part of No More Deaths; the UUA (national body) held is 2010 annual meeting in Phoenix where its president, the Rev. Peter Morales, and a future president, the Rev. Susan Frederick-Douglas, were both arrested as part of the protest of SB 1070, as was Kat Sinclair who subsequently provided testimony to the Justice Department following her stint in Joe Arpaio's jail. The UUA established a social-justice program called "Standing on the Side of Love" which includes immigration issues as part of its mandate. It seems the UUs and No More Deaths over the years have significantly influenced one another. No More Deaths, for example, has helped open the door for the UUs nationally to be on the front lines of immigration reform.

Early on, after several lengthy, aborted search and rescue missions to find missing migrants, No More Deaths decided to leave this job to others. We had learned that even long-established search and rescue organizations refused to initiate a search unless they had the last known location of the lost individual and in the vast southern Arizona desert, this information was seldom available. No

More Deaths volunteers had previously spent many hours in the desert to no avail. For one search, Walt Staton borrowed Gene's Toyota and drove close to the border chasing clues. When he returned, he stated the trip had been futile; he didn't have enough information to locate remains in that vast desert. Subsequently, most pleas were directed to *Derechos Humanos*, who usually chose to conduct these searches.

Started in 2006, The Missing Migrant Project was a small initiative established inside the Medical Examiner's office (ME). It was designed to organize information about missing people along the border. This effort was started by Dr. Bruce Anderson, Pima County Medical Examiner (forensic anthropologist) at the time and Dr. Robin Reineke also working in the ME's office (cultural anthropologist and graduate student). In 2013, Robin and three others grew the Missing Migrant Project into a non-profit, non-governmental organization named the Colibri Center for Human Rights.[166] Their work includes looking for lost migrants. Now information about missing migrants is shared among Colibri, Derechos Humanos, Humane Borders, Samaritans and No More Deaths. Both Derechos and No More Deaths have extensive information on their websites to assist anyone looking for a missing person, whether in the Arizona Desert, Mexico, or other locations. When sufficient information is available, help with migrant locations is sought by volunteers from any of these groups.

From its beginning, No More Deaths worked hard to establish and maintain a loose, but democratic organization following the tenants of Civil Initiative (from Sanctuary) and consensus decision making. Significant fundraising to support the growing programs started following the response to the arrests of Shanti and Daniel in 2006, when No More Deaths had a mailing list of around 3,000.

---

166 Colibri----also more about Colibri and Catholic Community Services (Casa Alitas).

Now more strategic planning, stricter organizational structure with a representational element from No More Deaths various working groups and regular community meetings characterize the organization. The summer budget for three months in 2004 was $25,000; the summer budget for 4 months in 2007 was $47,000. By 2015 it reached $300,000 for a year-round program, and now, following the increased interest after the 2016 election, the budget approaches $550,000. With a much broader base of financial support, the mailing list is now over 10,000. In the year following the election of Donald Trump, No More Deaths received more than $100,000 over the previous year. Funding comes from a wide variety of like-minded individuals and groups.

In the early years, the government utilized the concept of "prosecutorial discretion" when charging and prosecuting migrants. This meant they could consider an individual's circumstances when deciding to return them to Mexico, give them asylum, release them in the U.S., or send them on for prosecution.

Now, under Trump this policy has been discontinued. The latest effort at demolishing this policy came when (former) Attorney General Jeff Sessions announced the establishment of the administration's "zero-tolerance" policy. This meant that no one would escape being sent back home immediately. Only those with an asylum claim had any chance (though a small one) of remaining in America, and children were taken from these people at the border while the parents awaited an amnesty hearing or were sent home unaccompanied by their kids.

At first, the preponderance of people encountered were young men looking for work; later, because travel back and forth across the border to spend time with family had become so onerous, we began to encounter women and children seeking to reunite with family members still living and working in the U.S.

Now, many of the recent immigrants are mothers and children who not only seek to be reunited with family members but are also fleeing violence and poverty in their home countries of Guatemala, El Salvador, and Honduras. In addition, children under the age of 18 are sent alone in the hope they can gain asylum to escape conscription into gangs at home. If successful, they can work to send money home to their mothers and siblings.

Even during the early years, No More Deaths volunteers encountered individuals coming from Central America who in telling of the perilous times back home wanted to seek asylum. Now, as we see in the news, thousands of people are presenting themselves at the border seeking asylum. According to U.S. Citizenship and Immigration Services, a person applying for asylum must prove that he or she has a well-founded fear of persecution in their country of nationality because of their race, religion, nationality, social group or political opinion. There is strong concern that these criteria are being vigorously applied in order to limit the number of persons who qualify. The Trump administration has tried to say that family violence and other categories do not fit. It seems that court action is needed to clarify the definition of social group to include, for example, such persons as young people in danger of conscription by cartels. But this book is not about the current asylum issue. This book is about the migration into Southern Arizona that has been occurring primarily from Mexico for more than 15 years, and the humanitarian response.

Even so, although it looked like No More Deaths would not participate in the latest crisis of Central Americans arriving at the border, emails I receive indicate both Tucson and Phoenix No More Deaths are participating in giant protests against Trump policies regarding separation of children, refusal to offer asylum, conditions for asylum seekers, etc. Churches and other organizations in Tucson and Phoenix have stepped up to handle folks in transit. Shadow Rock United Church of Christ, for example, hosted more than 100 people on their way to Florida. Rincon United Church of Christ in Tucson hosted more than 500. Both churches had the help of other churches and organizations in their neighborhoods. The Red Cross provided cots. The December 2, 2018, issue of the *Arizona Republic* states that this "drop" included more than 5,000 persons, with more than 10 churches (many of them Hispanic) responding. One church hastily built showers to accommodate the needs. Later they reported that 14,500 people were dumped in Phoenix between December 21, 2018, and March 15, 2019, stretching the limits of the humanitarian response. It turns out it's all of a piece.

In 2000, 14 miles of physical barriers were constructed in the Border Patrol San Diego sector. The Secure Fence Act, passed by Congress in September 2006, provided for 700 miles of fencing. This was later modified to permit differing types of barriers depending on the terrain. In May 2011, DHS reported the completion of 649 miles—299 miles of vehicle barriers and 350 miles of pedestrian fence. In 2015, the GAO reported the government had completed the planned 652 miles of fencing. Many activists and border residents heaved a sigh of relief at the limited length of the fencing. The entire border is 1954 miles.

During Trump's presidential campaign, he claimed he would build the border wall and Mexico would pay for it. We all know how that worked out and he has since wrought havoc on the work of Congress. While legislation on climate change, gun control, infrastructure, election interference and other major issues go unresolved, Trump sticks to his tiresome mantra, "Build the wall."

We remember when Border Patrol had fewer than 500 agents to pursue immigrants. At various points Border Patrol ramped up hiring and training, but at no time more significantly than after the 9/11 attacks.

Now, according to Border Patrol data, 4,200 agents are assigned to the Tucson Sector, and the Nogales Station is the second largest in the country. Yet, with fewer people crossing, fewer people apprehended (in Arizona alone: 616,346 in 2000; 38,657 in 2017) and fewer deaths, what's the point? The total southern border has 16,605 agents. There is word out that 4,000 more agents are to be added soon, plus possibly 5,000-15,000 members of the military to help Border Patrol deal with thousands of Central American refugees. Yet, according to *USA Today*,[167] the number of persons in the U.S. illegally hit a 12-year low in 2016. In 2004, early in the humanitarian response, the number was 10.7 million. It reached a high point of 12.2 million in 2007, and in 2016 was back down to 10.7 million. Where is the logic?

Over the years, humanitarian groups met off and on with Border Patrol to discuss mutual issues. We discovered that as we told them our concerns, this information was turned into strategies to thwart our work. As a result, we would take a break from these meetings. In 2013, John Fife and Sarah Roberts presented the tenants of the Red Cross Code of Conduct[168] as a universally-recognized set of principles that we wanted Border Patrol to respect regarding the Southern Arizona humanitarian groups (especially No More Deaths). One of the tenants in the code "The Working Environment" was that "Governments should recognize and respect the independent humanitarian and impartial actions of NGHAs (non-governmental humanitarian agencies)." There was verbal assent by Border Patrol, but no written agreement. This issue was raised a few times over the ensuing years and the response was looking hopeful when, in 2017, any expectation of a formal agreement was dashed by the raid of Byrd Camp and the arrests of nine No More Deaths volunteers in the area of Ajo, Arizona.

No More Deaths and other humanitarians have always responded to needs as they became evident: When the people in Tucson and other areas of Southern Arizona realized what was happening in the southern desert, they quickly responded with water in the

---

167 Alan Gomez, "Number in US Illegally Hit 12-year low in 2016," *USA Today*, 11-28-2018, p. 1.
168 See Appendix C.

desert (Humane Borders, 2000), medical aid and Spanish speakers to assist migrants (Samaritans, 2002), and No More Deaths to provide services 24/7 in areas frequented by migrants and mapping larger and larger areas of service (2004). By 2006 they responded to needs in Nogales and other areas along the border. Local folks in Bisbee and Douglas established services at the ports of Naco and Douglas. Meanwhile, work was taking place in Sonora—at Benjamin Hill Migrant Center, along with the migrant centers in Nogales—*el Comedor, Juan Bosco* Migrant Shelter, *Grupo Beta*, etc.

Humanitarian organizations reached a heightened level of cooperation during their work in Ajo. Initially, Brother David and Samaritans moved in. They were followed by No More Deaths and a variety of other volunteers, including some from California. This followed multiple efforts in the previous four or five years in and around Tucson. During the work with BANWR, Samaritans, Humane Borders, and No More Deaths mounted a united effort to deal with U.S. Fish and Wildlife Service. During efforts surrounding SB 1070, the various groups held a two-day conference where they came together and made cooperation a priority and developed a joint effort to end Streamline.

Once Operation Streamline initiated court proceedings, we, along with other humanitarian groups, began to monitor "trials" of 70 or so migrants each weekday. We had learned that watchdog organizations found this government strategy to be ineffective in preventing illegal immigration. In addition, as late as 2015 when almost half of all federal prosecutions were made up of a crime of trespassing—improper entry and re-entry, questions of misplaced priorities still were being raised.

When we were challenged on BANWR, we responded with negotiations and resistance, starting more cooperative efforts among humanitarian groups. Moving along two tracks, the No More Deaths strategy in BANWR included working with the government at local, regional and federal levels as well as continuing to pursue with dogged persistence our presence with water on the Refuge. It seemed that things must be happening behind the scenes that, combined with our efforts, resulted in our continuing to work on the Refuge with no consequences. That is, until the arrests of Scott Warren and eight others on the Cabeza Prieta National Wildlife Refuge in 2017.

State passage of SB 1070 stimulated heightened focus on undocumented people living in Tucson and their needs; we worked with neighborhoods and business people under the banner "We Reject Racism." The outgrowth of that effort was "Keep Tucson Together" which has provided immigration services to hundreds of people. Phoenix No More Deaths responded to needs in the south-central desert by providing water, food, and first aid; they also raised money for the Douglas program and the Tucson Byrd Camp and have established a "Keep Phoenix Together" clinic to help migrants with federal applications for asylum, green cards, and DACA services.

By 2019, KTT has several distinct areas of work including: asylum, family unification, U.S. citizenship, DACA and other services. More than 150 people volunteer in various capacities. Cowan says that KTT now (2019) represents more than 400 people and families in removal proceedings and our lawyers see an average of 40 new people seeking legal representation every week. Recently, KTT has represented Nicaraguan asylum applicants and has been winning its cases. Currently, the demand for representation is overwhelming.

We try to take a broad view, recognizing the need for intense local services, but also the heightened need for outreach, public education, and making the political case for humane immigration policy.

Initially, many volunteers were needed to serve with No More Deaths at the border and in the desert. While migrants and their needs were our first concern, No More Deaths spent a great deal of time with the volunteers arriving from around the country—giving them the experience of the desert and the border, plus providing them with information to take back home to educate their communities (letters to editors, holding events, etc.).

Now, except for the massive numbers of Central Americans who are presenting themselves, both the numbers of border crossers and the numbers of volunteers are down. According to the Arizona Daily Star, more than a million apprehensions took place in the mid-2000s while fewer than 400,000 took place in FY 2017. No More Deaths must be more strategic in its efforts. We currently have a smaller volunteer corps of individuals who are very knowledgeable and well trained to do most of the work. Additional volunteers come in during high service times of the year. The focus on migrants continues through improving the services at camp and along the border, participating in search and rescue efforts, and reaching out to migrant needs in the Ajo Corridor. In addition, in 2017 and 2018, No More Deaths has extended its services into Northern Mexico—to the towns of Lukeville (right across the border from the Arizona town of Sonoyta), Altar, Caboca, and Sasabe. We provide volunteer time and food, medicine, dehydration kits, and other supplies to those migrant centers.

The numbers of volunteers who have stepped up to do this work is astounding. Each one knows this is a history we can be proud of, while at the same time, we know there is much more work to be done, many more hearts to change, and many more productive legal provisions to be enacted.

CHAPTER 109

Where Are We Going?

We refuse to be worn out.

— *LAUREN BERLANT*

A GREAT DEAL HAS CHANGED during the past 15 years. One significant change has been in the percentage of the citizenry that supports immigration. According to Gallup, in 2010, 57% of responders thought immigration was a good thing; 36% thought it was bad. In 2018, however, 84% of responders supported legal immigration, with only 13% not supportive of it.

The greatest challenge to the work of Southern Arizona humanitarians in 2018-2019, is the trials in federal court of nine No More Deaths volunteers. Throughout this book you have witnessed as No More Deaths has fought for its right to be in the desert—all the desert—along the southern border of our state. That area includes federal lands including wildlife preserves, state lands and tribal lands. Migrants traveling north do not make such distinctions and can be located hungry and thirsty, freezing or frying wherever find themselves. In the first trial of four volunteers in mid-January 2019, former assistant U.S. Attorney Robert Bartels testified: "No matter how you look at it, no one who is *not* a member of No More Deaths has been referred for prosecution." (Note: Others have been ticketed but U.S. attorneys have declined to prosecute.)

Cabeza Prieta Wildlife Refuge manager, Sid Slone admitted that he created the agency's first "do not issue" list in June 2017 to deny No More Deaths volunteers permits, even before permit language was changed to include that denial. He also instructed staff to notify him if anyone who "looked like they were with No More Deaths" came in seeking a permit. He also admitted that the creation of permit language forbidding humanitarian aid was a joint effort among U.S. Fish and Wildlife Service, U.S. Air Force, U.S. Marine Corps, and the Bureau of Land Management.

All this, in spite of the fact that U.S. Fish and Wildlife Service Officer Yurdi Aitkin testified about a meeting in July 2017 with the U.S. Attorney's Office, No More Deaths, Fish and Wildlife and other federal agencies where he understood that "the DOJ does not appear to want to prosecute violations by this group."[169] (Note: This is consistent with No More Deaths previous understanding of the stance of the U.S. Attorney's Office (see Part III).

Four trials were scheduled. one with four defendants, a second one with four defendants and two with Scott Warren to be held in May 2019. If the government prevails in its cases against these No More Deaths volunteers, the role of humanitarians providing services to migrants in Southern Arizona will likely be severely curtailed.

No More Deaths volunteers can find hope in the general support now present around the country as we wait for action in Congress. I see no slackening in the fervor of volunteers as they work day in and day out to save lives of innocent and beleaguered individuals crossing the Arizona desert. I believe they will continue to toil until the needed changes in our immigration system are made to allow for humane treatment of those migrants and asylum seekers who need to leave their homes, and whose work is needed and potentially

---

169 Reporting by Lyle Peachtree for No More Deaths, email: January 17, 2019.

welcome in our country. In addition, I believe they will follow through with the work that will be necessary once such legislation is passed. Henry Giroux writing in his 2018 book, *American Nightmare*, says: "In the end, there is no democracy without informed citizens, no justice without language critical of injustice, and no change without a broad-based movement of collective resistance." He also asks us to heed the words of the great abolitionist, Frederick Douglass:[170]

> It is not light that is needed, but fire; it is not the gentle shower, but thunder. We need the storm, the whirlwind, the earthquake. The feeling of the nation must be quickened; the conscience of the nation must be roused; the propriety of the nation must be startled; the hypocrisy of the nation must be exposed; and the crimes against God and man must be exposed and denounced. [171]

At the turn of the 20th century, valid hope existed that comprehensive immigration reform was possible. At the same time as No More Deaths worked on the ground to save migrant lives, the entire humanitarian movement worked tirelessly for immigration reform. In 2006 and 2007, Arizona Republican Senator John McCain worked across the aisle with Democratic Senator Ted Kennedy to write comprehensive immigration legislation. While his efforts failed, McCain continued to work throughout much of his life[172] to achieve this goal. While the remote Arizona desert often feels distanced from activities in Washington, as you saw in this account of No More Deaths, some public servants are paying attention.

---

170 Henry A. Giroux, *American Nightmare, Facing the Challenges of Fascism*, City Lights Books/Open Media Series, 2018.

171 Ibid.

172 McCain backed off his immigration reform efforts during his bid for president, and at other vulnerable times.

In 2018, shortly after McCain's death, the *Arizona Republic* titled a story about him, "McCain's Death a Blow to Immigration Reform." The article quoted Doris Meissner, now a senior fellow at the Migration Policy Institute:

> Senator McCain was a singularly important figure in all this and not only because of his political history and his viewpoints but, simply, his knowledge of the issues and the state that he comes from (which) gave him a degree of authenticity and authoritativeness on this that will simply be missing in the future, at least in the near term. So, for immigration, it's a big loss.

On his final day, at his home in Cornville, Arizona, Senator McCain said: "Believe always in the promise of America because nothing is impossible here."

Border Wall in Douglas 2019 (Mark Adams, Frontera de Cristo)

Brandon John Rick Gene

Love Not Borders

Jerry Zawada

Antonio Zapien

Isabel Garcia

Lois Martin, Jim and Stephanie Keenan   **Byrd Baylor and Maryada Vallet**

More No More Deaths Photos

**Laura Ilardo
and Chris**

Billie Foltz and Gene Lefebvre

Walt Emrys Staton

Migrant Family in Altar

**Jean Boucher and
Peter Ragan**

Maria Aparicio and Ollin

Sarah Roberts and Jim Walsh

Pancho Medina

Aguaton in Phoenix

620

AFTERWARD

ONE OF THE UNIQUE ASPECTS of this book is its reliance on volunteers to tell the story of No More Deaths response to the migration of people from the south into the United States. Here is some information about many of them.

In order of their initial contributions:

PART I:

1. **Dr. Norma Price**: Norma has lived in Tucson for more than ten years. She graduated from the University of Tennessee College of Medicine and spent her career as an oncologist and urgent care specialist in Atlanta, Georgia. She has served as a medical supervisor for No More Deaths and Tucson Samaritans ever since John Fife said, "We need a medical doctor." In that role she has trained hundreds of volunteers planning to work in the desert with ill and injured migrants. She collaborated with two fellow activists on the book, *Crossing with the Virgin*, and was named "Hero of Health and Human Rights" by Physicians for Human Rights in 2017.

2. **Maryada Vallet:** A pioneer volunteer with No More Deaths, Maryada has a Bachelor's Degree from Azusa Pacific University and a Master's Degree in Public Health from

UCLA. Currently, she is earning on a PhD at the University of Arizona. She works as a design, monitoring and evaluation specialist for Tango International providing technical assistance to NGOs.

3. **Jim Corbett:** Jim received a Master's Degree in Philosophy from Harvard University and went on to develop the philosophical basis for humanitarian activism in Southern Arizona termed, "civil initiative." He has been called a philosopher, spiritual warrier and Quaker prophet (*Friends Journal*). He taught philosophy at Cochise College; he wrote two books: *Goatwalking* and *Sanctuary for all Life*. He died in August 2001.

4. **Jim Walsh:** Jim volunteers for the Tucson Food Bank and is a steady volunteer for No More Deaths. Jim is a trained social worker and spent a number of years working on environmental and human rights in Korea and Kenya. He makes a mean pot of beans and loves to hike with his partner, Sarah Roberts.

5. **Steve Johnston**: Steve has a Bachelor's Degree from Southwestern at Memphis (now Rhodes College), Tennessee. From 1970-1974 he was a press officer at Penguin Books in London. He's the co-founder of Writers and Readers Publishing Cooperative, London, 1974. He volunteered in various low-income and homelessness-related projects in Nashville, Tennessee from 1979-1990, and at Casa Maria Hospitality House in Tucson from 1990-2004. He's been a No More Deaths volunteer from 2005 to present.

6. **Guadalupe Castillo:** "Lupe" graduated from the University of Arizona with a Master's Degree in History, and taught at Pima Community College in Tucson, Arizona for 30 years. She was active with the Manzo Council in the earliest days of organized migrant assistance in Southern Arizona (in the 1970s). She has been active in No More Deaths and Tucson Samaritans as well as other humanitarian groups. In 2011, she received the YMCA Lifetime Achievement Award as an immigration activist.

7. **The Rev. Gene Lefebvre:** Gene graduated from the University of Arizona in business. Then, following three years of study, Gene graduated from San Francisco Theological Seminary. A retired Presbyterian minister, he has served churches in Salinas, California and Phoenix, Arizona. Gene is a long-time civil-rights activist, and a co-founder of No More Deaths. He received the Freedom from Fear Award in 2012 and the Ann Burton and Tim Driver Award for Excellence in Nonviolent Direct Action in Retirement in 2016. He lives in Phoenix and continues to play a supportive role with No More Deaths.

8. **Antonio Zapien:** Antonio was born in Mexico, moved to the U.S. where he became a citizen. He taught in the agriculture department at the University of Arizona and currently resides in Mexico where he volunteers for the orphanage where he was placed as a child by his mother, so he could receive an education.

9. **Dr. Cecile Lumer:** Cecile is a botanist who taught at Cochise College in Sierra Vista, Arizona, and was curator of the Cochise County Herbarium. Along with others, she founded and pursued the work of serving migrants at the border station in Naco, Arizona. In retirement, she returned to her home in New York state.

10. **Annie Olson Swanson:** Annie has a Master's in International Affairs from the School of International Service at American University in Washington D.C. She was a volunteer coordinator for No More Deaths for desert aid to migrants and currently lives in New Jersey with her husband and two young children.

PART II:

11. **Kathryn Ferguson:** Kathryn, a volunteer with Tucson Samaritans, was a dancer, artist, film-maker, author and

much more. She studied at the University of Arizona. Her most recent artistic expression was *The Haunting of the Mexican Border.* Kathryn was working on another book when she died in Spring of 2017.

12. **Jean and Charlie Rooney:** Former Catholic nun and priest, they spent fifty years in Detroit in ministry and teaching, then moved to Tucson to continue their activist work. They adopted two Colombian children.

13. **Stephanie and Jim Keenan:** Kindergarten teacher and fishereman, they retired to Tucson and became involved with No More Deaths. Jim is an avid biker and Stephanie a musician.

14. **Dan Millis:** Dan taught Spanish at Verde Valley School in Sedona; volunteered full-time for No More Deaths for an entire year; and currently works for Sierra Club in Southern Arizona, observing and reporting on the effects of the border wall as a representative for border environmental issues.

15. **The Rev. John Fife:** John is a retired Presbyterian minister and human rights activist in Tucson, Arizona. John served as a minister for 35 years at Southside Presbyterian Church in Tucson. In 1992, Fife was elected moderator of the General Assembly of the Presbyterian Church (USA). He is now a pastor emeritus at Southside Presbyterian Church. In the 1980s, John co-founded the Sanctuary Movement in the United States. The movement organized over 500 churches to help Central American refugees cross the border and find sanctuary in the U.S., in defiance of federal law. In 1986, Fife was convicted, along with seven other people, of violating federal immigration laws and served five years' probation. In 2004 a group of humanitarian leaders in Tucson formed No More Deaths to attempt to end the deaths of immigrants along the U.S/Mexico border. John was among the leaders of that effort and continues to work closely with No More Deaths.

16. **The Rev. Diane Dowgiert:** Diane is an ordained minister in the Unitarian Universalist Church. She spent ten years as pastor of the Unitarian Universalist Church of Tucson (UUCT). She oversaw No More Deaths becoming a ministry of UUCT. For two years, she served as interim minister at the Greensboro UU Church and as of August 2018, serves as interim minister of the UU Society in Coralville, Iowa.

17. **The Rev. Walt Emrys Staton:** Walt was one of the early volunteers for No More Deaths and helped with its organization and strategy. He completed his seminary work at Claremont School of Theology. From Claremont, Emrys moved back to Tucson and then to Phoenix where he served two years as director of pastoral care and justice with the First Unitarian Church of Phoenix. He is currently moving onto a career in hospital chaplaincy.

PART III:

18. **john heid:** John is a Quaker who spent several years with Christian Peacemaker Teams (CPT). Following time with CPT in Douglas, Arizona, john moved to Tucson to work with No More Deaths. Currently he is living and volunteering with No More Deaths in Ajo Arizona. He has been active in the peace movement and is an avid birder.

19. **Kevin Riley:** When Kevin left No More Deaths, he studied to be come an EMT and now is a nurse living in New Jersey.

PART IV:

20. **David Joseph Hill:** David has a Degree in Literature from Massachusetts Institute of Technology. After serving as a

volunteer coordinator for No More Deaths, he moved to Nogales where he makes a living as an editor and volunteers with No More Deaths in several capacities, including managing the returned belongings project.

21. **Kat Bucciantini**: Kat received her Master's Degree in Nursing from the University of Illinois, in Chicago and has a specialty in Hospice care. She works at a federally qualified health center (FQHC) called Wallace Medical Concern that serves an underserved population outside of Portland, Oregon. Many of its patients are migrants. Soon she will start working for Providence Hospice in Portland.

22. **Sarah Launius**: Sarah is an early and consistent volunteer with No More Deaths and is currently at work on her PhD in the Geography and Development Department at UA. Her undergraduate degree is from Prescott College. She and Geoff Boyce led media relations for No More Deaths for many years. In the early years she volunteered regularly at Byrd Camp and helped establish many of the group's protocols.

23. **Geoff Boyce**: Geoff's undergraduate degree is from Prescott College. He recently completed his PhD at UA and now works with a consortium at Earlham College Border Studies Institute researching migration around the world, along with fellow No More Deaths volunteer, Kate Morgan.

24. **Asa Duffee:** No information available.

PART V:

25. **Carlotta Wray**: Lives near Arivaca, Arizona. She moved from Mexico to Southern Arizona and married a member of the Tohono O'odham Nation. She is active with No More Deaths in Southern Arizona.

26. **Laura Ilardo:** Laura has a Master's Degree in Social Work from the University of Michigan. She is a licensed social worker and worked for any years at Thunderbird High School in Phoenix, Arizona. Laura started Phoenix No More Deaths and maintains its Facebook page. She also manages the Phoenix clinic to assist migrants with securing legal "papers," especially DACA recipients. Currently she is adjunct faculty at Rio Salado Community College in Phoenix.

27. **Chris Fleischman**: Consulting engineer (aircraft). Essential to Phoenix No More Deaths organizing regular field services to migrants. Political activist.

28. **Dr. Scott Warren:** Scott is a professor in the Geography Department at Arizona State University. He lives in Ajo, Arizona, and is a leader for No More Deaths in humanitarian efforts there. In January 2019, he is on trial for his humanitarian work in Ajo.

ADDITIONAL INDIVIDUALS WHOSE WORK INSPIRED THIS BOOK:

29. **Jean Boucher**: After serving as a volunteer coordinator for No More Deaths, Jean attended George Mason University in Fairfax, Virginia, receiving a PhD in Sociology. Then he went to Michigan State University as a visiting assistant professor teaching sociology. In 2019, he is working at the Clean Energy Research Center at the University of British Columbia.

30. **Lucy Zhang:** Lucy spent two periods of time with No More Deaths. She graduated from Duke University, finished her Doctor of Jurisprudence degree, and is now an attorney living in London.

31. **Rick Ufford Chase:** A co-founder of No More Deaths, Rick graduated from Colorado College and subsequently received honorary degrees from Hastings, Bloomfield, and Austin Colleges plus Eden Theological Seminary. He received the Dignitas Humana Award for human rights work from St. John's School of Theology and Seminary. He founded No More Deaths in 2004 and was moderator of the General Assembly of the Presbyterian Church for two years. He and his wife, Kitty, are trained as reservist workers for Christian Peacemaker Teams (CPT). Currently, he and Kitty serve as co-directors of the Stony Point Center in New York state.

32. **Maureen and Jim Marx:** Maureen and Jim are No More Deaths volunteers since 2008. Maureen is a registered nurse and works tirelessly making survival kits for migrants. Jim is a former school principal and counselor. He has spent many hours and days in the desert at Byrd Camp and now works with finance, staffing, and other behind-the-scenes challenges for No More Deaths.

33. **Attorney Andy Silverstein:** Providing legal support to No More Deaths is attorney Andy Silverman, UA graduate and recipient of his JD degree from the UA College of Law in 1969. Since 2001, Andy has been Joseph P. Livermore Professor of Law and Director of Clinical Program at the James E. Rogers College of Law at UA. He has written many publications and has served on a number of community boards of directors.

34. **Attorney Margo Cowen:** An immigrant rights activist since the 1970s, Margo is a founder of No More Deaths and other humanitarian organizations in Tucson, Arizona. In 2015, she received the Church Women United Human Rights Award and in 2018 she received the Pro Bono Champion Award from the American Immigration Law Association. Margo is indefatigable in her defense and support of migrants. She has worked as a Pima County defense attorney since 2004.

35. **Catherine Gaffney:** Catherine has been a volunteer at Byrd Camp for several years. She is currently a leader among the young adult volunteers for No More Deaths.

36. **Sarah Roberts, R.N.** Sarah is a No More Deaths co-founder who lives with her partner, Jim Walsh. Sarah is a nurse at Tucson Public Schools and at a local hospital where she encounters and provides follow-up services to migrants. Sarah provides volunteer training for No More Deaths, Samaritans and other humanitarians in first aid and emergency medical aid to those working in the field. She also answers phones from volunteers in the field when there are questions about specific assistance needed or whether to contact Border Patrol and start driving sick or injured migrants toward the nearest hospital. She works closely with Dr. Norma Price and other health professionals to support humanitarian work in the field.

37. **Jerry Zawada:** Father Jerry Zawada was a nuclear resister, peace-and-justice activist, Franciscan friar. He died recently at the age of eighty. Father Jerry started the Dignity Bag project, a collaboration between No More Deaths and other groups. The project has raised money to buy sturdy canvas tote bags made by the women of the DouglasPrieta Works sewing cooperative, for use by people deported across the border. Throughout his life, Jerry worked with the homeless, war refugees and survivors of torture around the country. He was imprisoned repeatedly for nonviolent protests of nuclear weapons and torture training.

While writing this book, I felt very grateful to the many people who clipped newspaper articles, read early drafts, edited various chapters, provided contributions, and made suggestions for improvement of the manuscript. This includes volunteers for No More Deaths and friends where I currently live at the Beatitudes Campus in Phoenix. I am indebted to you all.

Sincere thanks to the photographers who contributed to this work: Gene McWhorter, Paula McPheeters, Chris Fleischman, Laura Ilardo, Mark Adams, Dan Millis, Cecile Lumer, and Gene and Sue Lefebvre. Special thanks to Steve and Paige Johnston who took many of the photos labeled "No More Deaths," and to professional photographer Michael Hyatt who provided more than a dozen photos to support the text. As a professional photographer, he was present at many significant events in the life of No More Deaths and recorded them for posterity.

Appendix

Bills Enacted Affecting *Chicanx*, Indigenous and Immigrant Residents
Arizona Legislature 2004-2010
Figure I

BETWEEN 2004-2010 ARIZONA VOTERS AND politicians implemented over 30 laws designed to disenfranchise *Chicanx*, indigenous and immigrant residents and to render everyday life increasingly difficult for non-citizens and their families (see figure 1). Combined, these laws: prohibit ethnic studies curricula (and specifically Mexican American Studies) in public k-12 schools; deny any social service assistance to undocumented residents or their children (regardless of whether or not the latter are eligible U.S. citizens); force all state-funded social service providers to act as immigration police by reporting anyone they suspect of being unlawfully present; make English the official language of the State of Arizona; mandate that all employers check all employees' eligibility to work against a federal immigration database; make it a state crime to work without federal authorization; and authorize the state to use trespassing and smuggling laws to criminally prosecute undocumented immigrants. Additional voter-passed propositions prohibit bilingual public-school instruction; deny undocumented individuals any damages as an outcome of civil litigation; deny in-state tuition and prohibit any type of public tuition assistance to undocumented youth.

Year	Bill	Description
2004	SB 1345	Prohibiting undocumented people ownership of firearms.
2005	SB 1372	Local law enforcement empowered to enforce trafficking laws.
2005	HB 2592	Prohibition of an AZ county building "work centers" which facilitate employment of undocumented people.
2005	HB 2259	Immigration status factored into sentencing of an arrestee.
2006	SB 1167	Making English AZ's official language and requiring all government functions to be conducted in English.
2006	HB 2448	Prohibiting undocumented people to receive health benefits.
2006	SB 1137	Prohibiting eligibility of undocumented people for "Comprehensive Care for the Elderly."
2007	SB 1157	Turn presence of undocumented people in AZ into criminal offense of trespass.
2007	HB 2202	Establish division of adult education within Dept. of Education for teaching English to foreigners and the Americanization of participating parties.
2007	HB 2779	Prohibits employers (with penalty) from knowingly hiring undocumented people and requires use of "Basic Pilot Program" to determine potential employee's status.
2007	HB 2391	Prohibits undocumented people from acquiring a liquor license.
2007	SB 1291	Prohibits participation of undocumented people on the AZ Board of Appraisals.
2007	HB 2016	Law enforcement allowed to detain undocumented people as material witnesses of a crime.

2007	HB 2781	Allies Dept. of Corrections with Gang and Immigration Intelligence Team, with $10 million allocated to the latter.
2007	HB 2787	Bail may be withheld for any arrestee that law enforcement has "probable cause" is an undocumented person.
2007	SB 1265	Allowance for law enforcement to determine an arrestee's citizenship status.
2007	HB 2467	Requires proof of citizenship and/or legal status to receive public assistance.
2008	HB 2403	Requires proof of citizenship for voter registration.
2008	HB 2486	Changes definition of "prohibited possessor" further restricting who may own a firearm for hunting purposes to exclude undocumented people.
2008	SB 1096	Appropriates $40.7 million for controversial English immersion programs in AZ.
2008	HB 2745	Employers required to use E-verify to check status of potential employees.
2008	HB 2842	Expands human trafficking to include use of property or "drop houses."
2009	SB 1188	Funds for English as a Second Language programming and immigration enforcement.
2009	SB1001	Allocation of $10 million to Gang and Immigration Intelligence Team. (held in rules until 2nd special session, at which point it was enacted)
2009	HB 2008	Specifies identification requirements to receive public benefits, and requires health workers to aid in immigration enforcement. (held in rules until 3rd special session, at which point it was enacted)
2009	HB 2426	Prohibits AZ involvement in RealID Act or Federal Western Hemisphere Travel Initiative.
2009	HB 2306	Prohibits undocumented people from acquiring an AZ business license.
2009	HB 2569	Increased penalties for human smuggling.
2009	SB 1281	Expands the definitions of sex trafficking and forced labor.

2010	SB 1282	Extends the definition of human smuggling.
2010	HB 2281	Prohibits Ethnic Studies curriculum in public schools.
2010	SB 1070	So-called "Support Our Law Enforcement and Safe Neighborhoods Act."
2010	HB 2162	Amendments to SB 1070 wording regarding "reasonable suspicion" as well as establishing punitive fines.

Figure 1. ATE bills enacted (or "chaptered") in Arizona State Legislature 2004-2010. Excluding voter petitions and proposed bills vetoed during that same time period. (Arizona State Legislature and National Conference of State Legislatures.) [173]

---

[173] Geoffrey Boyce, Sarah Launius, and Adam O. Aguirre, "Drawing the Line: Spatial Strategies of Community and Resistance in Post-SB 1070 Arizona," School of Geography and Development, University of Arizona, published in *ACME*, An International Journal for Critical Geographies, 2017.

UNITARIAN UNIVERSALIST SEVEN PRINCIPLES

WE, THE MEMBER CONGREGATIONS OF the Unitarian Universalist Association, covenant to affirm and promote:

- The inherent worth and dignity of every person
- Justice, equity and compassion in human relations
- Acceptance of one another and encouragement to spiritual growth in our congregations
- A free and responsible search for truth and meaning
- The right of conscience and the use of the democratic process within our congregations and in society at large
- The goal of world community with peace, liberty and justice for all.
- Respect for the interdependent web of all existence of which we are a part.

RED CROSS CODE OF CONDUCT

THE FOLLOWING CODE OF CONDUCT has been developed by the Red Cross and Red Crescent Movement to cover Non-Governmental Humanitarian Agencies (NGAHs) in disaster response. No More Deaths proposes that this same code be applied to humanitarian actions in the current crisis along the southern U.S. and Mexico border. A disaster in this document refers to "a calamitous event resulting in loss of life, great human suffering and distress, and large-scale material damage. Non-relevant sections not included.

The Code of Conduct:

1. The right to receive humanitarian assistance, and to offer it, is a fundamental humanitarian principle which should be enjoyed by all citizens of all countries.
2. Aid is given regardless of the race, creed or nationality of the recipients and without adverse distinction of any kind. Aid priorities are calculated on the basis of need alone.
3. Aid will not be used to further a particular political or religious standpoint.
4. We shall endeavor not to act as instruments of government foreign policy.
5. We shall respect culture and custom.

6. We shall attempt to build disaster response on local capabilities.

7. Ways shall be found to involve program beneficiaries in the management of relief aid.

8. Relief aid must strive to reduce future vulnerabilities to disaster s well as meeting basic needs.

9. We hold ourselves accountable to both those we seek to assist and those from whom we accept resources.

10. In our information, publicity and advertising activities, we shall recognize disaster victims as dignified humans, not hopeless objects.

The Working Environment:

1. Governments should recognize and respect the independent, humanitarian and impartial actions of NGHAs.

2. Host governments should facilitate rapid access to disaster victims for NGHAs.

3. Governments should facilitate the timely flow of relief goods and information during disasters.

4. Governments should seek to provide a coordinated disaster information and planning service.

5. Disaster relief in the event of armed conflict is governed by the relevant government.

AFFILIATED HUMANITARIAN ORGANIZATIONS

NO MORE DEATHS/*NO MAS MUERTES* is not the only organization working to end death and suffering in the U.S./Mexico borderlands. We are but one member of an extended and ever-growing team of diverse people and initiatives doing this important work Here are some of the organizations that make up our working partners and friends we work together with in the field.

<u>Southern-Arizona Based</u>

BorderLinks
620 South 6th Ave.
Tucson, AZ 85701
520-628-8263
info@borderlinks.org

Coalicion de Derechos Humanos
225 E. 26th St., #2
Tucson, AZ
520-770-1373
derechoshumanosaz.net

Colibri Center for Human Rights
Mailing Address:

3849 E. Broadway Blvd., #206
520-724-8644
Physical Location:
2825 E. District St.
Tucson, AZ 85714

Green Valley Samaritans
The Good Shepherd Church
1775 S. La Canada
Sahuarita, AZ 85629
520-549-8903
Tucsonsamaritans.ordg

Humane Borders
243 W. 33rd. St.
Tucson, AZ85713
P.O. Box 27024
Tucson, AZ 85726
520-398-5063
info@humaneborders.org

No More Deaths/*No Mas Muertes*
Sponsor: Unitarian Universalist Church of Tucson
4831 E. 22nd St., Tucson, AZ 85711
Office: St. Mark's Presbyterian Church
3809 E. 3rd St., Tucson, AZ 85716-4611
(520) 495-5583
action@nomoredeaths.org

Mariposas Sin Fronteras
317 W. 23rd St.
Tucson 85713-1541
520-955-8165
mariposasinfronteras.net

People Helping People
P.O. Box 826
Arivaca, AZ 85601
520-398-3093
phparivaca.org

Protection Network Action Fund
225 E. 22nd St., Ste. #2
Tucson, AZ 85713
520-770-1373
derechoshumanos.net/protection-network-action

School of the Americas Watch
733 E. Euclid St. NW
Washington, D.C.
202-234-3440
m.me/closethesoa

Southside Workers Center
312 W. 23rd St.
Tucson, AZ 85713
520-955-8165
southsidecentro@gmail.com

Tucson Samaritans
c/o Southside Presbyterian Church
317 W. 23rd St.
Tucson, AZ 85713
tucsonsamaritans.org

Border-Wide:

Aguilas del Desierto
760-521-3760
See Facebook: Aguilas del Desierto

Border Angels
P.O.Box 86598
San Diego, CA 92138
619-487-0248
info@borderangels.org

Sierra Club Borderlands Campaign
See Facebook: Sierra Club Borderlands Campaign

South Texas Human Rights Center
117 E. Miller
Falfurrias, TX 78355
361-325-2555
southtexashumanrights.org

No More Deaths Awards

- <u>Oscar Romero Foundation Prize</u> to No More Deaths, Shanti Sells and Daniel Strauss, from the Rothco Chapel for humanitarian rights work. 2007
- <u>Dignita Humana Award for Human Rights</u> to Rick Ufford-Chase from St. John's School of Theology and Seminary. 2007
- <u>Freedom from Fear Award</u> to Sarah Roberts and Gene Lefebvre from the Public Interest Project. 2012
- <u>Wilton Peace Prize</u> to No More Deaths for their contribution to peace and human progress from the Unitarian Universalist Association. 2012
- <u>Ann Barstow and Tom Driver Award for Excellent Direct Action in Retirement,</u> to Gene Lefebvre. 2016.
- <u>Wilton Peace Prize</u> by the Unitarian Universalist Association (UUA) to No More Deaths. 2012. "The work of your all-volunteer-led organization embodies the very spirit of being the change one wishes to see in the world. $1,500 prize. www.standingontthe sideoflove.org.
- <u>Arizona Chapter Pro-Bono Champion Award to attorney</u> Margo Cowan from the American Immigration Lawyers Association. Margo is one of the co-founders of No More Deaths and the pro bono attorney for both No More Deaths

and Samaritans. She was recognized in June 2018 at their annual conference, honoring her years of pro bono service.

* Heroes of Health and Human Rights Award, from Physicians for Human Rights, to Norma Price, MD, volunteer with No More Deaths, Tucson Samaritans, and other humanitarian organizations in Tucson. Norma was recognized at their annual gala in New York in May 2018. The gala honors health professionals working on the front lines to defend human rights. Norma was one of three people to receive the award.

48128321R00375

Made in the USA
San Bernardino, CA
15 August 2019